# MAD LOVE



Kazusa Takashima

Volume 4

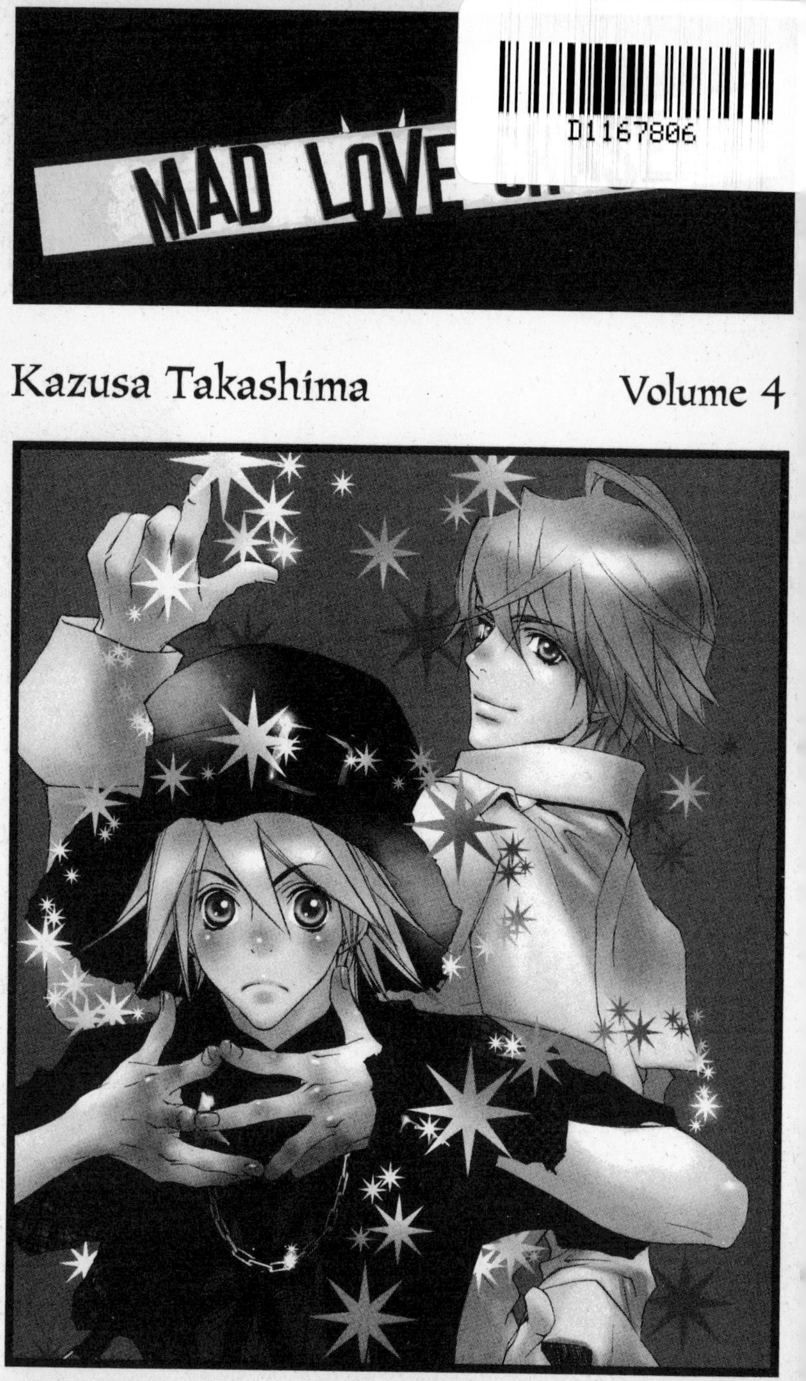

*Harlem Beat Wa Yoakemade -Mad Love Chase- Volume 4*
Created by Kazusa TAKASHIMA

Translation & Adaptation - Katherine Schilling
Retouch and Lettering - Star Print Brokers
Production Artist - Michael Paolilli
Graphic Designer - Al-Insan Lashley

Editor - Lillian Diaz-Przybyl
Print Production Manager - Lucas Rivera
Managing Editor - Vy Nguyen
Senior Designer - Louis Csontos
Art Director - Al-Insan Lashley
Director of Sales and Manufacturing - Allyson De Simone
Associate Publisher - Marco F. Pavia
President and C.O.O. - John Parker
C.E.O. and Chief Creative Officer - Stu Levy

A  Manga

TOKYOPOP Inc.
5900 Wilshire Blvd. Suite 2000
Los Angeles, CA 90036

E-mail: info@TOKYOPOP.com
Come visit us online at www.TOKYOPOP.com

HARLEM BEAT WA YOAKEMADE Volume 4
© Kazusa TAKASHIMA 2007 First published in Japan in
2007 by KADOKAWA SHOTEN PUBLISHING CO., LTD., Tokyo.
English translation rights arranged with
KADOKAWA SHOTEN PUBLISHING CO., LTD., Tokyo
through TUTTLE–MORI AGENCY, INC., Tokyo.
English text copyright © 2010 TOKYOPOP Inc.

ISBN: 978-1-4278-1601-6

First TOKYOPOP printing: September 2010
10 9 8 7 6 5 4 3 2 1
Printed in the USA

# MAD LOVE CHASE

## Volume.4

### by Kazusa TAKASHIMA

HAMBURG // LONDON // LOS ANGELES // TOKYO

# Story Summary

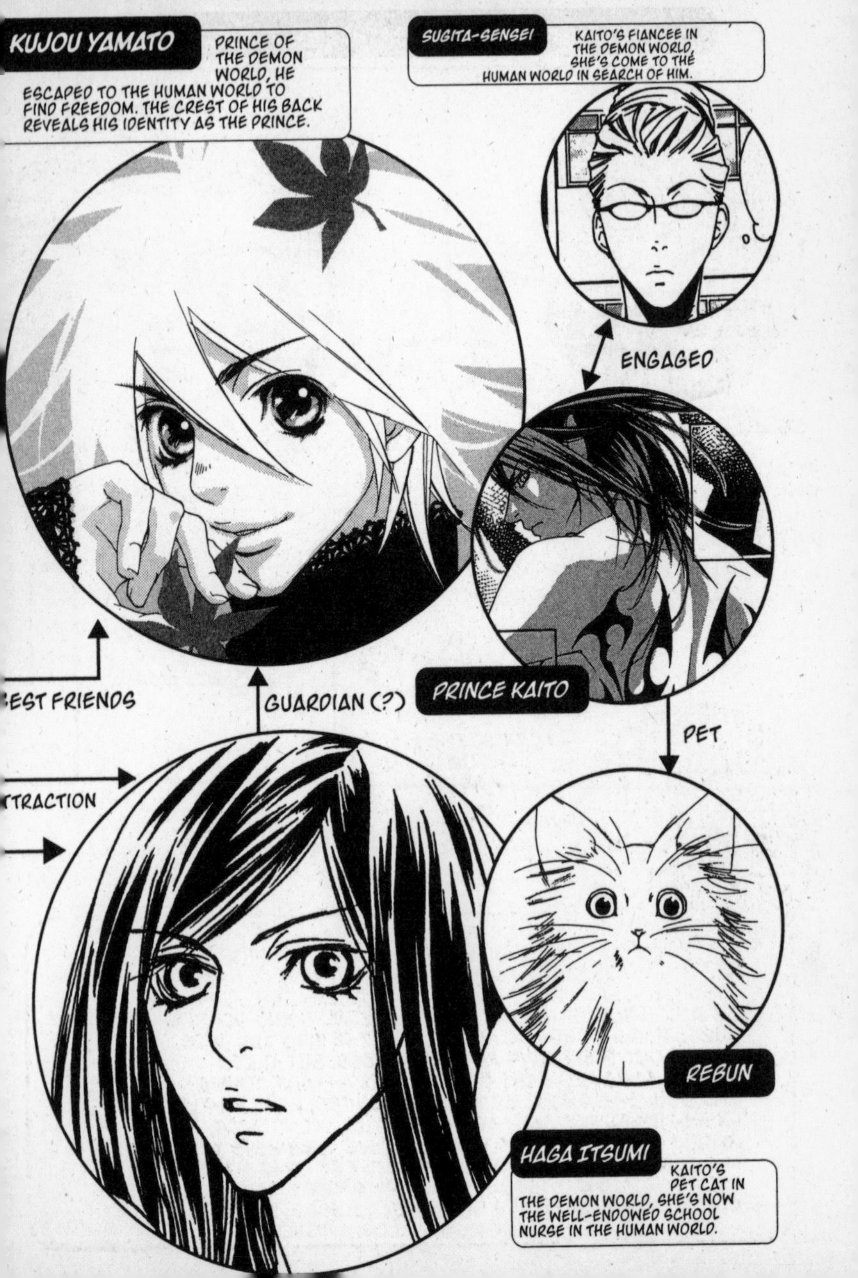
KUJOU YAMATO
PRINCE OF THE DEMON WORLD, HE ESCAPED TO THE HUMAN WORLD TO FIND FREEDOM. THE CREST OF HIS BACK REVEALS HIS IDENTITY AS THE PRINCE.
SUGITA-SENSEI
KAITO'S FIANCEE IN THE DEMON WORLD, SHE'S COME TO THE HUMAN WORLD IN SEARCH OF HIM.
ENGAGED
PRINCE KAITO
PET
EST FRIENDS
GUARDIAN (?)
TTRACTION
REBUN
HAGA ITSUMI
KAITO'S PET CAT IN THE DEMON WORLD, SHE'S NOW THE WELL-ENDOWED SCHOOL NURSE IN THE HUMAN WORLD.

# Character Relations

## THE THREE AGENTS FROM THE DEMON WORLD

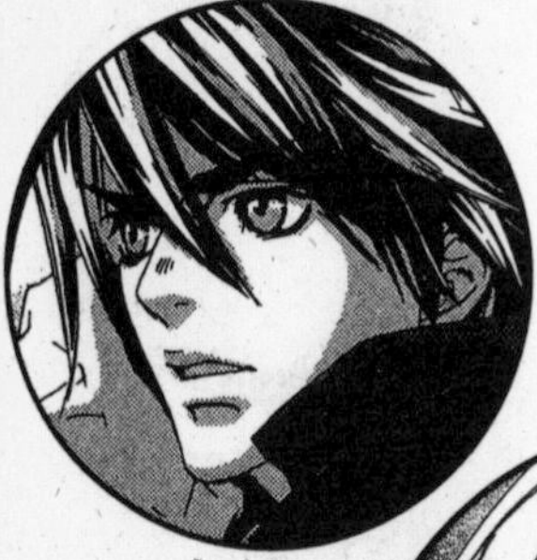

KISARAGI TOUMA

STOIC AND SHORT-TEMPERED, BUT CARES DEEPLY FOR HIS COMRADES.

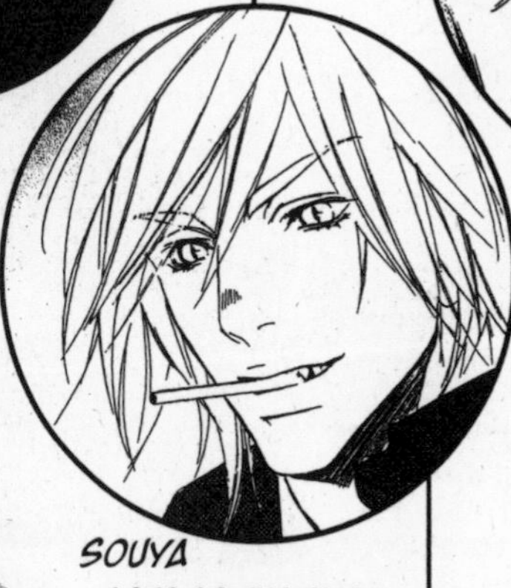

SOUYA

ACTS AS THE FLIRTY JANITOR IN THE HUMAN WORLD, BUT IS STILL THE THREESOME'S COOL-HEADED LEADER.

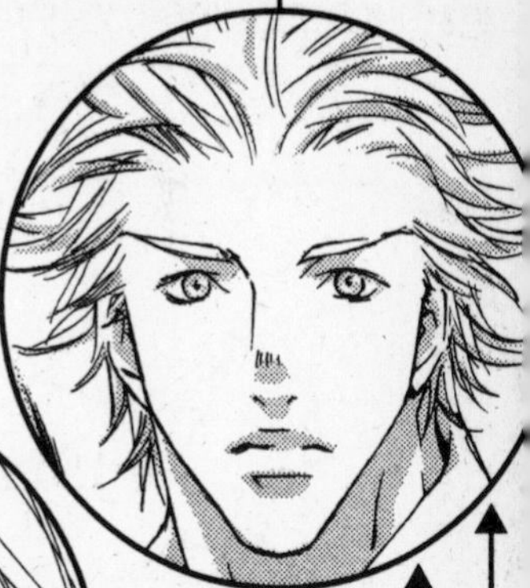

ASAKURA TAIKI

CAME TO THE HUMAN WORLD IN PURSUIT OF KAITO, BUT SOMEHOW ENDED UP AS YAMATO'S BEST FRIEND.

SOME SORT OF

ONE-SIDED CRUSH ♡

## STORY

ON THE DAY OF HIS ARRANGED MARRIAGE, THE PRINCE OF THE DEMON WORLD, KAITO, ALONG WITH HIS PET CAT REBUN, ESCAPED INTO THE HUMAN WORLD. NOW POSING AS A HIGH SCHOOL STUDENT NAMED YAMATO AND SCHOOL NURSE HAGA-SENSEI RESPECTIVELY, THE TWO ARE ABLE TO LIVE OUT THEIR DAYS AS THEY PLEASE. BUT THREE MESSENGERS FROM THE DEMON WORLD--TAIKI, TOUMA, AND SOUYA--AS WELL AS KAITO'S FIANCÉE, PRINCESS VIITA (NOW SUGITA-SENSEI), ARE IN HOT PURSUIT TO DRAG THE PRINCE BACK HOME! BUT THE ONLY CLUE THEY HAVE TO THE PRINCE'S TRUE IDENTITY IS THE CREST ON HIS BACK. WHILE YAMATO STRUGGLES TO KEEP HIS IDENTITY A SECRET, SOMETHING IS CHANGING IN HIS FRIENDSHIP WITH TAIKI...

# TABLE OF CONTENTS

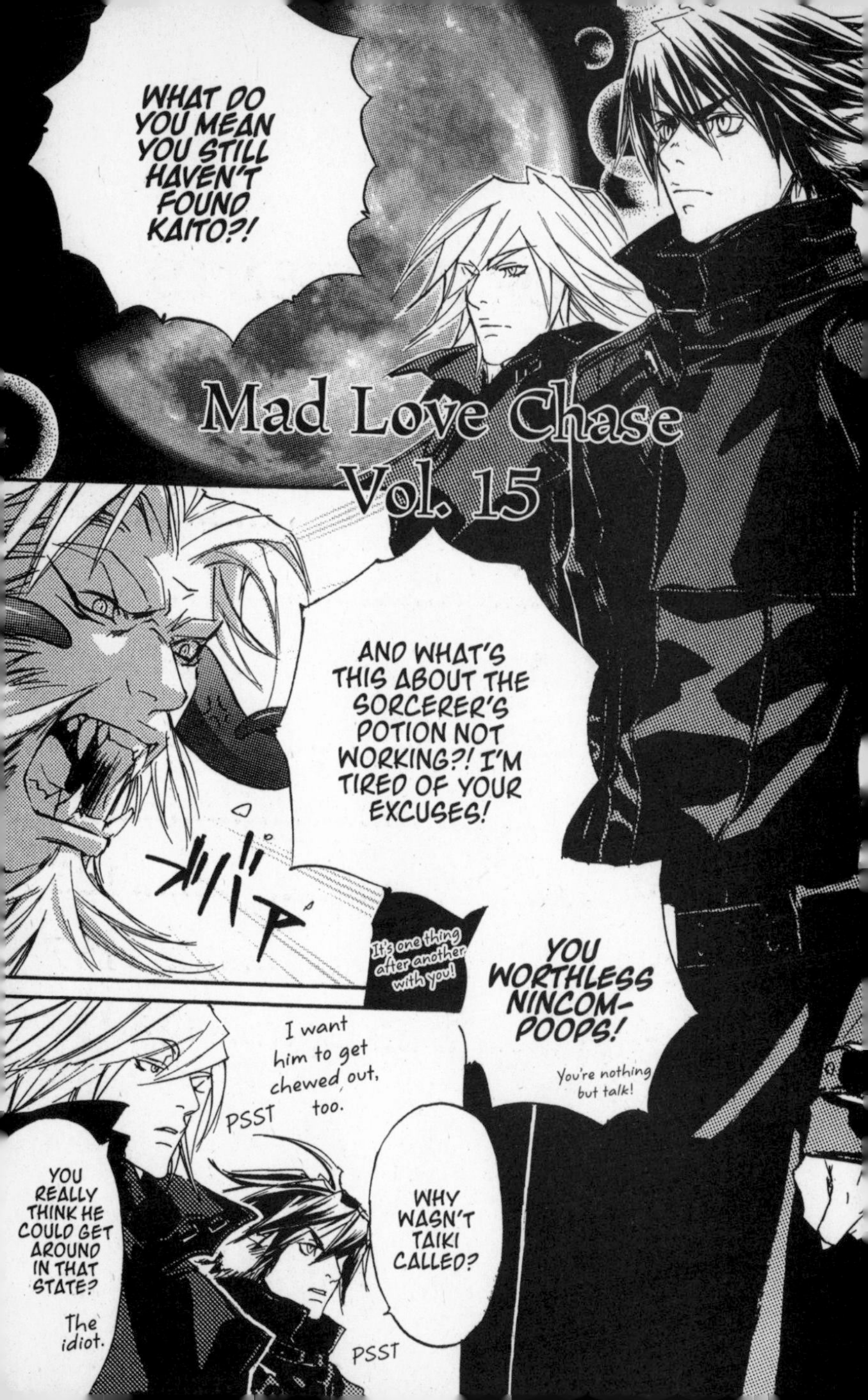
WHAT DO YOU MEAN YOU STILL HAVEN'T FOUND KAITO?!
Mad Love Chase
Vol. 15
AND WHAT'S THIS ABOUT THE SORCERER'S POTION NOT WORKING?! I'M TIRED OF YOUR EXCUSES!
YOU WORTHLESS NINCOM-POOPS!
You're nothing but talk!
It's one thing after another with you!
I want him to get chewed out, too.
PSST
WHY WASN'T TAIKI CALLED?
YOU REALLY THINK HE COULD GET AROUND IN THAT STATE?
The idiot.
PSST

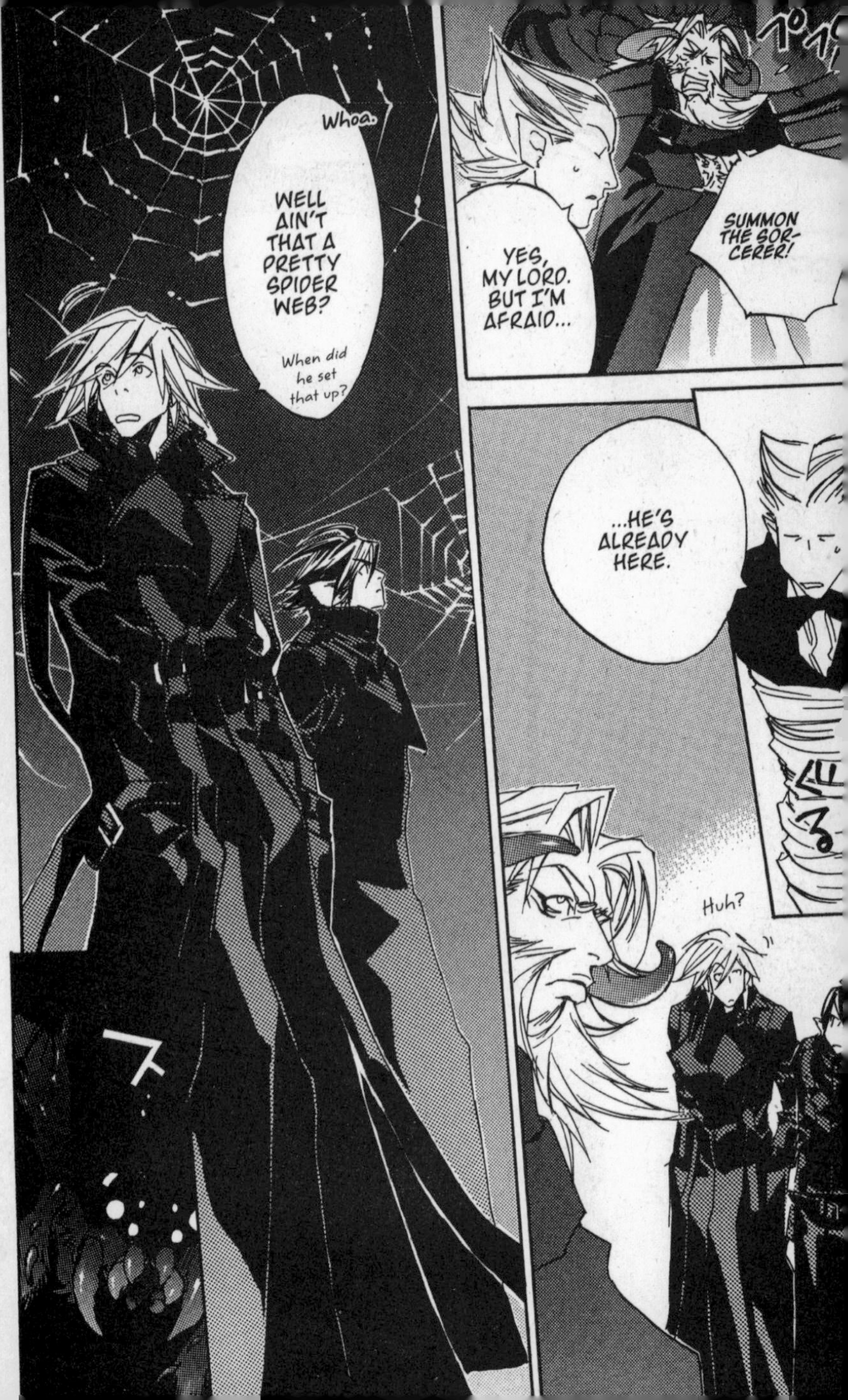
SUMMON THE SORCERER!
YES, MY LORD. BUT I'M AFRAID...
...HE'S ALREADY HERE.
Huh?
Whoa.
WELL AIN'T THAT A PRETTY SPIDER WEB?
When did he set that up?

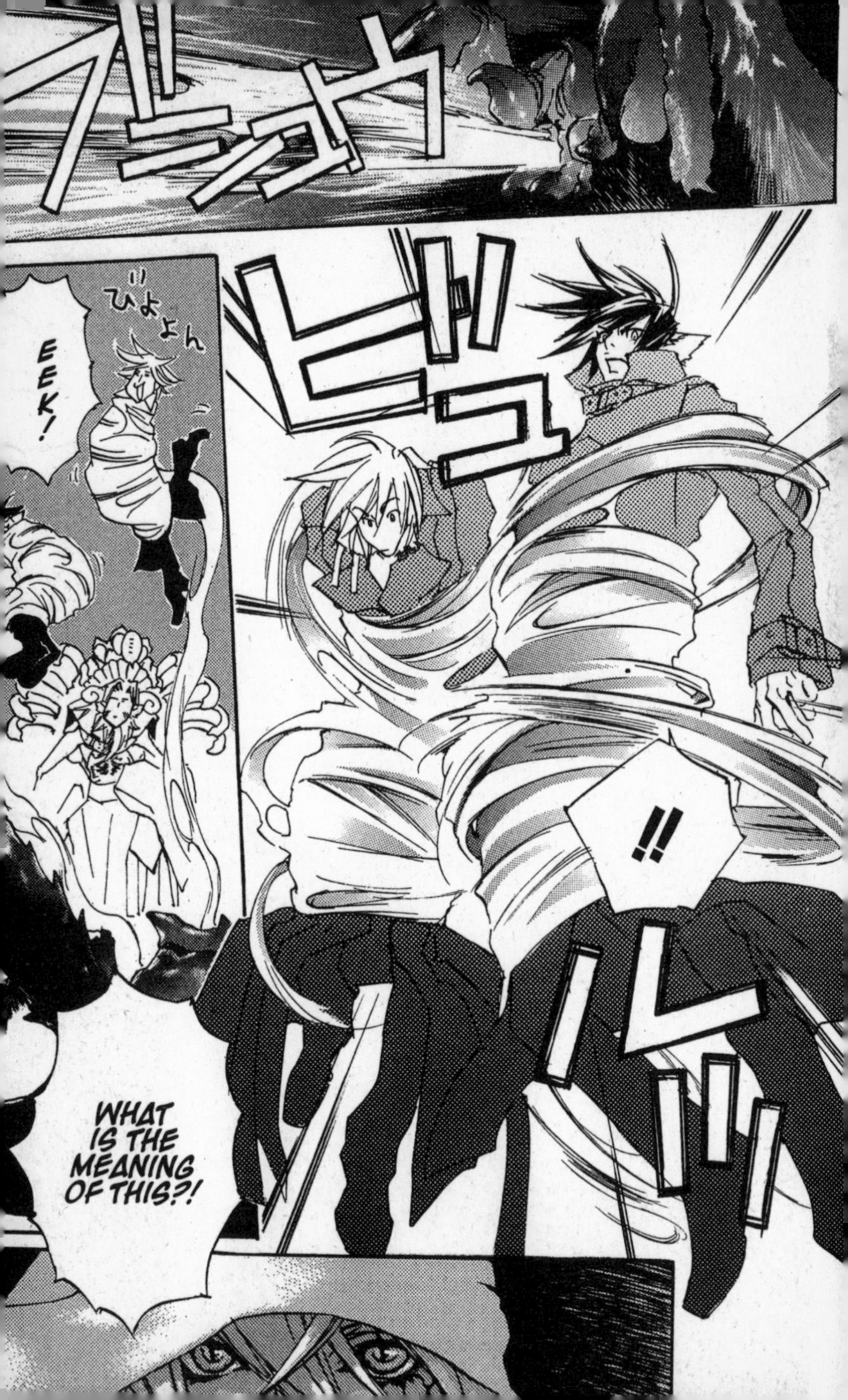

!!
EEK!
WHAT IS THE MEANING OF THIS?!

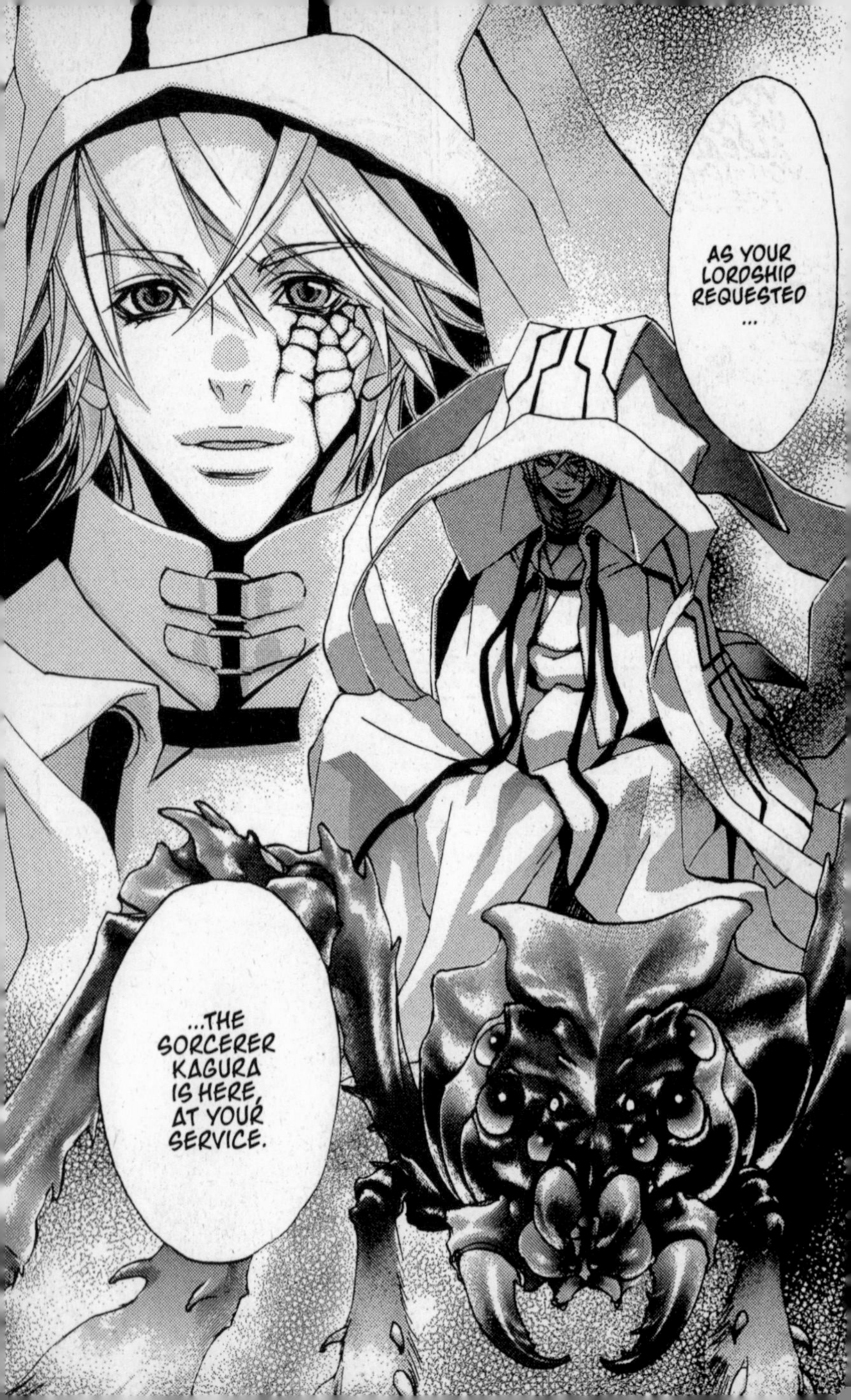
AS YOUR LORDSHIP REQUESTED ...
...THE SORCERER KAGURA IS HERE, AT YOUR SERVICE.

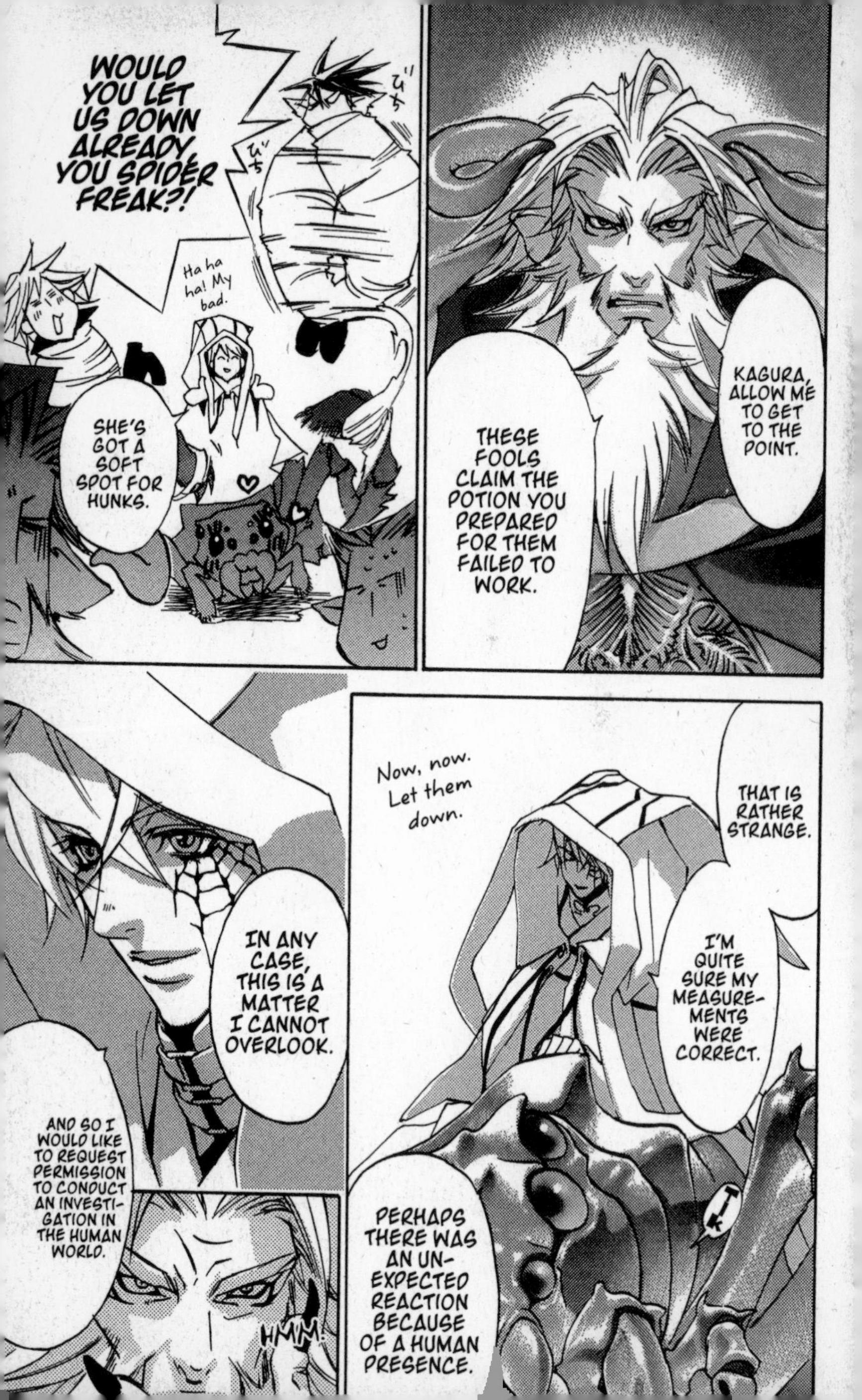
KAGURA, ALLOW ME TO GET TO THE POINT.
THESE FOOLS CLAIM THE POTION YOU PREPARED FOR THEM FAILED TO WORK.
WOULD YOU LET US DOWN ALREADY, YOU SPIDER FREAK?!
Ha ha ha! My bad.
SHE'S GOT A SOFT SPOT FOR HUNKS.
THAT IS RATHER STRANGE.
Now, now. Let them down.
I'M QUITE SURE MY MEASUREMENTS WERE CORRECT.
TIK
PERHAPS THERE WAS AN UNEXPECTED REACTION BECAUSE OF A HUMAN PRESENCE.
IN ANY CASE, THIS IS A MATTER I CANNOT OVERLOOK.
AND SO I WOULD LIKE TO REQUEST PERMISSION TO CONDUCT AN INVESTIGATION IN THE HUMAN WORLD.
HMM!

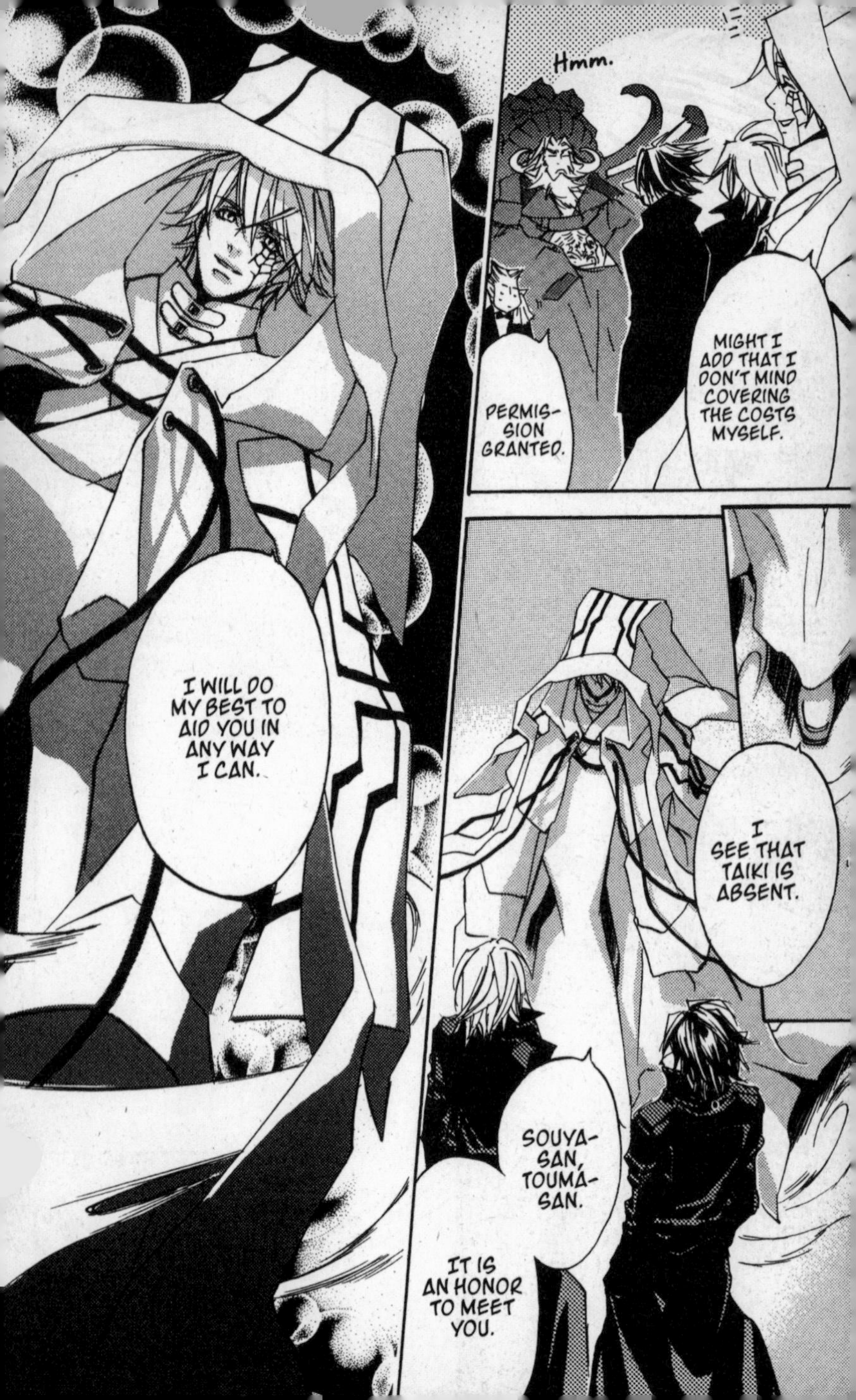
Hmm.
MIGHT I ADD THAT I DON'T MIND COVERING THE COSTS MYSELF.
PERMIS-SION GRANTED.
I SEE THAT TAIKI IS ABSENT.
SOUYA-SAN, TOUMA-SAN.
IT IS AN HONOR TO MEET YOU.
I WILL DO MY BEST TO AID YOU IN ANY WAY I CAN.

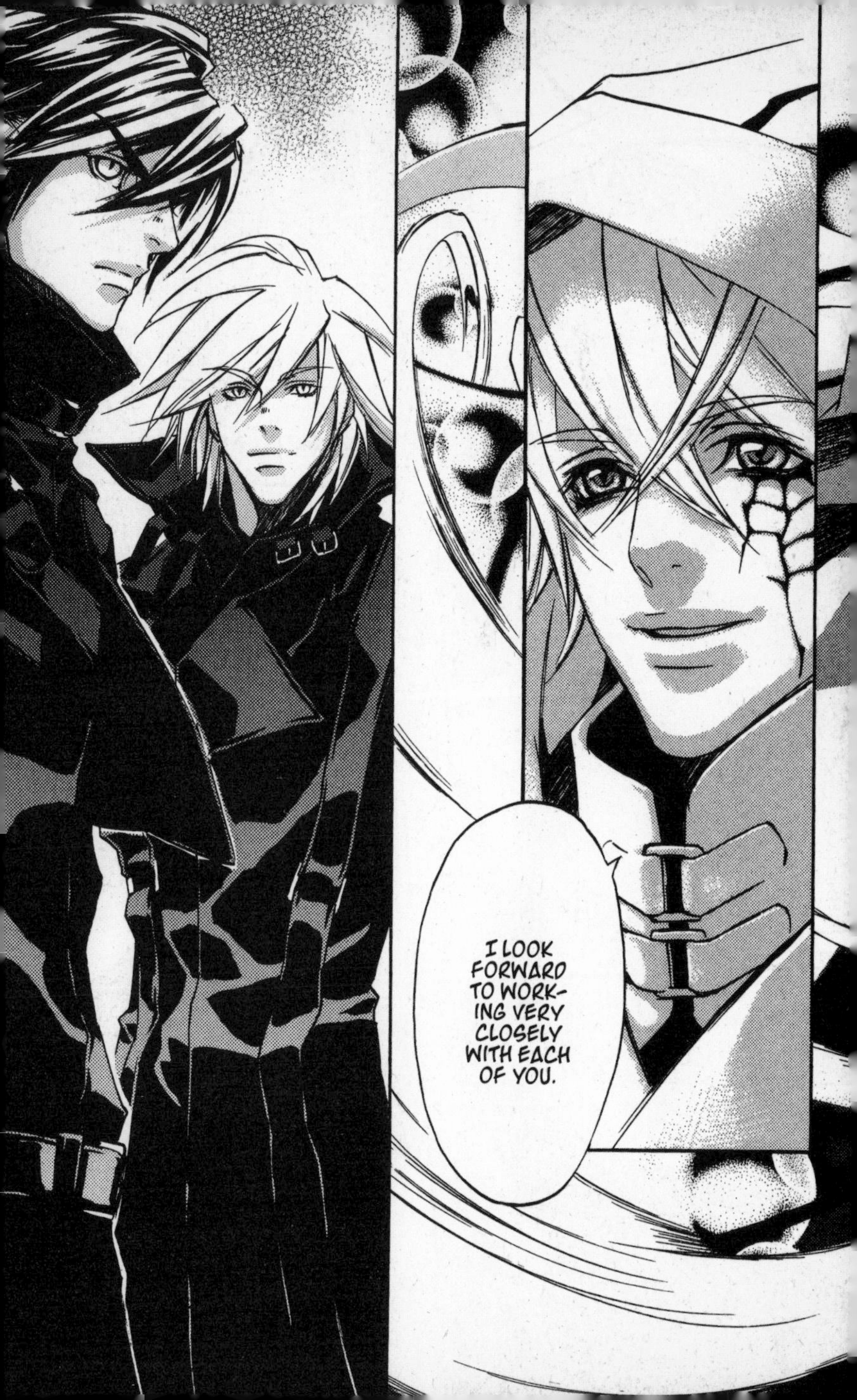
I LOOK FORWARD TO WORKING VERY CLOSELY WITH EACH OF YOU.

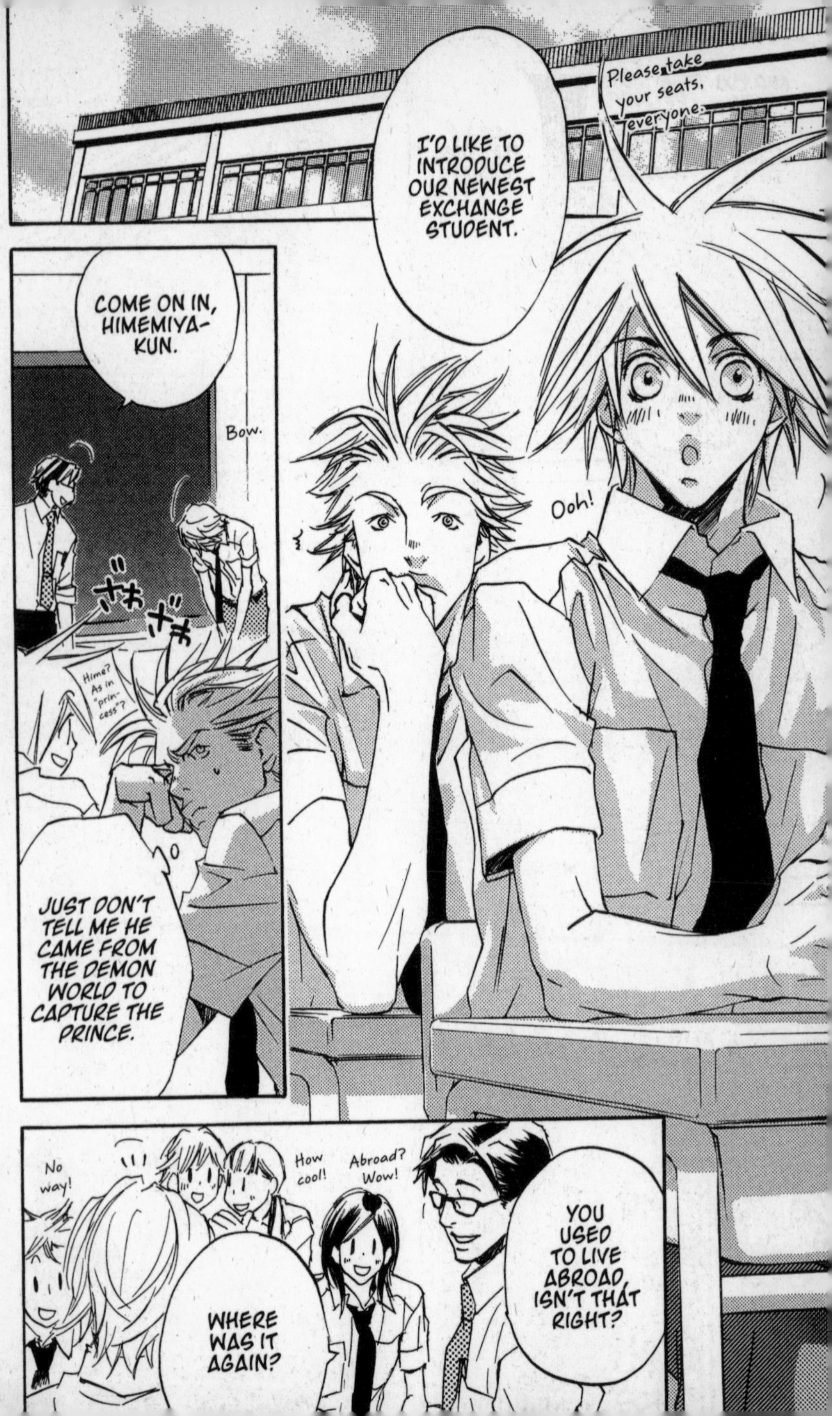

Please take your seats, everyone.
I'D LIKE TO INTRODUCE OUR NEWEST EXCHANGE STUDENT.
Ooh!
COME ON IN, HIMEMIYA-KUN.
Bow.
ザわ ザわ
Hime? As in "princess"?
JUST DON'T TELL ME HE CAME FROM THE DEMON WORLD TO CAPTURE THE PRINCE.
YOU USED TO LIVE ABROAD, ISN'T THAT RIGHT?
Abroad? Wow!
How cool!
WHERE WAS IT AGAIN?
No way!

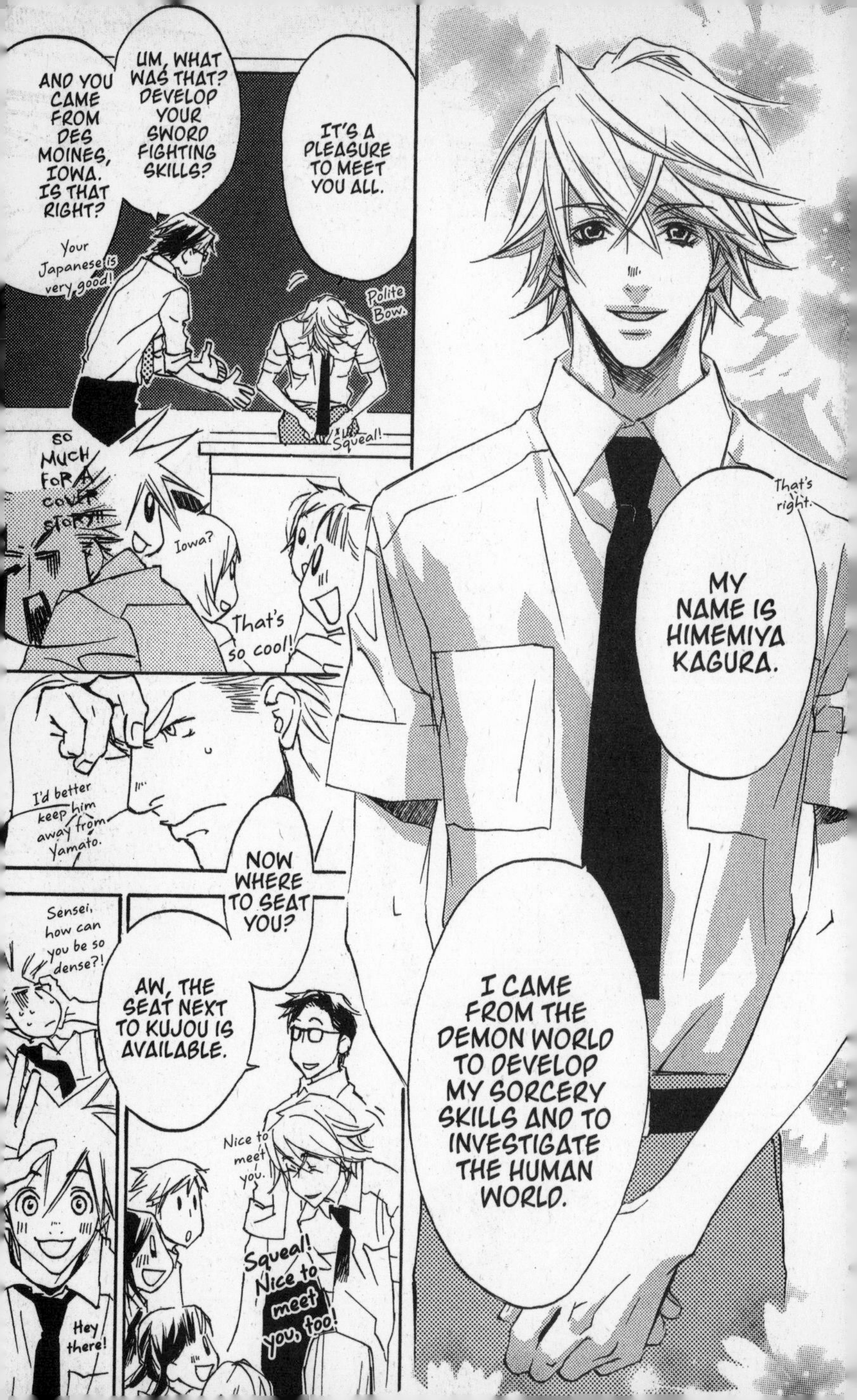
That's right.
MY NAME IS HIMEMIYA KAGURA.
I CAME FROM THE DEMON WORLD TO DEVELOP MY SORCERY SKILLS AND TO INVESTIGATE THE HUMAN WORLD.
IT'S A PLEASURE TO MEET YOU ALL.
Polite Bow.
Squeal!
UM, WHAT WAS THAT? DEVELOP YOUR SWORD FIGHTING SKILLS?
AND YOU CAME FROM DES MOINES, IOWA. IS THAT RIGHT?
Your Japanese is very good!
Iowa?
That's so cool!
SO MUCH FOR A COVER STORY!!
I'd better keep him away from Yamato.
NOW WHERE TO SEAT YOU?
AW, THE SEAT NEXT TO KUJOU IS AVAILABLE.
Sensei, how can you be so dense?!
Nice to meet you.
Squeal! Nice to meet you, too!
Hey there!

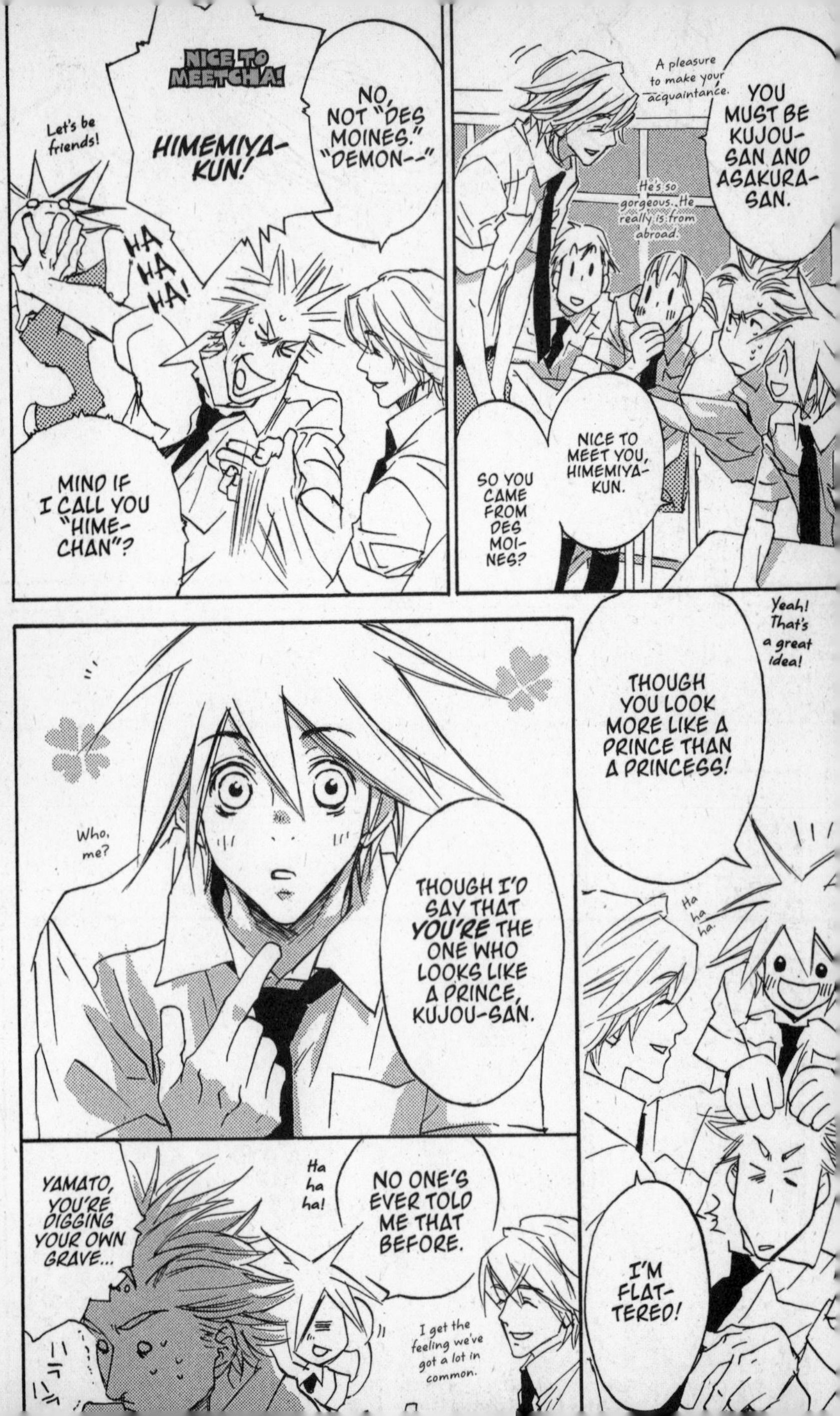
A pleasure to make your acquaintance.
YOU MUST BE KUJOU-SAN AND ASAKURA-SAN.
He's so gorgeous. He really is from abroad.
NICE TO MEET YOU, HIMEMIYA-KUN.
SO YOU CAME FROM DES MOINES?
NO, NOT "DES MOINES." "DEMON--"
NICE TO MEETCHA!
HIMEMIYA-KUN!
Let's be friends!
HA HA HA!
MIND IF I CALL YOU "HIME-CHAN"?
Yeah! That's a great idea!
THOUGH YOU LOOK MORE LIKE A PRINCE THAN A PRINCESS!
Ha ha ha.
I'M FLAT-TERED!
Who, me?
THOUGH I'D SAY THAT YOU'RE THE ONE WHO LOOKS LIKE A PRINCE, KUJOU-SAN.
NO ONE'S EVER TOLD ME THAT BEFORE.
Ha ha ha!
I get the feeling we've got a lot in common.
YAMATO, YOU'RE DIGGING YOUR OWN GRAVE...

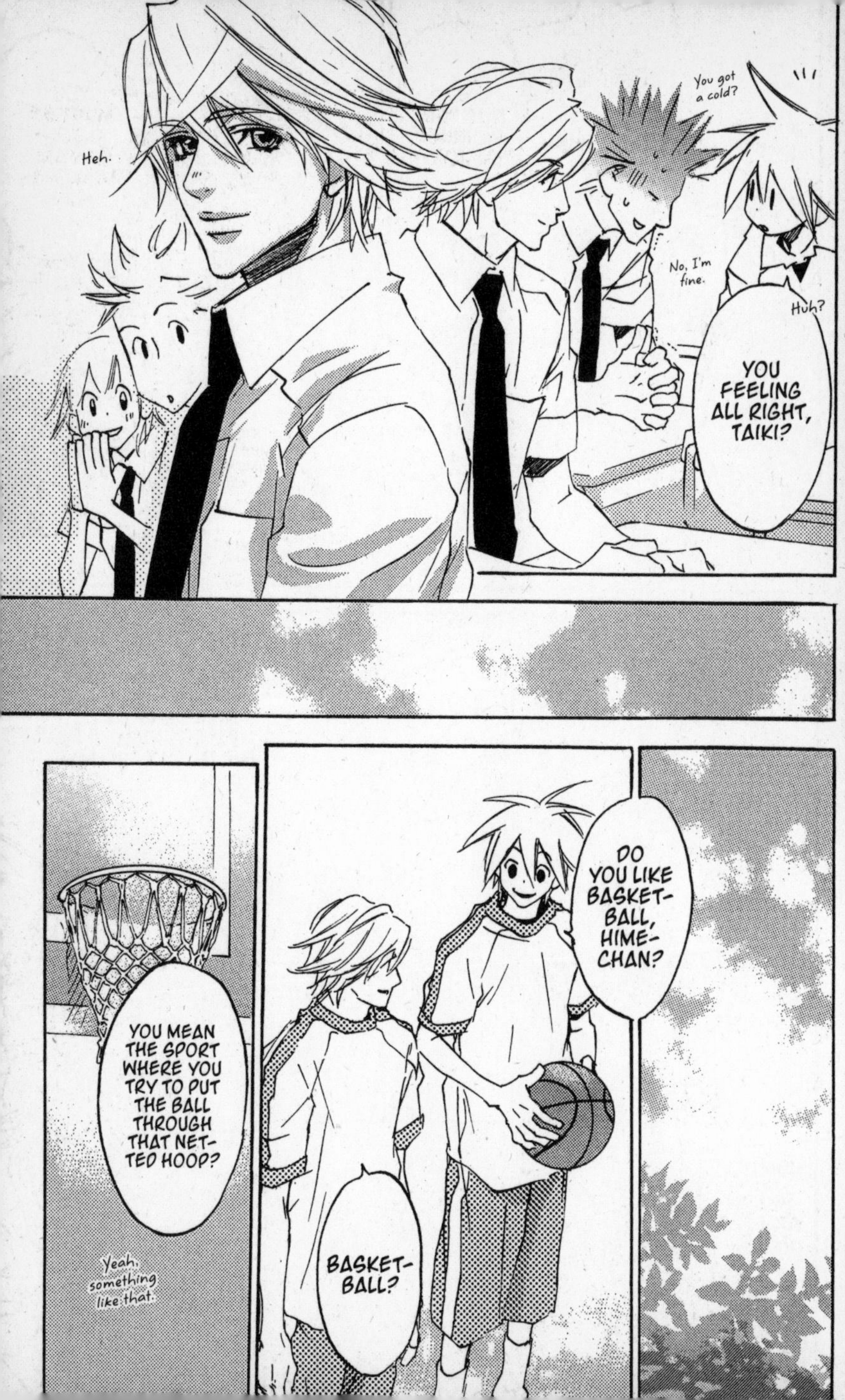
YOU FEELING ALL RIGHT, TAIKI?
Huh?
You got a cold?
No, I'm fine.
Heh.
DO YOU LIKE BASKET-BALL, HIME-CHAN?
BASKET-BALL?
YOU MEAN THE SPORT WHERE YOU TRY TO PUT THE BALL THROUGH THAT NET-TED HOOP?
Yeah, something like that.

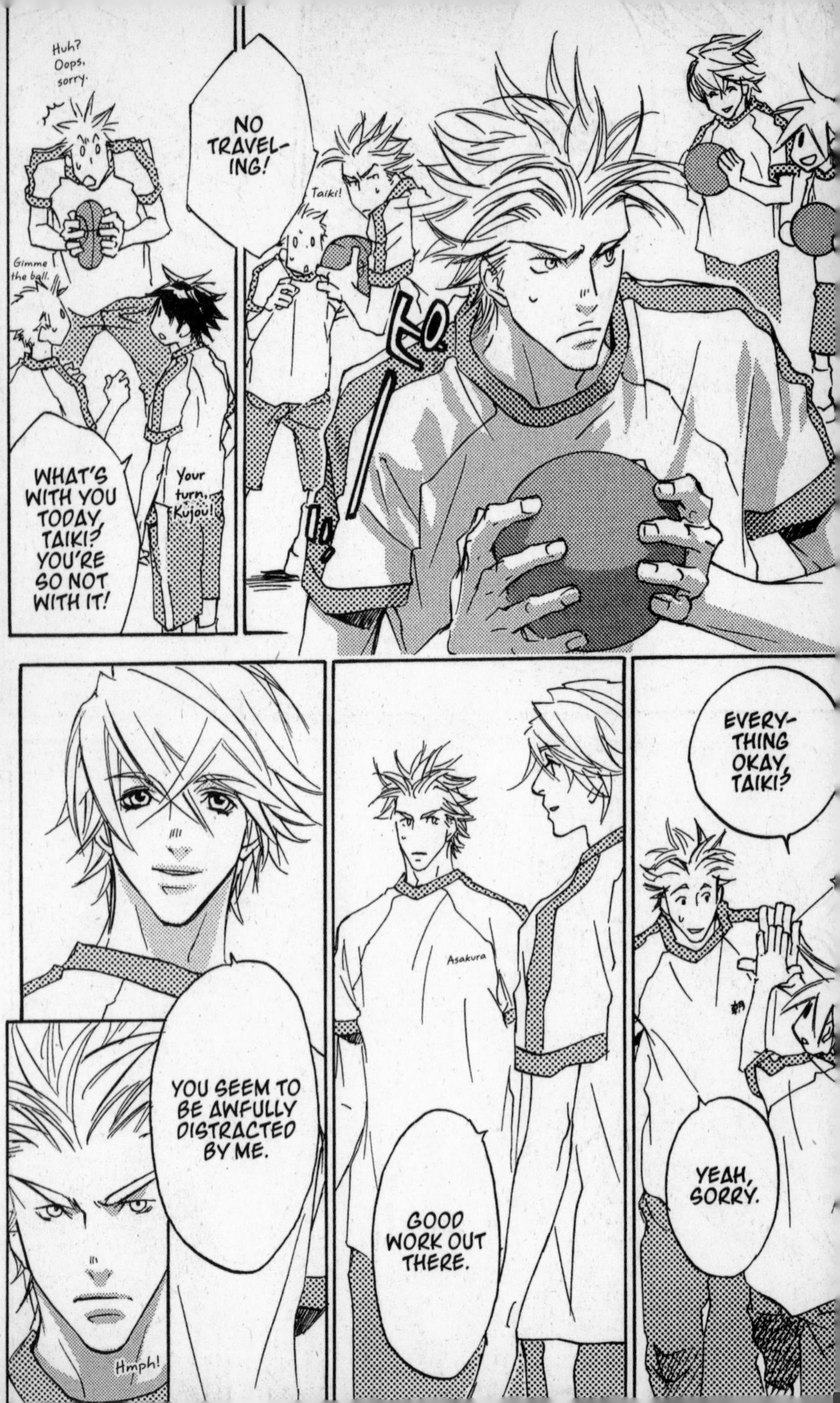
NO TRAVEL-ING!
Taiki!
Huh? Oops, sorry.
Gimme the ball.
WHAT'S WITH YOU TODAY, TAIKI? YOU'RE SO NOT WITH IT!
Your turn, Kujou!
EVERY-THING OKAY, TAIKI?
YEAH, SORRY.
Asakura
GOOD WORK OUT THERE.
YOU SEEM TO BE AWFULLY DISTRACTED BY ME.
Hmph!

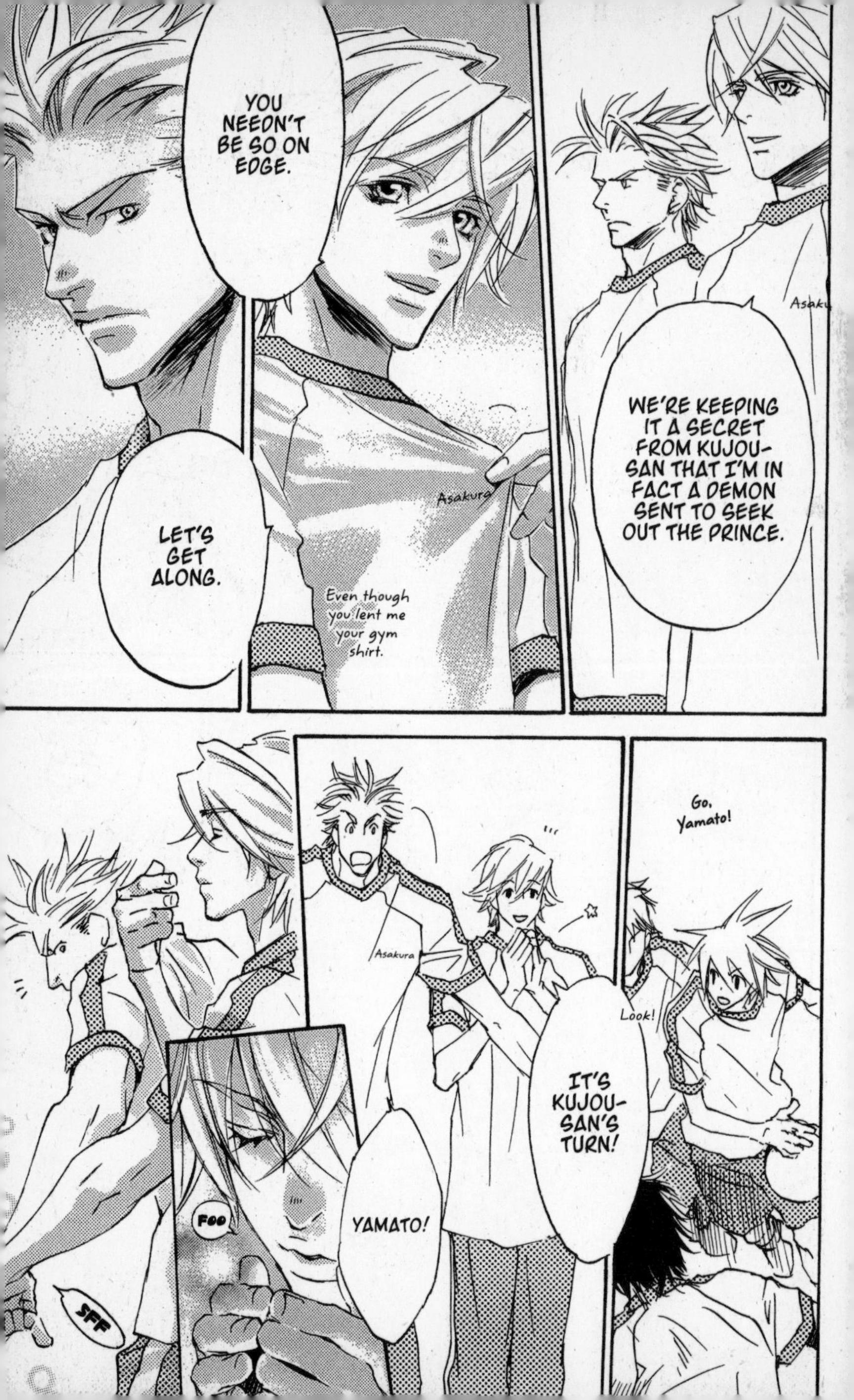
WE'RE KEEPING IT A SECRET FROM KUJOU-SAN THAT I'M IN FACT A DEMON SENT TO SEEK OUT THE PRINCE.
YOU NEEDN'T BE SO ON EDGE.
Asakura
Even though you lent me your gym shirt.
LET'S GET ALONG.
Go, Yamato!
Look!
Asakura
IT'S KUJOU-SAN'S TURN!
YAMATO!
FOO
SFF

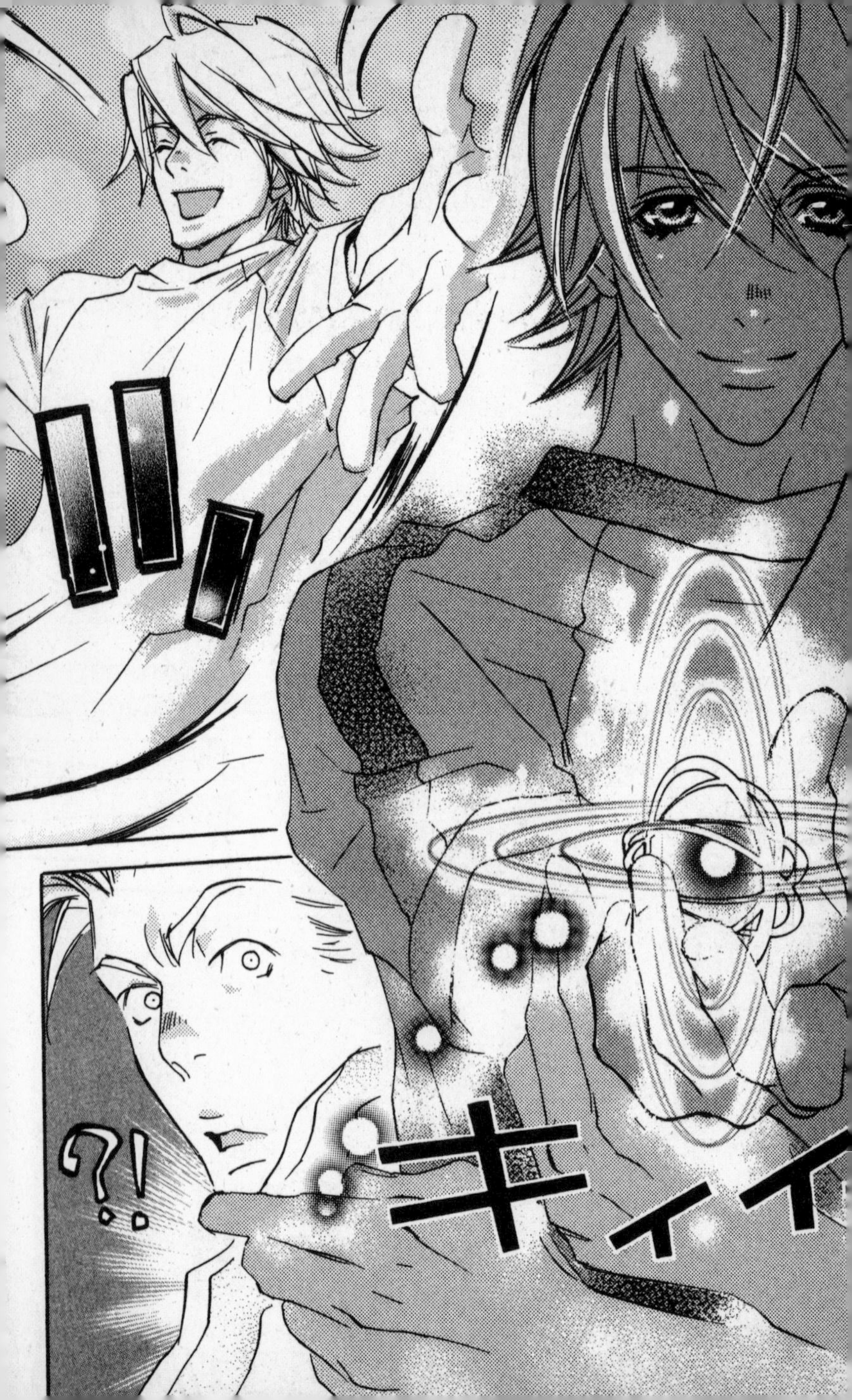
キイイ
?!

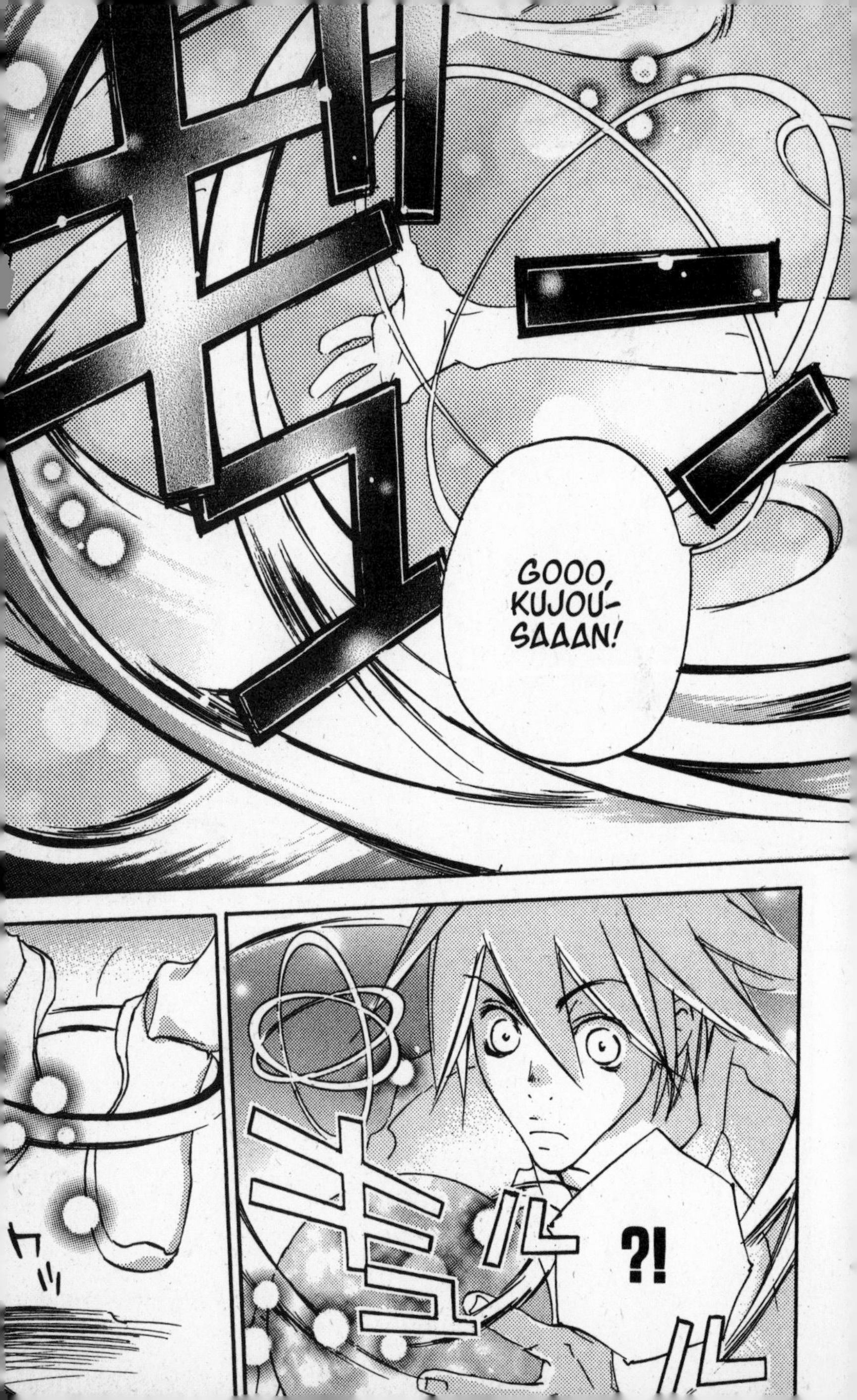
GOOO, KUJOU-SAAAN!
?!

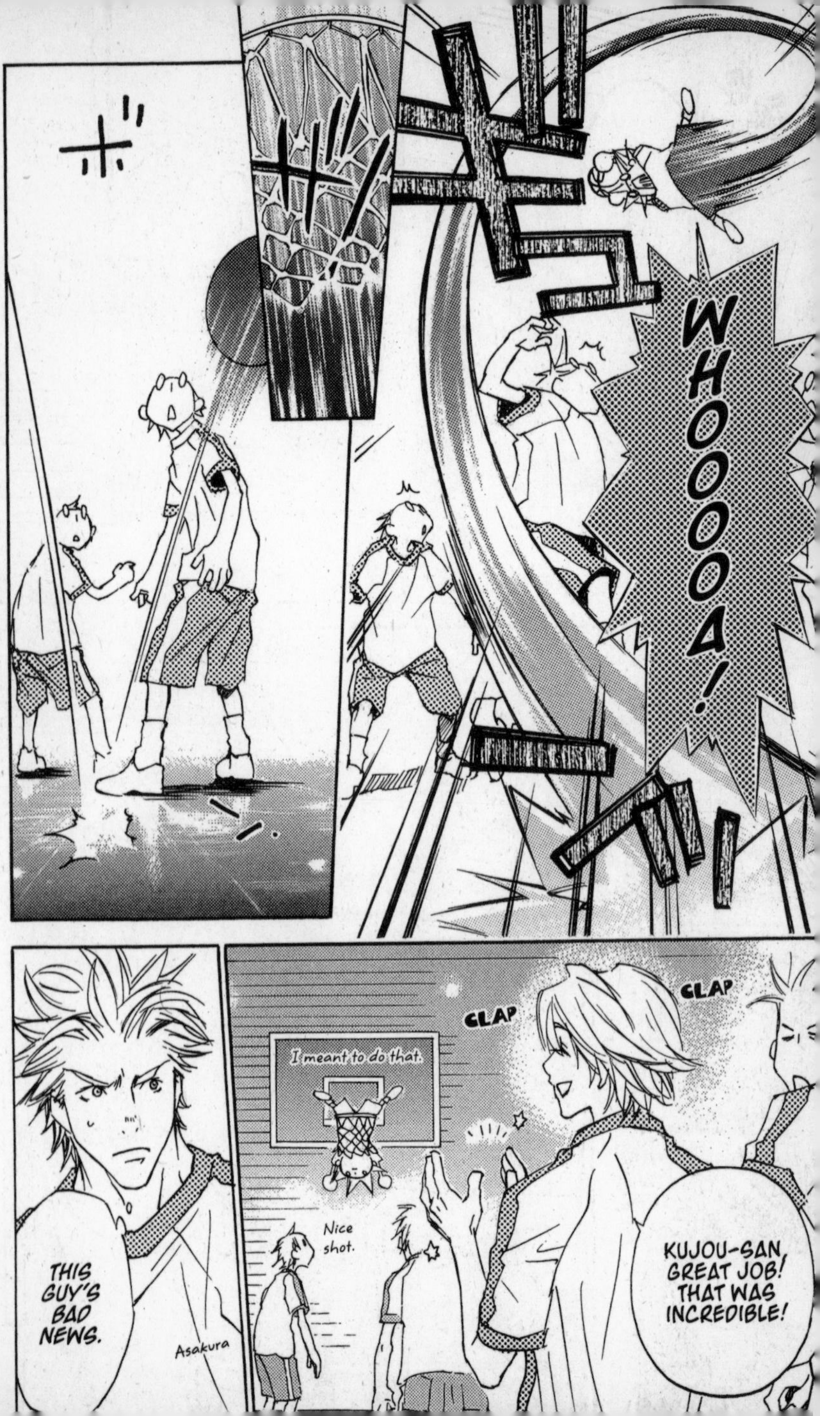
WHOOOOA!!
GLAP
GLAP
KUJOU-SAN, GREAT JOB! THAT WAS INCREDIBLE!
I meant to do that.
Nice shot.
THIS GUY'S BAD NEWS.
Asakura

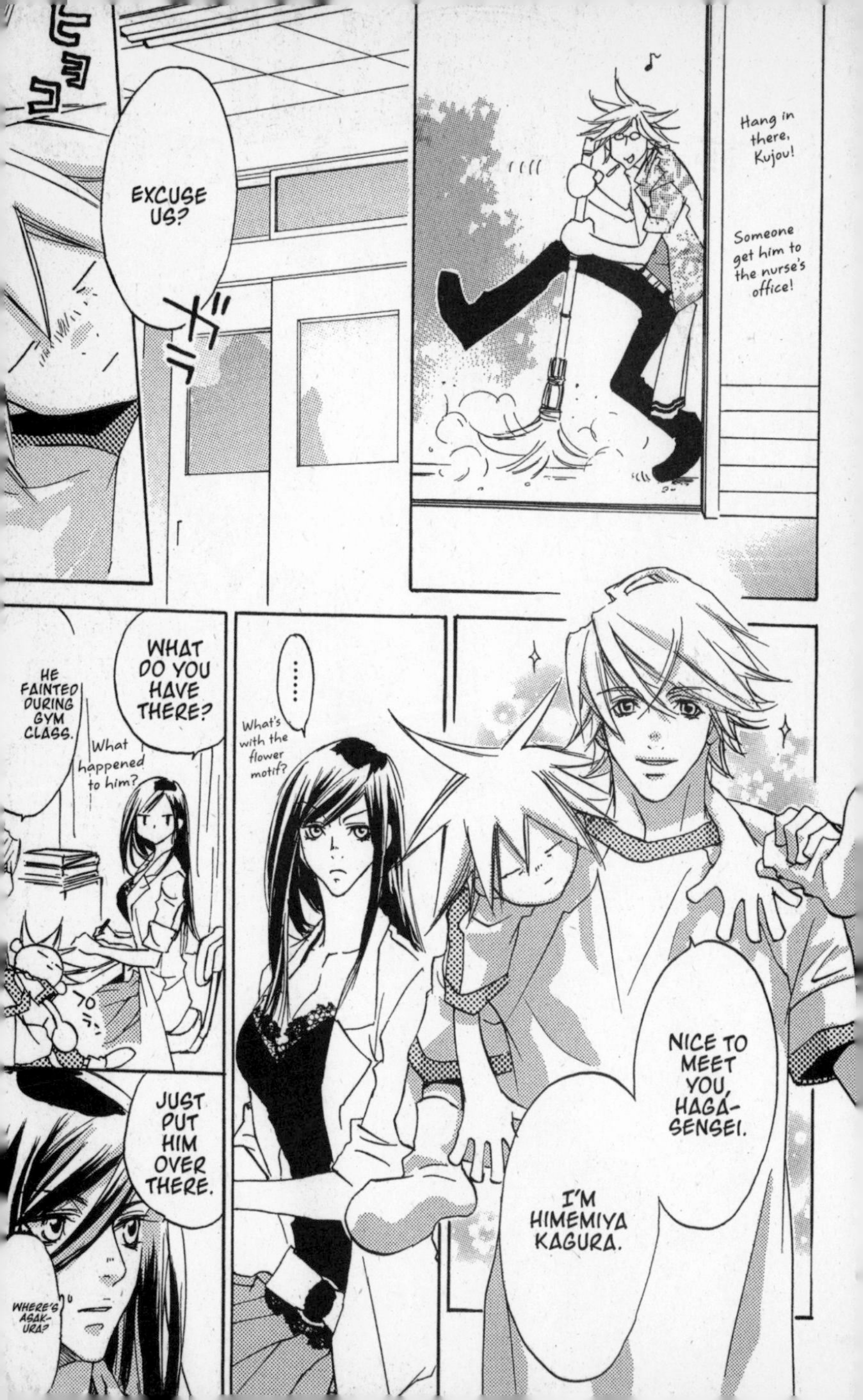
Hang in there, Kujou!
Someone get him to the nurse's office!
EXCUSE US?
NICE TO MEET YOU, HAGA-SENSEI.
I'M HIMEMIYA KAGURA.
......
What's with the flower motif?
WHAT DO YOU HAVE THERE?
HE FAINTED DURING GYM CLASS.
What happened to him?
JUST PUT HIM OVER THERE.
WHERE'S ASAKURA?

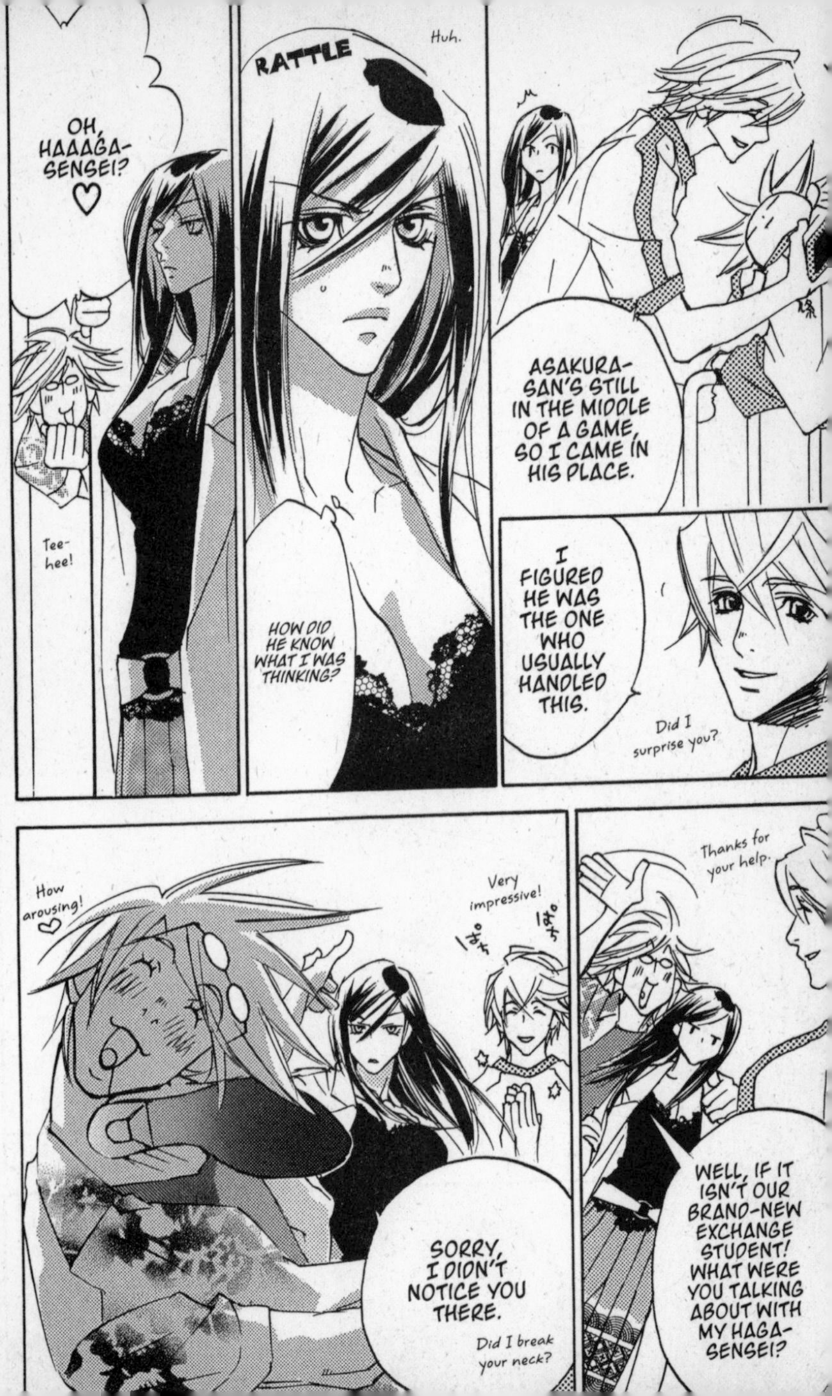
Huh.
ASAKURA-SAN'S STILL IN THE MIDDLE OF A GAME, SO I CAME IN HIS PLACE.
I FIGURED HE WAS THE ONE WHO USUALLY HANDLED THIS.
Did I surprise you?
RATTLE
HOW DID HE KNOW WHAT I WAS THINKING?
OH, HAAAGA-SENSEI? ♡
Tee-hee!
Thanks for your help.
WELL, IF IT ISN'T OUR BRAND-NEW EXCHANGE STUDENT! WHAT WERE YOU TALKING ABOUT WITH MY HAGA-SENSEI?
Very impressive!
ぱち ぱち
How arousing! ♡
SORRY, I DIDN'T NOTICE YOU THERE.
Did I break your neck?

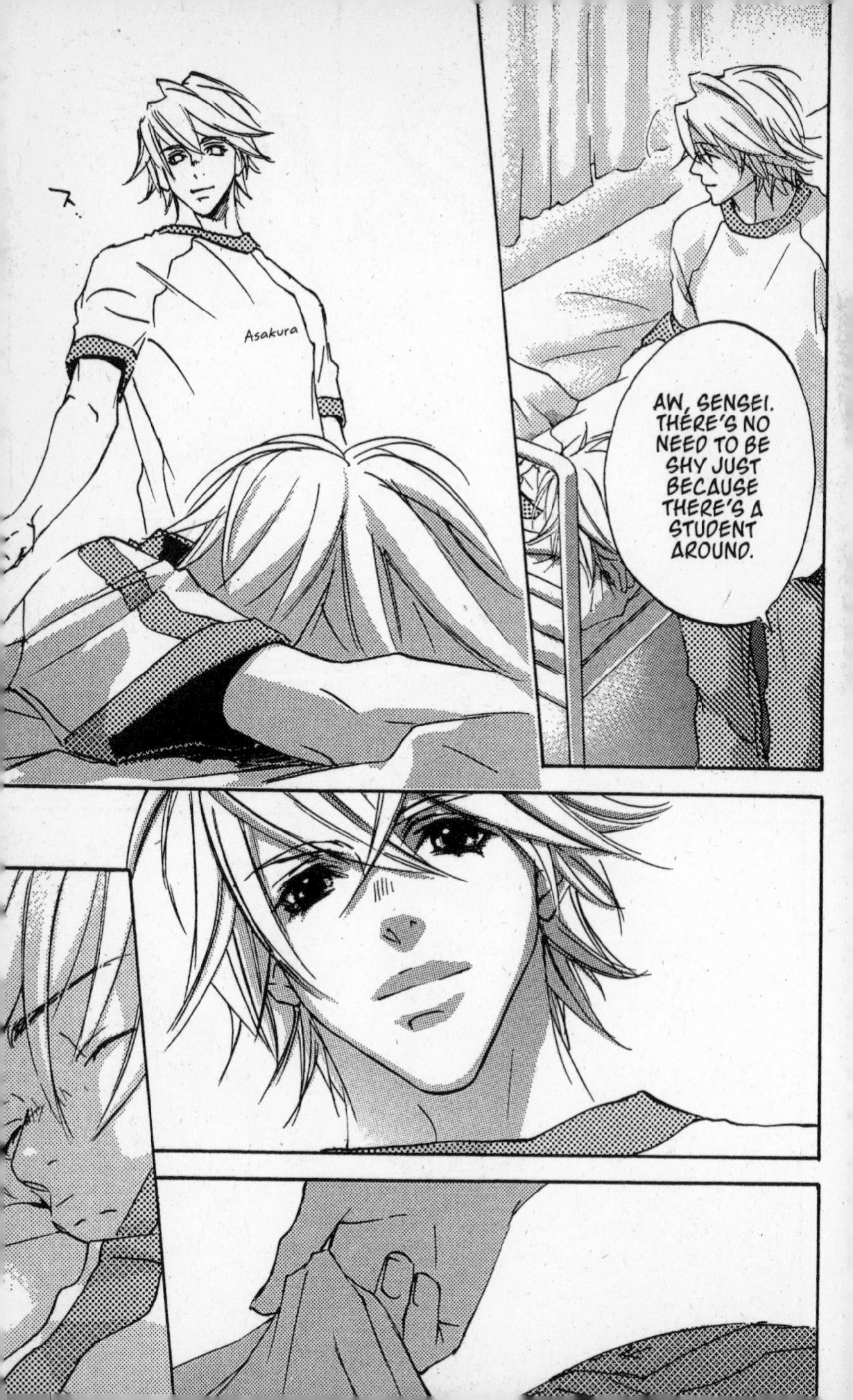
AW, SENSEI. THERE'S NO NEED TO BE SHY JUST BECAUSE THERE'S A STUDENT AROUND.
Asakura

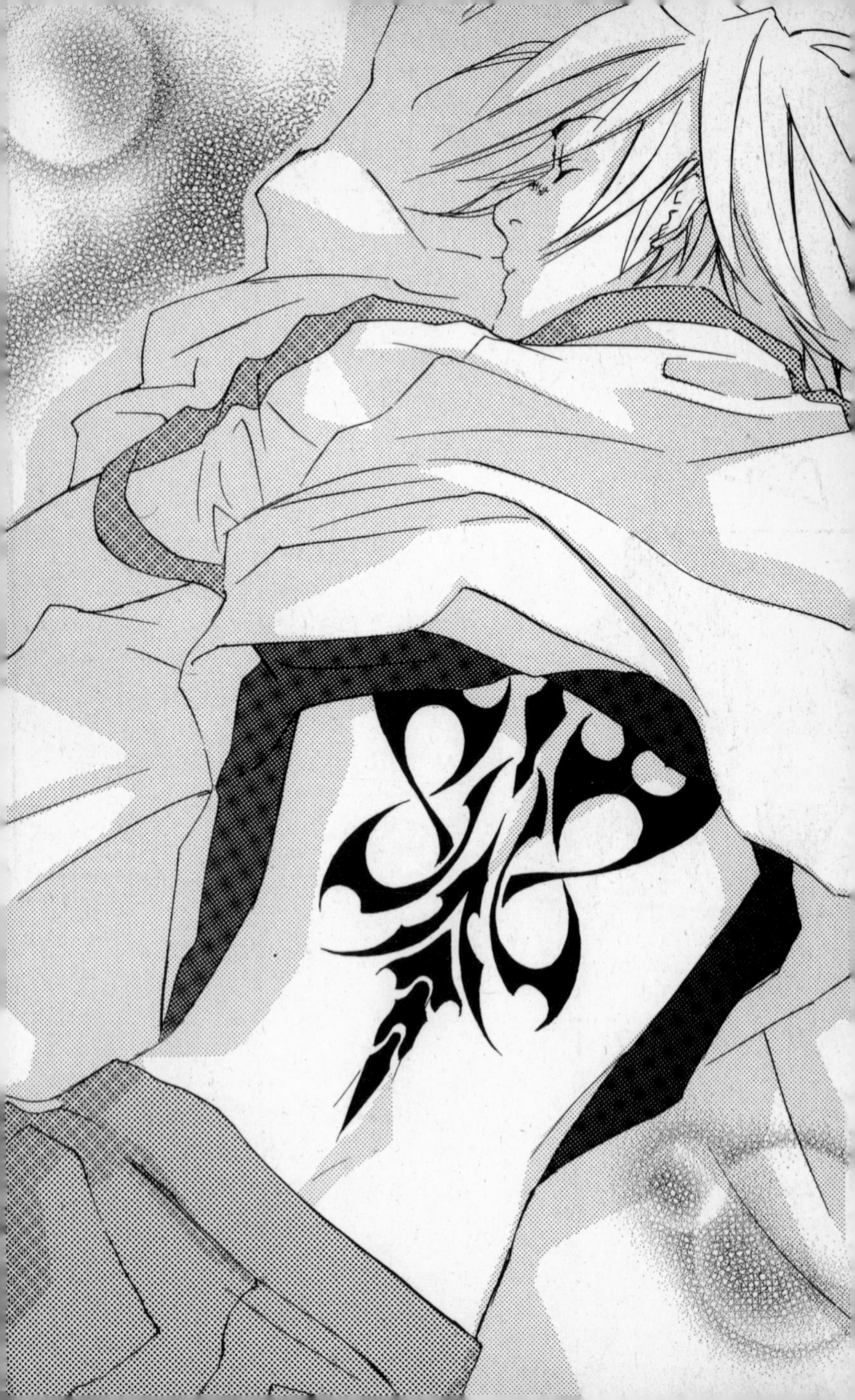

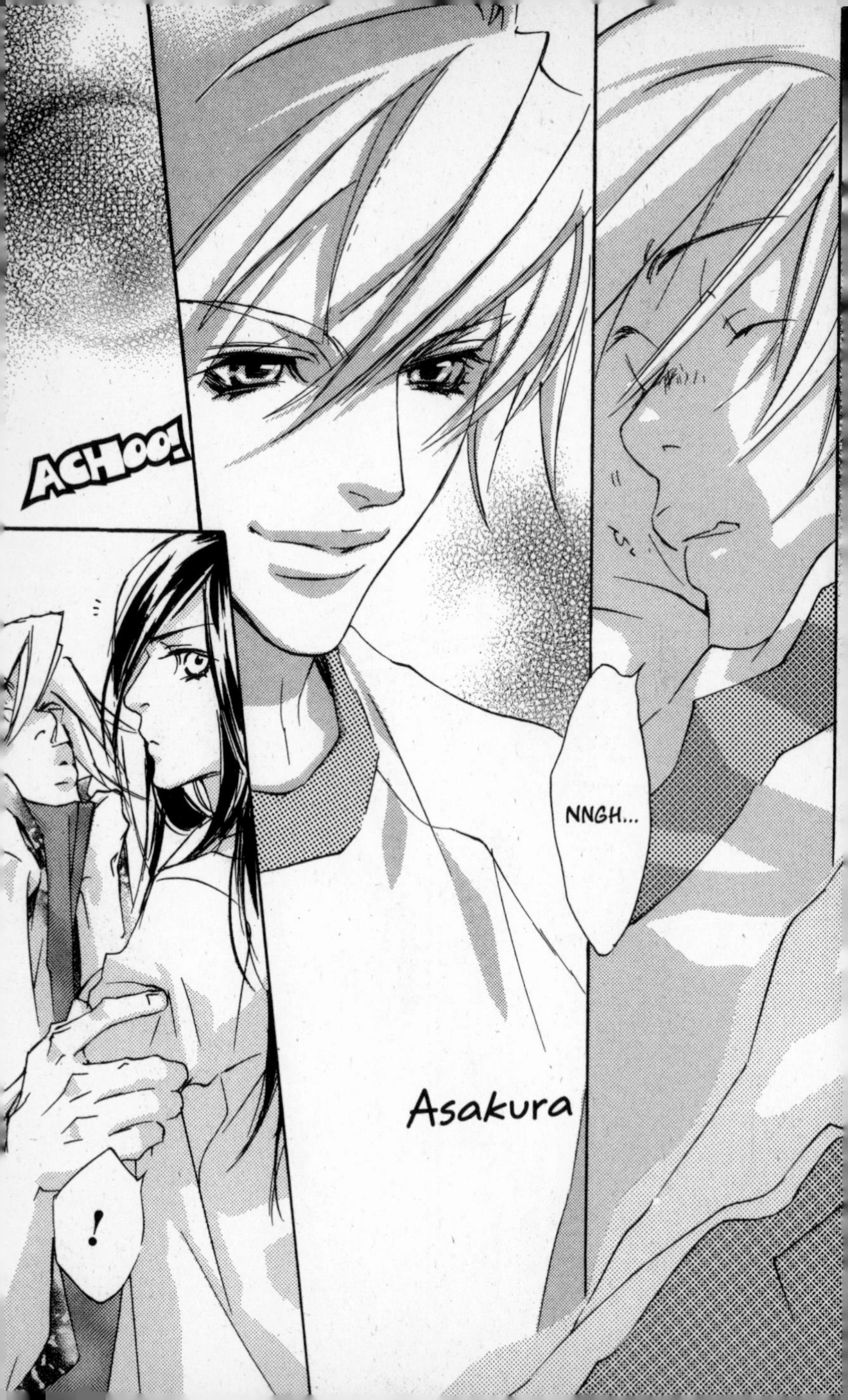
NNGH...
Asakura
ACHOO!
!

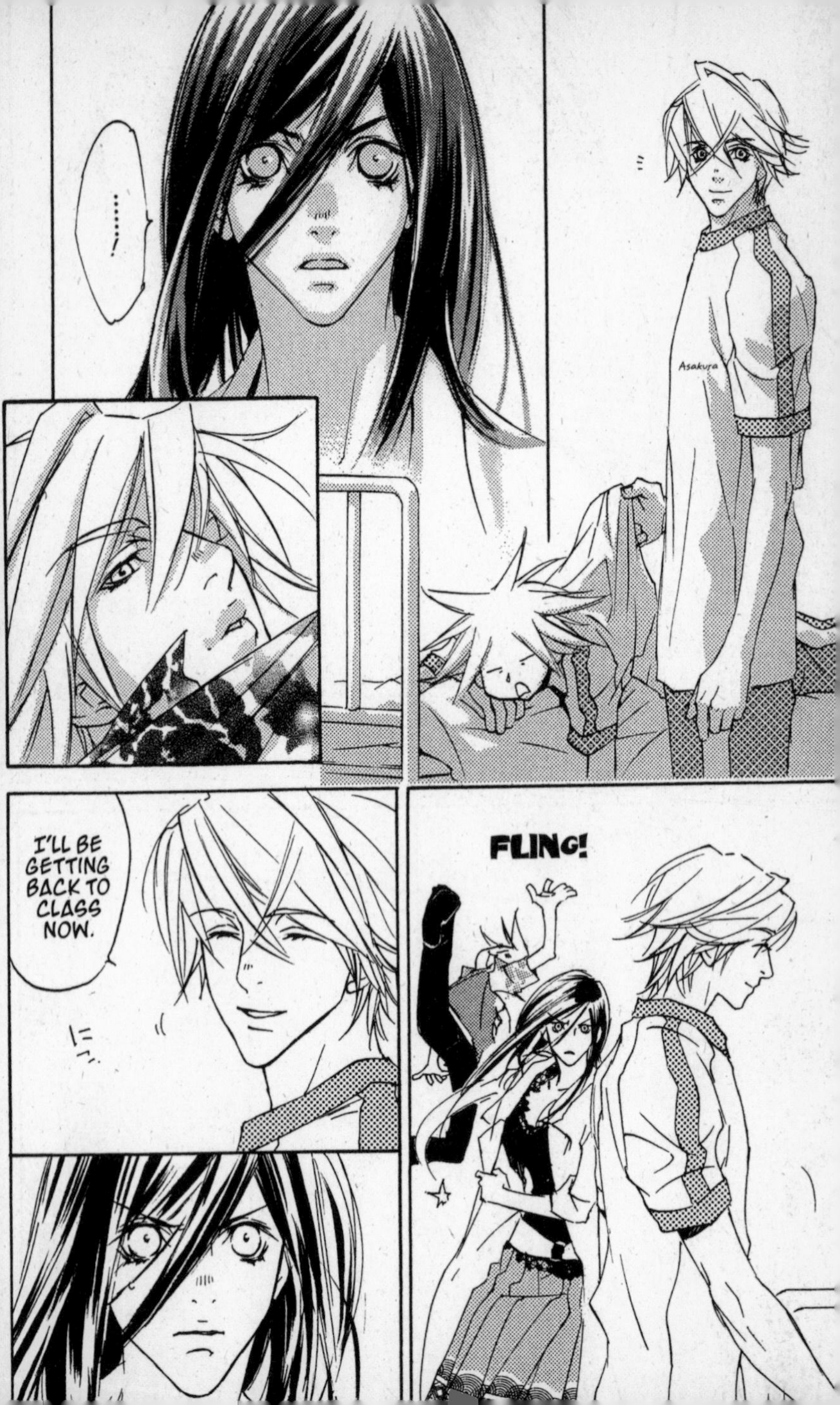
......!
Asakura
I'LL BE GETTING BACK TO CLASS NOW.
FLING!

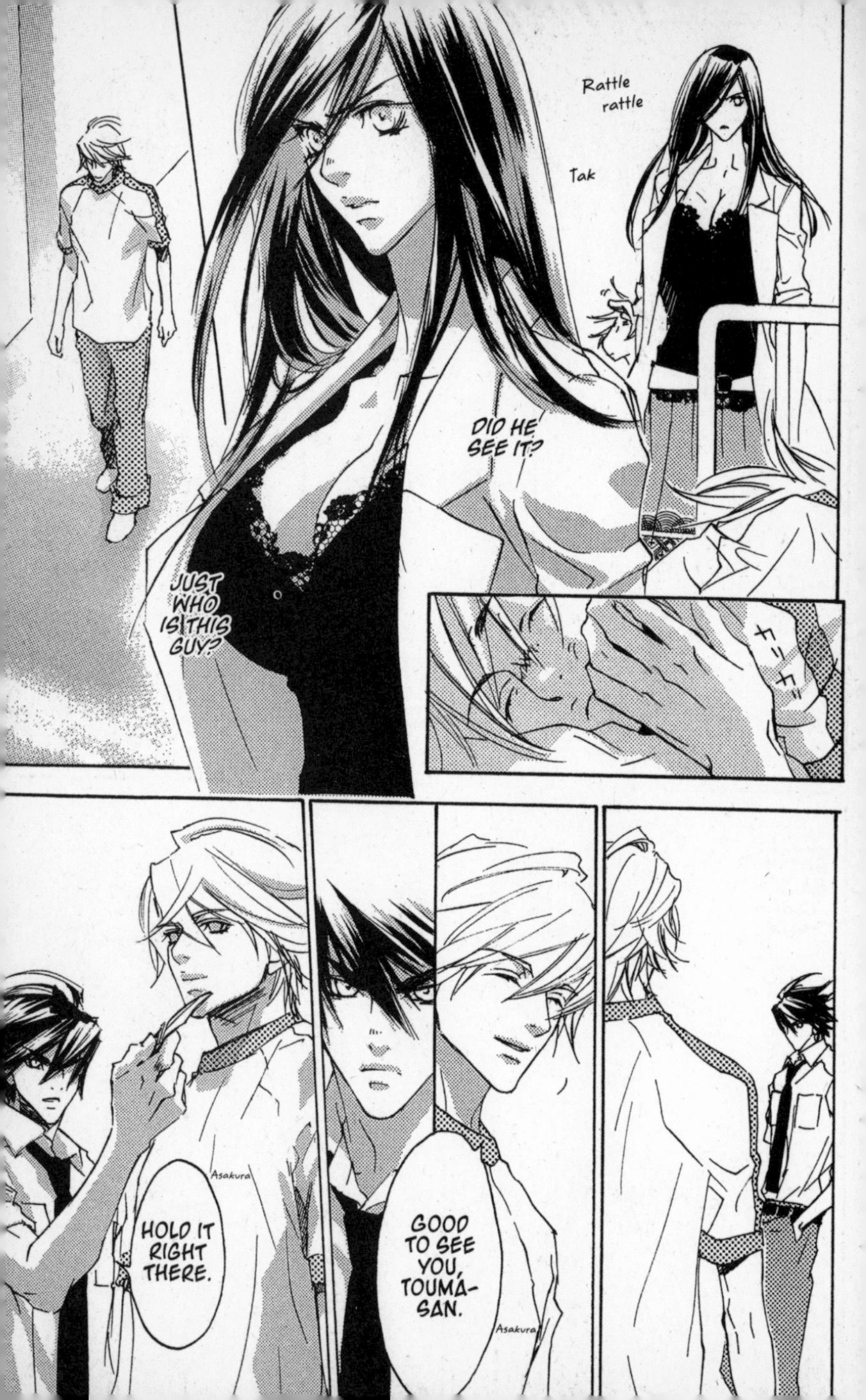
Rattle rattle
Tak
DID HE SEE IT?
JUST WHO IS THIS GUY?
GOOD TO SEE YOU, TOUMA-SAN.
Asakura
Asakura
HOLD IT RIGHT THERE.

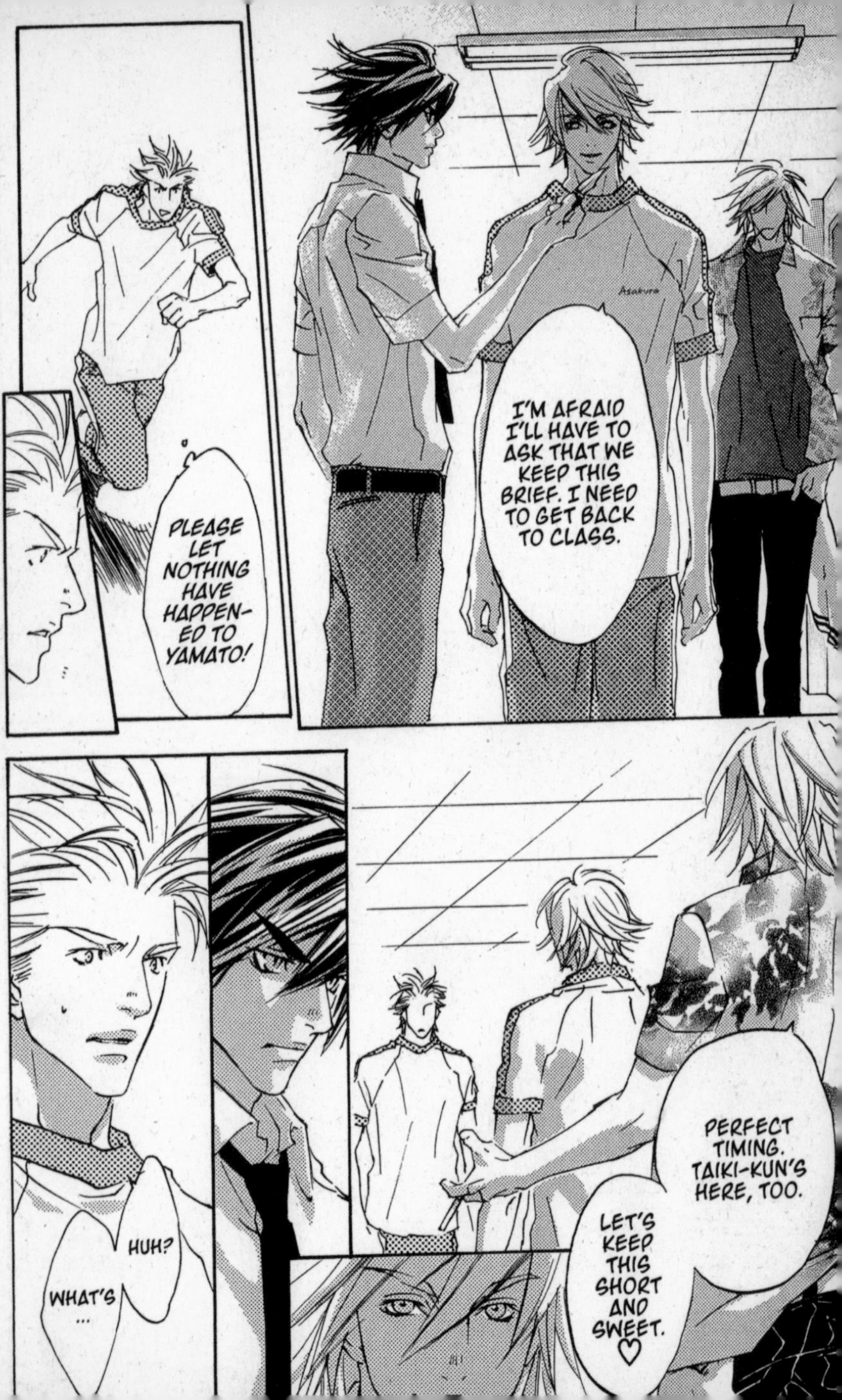
I'M AFRAID I'LL HAVE TO ASK THAT WE KEEP THIS BRIEF. I NEED TO GET BACK TO CLASS.
PLEASE LET NOTHING HAVE HAPPEN-ED TO YAMATO!
PERFECT TIMING. TAIKI-KUN'S HERE, TOO.
LET'S KEEP THIS SHORT AND SWEET. ♡
HUH?
WHAT'S ...

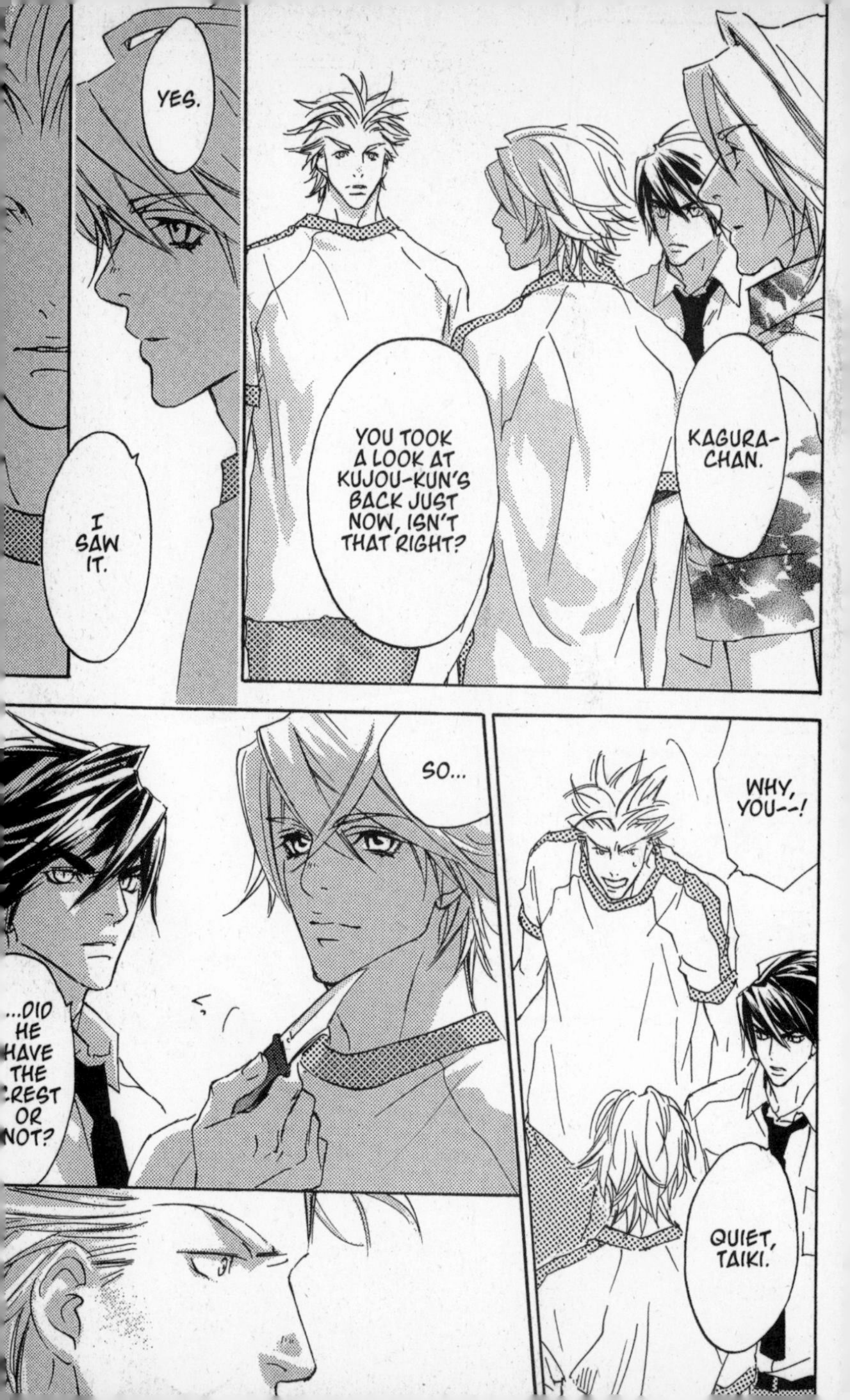
KAGURA-CHAN.
YOU TOOK A LOOK AT KUJOU-KUN'S BACK JUST NOW, ISN'T THAT RIGHT?
YES.
I SAW IT.
WHY, YOU--!
QUIET, TAIKI.
SO...
...DID HE HAVE THE CREST OR NOT?

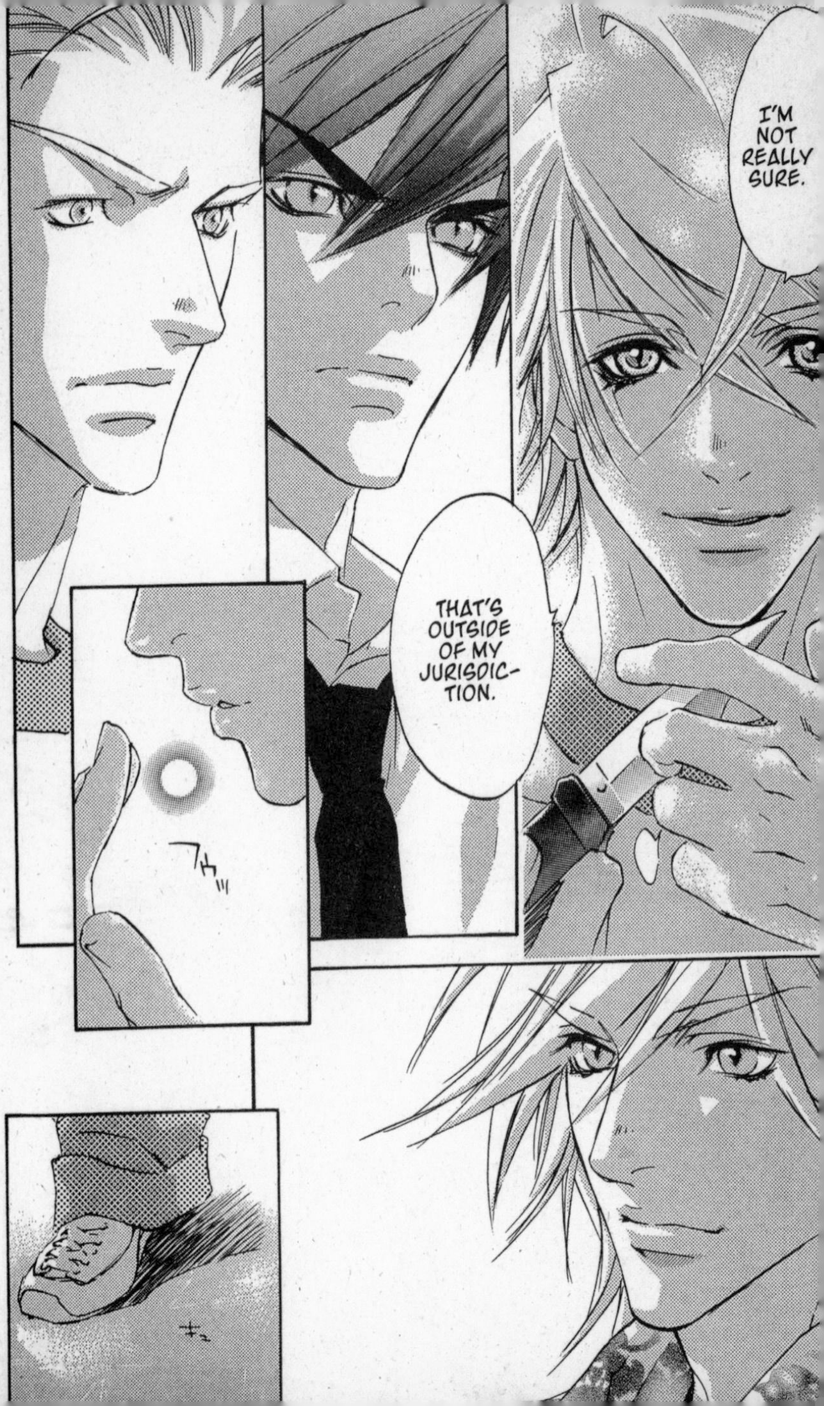
I'M NOT REALLY SURE.
THAT'S OUTSIDE OF MY JURISDICTION.

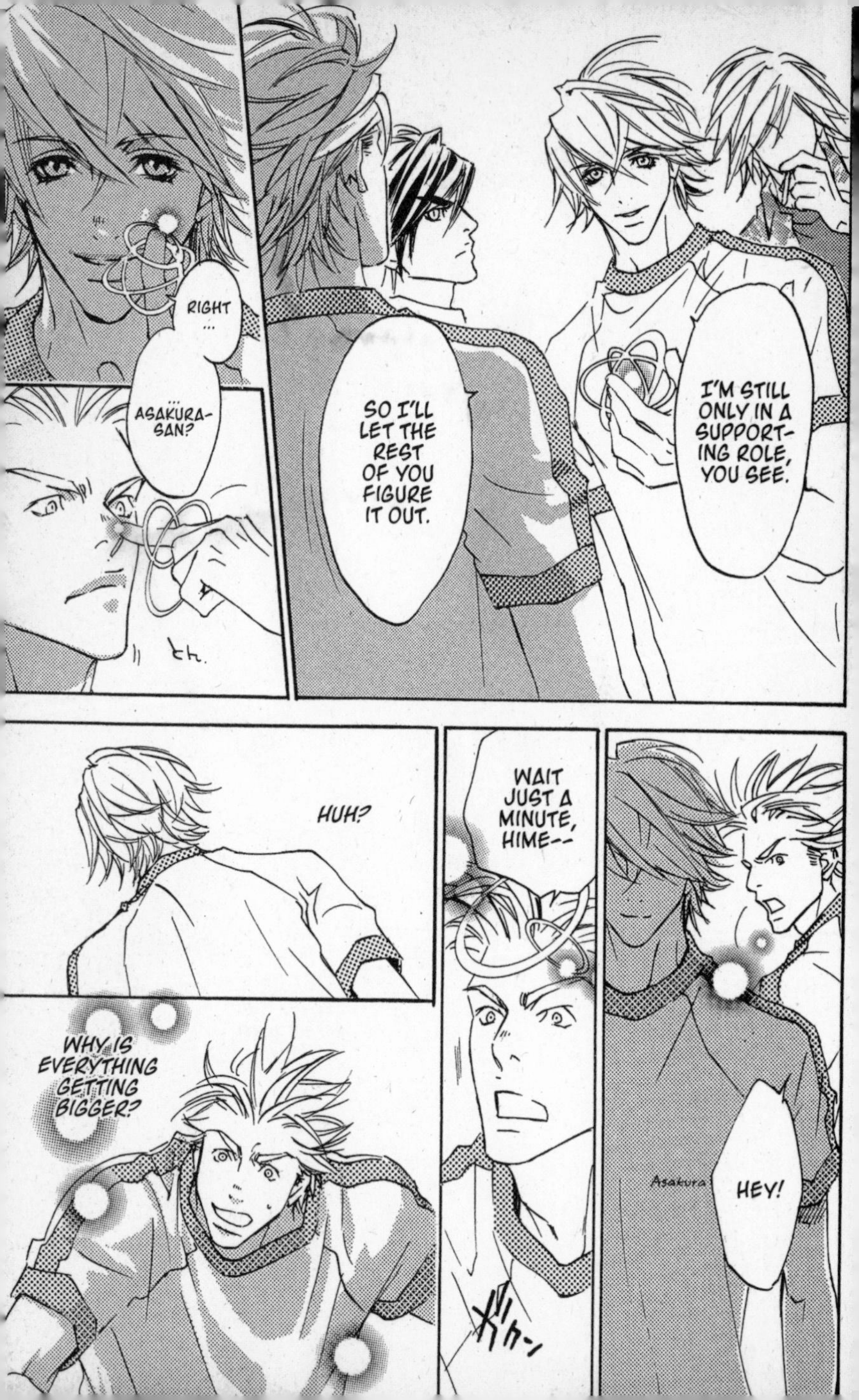
I'M STILL ONLY IN A SUPPORTING ROLE, YOU SEE.
SO I'LL LET THE REST OF YOU FIGURE IT OUT.
RIGHT...
...ASAKURA-SAN?
とん.
HEY!
Asakura
WAIT JUST A MINUTE, HIME--
HUH?
WHY IS EVERYTHING GETTING BIGGER?

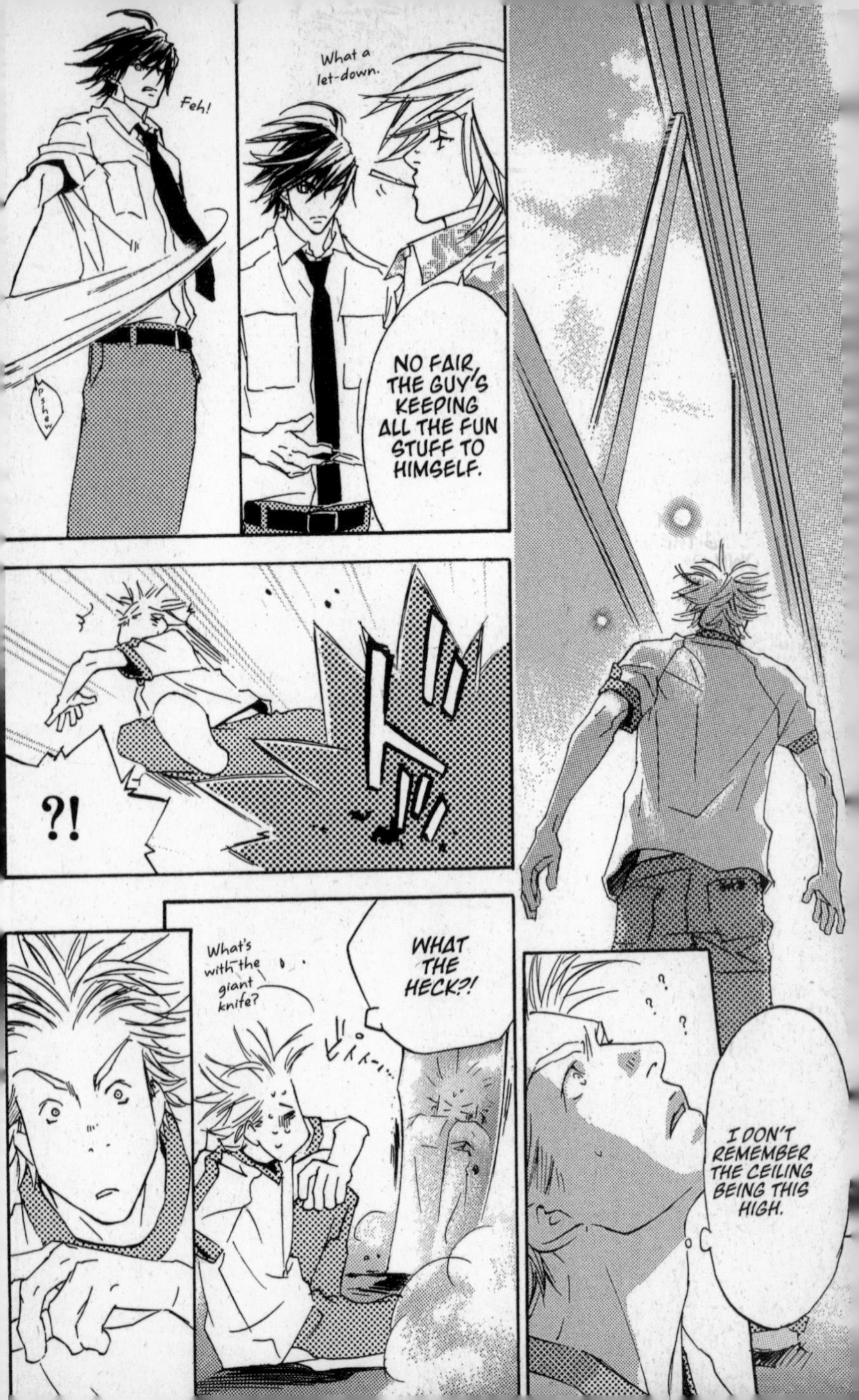
What a let-down.
NO FAIR, THE GUY'S KEEPING ALL THE FUN STUFF TO HIMSELF.
Feh!
Pshew
?!
I DON'T REMEMBER THE CEILING BEING THIS HIGH.
WHAT THE HECK?!
What's with the giant knife?

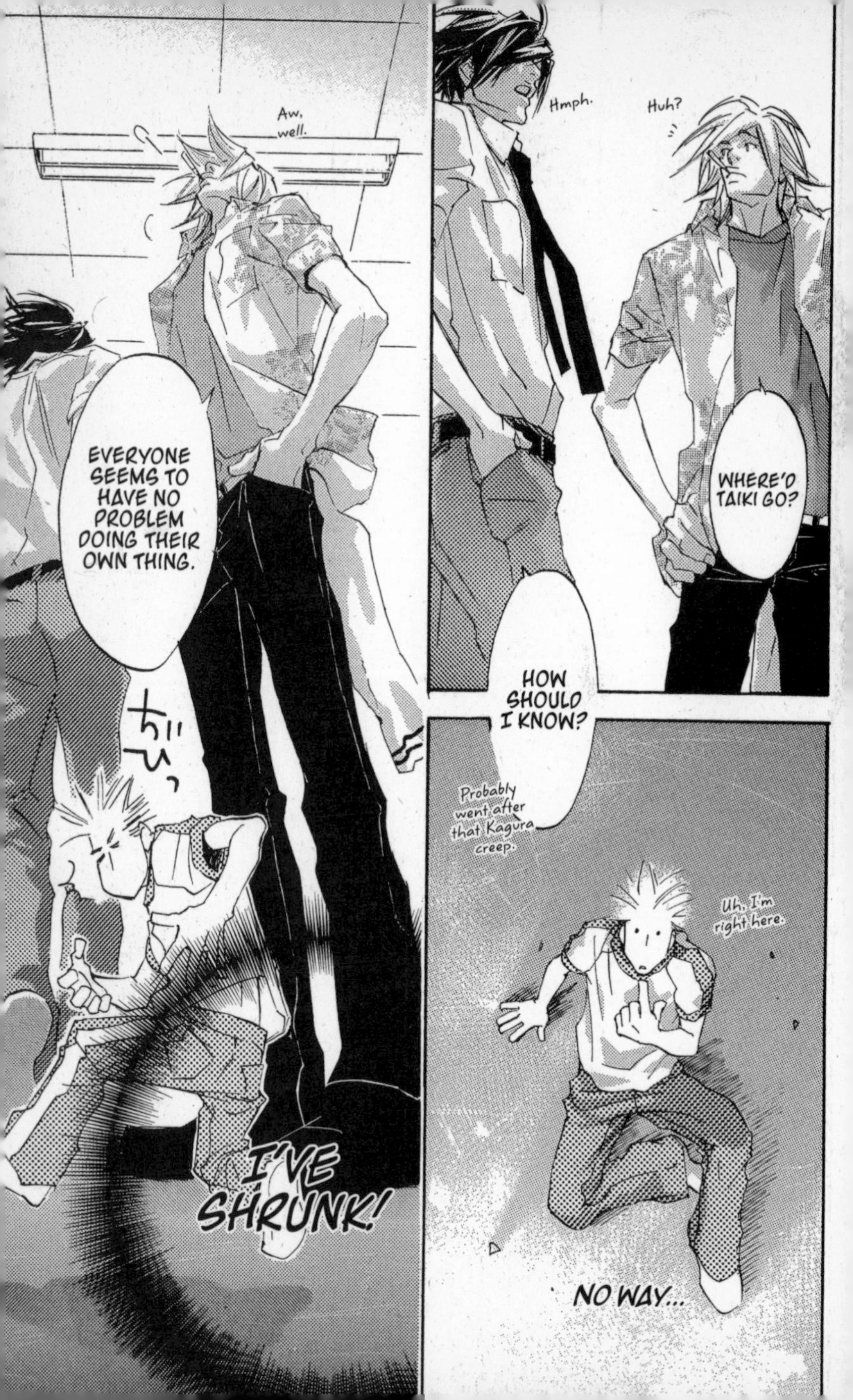

Huh?
Hmph.
WHERE'D TAIKI GO?
HOW SHOULD I KNOW?
Probably went after that Kagura creep.
Uh, I'm right here.
NO WAY...
Aw, well.
EVERYONE SEEMS TO HAVE NO PROBLEM DOING THEIR OWN THING.
I'VE SHRUNK!

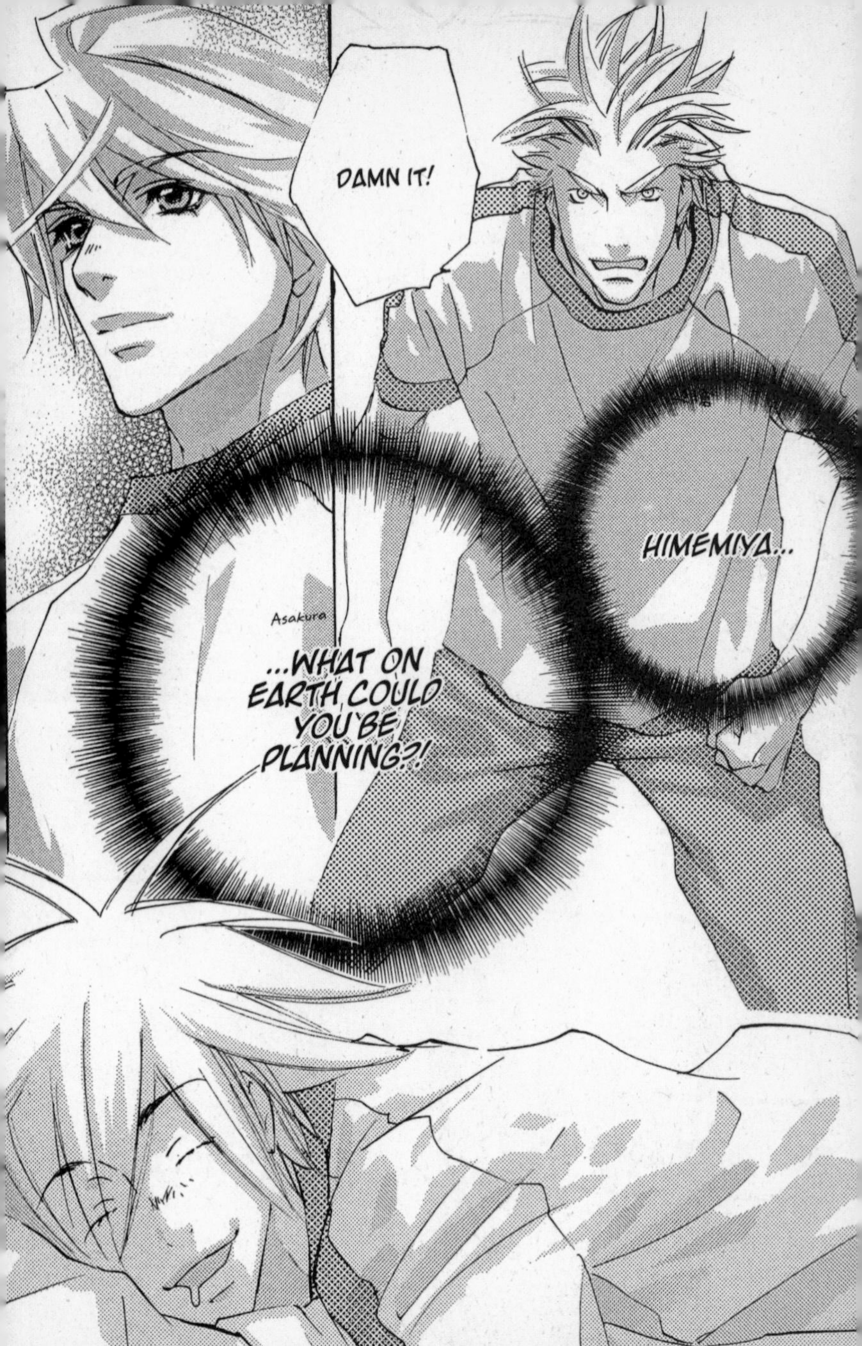
DAMN IT!
HIMEMIYA...
Asakura
...WHAT ON EARTH COULD YOU BE PLANNING?!

★vol.15★End

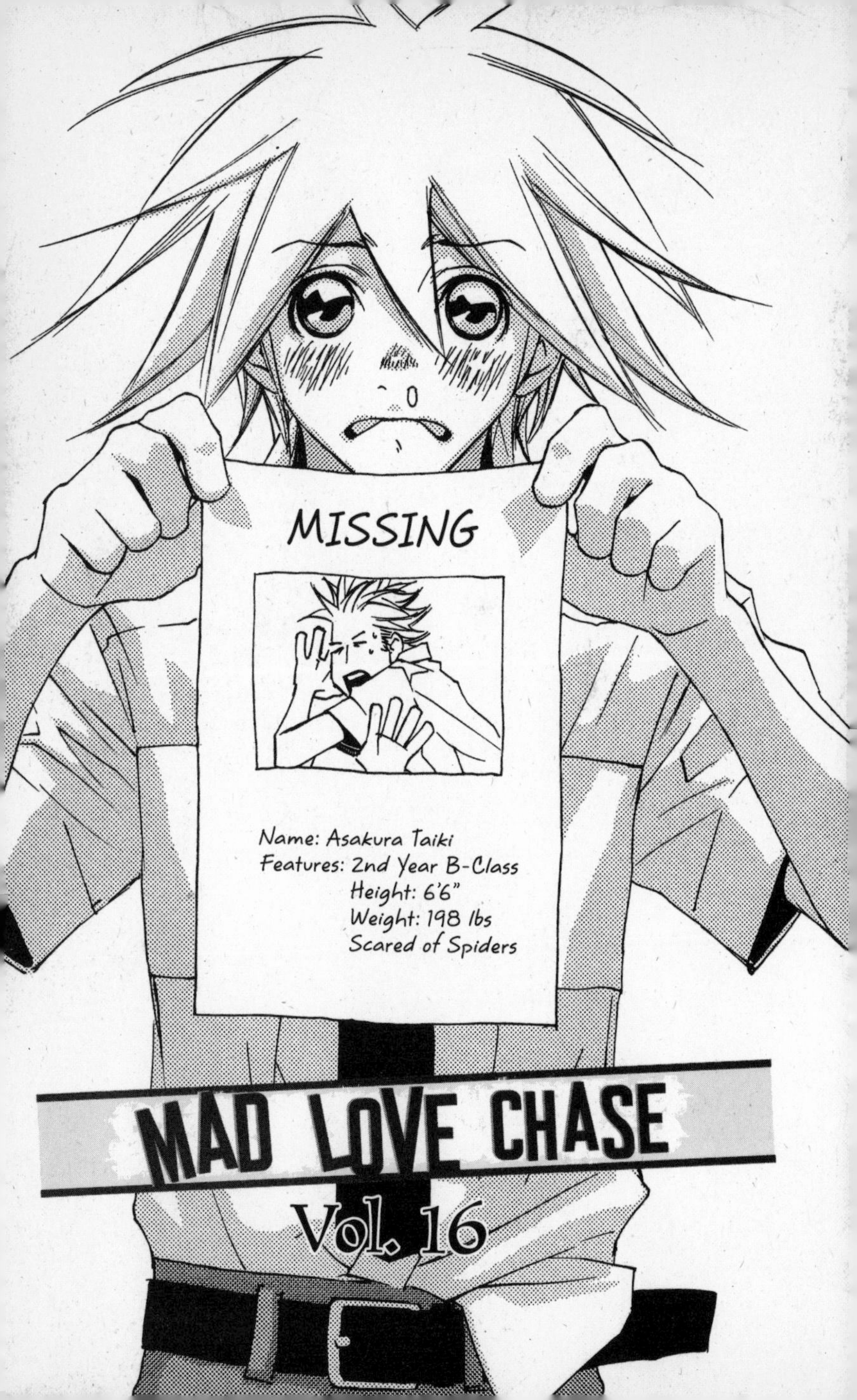
MISSING
Name: Asakura Taiki
Features: 2nd Year B-Class
Height: 6'6"
Weight: 198 lbs
Scared of Spiders
MAD LOVE CHASE
Vol. 16

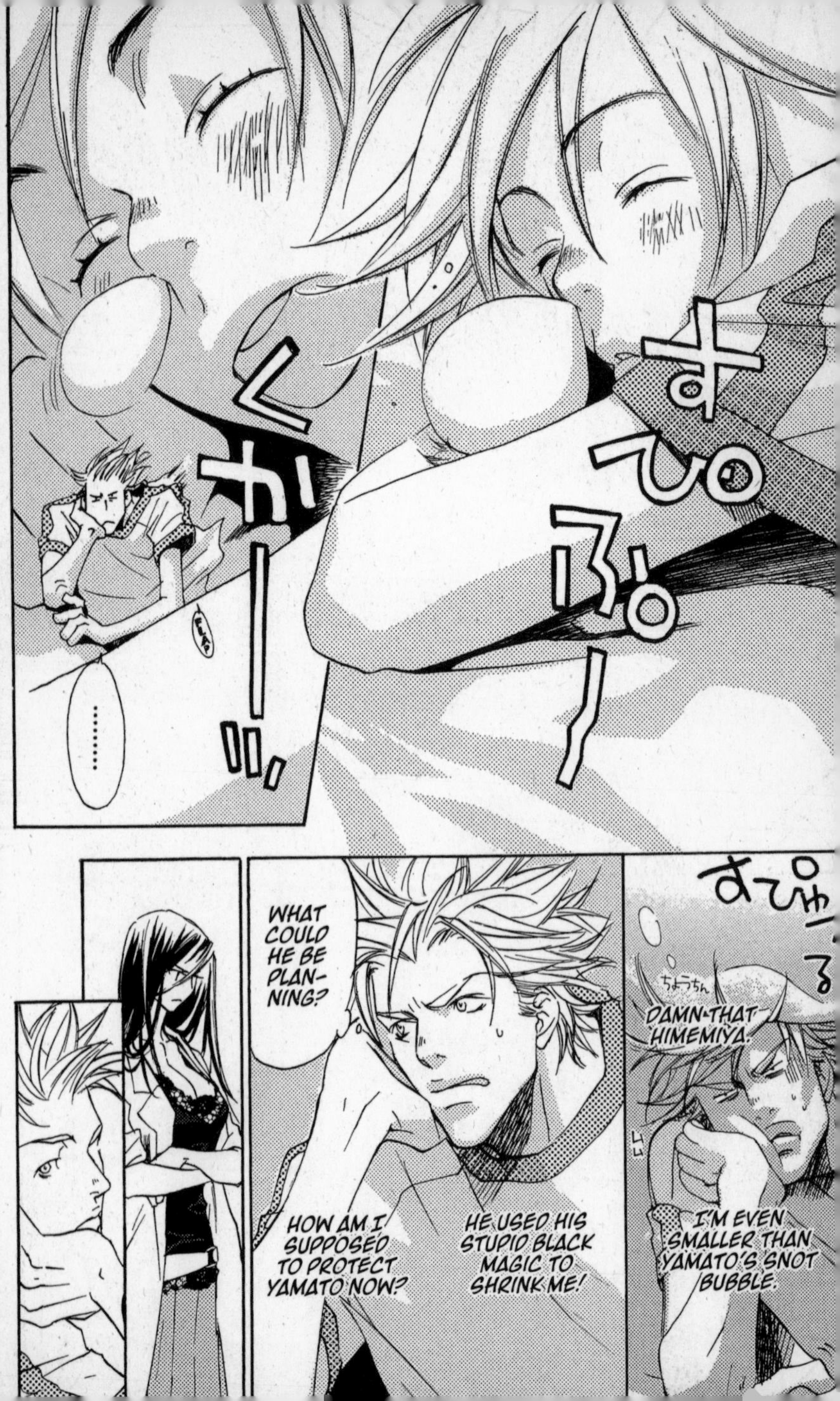
すぴーふー
くかー
FLAP
......
すぴゅ～る
ちょうちん
DAMN THAT HIMEMIYA.
I'M EVEN SMALLER THAN YAMATO'S SNOT BUBBLE.
HE USED HIS STUPID BLACK MAGIC TO SHRINK ME!
HOW AM I SUPPOSED TO PROTECT YAMATO NOW?
WHAT COULD HE BE PLANNING?

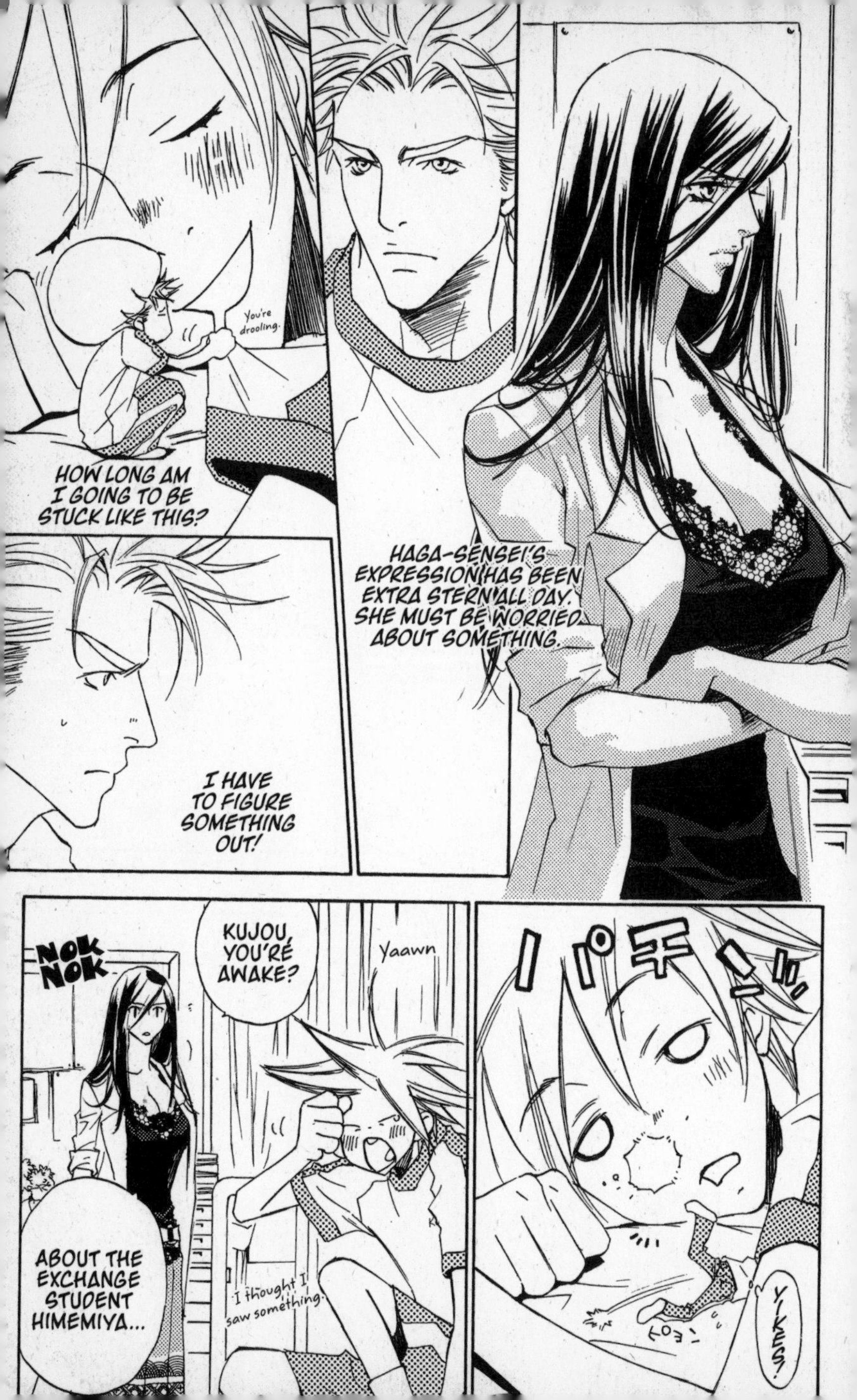
HAGA-SENSEI'S EXPRESSION HAS BEEN EXTRA STERN ALL DAY. SHE MUST BE WORRIED ABOUT SOMETHING.
You're drooling.
HOW LONG AM I GOING TO BE STUCK LIKE THIS?
I HAVE TO FIGURE SOMETHING OUT!
パチ
YIKES!
Yaawn
KUJOU, YOU'RE AWAKE?
I thought I saw something.
NOK NOK
ABOUT THE EXCHANGE STUDENT HIMEMIYA...

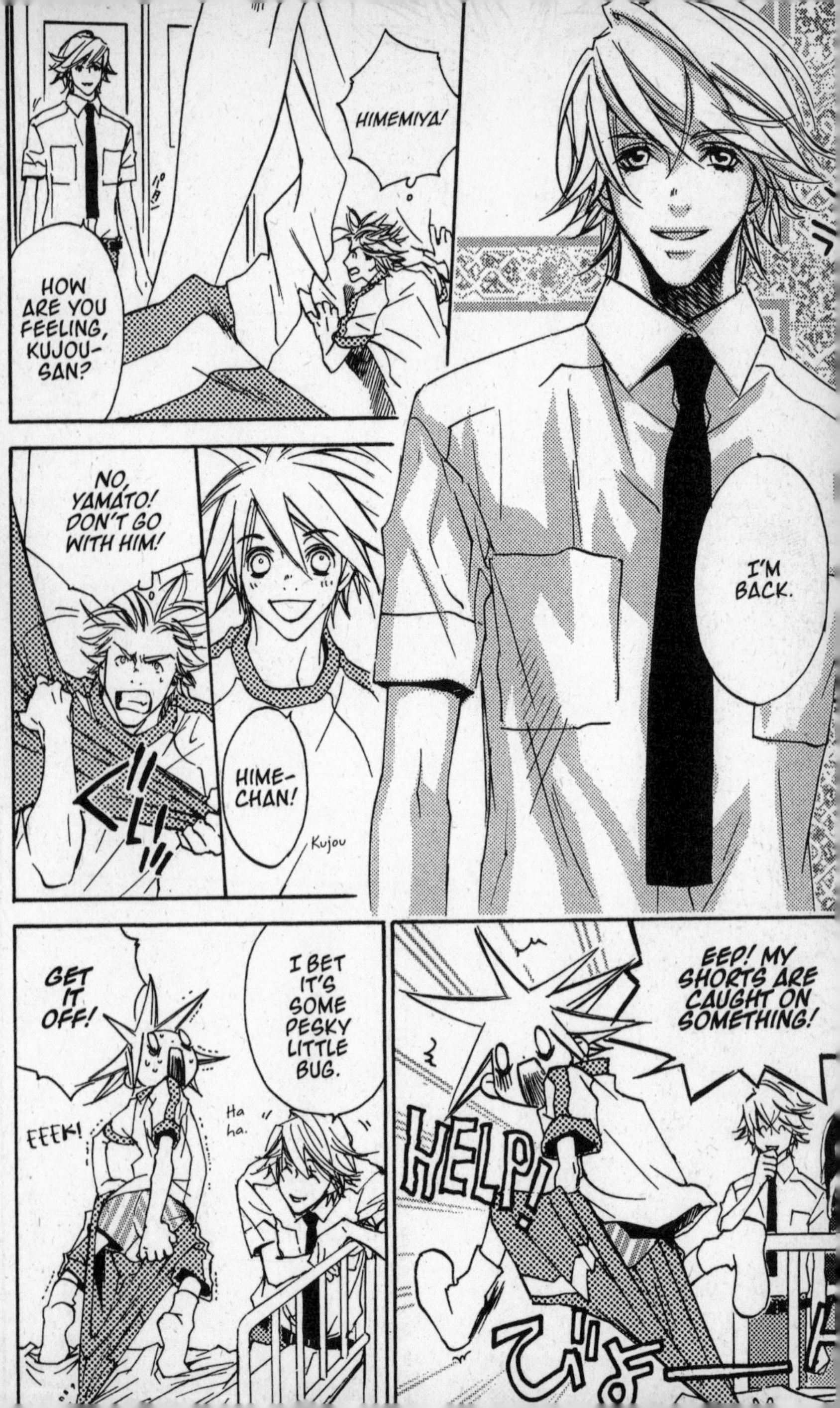
I'M BACK.
HIMEMIYA!
HOW ARE YOU FEELING, KUJOU-SAN?
HIME-CHAN!
Kujou
NO, YAMATO! DON'T GO WITH HIM!
EEP! MY SHORTS ARE CAUGHT ON SOMETHING!
HELP!
I BET IT'S SOME PESKY LITTLE BUG.
GET IT OFF!
Ha ha.
EEEK!

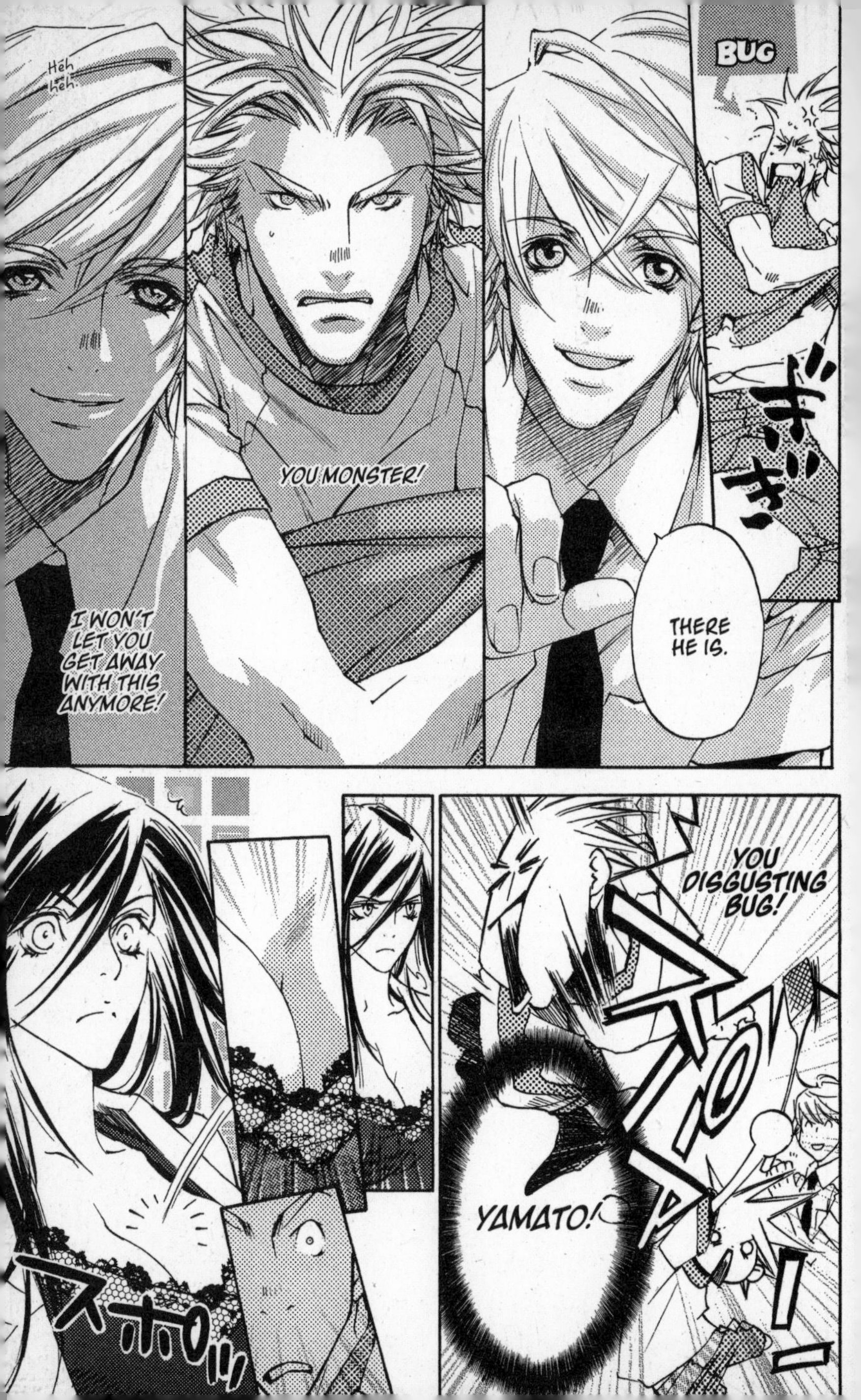
BUG
THERE HE IS.
YOU MONSTER!
Heh heh.
I WON'T LET YOU GET AWAY WITH THIS ANYMORE!
YOU DISGUSTING BUG!
YAMATO!

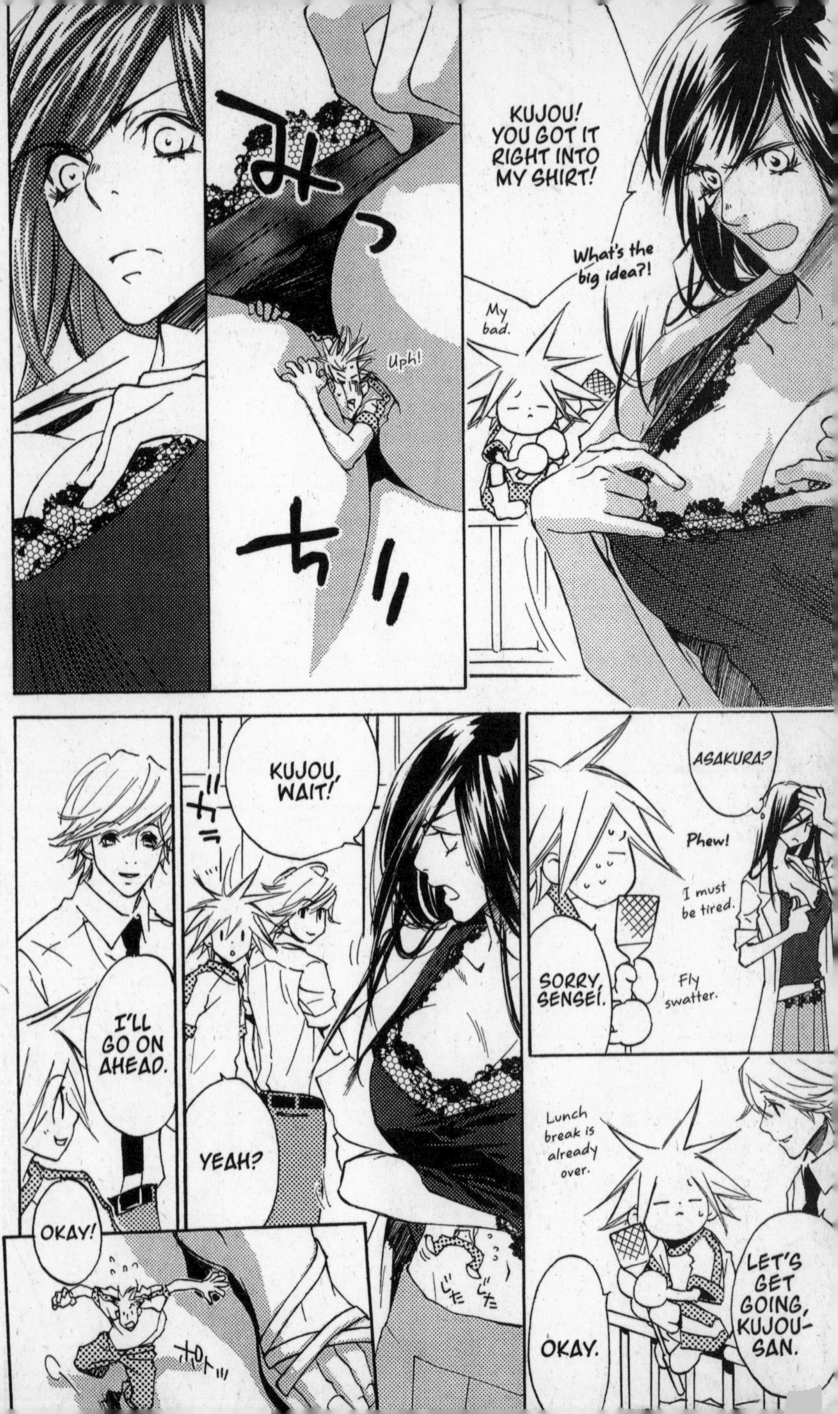
KUJOU! YOU GOT IT RIGHT INTO MY SHIRT!
What's the big idea?!
My bad.
みっ
ちり
Uph!
ASAKURA?
Phew!
I must be tired.
SORRY, SENSEI.
Fly swatter.
Lunch break is already over.
LET'S GET GOING, KUJOU-SAN.
OKAY.
KUJOU, WAIT!
YEAH?
I'LL GO ON AHEAD.
OKAY!
じたじた

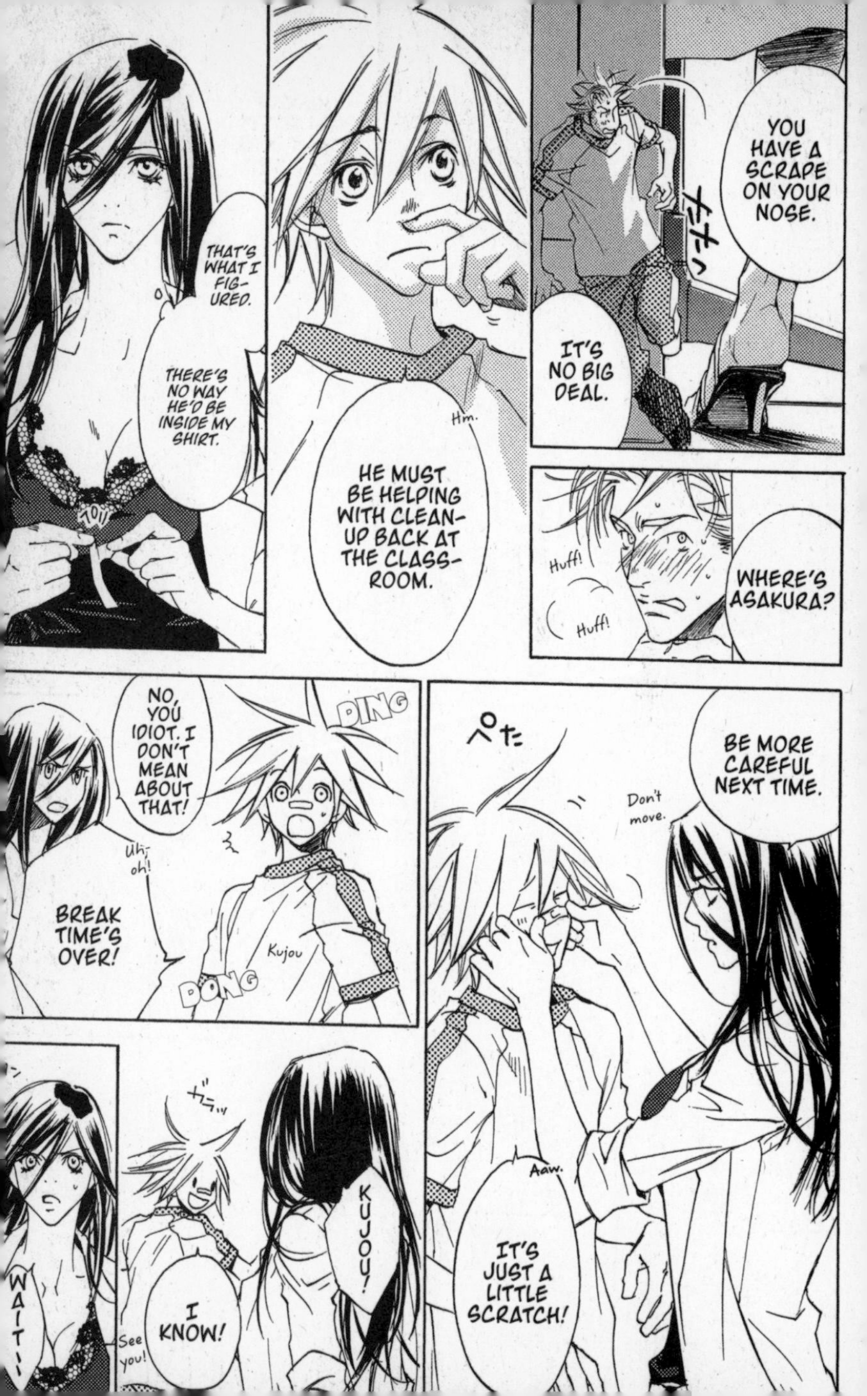
YOU HAVE A SCRAPE ON YOUR NOSE.
IT'S NO BIG DEAL.
WHERE'S ASAKURA?
Huff!
Huff!
Hm.
HE MUST BE HELPING WITH CLEAN-UP BACK AT THE CLASSROOM.
THAT'S WHAT I FIGURED.
THERE'S NO WAY HE'D BE INSIDE MY SHIRT.
BE MORE CAREFUL NEXT TIME.
ぺた
Don't move.
Aaw.
IT'S JUST A LITTLE SCRATCH!
DING
NO, YOU IDIOT. I DON'T MEAN ABOUT THAT!
Uh-oh!
BREAK TIME'S OVER!
Kujou
DONG
KUJOU!
I KNOW!
See you!
WAIT!

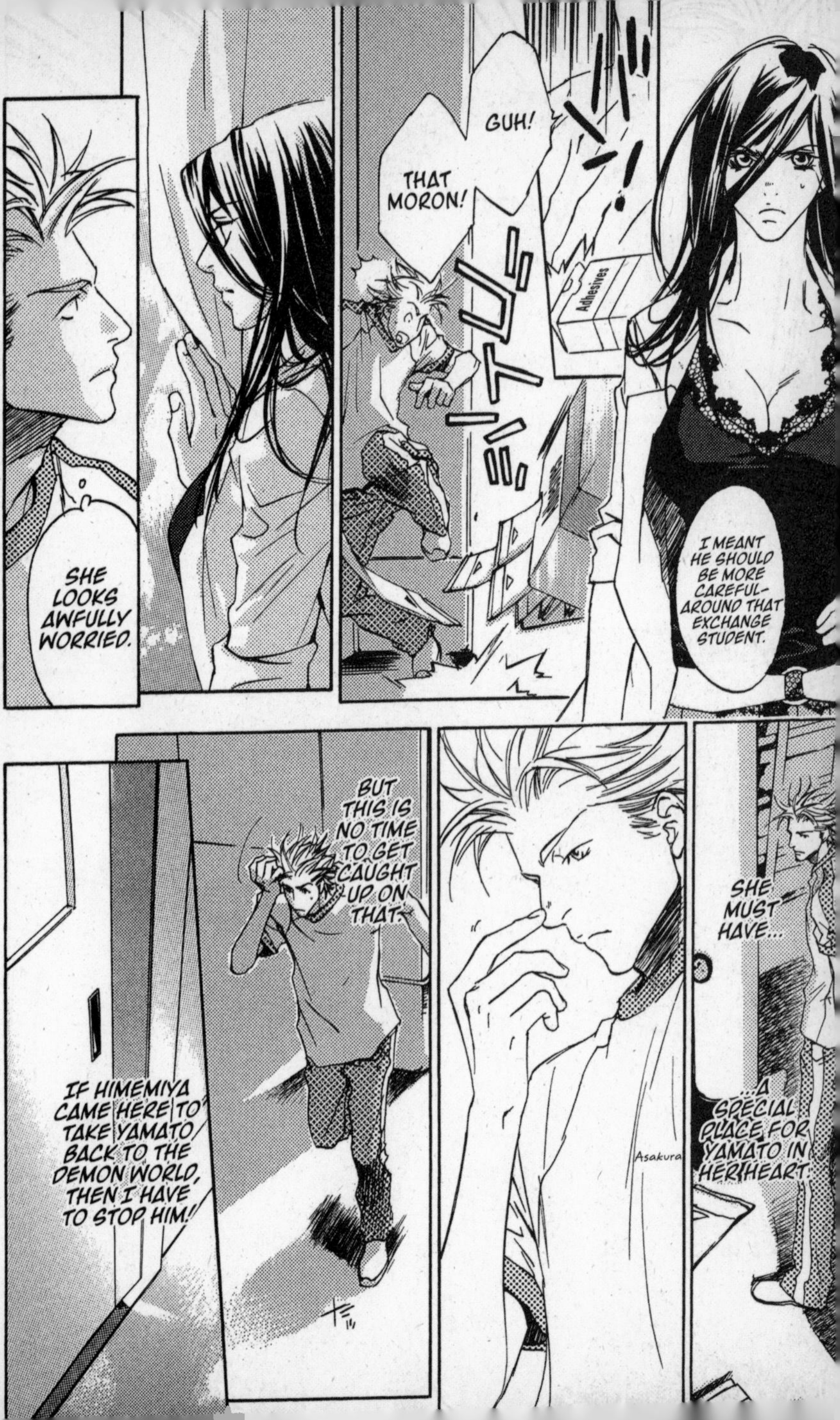
I MEANT HE SHOULD BE MORE CAREFUL-AROUND THAT EXCHANGE STUDENT.
GUH!
THAT MORON!
Adhesives
SHE LOOKS AWFULLY WORRIED.
SHE MUST HAVE...
...A SPECIAL PLACE FOR YAMATO IN HER HEART.
Asakura
BUT THIS IS NO TIME TO GET CAUGHT UP ON THAT.
IF HIMEMIYA CAME HERE TO TAKE YAMATO BACK TO THE DEMON WORLD, THEN I HAVE TO STOP HIM!

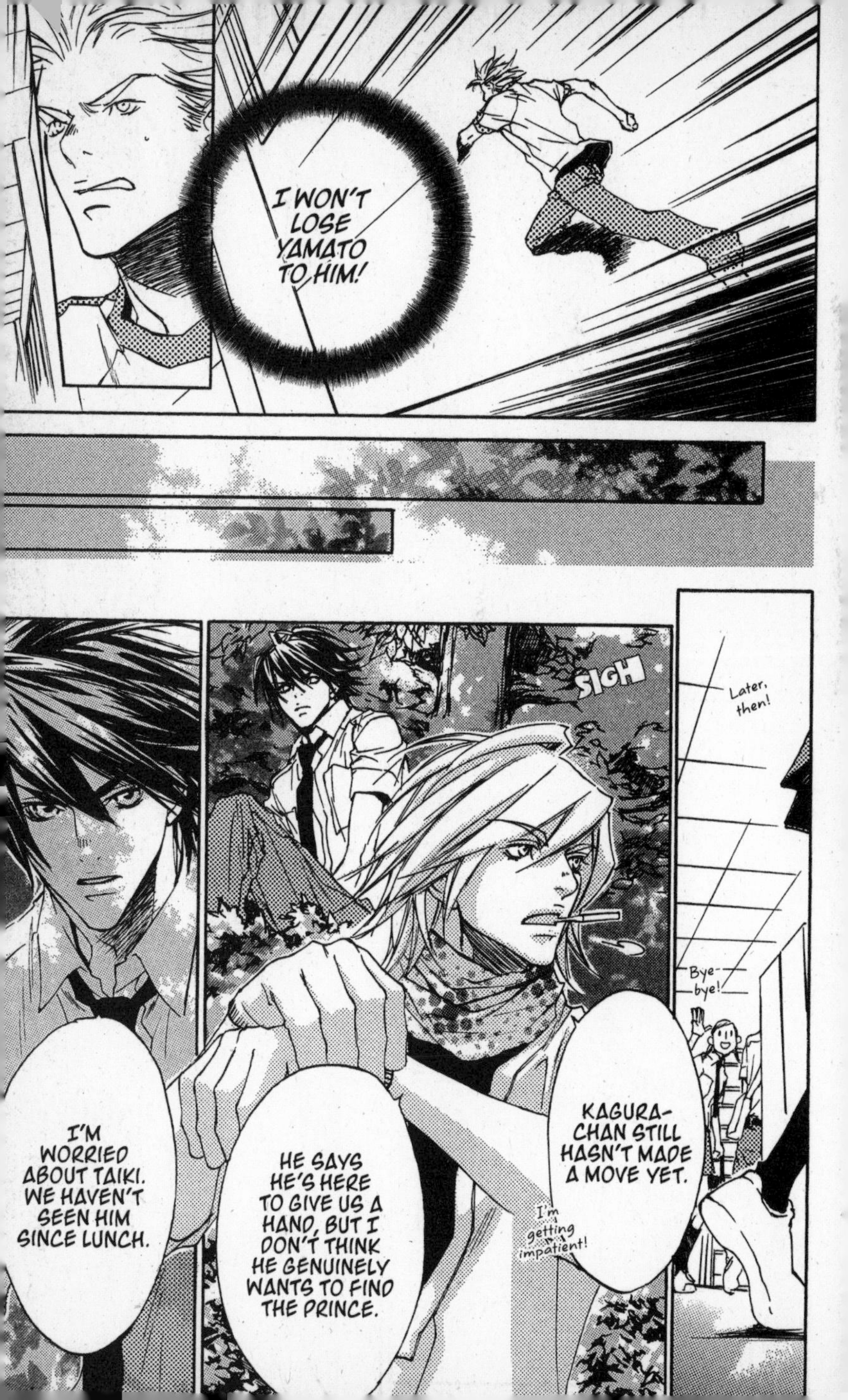
I WON'T LOSE YAMATO TO HIM!
Later, then!
Bye-bye!
SIGH
KAGURA-CHAN STILL HASN'T MADE A MOVE YET.
I'm getting impatient!
HE SAYS HE'S HERE TO GIVE US A HAND, BUT I DON'T THINK HE GENUINELY WANTS TO FIND THE PRINCE.
I'M WORRIED ABOUT TAIKI. WE HAVEN'T SEEN HIM SINCE LUNCH.

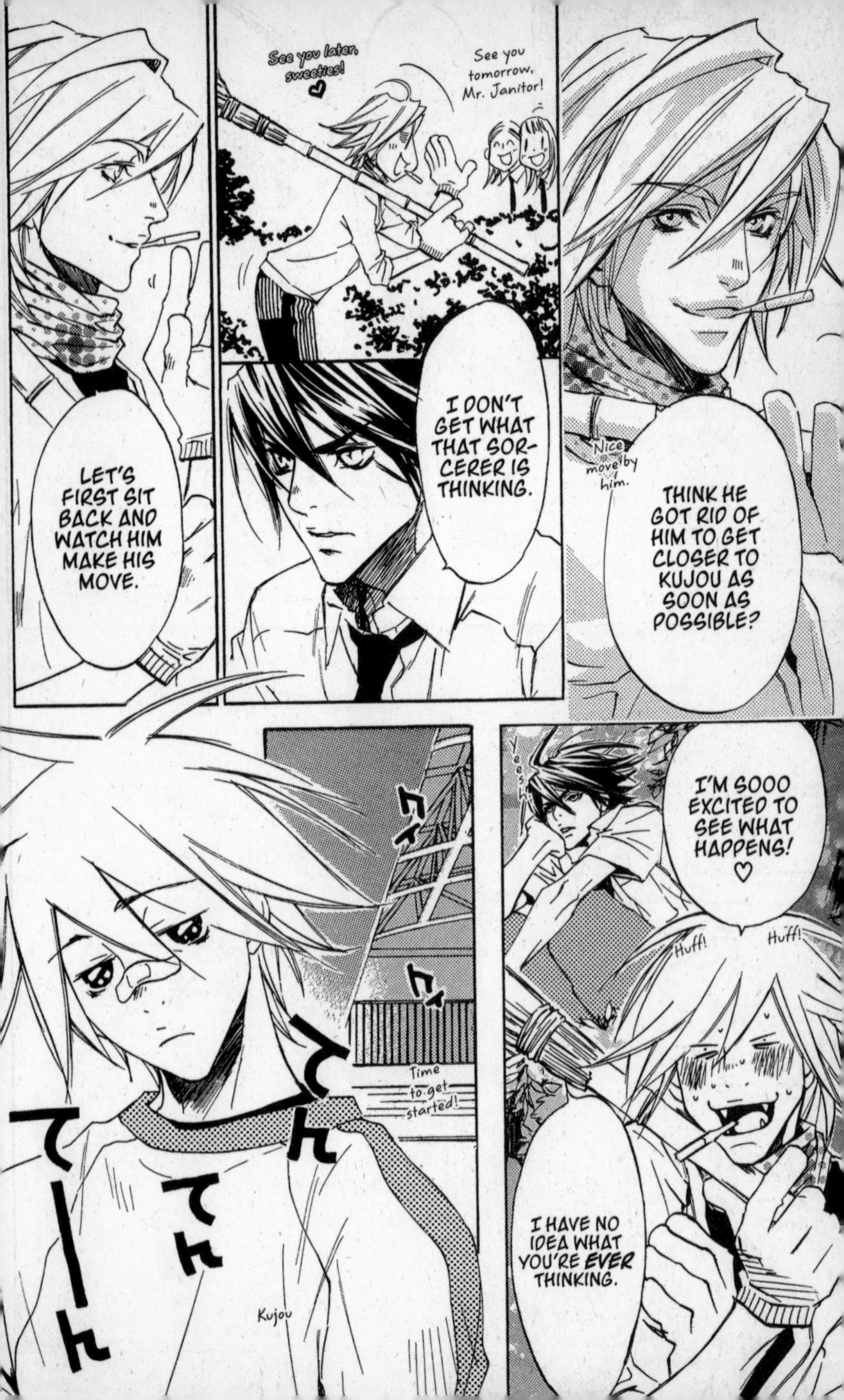
Nice move by him.
THINK HE GOT RID OF HIM TO GET CLOSER TO KUJOU AS SOON AS POSSIBLE?
See you tomorrow, Mr. Janitor!
See you later, sweeties! ♡
I DON'T GET WHAT THAT SORCERER IS THINKING.
LET'S FIRST SIT BACK AND WATCH HIM MAKE HIS MOVE.
I'M SOOO EXCITED TO SEE WHAT HAPPENS! ♡
Yeesh
Huff! Huff!
I HAVE NO IDEA WHAT YOU'RE *EVER* THINKING.
Time to get started!
てん
てん
てーん
Kujou

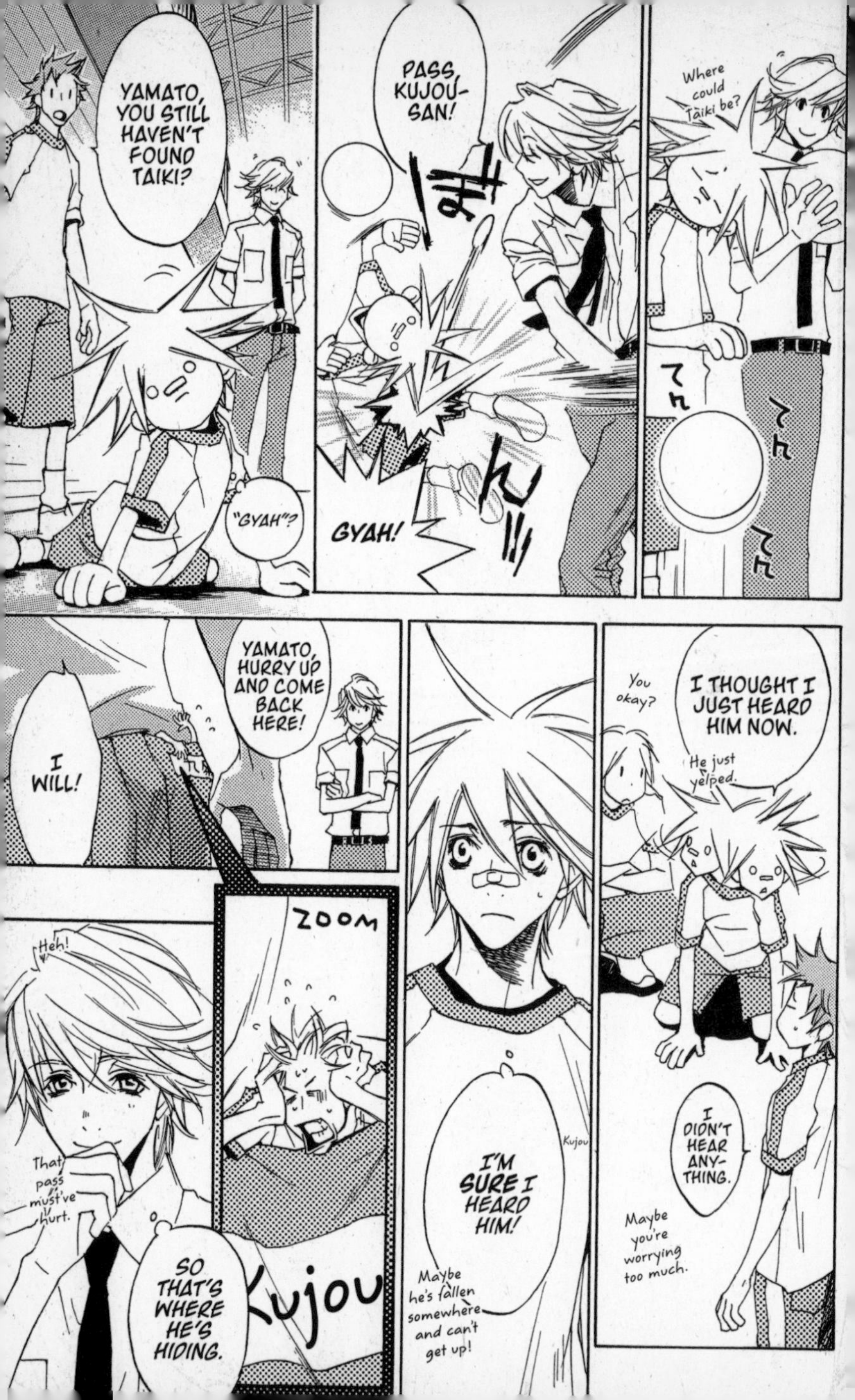
Where could Taiki be?
てれ
てれ
てれ
PASS, KUJOU-SAN!
GYAH!
YAMATO, YOU STILL HAVEN'T FOUND TAIKI?
"GYAH"?
You okay?
I THOUGHT I JUST HEARD HIM NOW.
He just yelped.
I DIDN'T HEAR ANYTHING.
Maybe you're worrying too much.
Kujou
I'M SURE I HEARD HIM!
Maybe he's fallen somewhere and can't get up!
YAMATO, HURRY UP AND COME BACK HERE!
I WILL!
ZOOM
Kujou
Heh!
That pass must've hurt.
SO THAT'S WHERE HE'S HIDING.

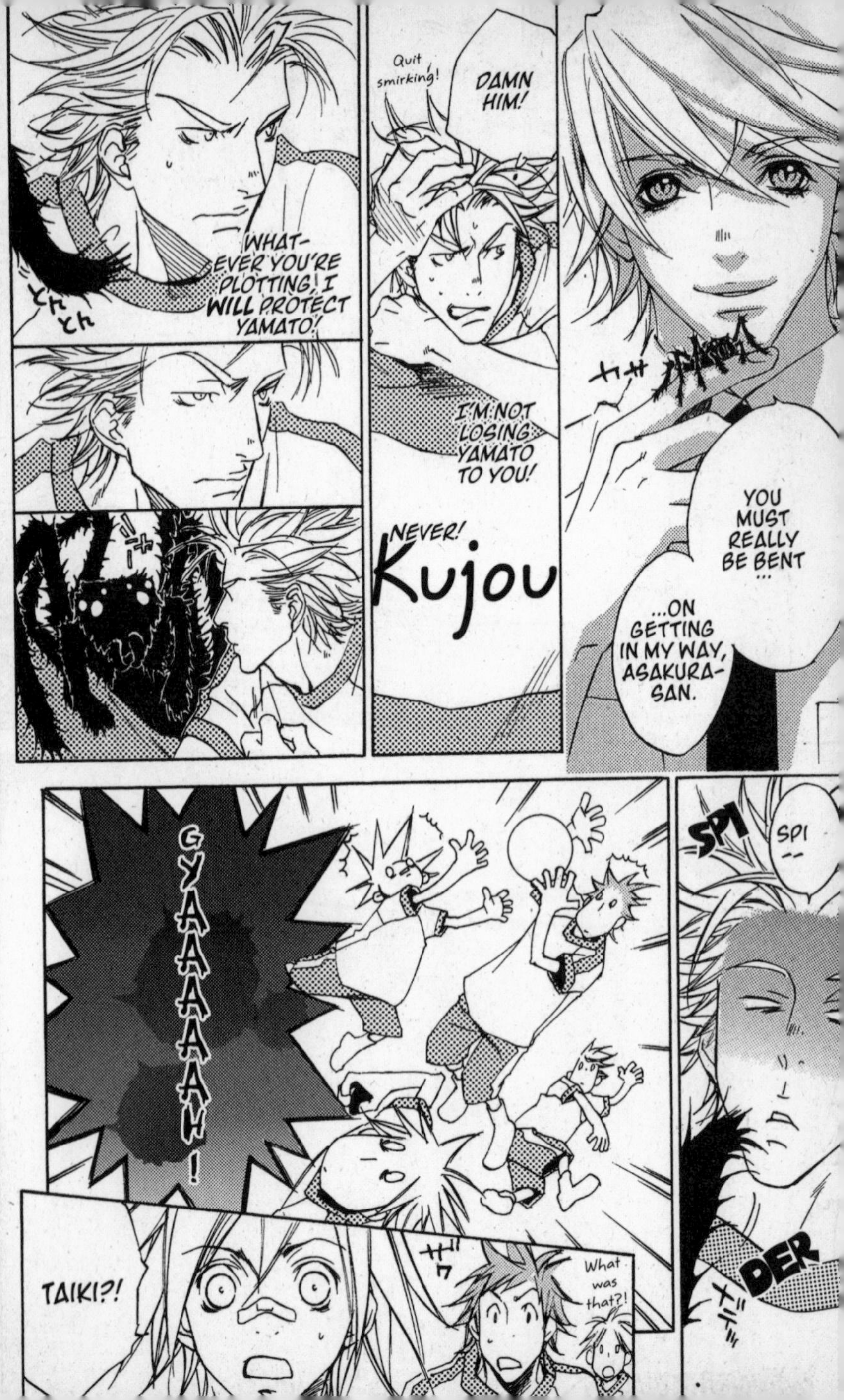
YOU MUST REALLY BE BENT...
...ON GETTING IN MY WAY, ASAKURA-SAN.
Quit smirking!
DAMN HIM!
I'M NOT LOSING YAMATO TO YOU!
NEVER! Kujou
WHATEVER YOU'RE PLOTTING, I WILL PROTECT YAMATO!
SPI--
SPI
DER
GYAAAAAAAH!
What was that?!
TAIKI?!

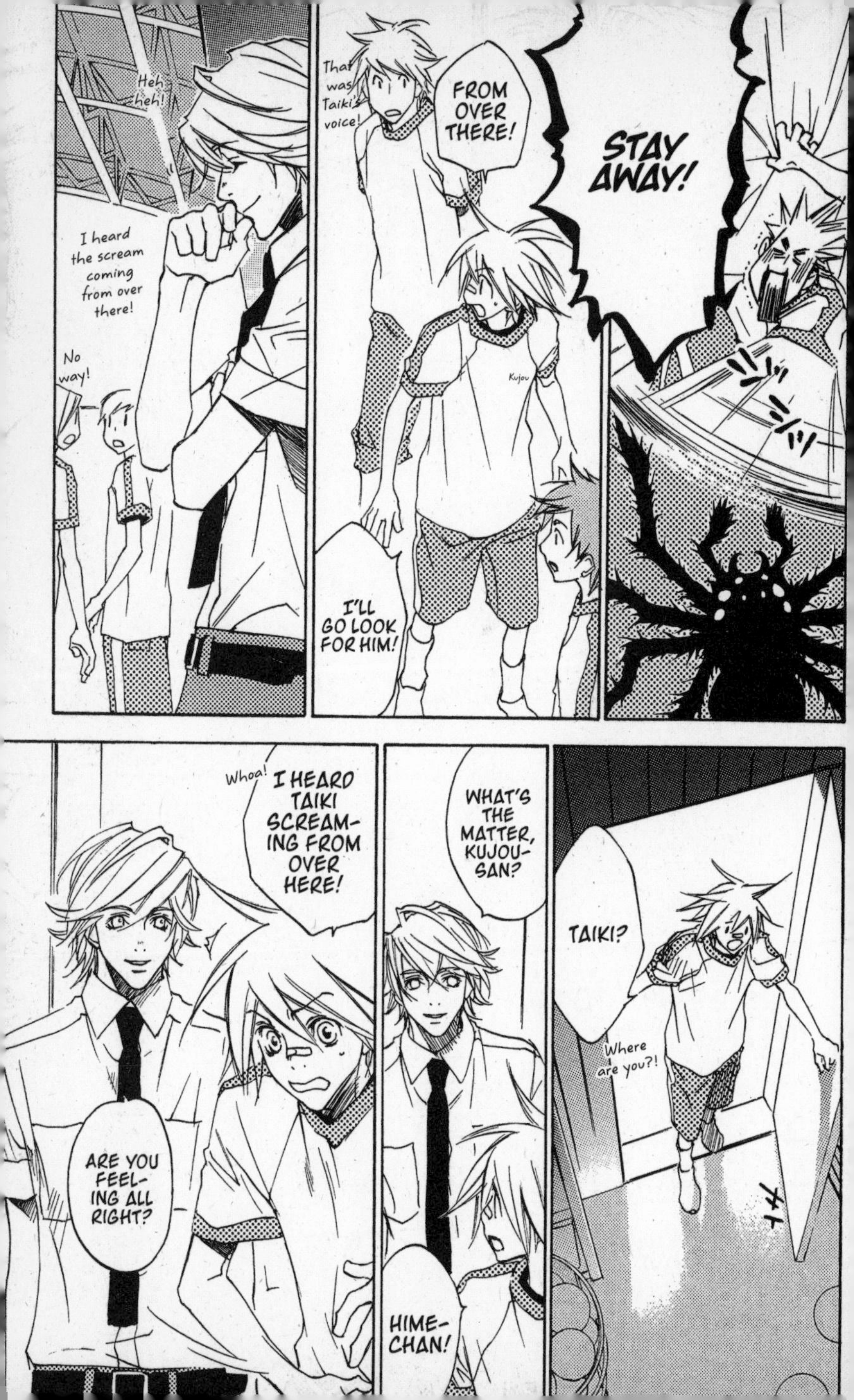
STAY AWAY!
That was Taiki's voice!
FROM OVER THERE!
I'LL GO LOOK FOR HIM!
Heh heh!
I heard the scream coming from over there!
No way!
TAIKI?
Where are you?!
WHAT'S THE MATTER, KUJOU-SAN?
HIME-CHAN!
Whoa!
I HEARD TAIKI SCREAMING FROM OVER HERE!
ARE YOU FEELING ALL RIGHT?

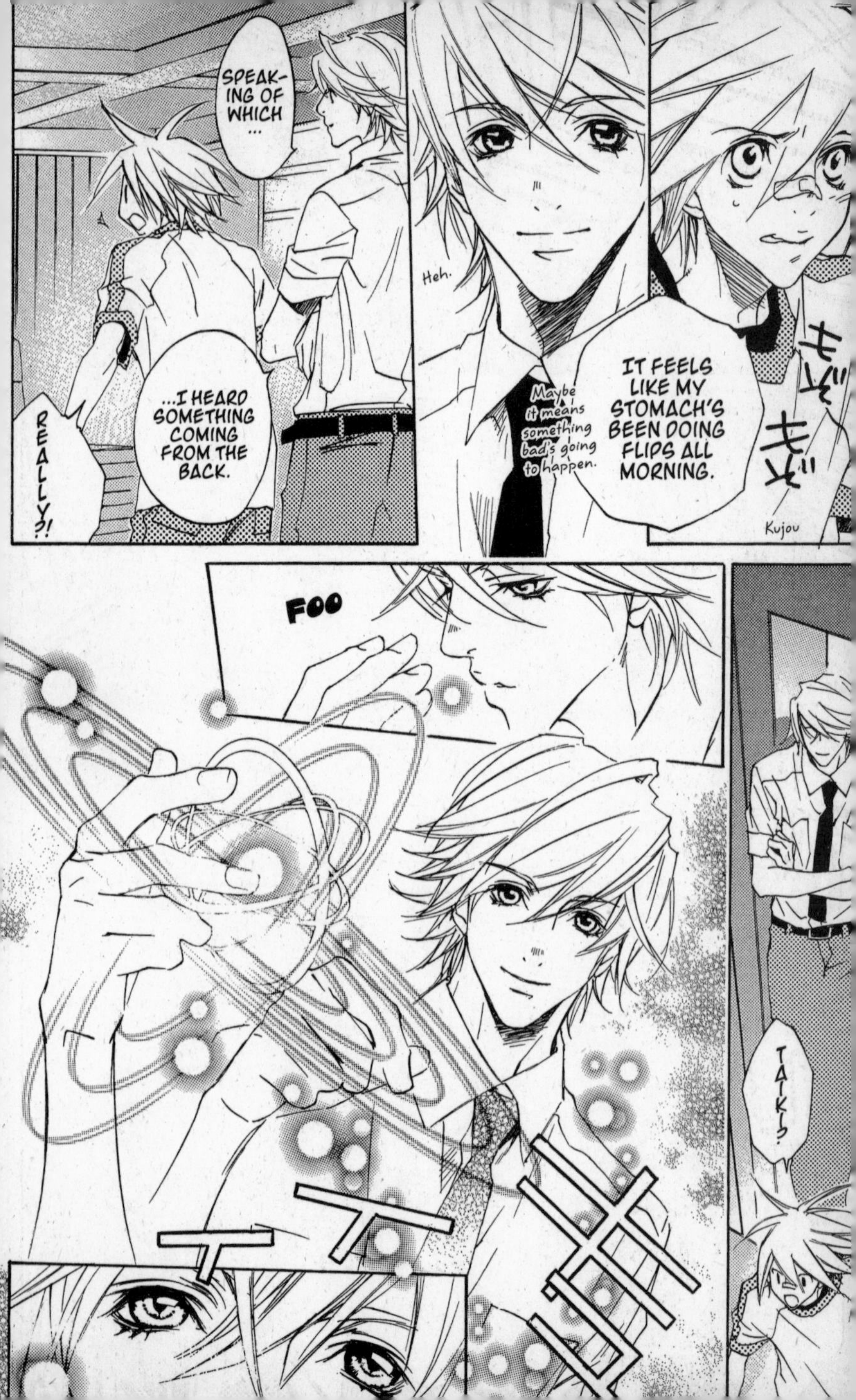
Kujou
IT FEELS LIKE MY STOMACH'S BEEN DOING FLIPS ALL MORNING.
Maybe it means something bad's going to happen.
Heh.
SPEAK-ING OF WHICH ...
...I HEARD SOMETHING COMING FROM THE BACK.
REALLY?!
TAIKI?
FOO

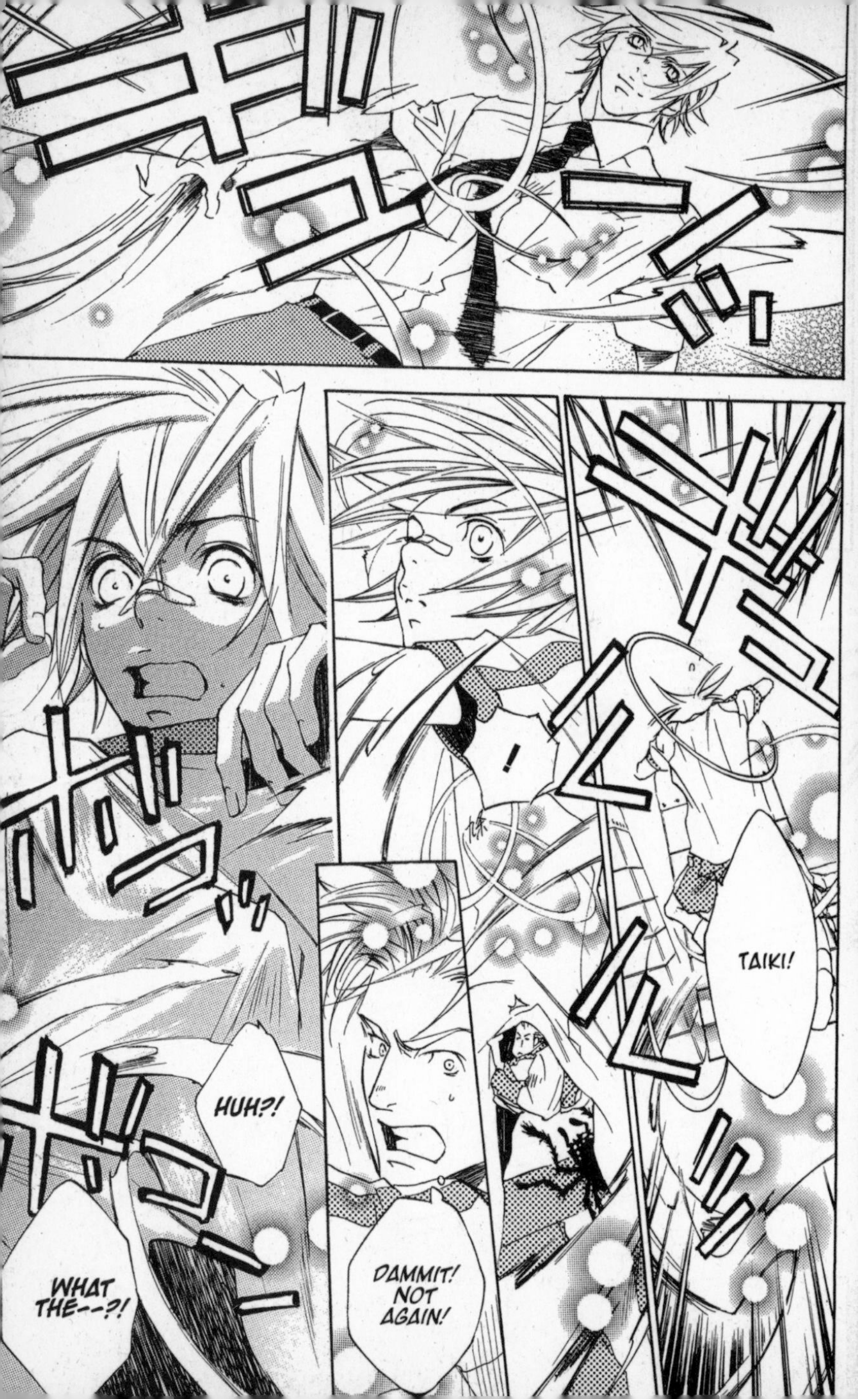
TAIKI!
!
DAMMIT! NOT AGAIN!
HUH?!
WHAT THE--?!

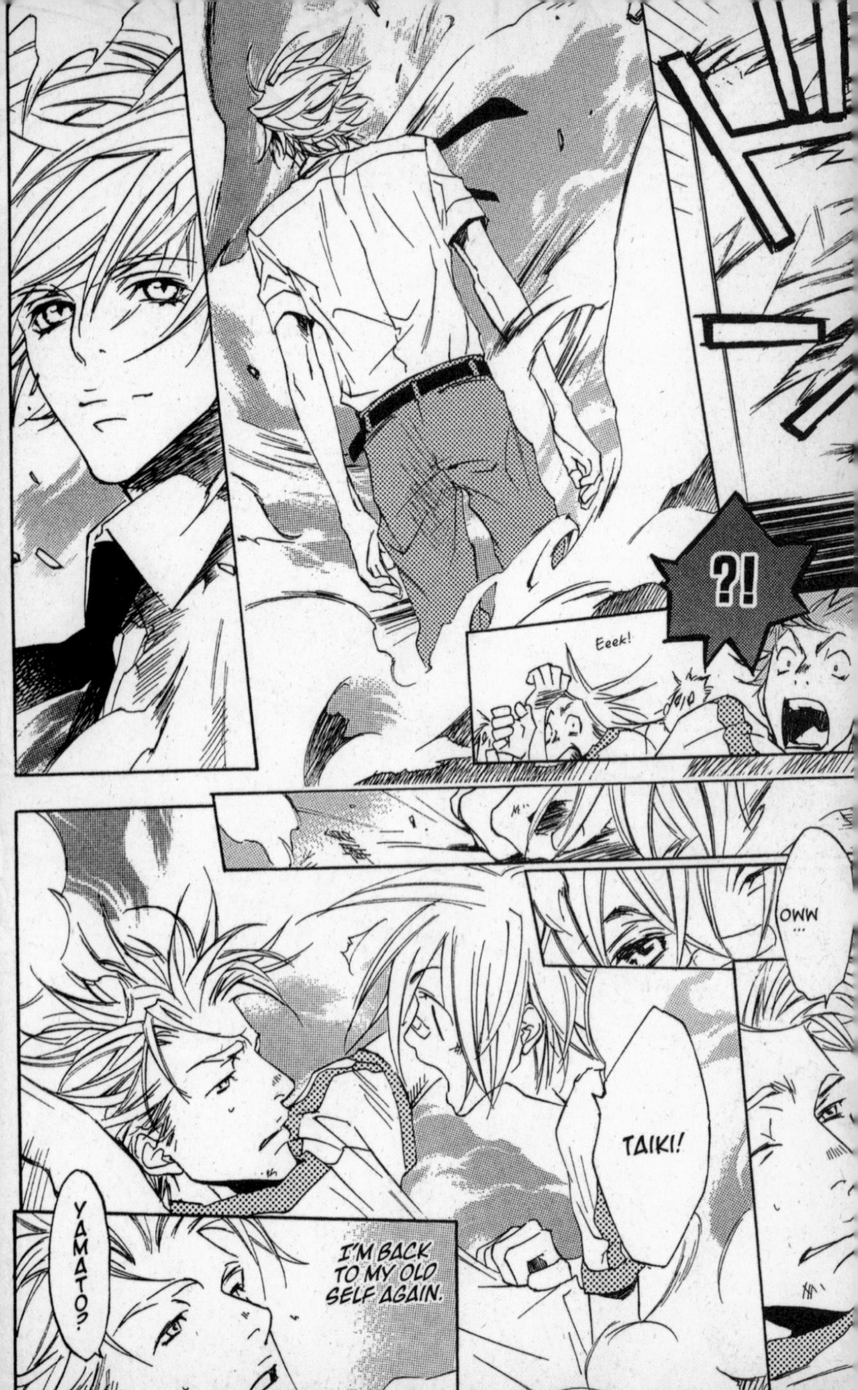
?!
Eeek!
OWW...
TAIKI!
YAMATO?
I'M BACK TO MY OLD SELF AGAIN.

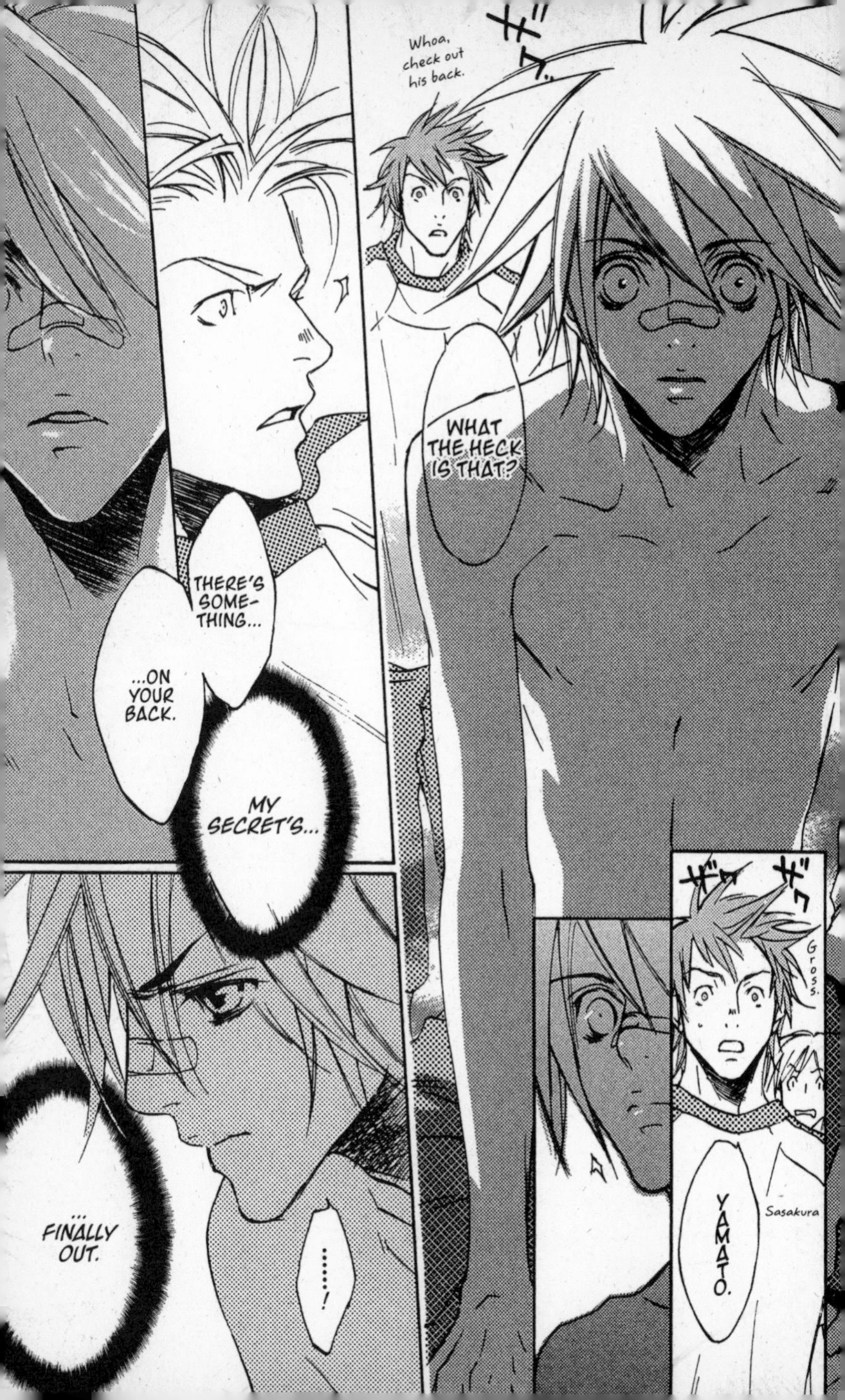
Whoa, check out his back.
WHAT THE HECK IS THAT?
THERE'S SOMETHING...
...ON YOUR BACK.
MY SECRET'S...
Gross.
Sasakura
YAMATO.
......!
... FINALLY OUT.

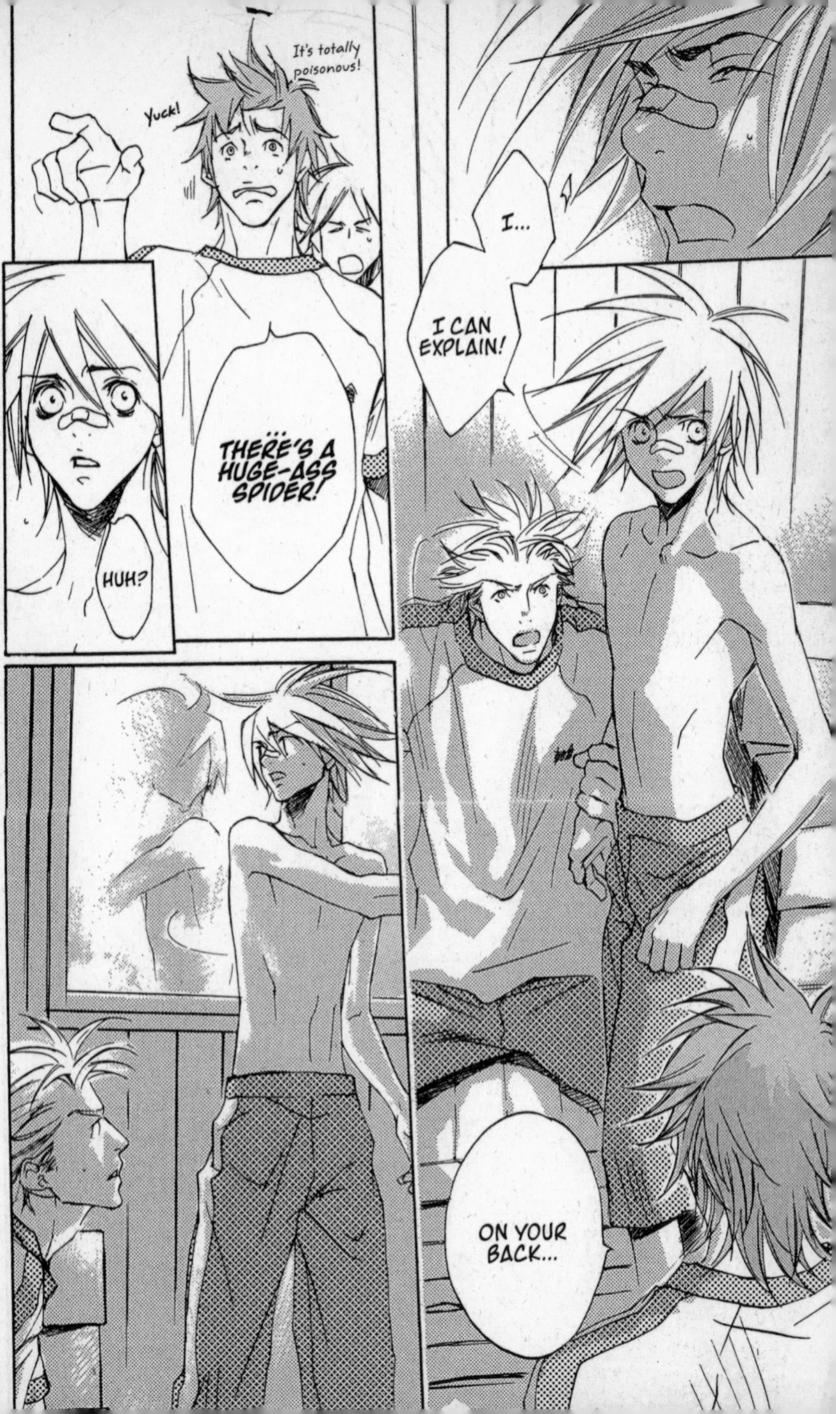
I...
I CAN EXPLAIN!
ON YOUR BACK...
It's totally poisonous!
Yuck!
... THERE'S A HUGE-ASS SPIDER!
HUH?

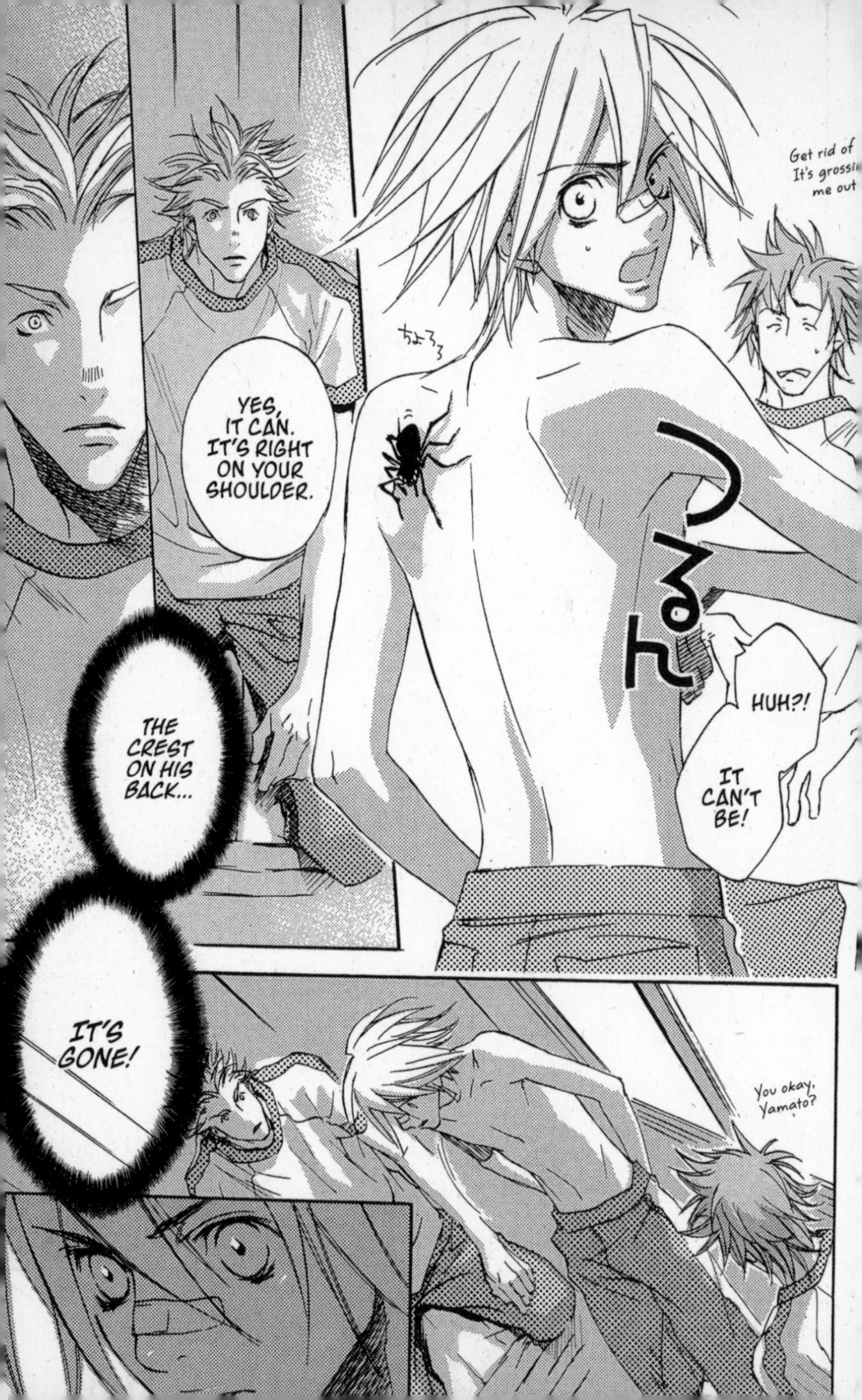
Get rid of
It's grossi
me out
つるん
HUH?!
IT CAN'T BE!
ちょろろ
YES, IT CAN. IT'S RIGHT ON YOUR SHOULDER.
THE CREST ON HIS BACK...
IT'S GONE!
You okay, Yamato?

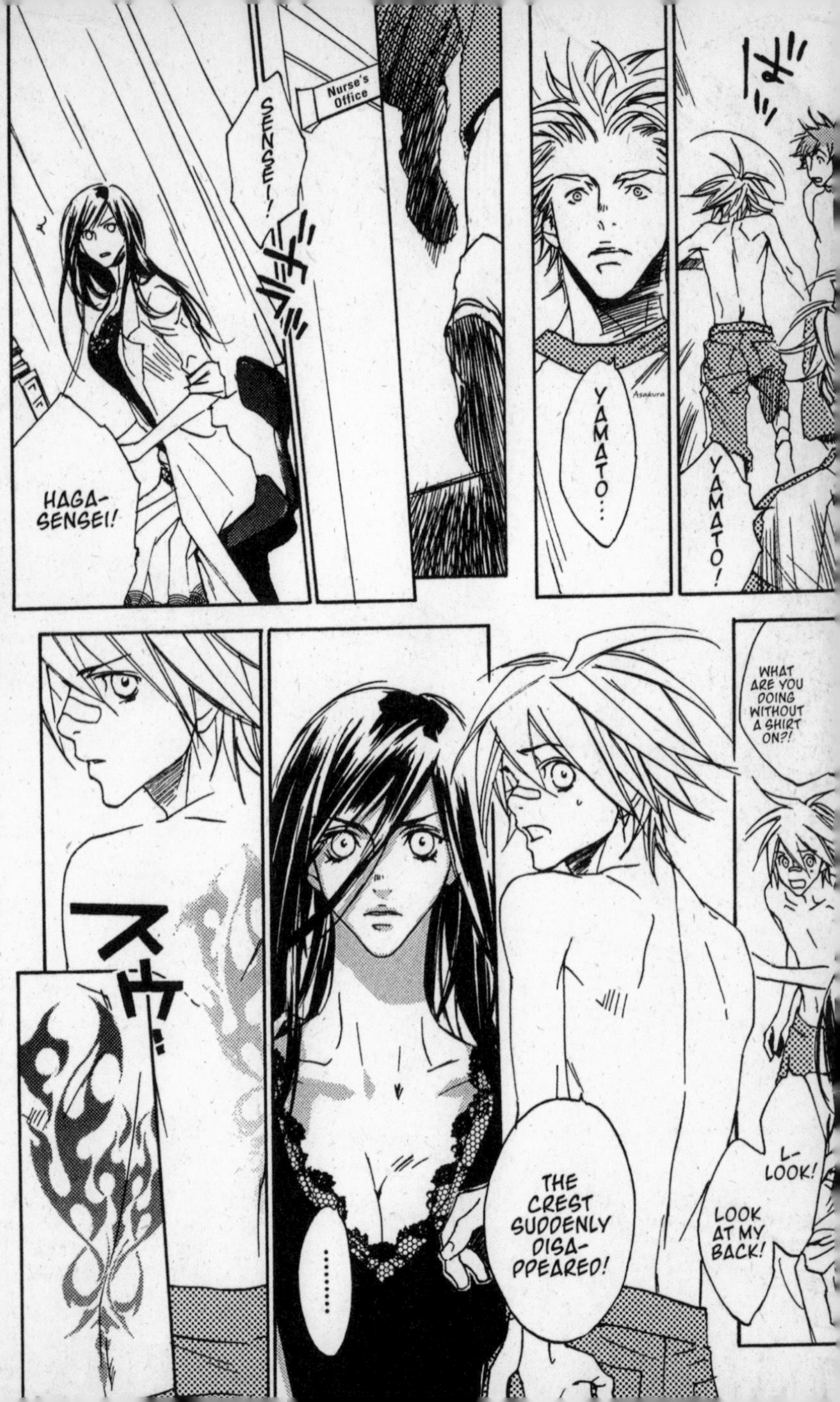
YAMATO!
Asakura
YAMATO...
Nurse's Office
SENSEI!
HAGA-SENSEI!
WHAT ARE YOU DOING WITHOUT A SHIRT ON?!
L-LOOK!
LOOK AT MY BACK!
THE CREST SUDDENLY DISAPPEARED!
......

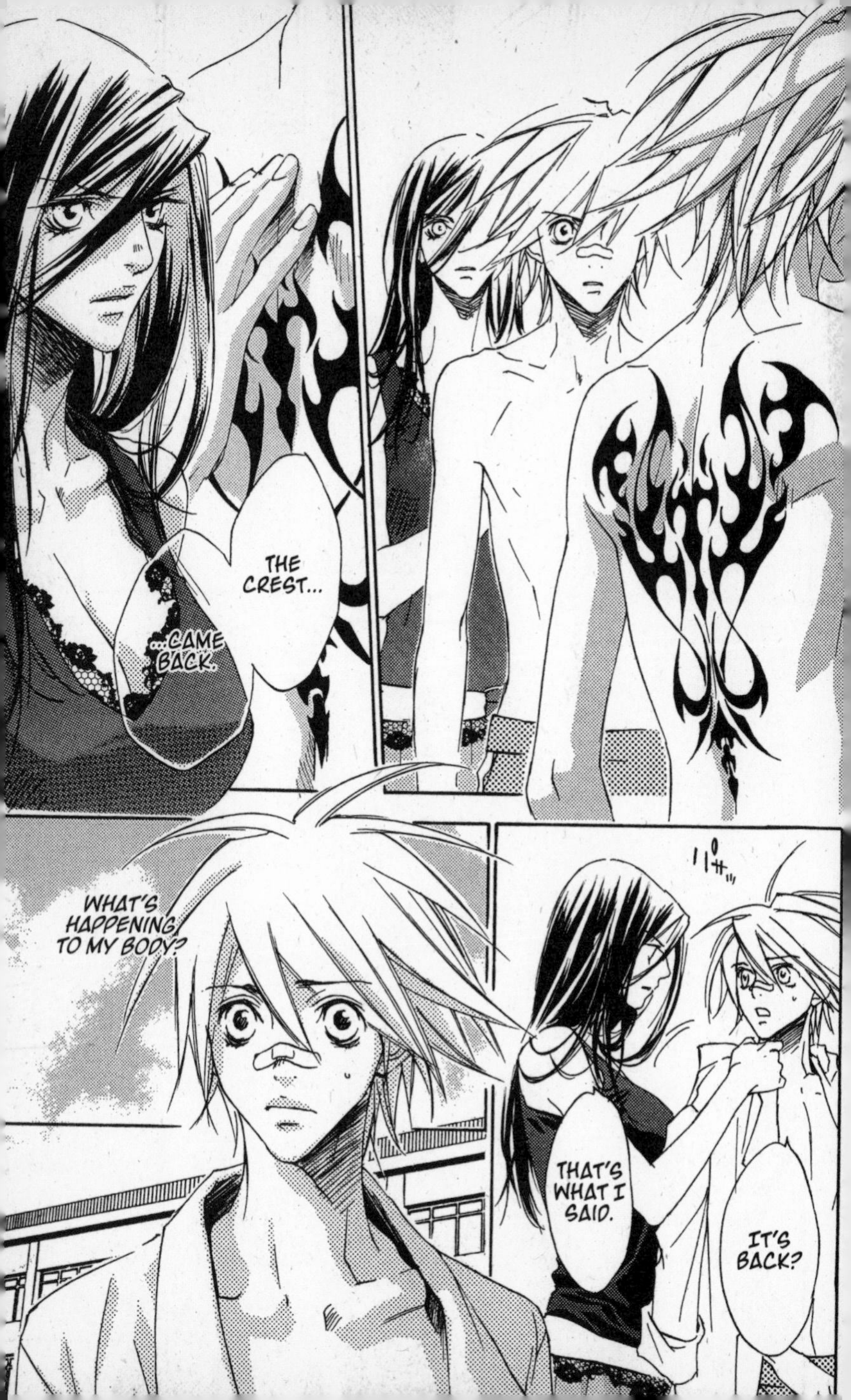
THE CREST...
...CAME BACK.
ハッ
IT'S BACK?
THAT'S WHAT I SAID.
WHAT'S HAPPENING TO MY BODY?

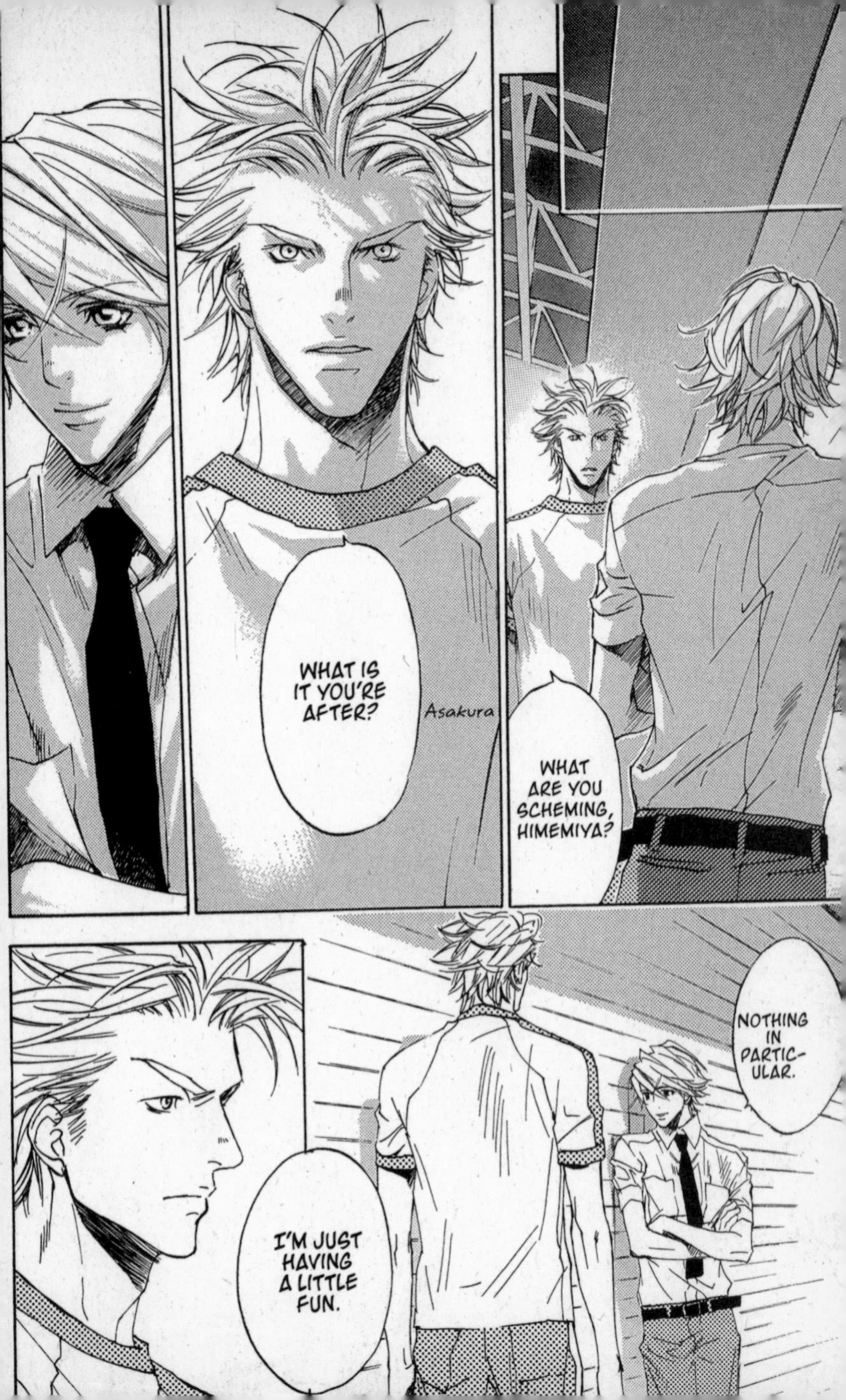
WHAT ARE YOU SCHEMING, HIMEMIYA?
WHAT IS IT YOU'RE AFTER?
Asakura
NOTHING IN PARTIC- ULAR.
I'M JUST HAVING A LITTLE FUN.

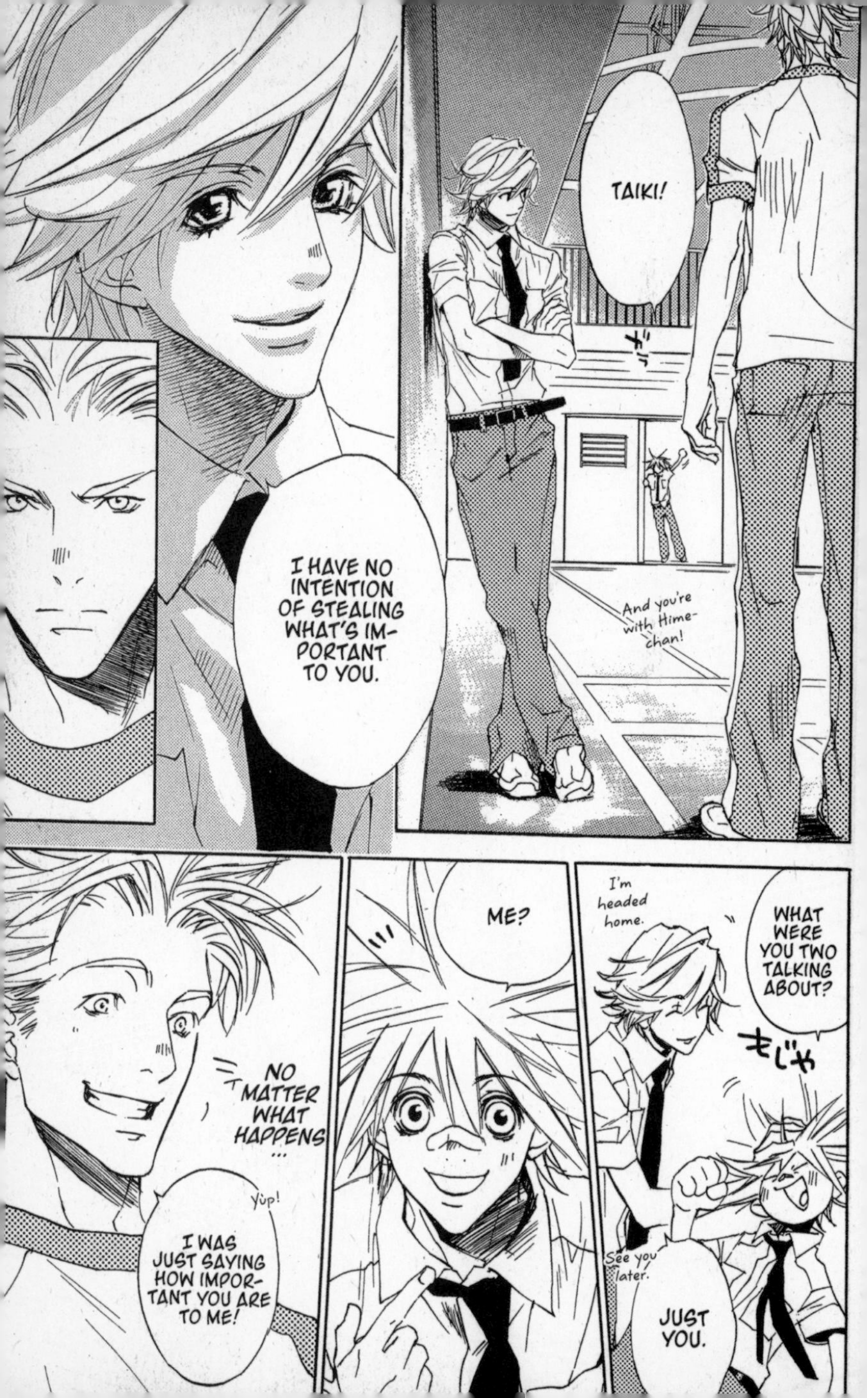
TAIKI!
And you're with Hime-chan!
I HAVE NO INTENTION OF STEALING WHAT'S IMPORTANT TO YOU.
WHAT WERE YOU TWO TALKING ABOUT?
I'm headed home.
もじゃ
See you later.
JUST YOU.
ME?
NO MATTER WHAT HAPPENS...
Yup!
I WAS JUST SAYING HOW IMPORTANT YOU ARE TO ME!

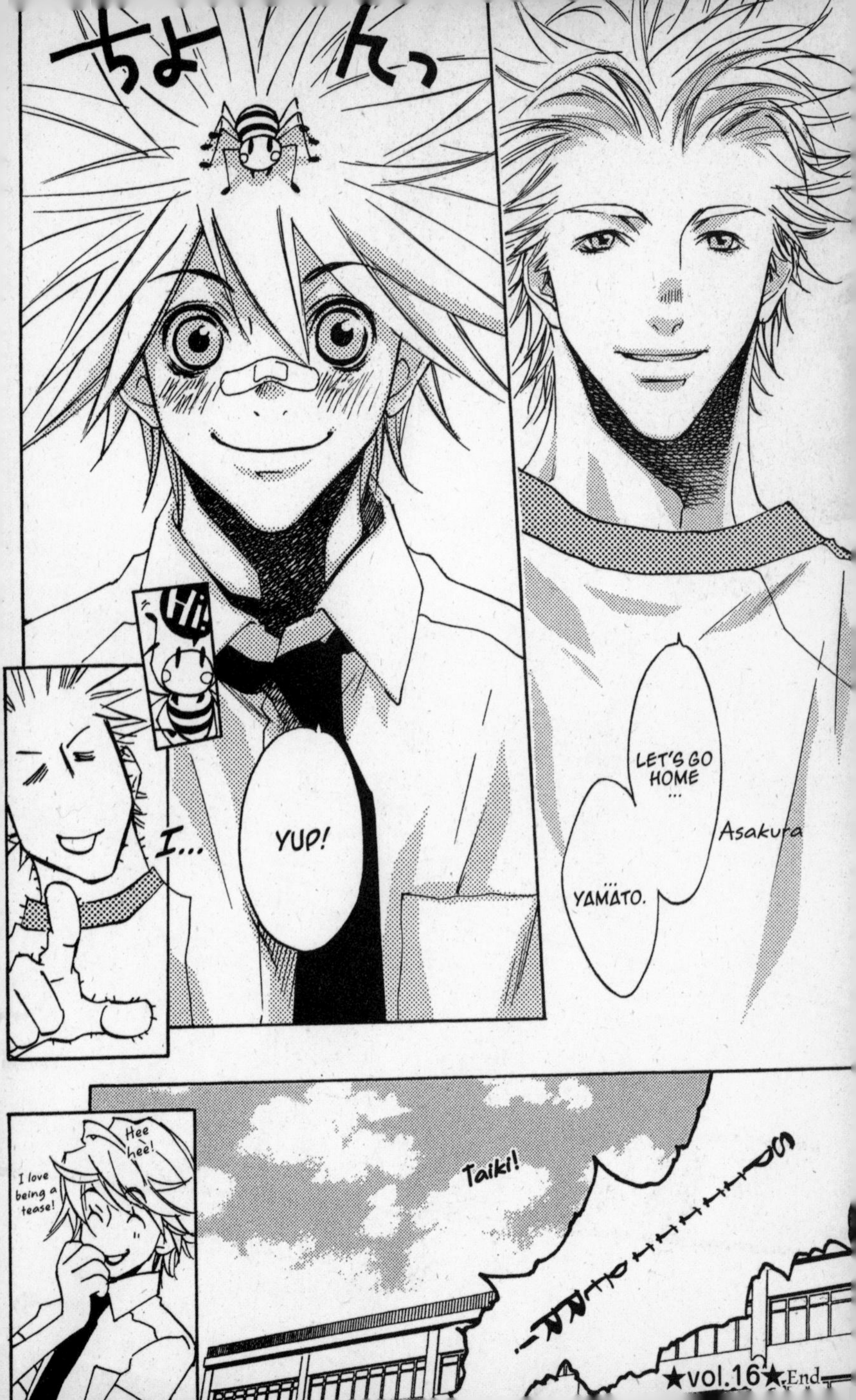
LET'S GO HOME... ...YAMATO.
Asakura
ちょんっ
YUP!
Hi!
I...
Taiki!
Hee hee!
I love being a tease!
★vol.16★.End

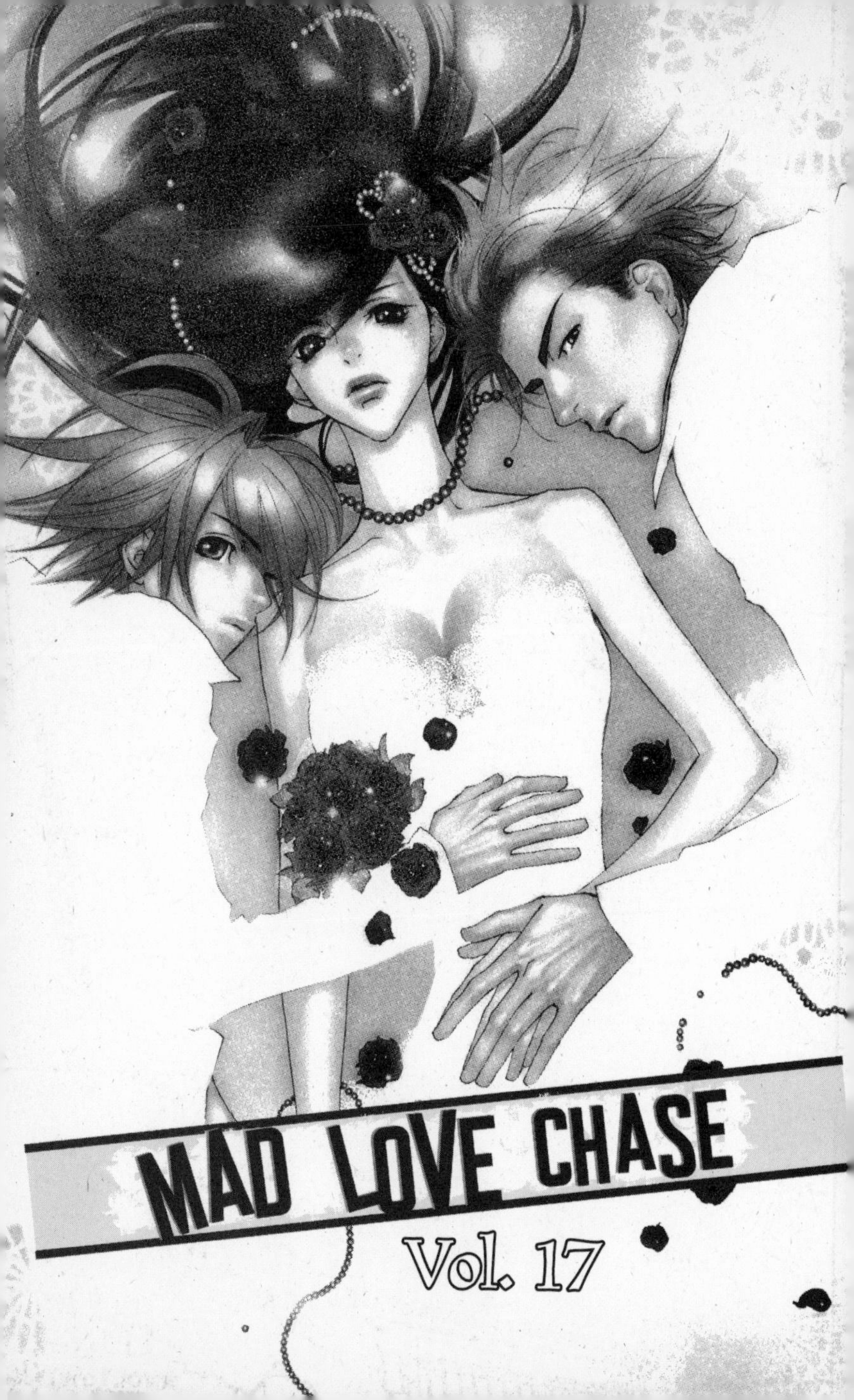
MAD LOVE CHASE
Vol. 17

MAD LOVE CHASE

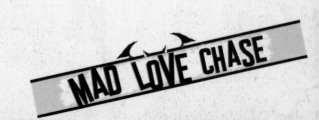

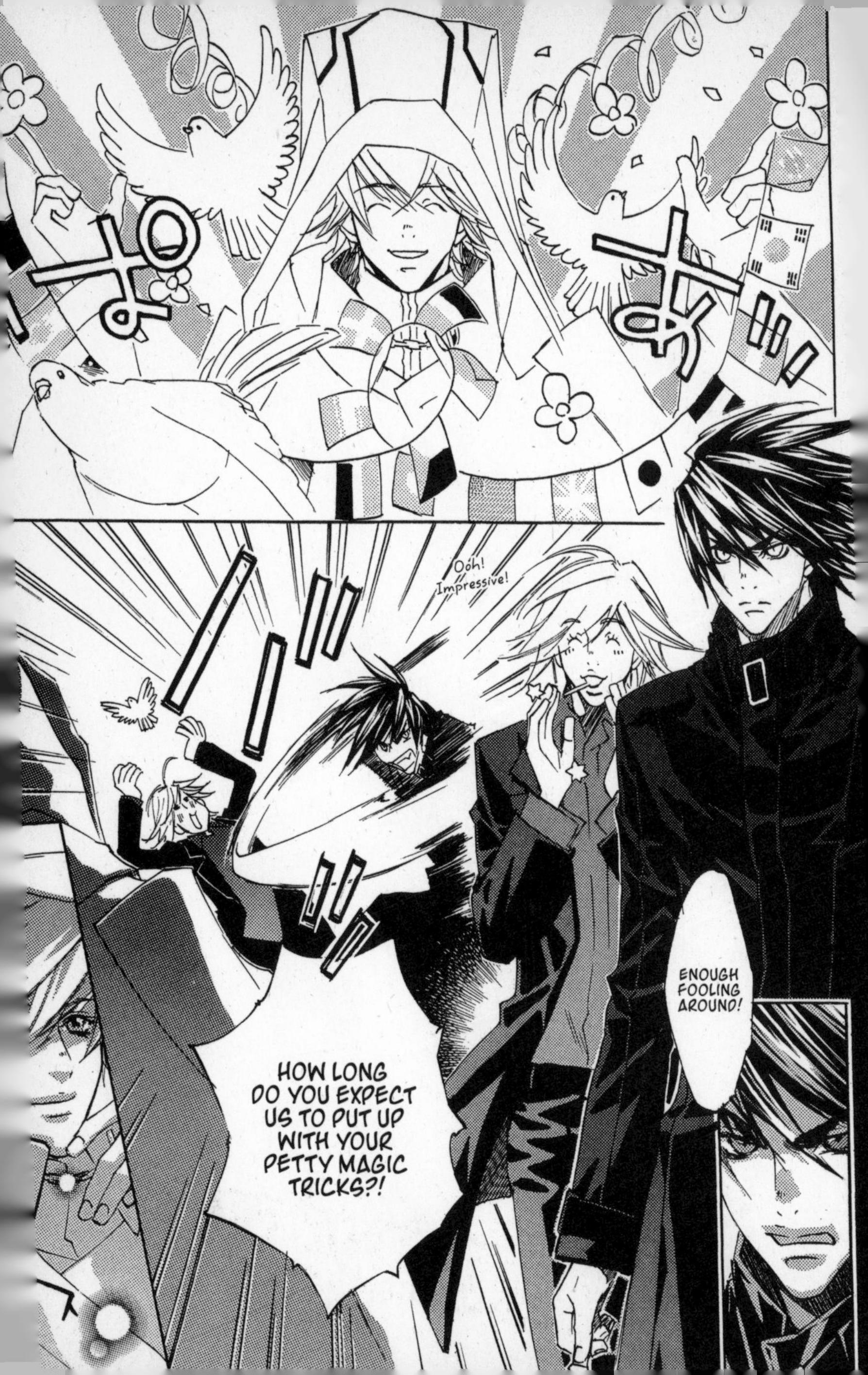
Ooh! Impressive!
ENOUGH FOOLING AROUND!
HOW LONG DO YOU EXPECT US TO PUT UP WITH YOUR PETTY MAGIC TRICKS?!

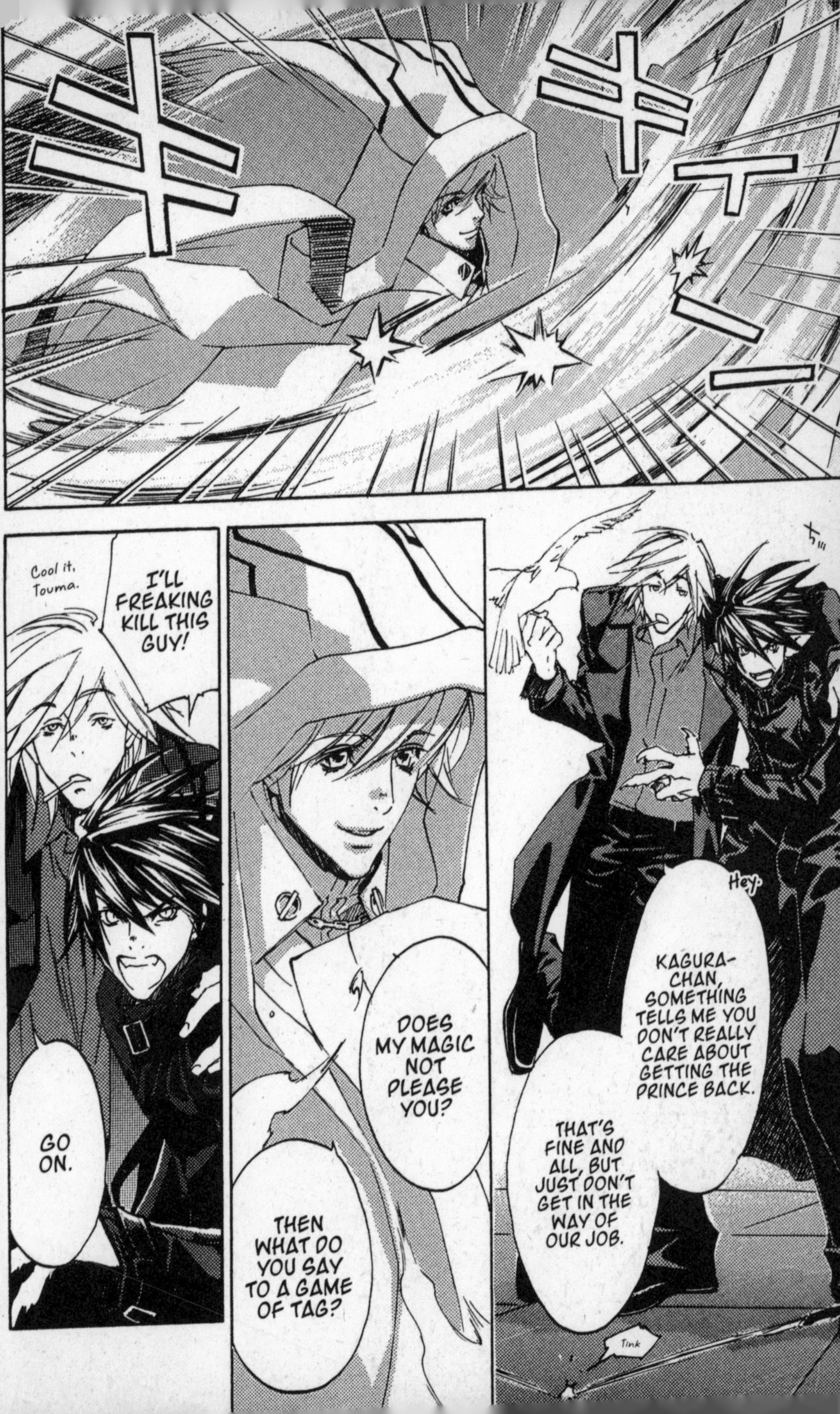
Hey.
KAGURA-CHAN, SOMETHING TELLS ME YOU DON'T REALLY CARE ABOUT GETTING THE PRINCE BACK.
THAT'S FINE AND ALL, BUT JUST DON'T GET IN THE WAY OF OUR JOB.
Tink
DOES MY MAGIC NOT PLEASE YOU?
THEN WHAT DO YOU SAY TO A GAME OF TAG?
I'LL FREAKING KILL THIS GUY!
Cool it, Touma.
GO ON.

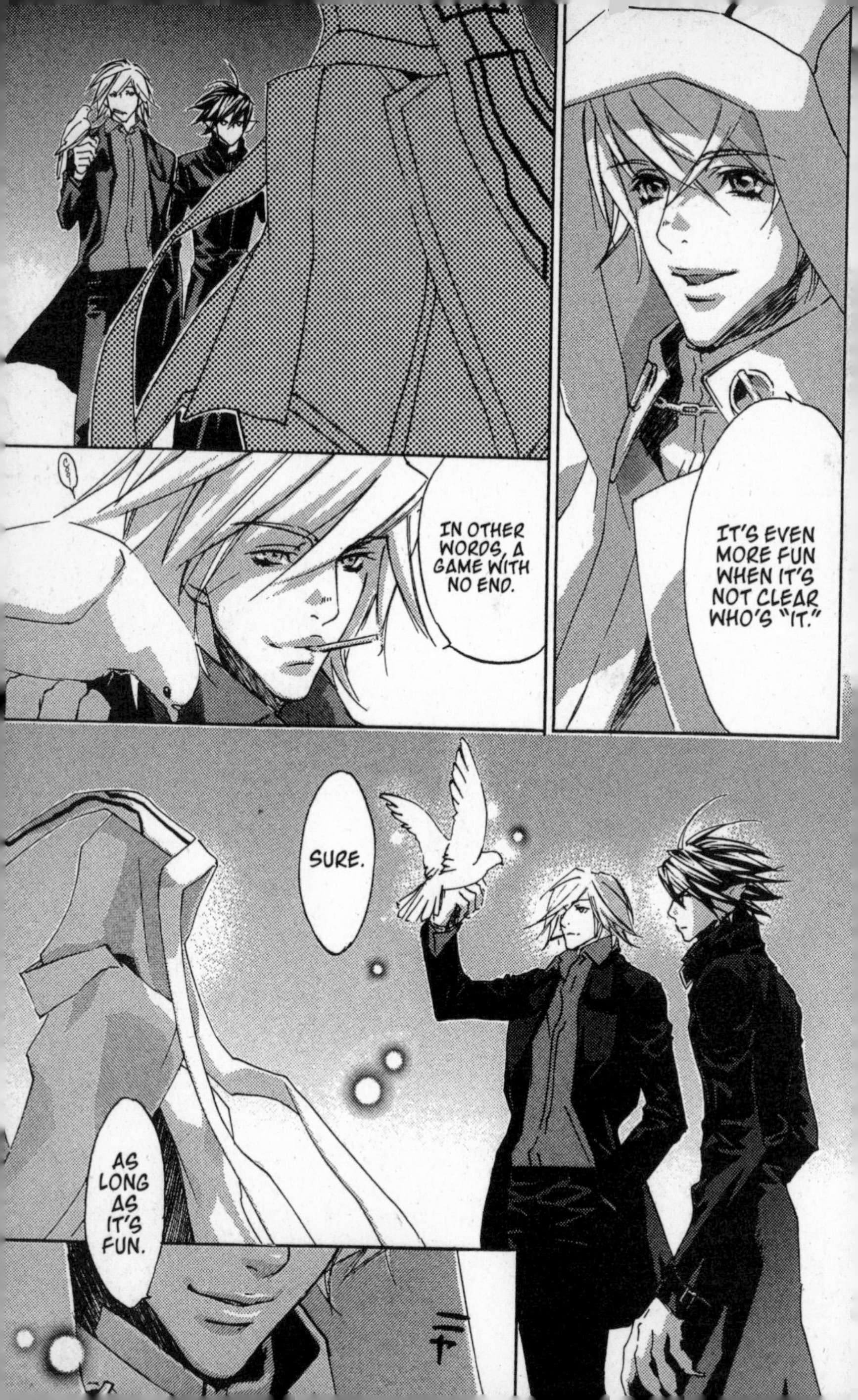
IT'S EVEN MORE FUN WHEN IT'S NOT CLEAR WHO'S "IT."
IN OTHER WORDS, A GAME WITH NO END.
SURE.
AS LONG AS IT'S FUN.

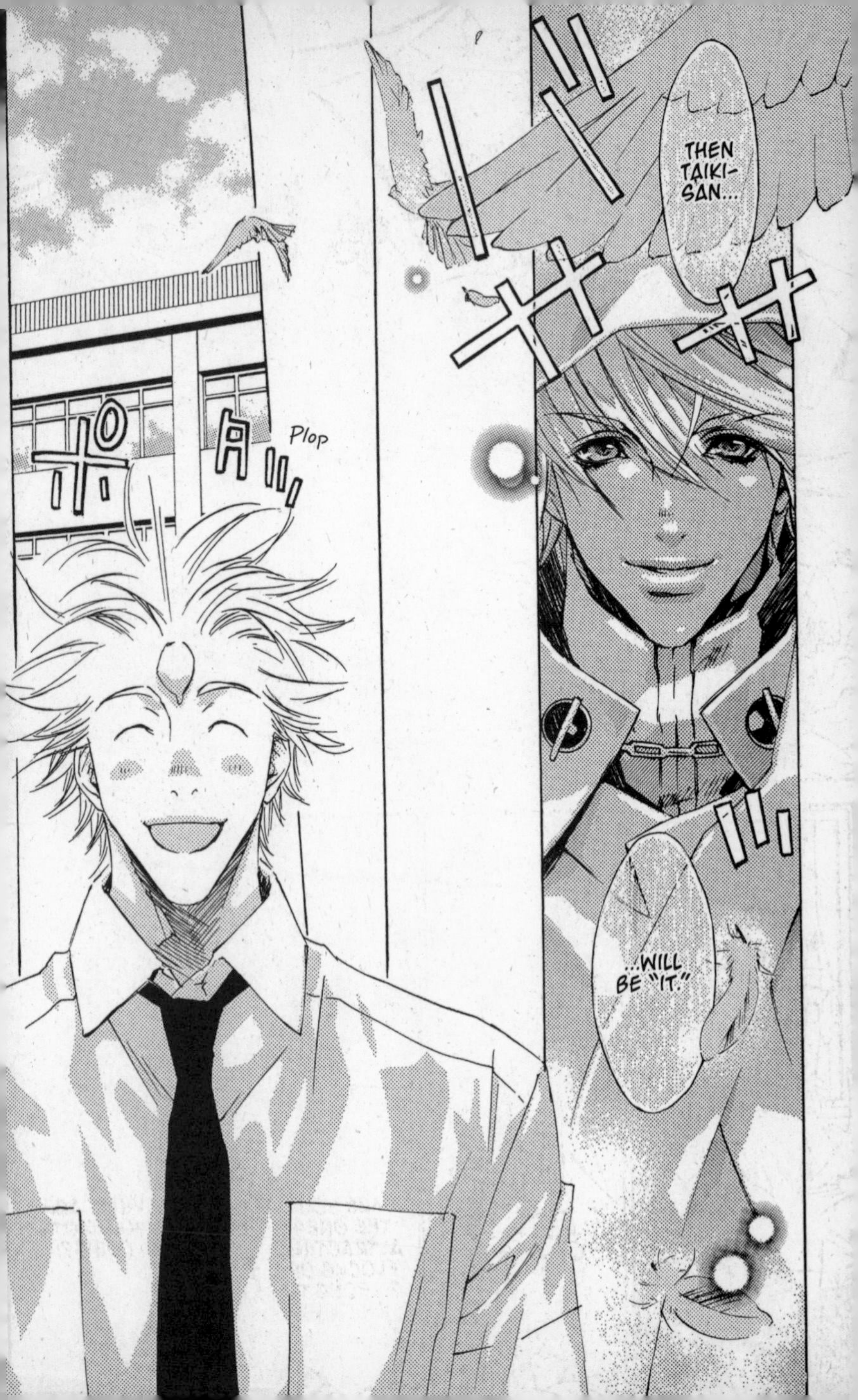
THEN TAIKI-SAN...
...WILL BE "IT."
Plop

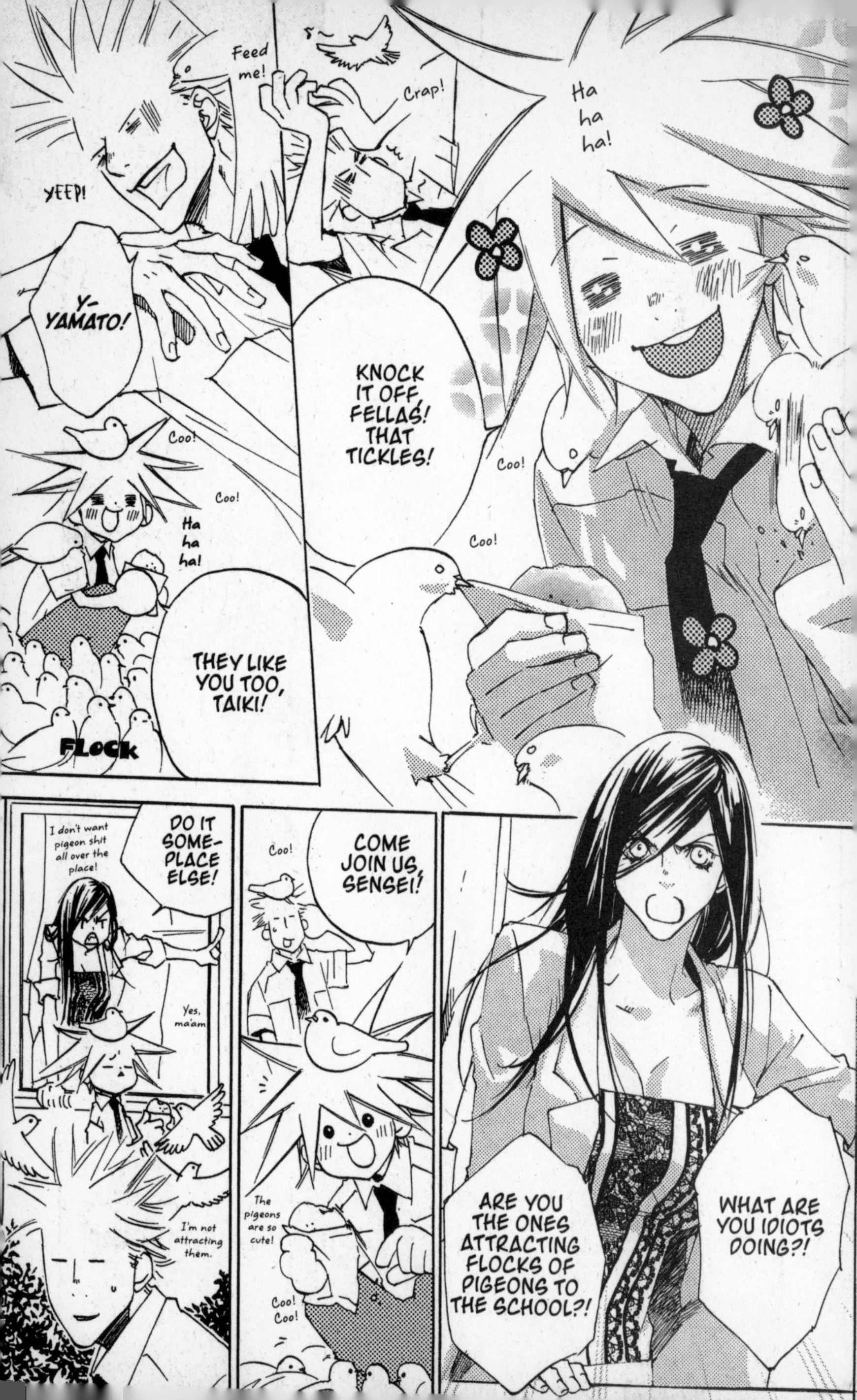
Ha ha ha!
KNOCK IT OFF, FELLAS! THAT TICKLES!
Coo!
Coo!
Feed me!
Crap!
YEEP!
Y-YAMATO!
Coo!
Coo!
Ha ha ha!
THEY LIKE YOU TOO, TAIKI!
FLOCK
WHAT ARE YOU IDIOTS DOING?!
ARE YOU THE ONES ATTRACTING FLOCKS OF PIGEONS TO THE SCHOOL?!
COME JOIN US, SENSEI!
Coo!
The pigeons are so cute!
Coo! Coo!
DO IT SOMEPLACE ELSE!
I don't want pigeon shit all over the place!
Yes, ma'am
I'm not attracting them.

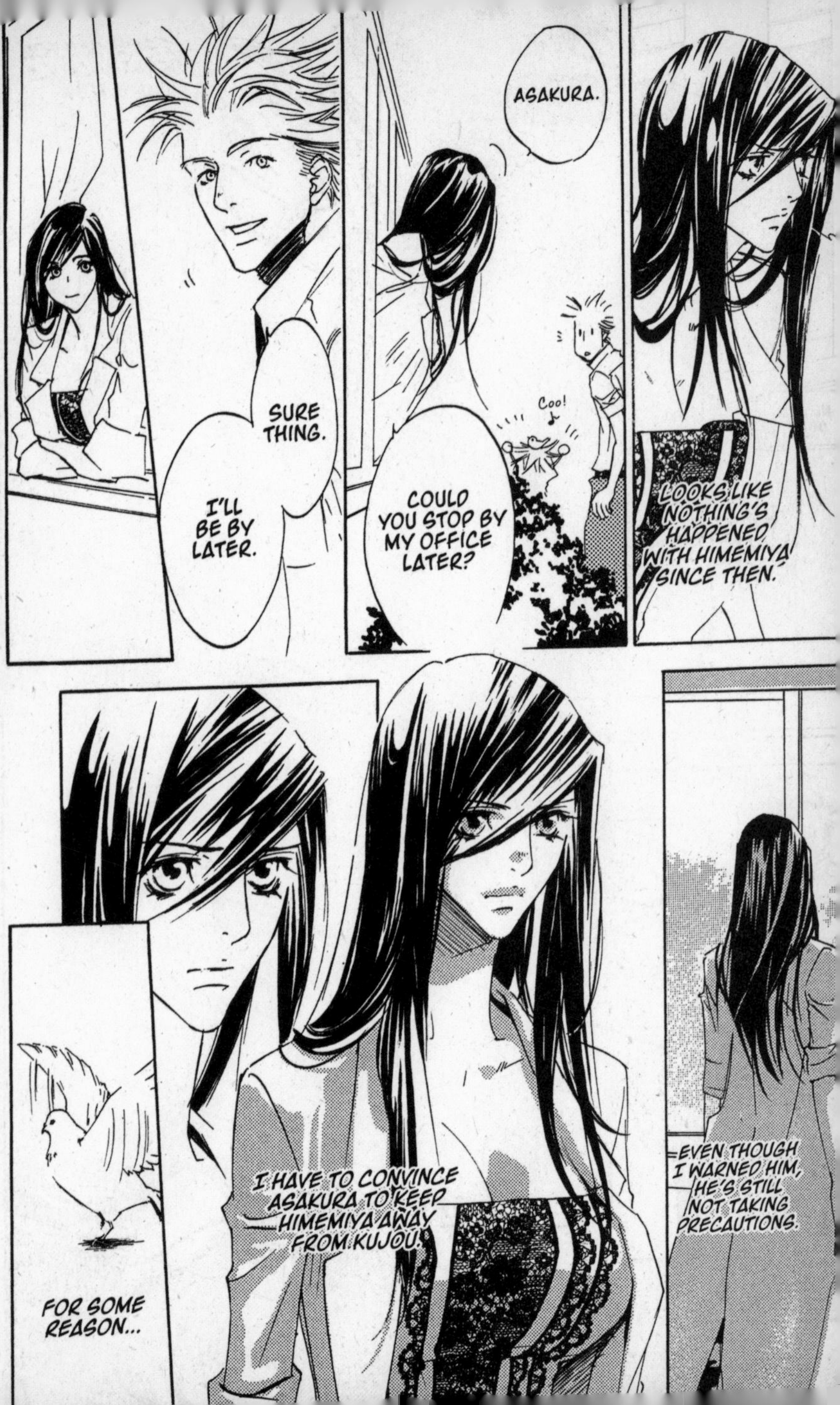
LOOKS LIKE NOTHING'S HAPPENED WITH HIMEMIYA SINCE THEN.
ASAKURA.
COULD YOU STOP BY MY OFFICE LATER?
Coo!
SURE THING.
I'LL BE BY LATER.
EVEN THOUGH I WARNED HIM, HE'S STILL NOT TAKING PRECAUTIONS.
I HAVE TO CONVINCE ASAKURA TO KEEP HIMEMIYA AWAY FROM KUJOU.
FOR SOME REASON...

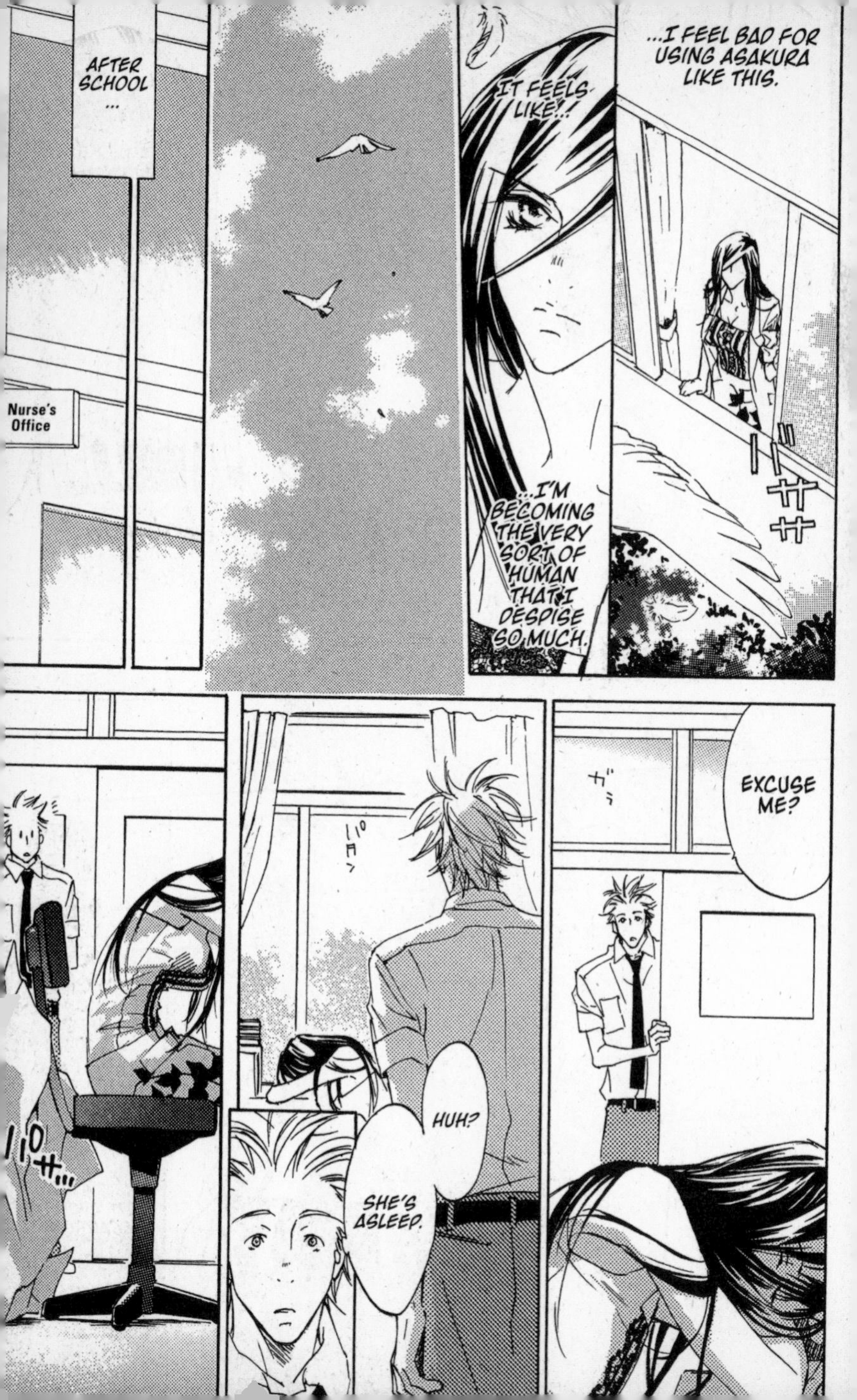
...I FEEL BAD FOR USING ASAKURA LIKE THIS.
IT FEELS LIKE...!
...I'M BECOMING THE VERY SORT OF HUMAN THAT I DESPISE SO MUCH.
AFTER SCHOOL ...
Nurse's Office
EXCUSE ME?
HUH?
SHE'S ASLEEP.

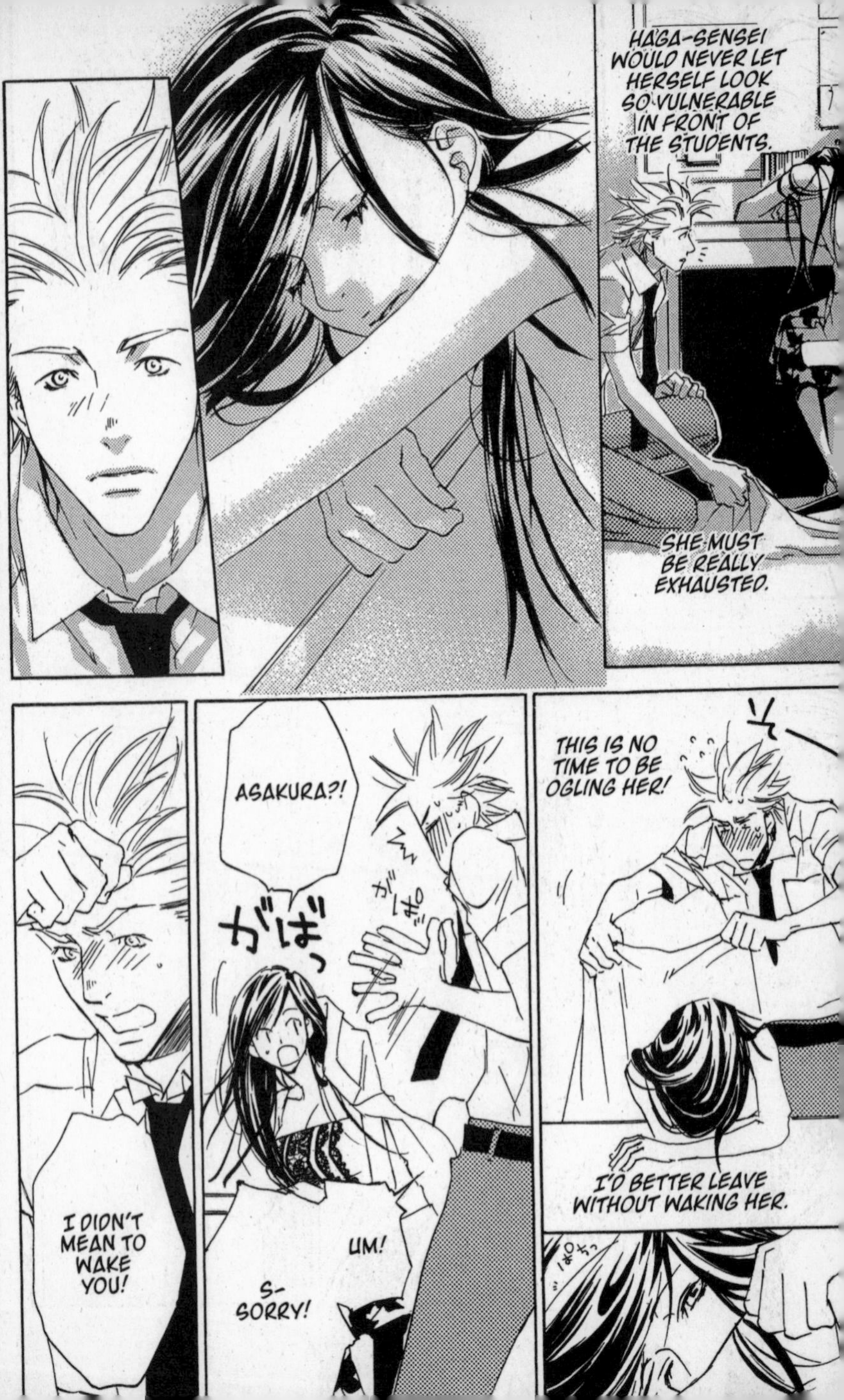
HAGA-SENSEI WOULD NEVER LET HERSELF LOOK SO VULNERABLE IN FRONT OF THE STUDENTS.
SHE MUST BE REALLY EXHAUSTED.
THIS IS NO TIME TO BE OGLING HER!
I'D BETTER LEAVE WITHOUT WAKING HER.
ぱちっ
ASAKURA?!
がばっ
がばっ
UM!
S-SORRY!
I DIDN'T MEAN TO WAKE YOU!

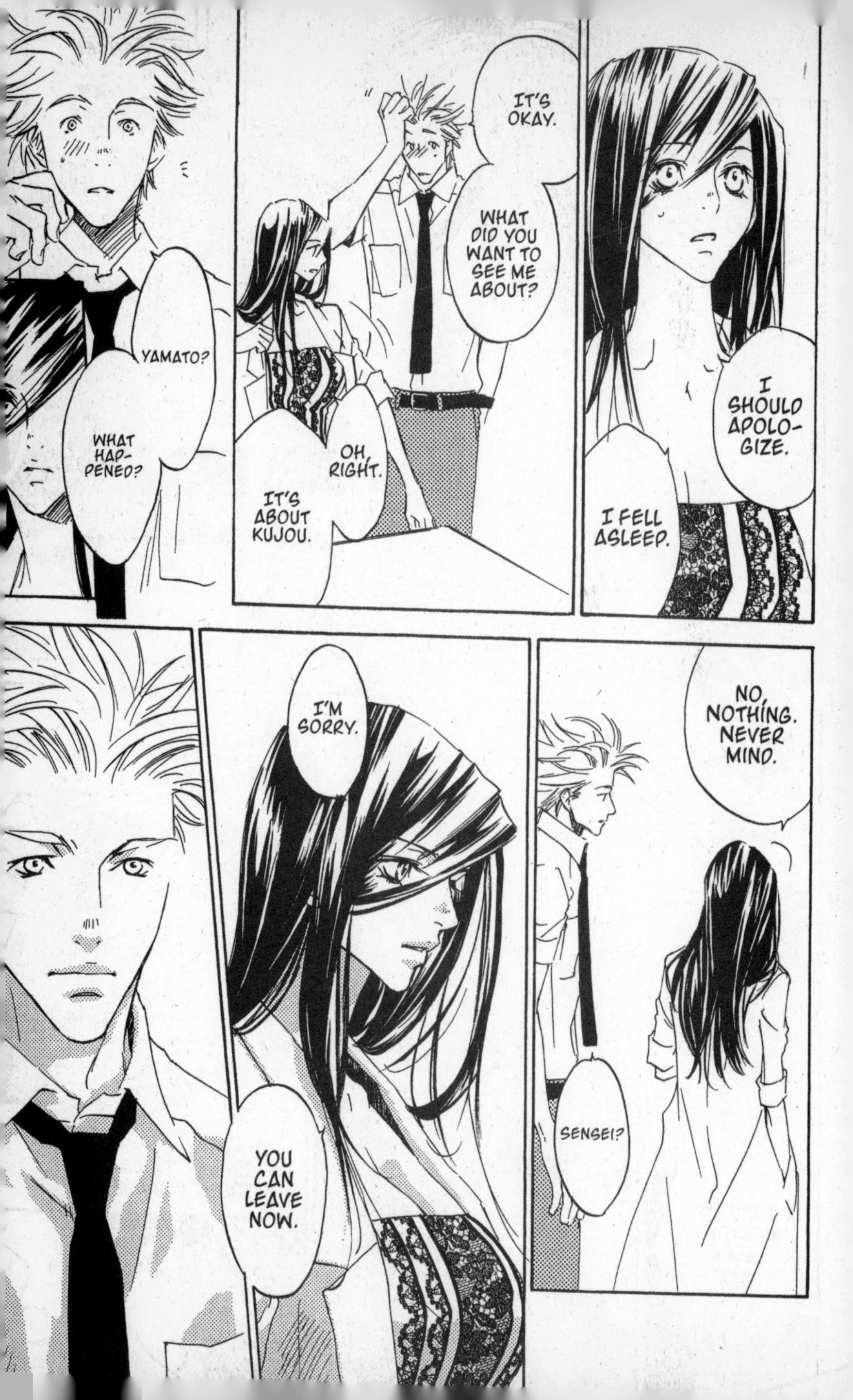
I SHOULD APOLOGIZE.
I FELL ASLEEP.
IT'S OKAY.
WHAT DID YOU WANT TO SEE ME ABOUT?
OH, RIGHT.
IT'S ABOUT KUJOU.
YAMATO?
WHAT HAPPENED?
NO, NOTHING. NEVER MIND.
SENSEI?
I'M SORRY.
YOU CAN LEAVE NOW.

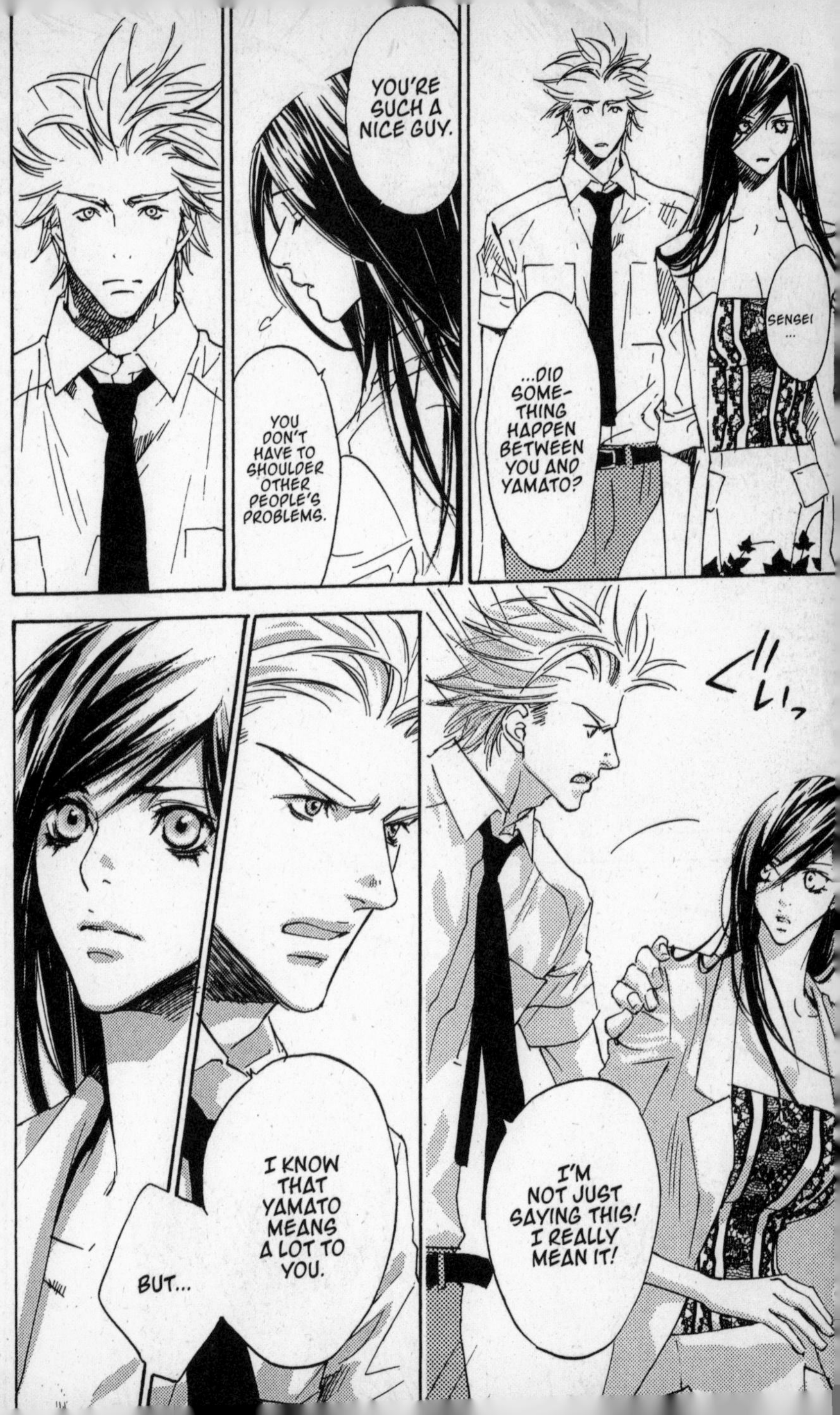
SENSEI...
...DID SOMETHING HAPPEN BETWEEN YOU AND YAMATO?
YOU'RE SUCH A NICE GUY.
YOU DON'T HAVE TO SHOULDER OTHER PEOPLE'S PROBLEMS.
ぐいっ
I'M NOT JUST SAYING THIS! I REALLY MEAN IT!
I KNOW THAT YAMATO MEANS A LOT TO YOU.
BUT...

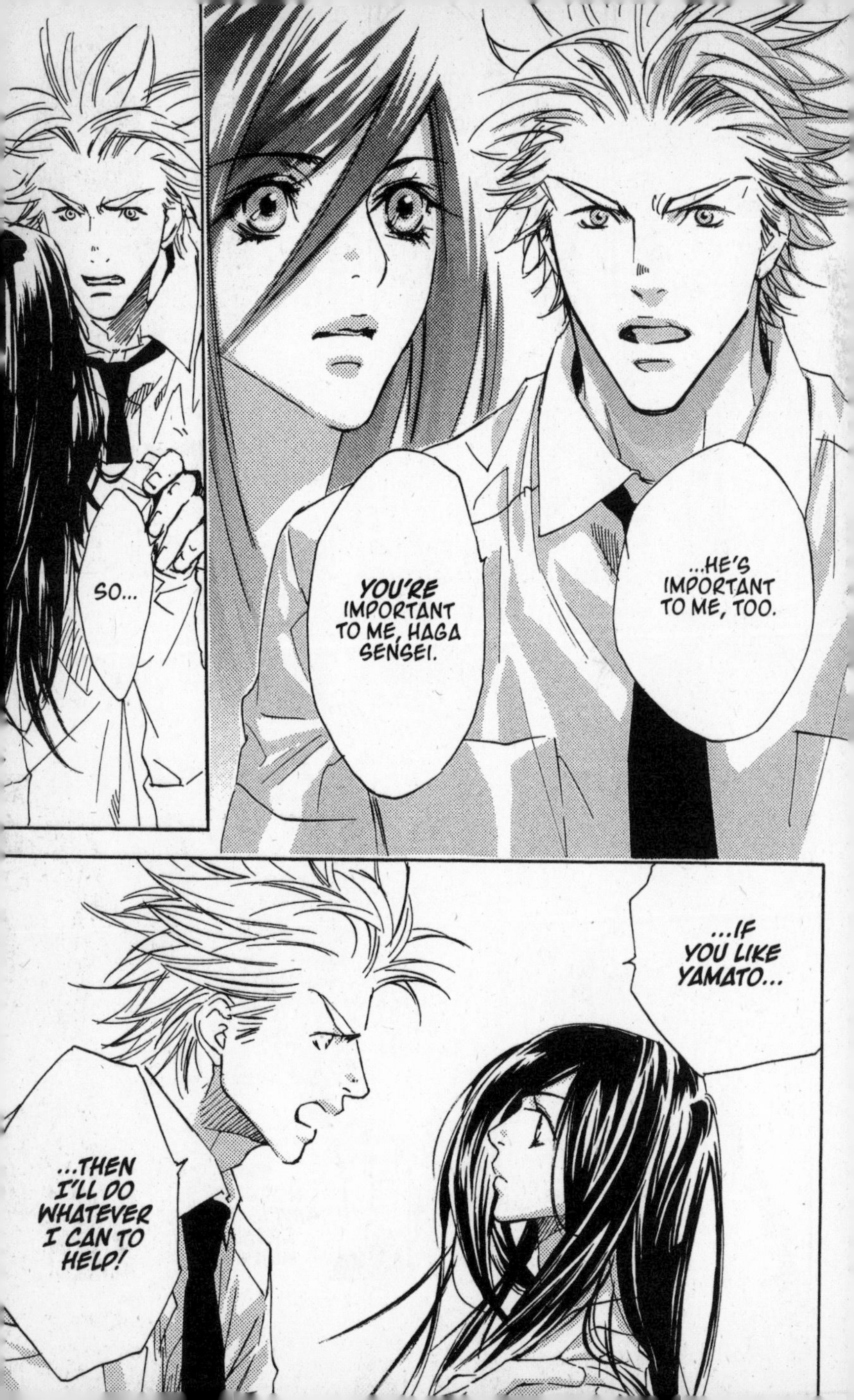
...HE'S IMPORTANT TO ME, TOO.
YOU'RE IMPORTANT TO ME, HAGA SENSEI.
SO...
...IF YOU LIKE YAMATO...
...THEN I'LL DO WHATEVER I CAN TO HELP!

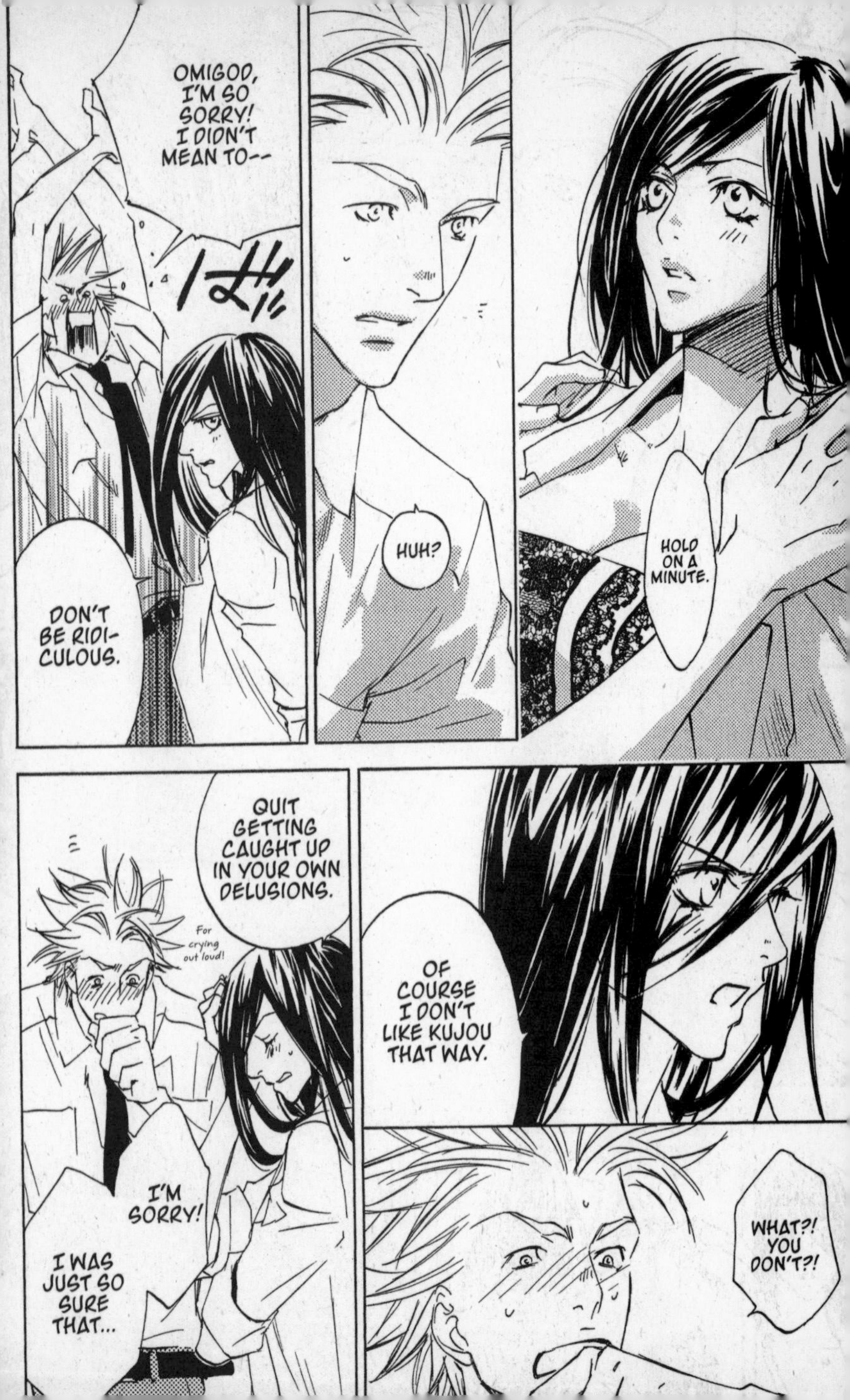
HOLD ON A MINUTE.
HUH?
OMIGOD, I'M SO SORRY! I DIDN'T MEAN TO--
DON'T BE RIDICULOUS.
OF COURSE I DON'T LIKE KUJOU THAT WAY.
WHAT?! YOU DON'T?!
QUIT GETTING CAUGHT UP IN YOUR OWN DELUSIONS.
For crying out loud!
I'M SORRY!
I WAS JUST SO SURE THAT...

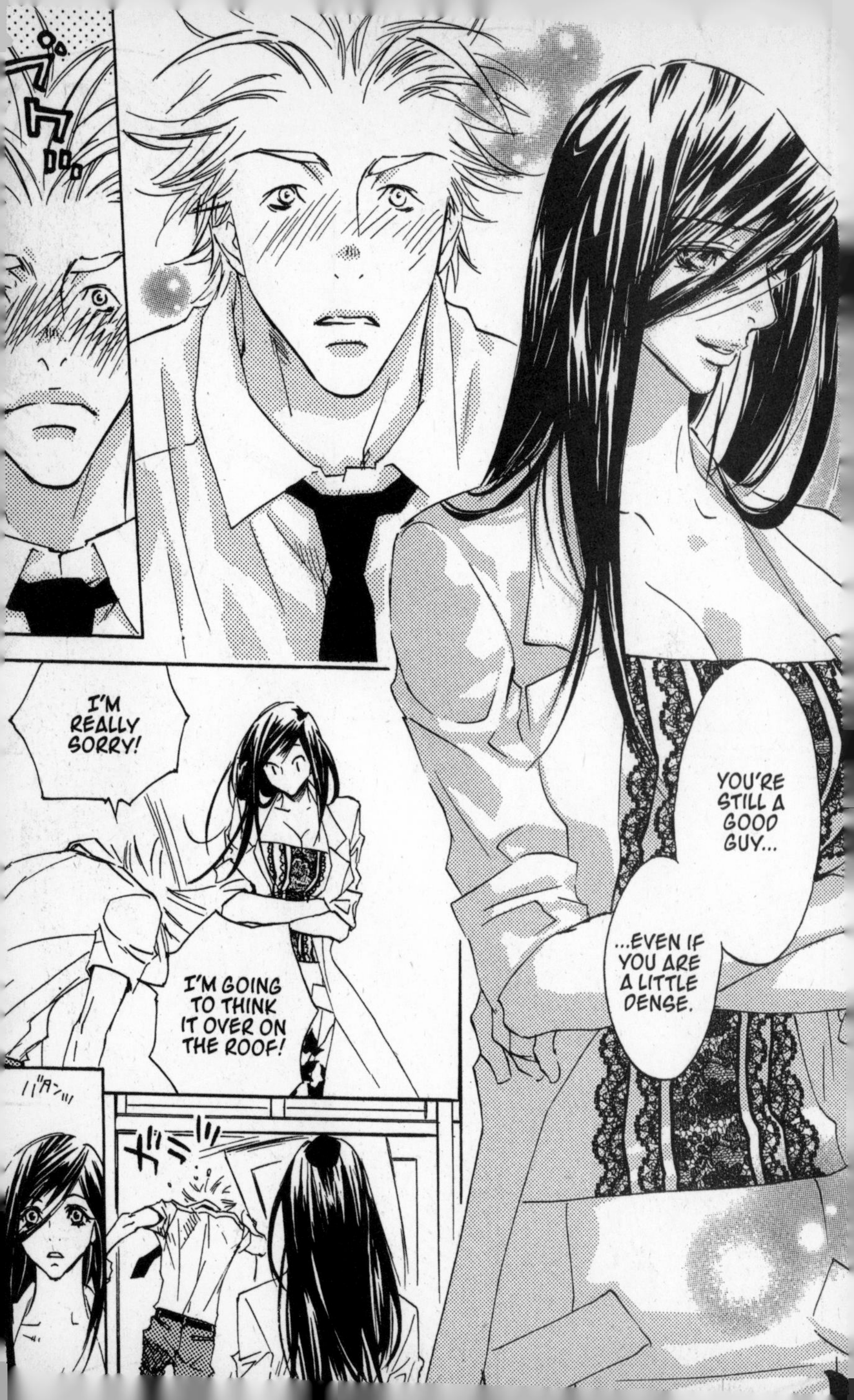
YOU'RE STILL A GOOD GUY...
...EVEN IF YOU ARE A LITTLE DENSE.
I'M REALLY SORRY!
I'M GOING TO THINK IT OVER ON THE ROOF!

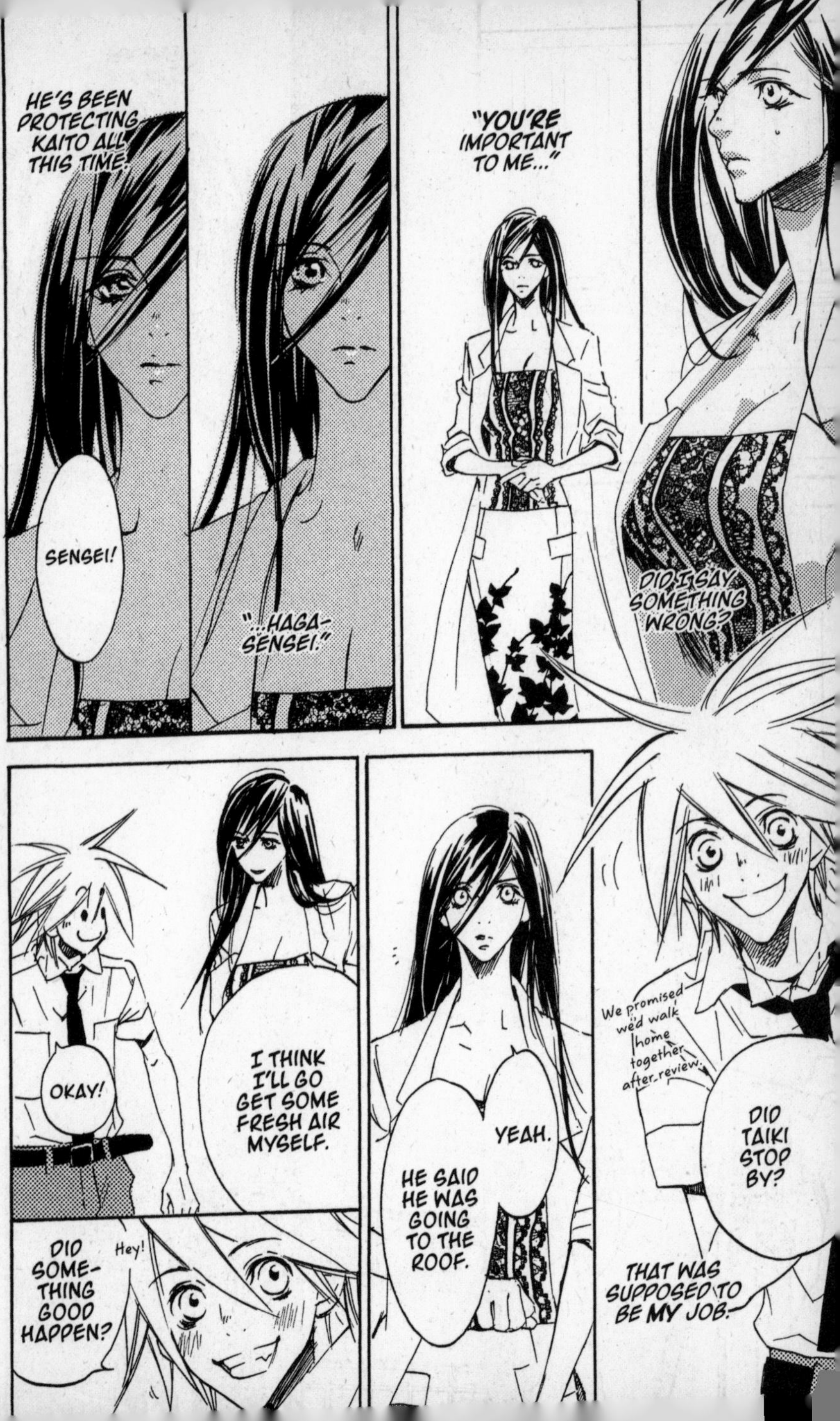
DID I SAY SOMETHING WRONG?
"YOU'RE IMPORTANT TO ME..."
"...HAGA-SENSEI."
HE'S BEEN PROTECTING KAITO ALL THIS TIME.
SENSEI!
DID TAIKI STOP BY?
We promised we'd walk home together after review.
THAT WAS SUPPOSED TO BE MY JOB.
YEAH.
HE SAID HE WAS GOING TO THE ROOF.
I THINK I'LL GO GET SOME FRESH AIR MYSELF.
OKAY!
Hey!
DID SOMETHING GOOD HAPPEN?

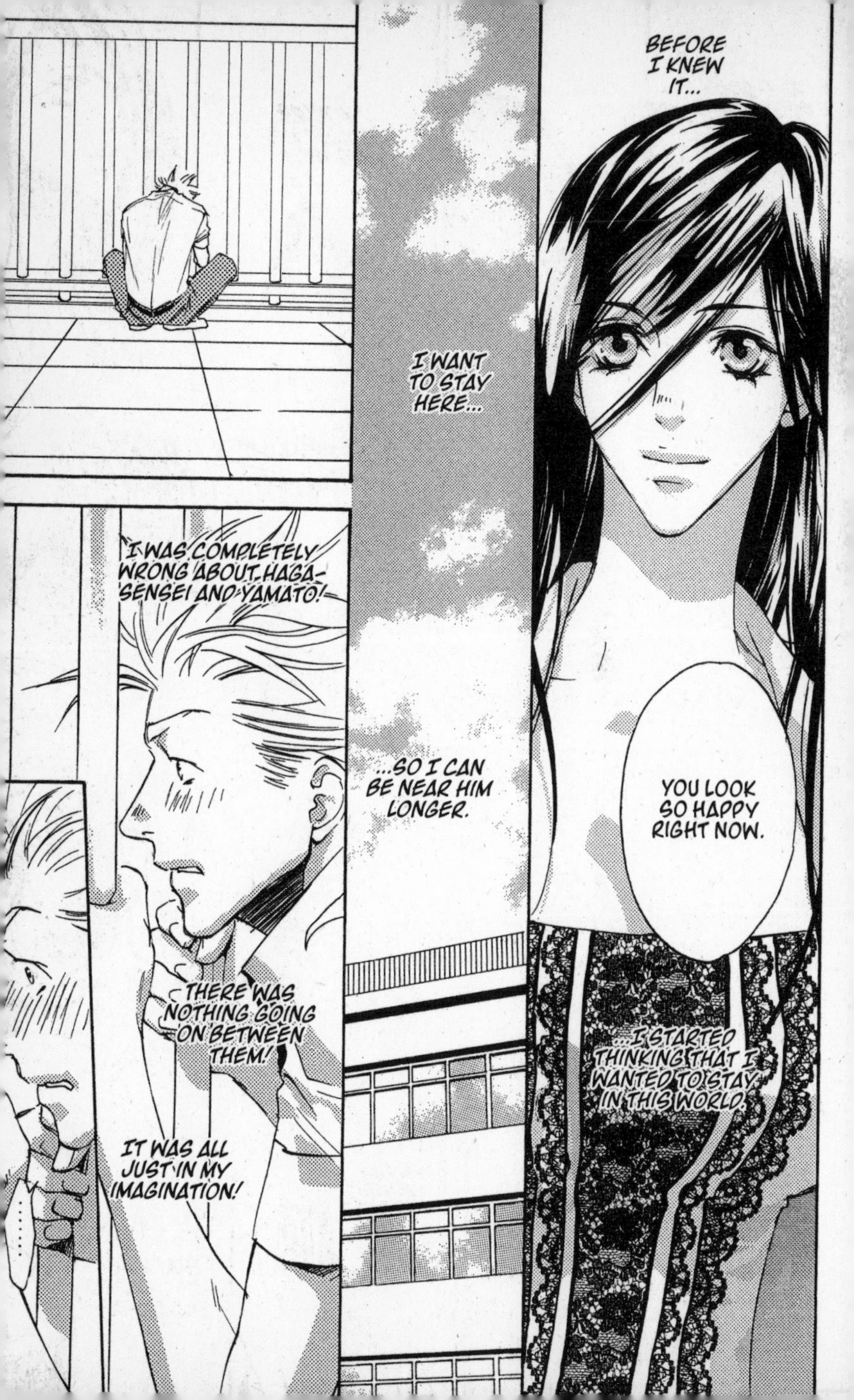
BEFORE I KNEW IT...
YOU LOOK SO HAPPY RIGHT NOW.
...I STARTED THINKING THAT I WANTED TO STAY IN THIS WORLD.
I WANT TO STAY HERE...
...SO I CAN BE NEAR HIM LONGER.
I WAS COMPLETELY WRONG ABOUT HAGA-SENSEI AND YAMATO!
THERE WAS NOTHING GOING ON BETWEEN THEM!
IT WAS ALL JUST IN MY IMAGINATION!

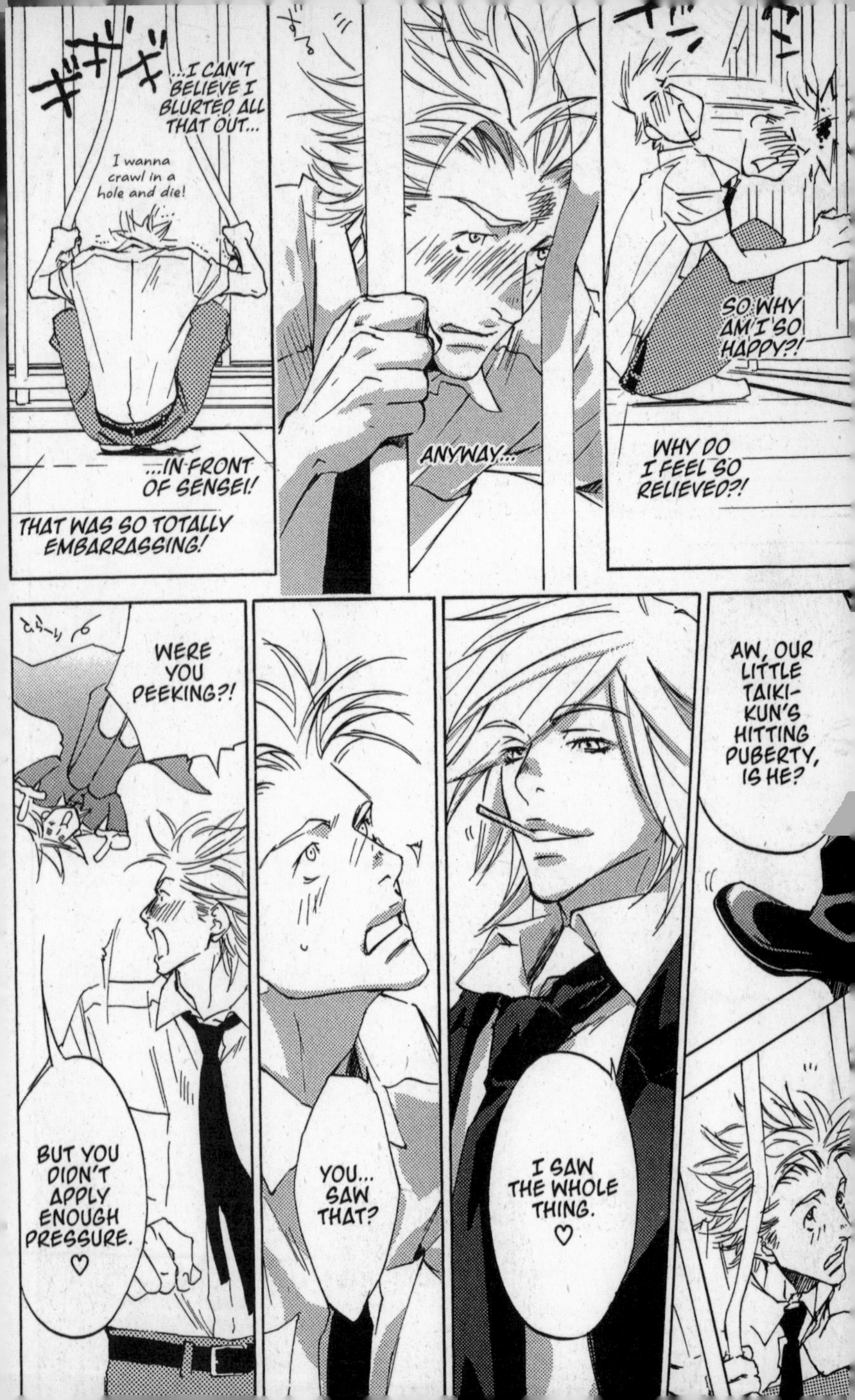
SO WHY AM I SO HAPPY?!
WHY DO I FEEL SO RELIEVED?!
ANYWAY...
...I CAN'T BELIEVE I BLURTED ALL THAT OUT...
I wanna crawl in a hole and die!
...IN FRONT OF SENSEI!
THAT WAS SO TOTALLY EMBARRASSING!
AW, OUR LITTLE TAIKI-KUN'S HITTING PUBERTY, IS HE?
I SAW THE WHOLE THING. ♡
YOU... SAW THAT?
WERE YOU PEEKING?!
BUT YOU DIDN'T APPLY ENOUGH PRESSURE. ♡

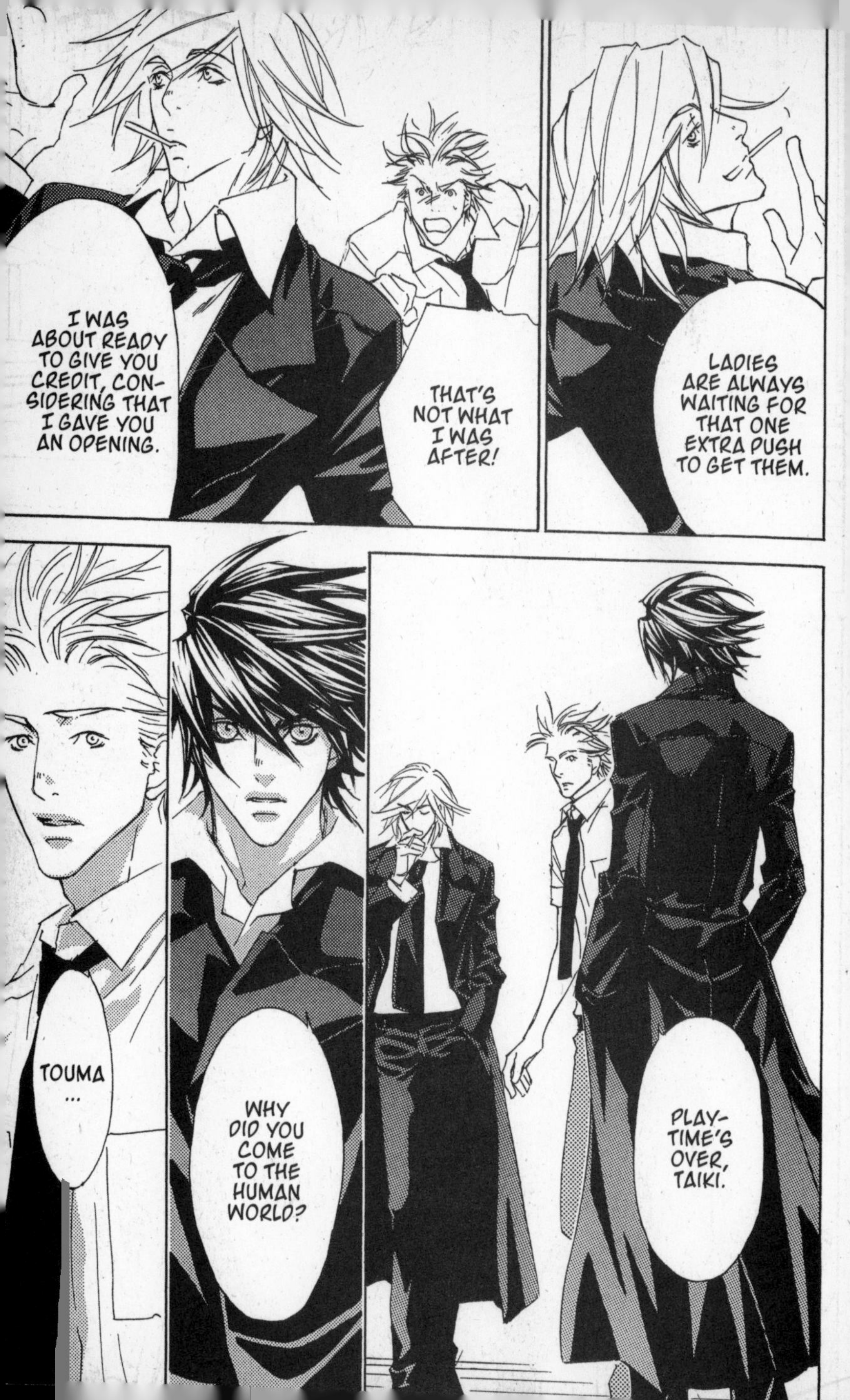
LADIES ARE ALWAYS WAITING FOR THAT ONE EXTRA PUSH TO GET THEM.
THAT'S NOT WHAT I WAS AFTER!
I WAS ABOUT READY TO GIVE YOU CREDIT, CON-SIDERING THAT I GAVE YOU AN OPENING.
PLAY-TIME'S OVER, TAIKI.
WHY DID YOU COME TO THE HUMAN WORLD?
TOUMA ...

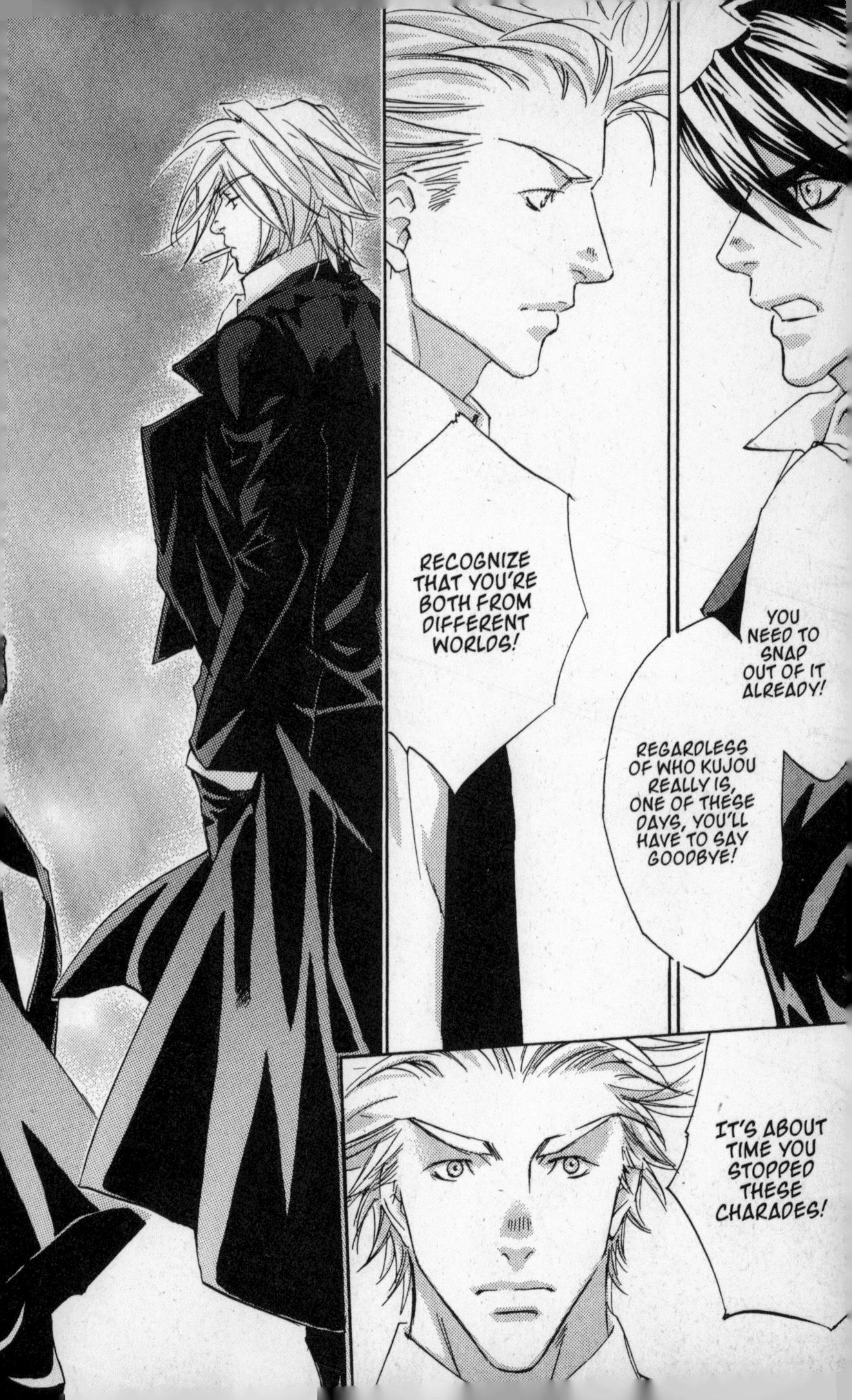
YOU NEED TO SNAP OUT OF IT ALREADY!
REGARDLESS OF WHO KUJOU REALLY IS, ONE OF THESE DAYS, YOU'LL HAVE TO SAY GOODBYE!
RECOGNIZE THAT YOU'RE BOTH FROM DIFFERENT WORLDS!
IT'S ABOUT TIME YOU STOPPED THESE CHARADES!

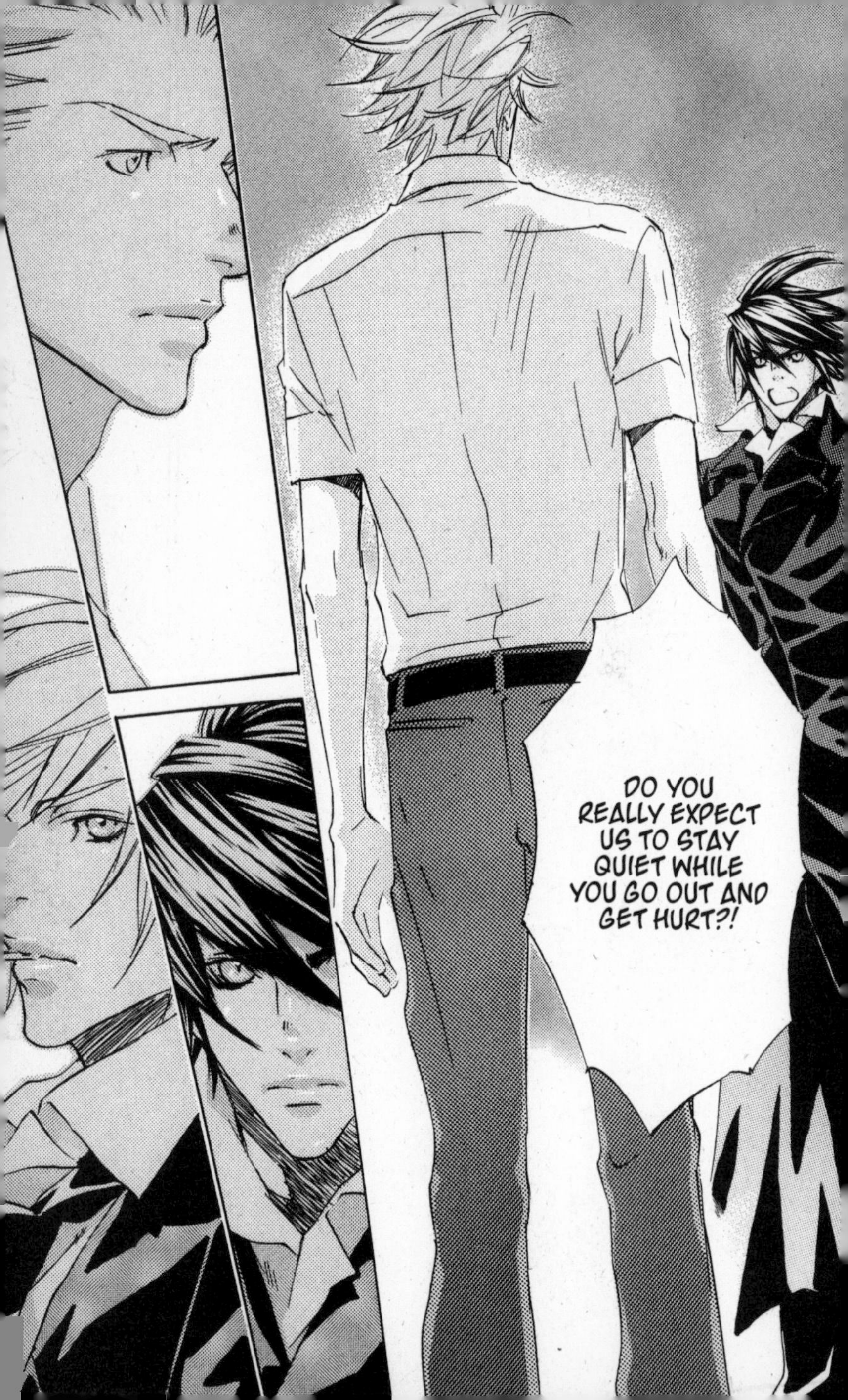
DO YOU REALLY EXPECT US TO STAY QUIET WHILE YOU GO OUT AND GET HURT?!

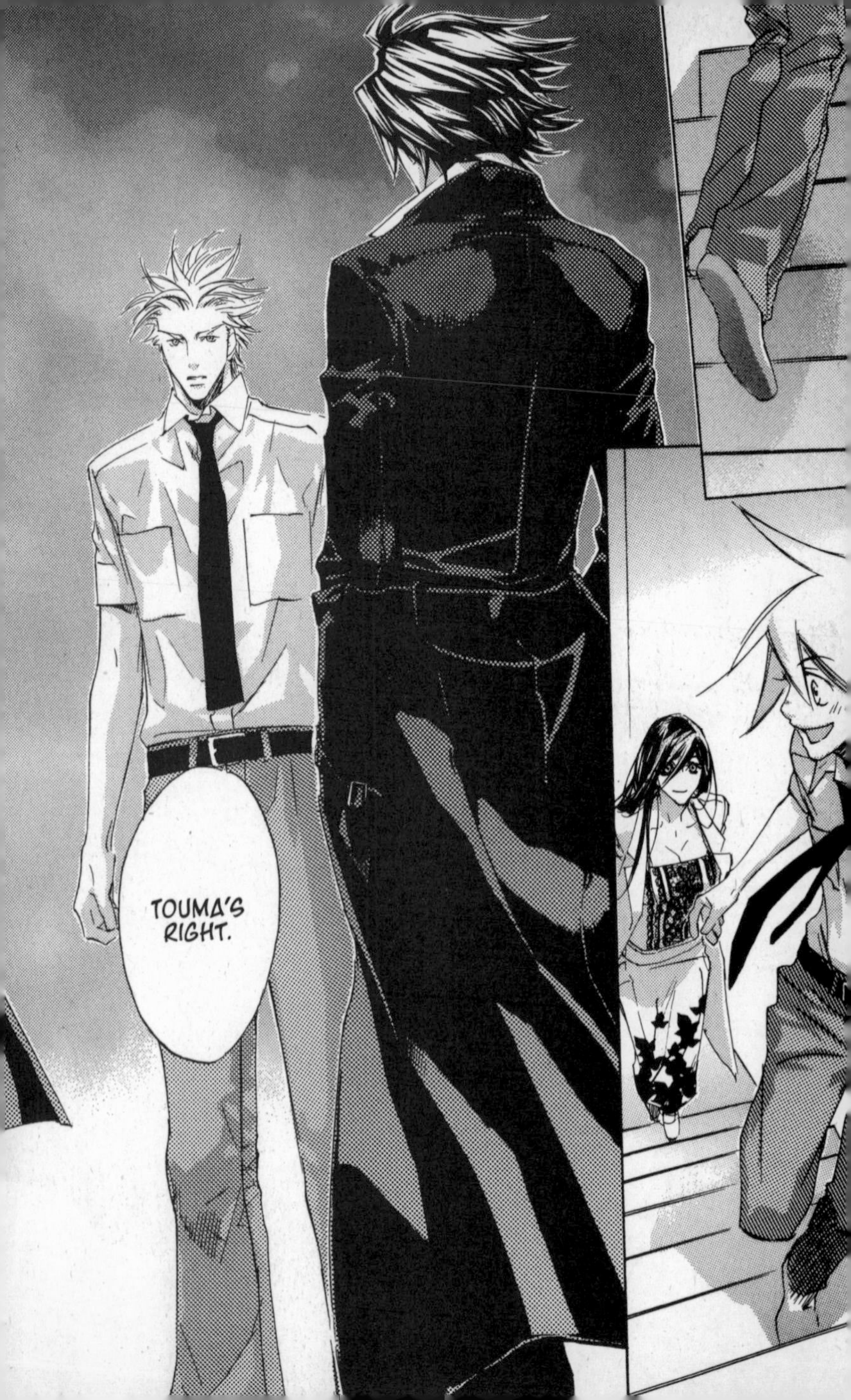
TOUMA'S RIGHT.

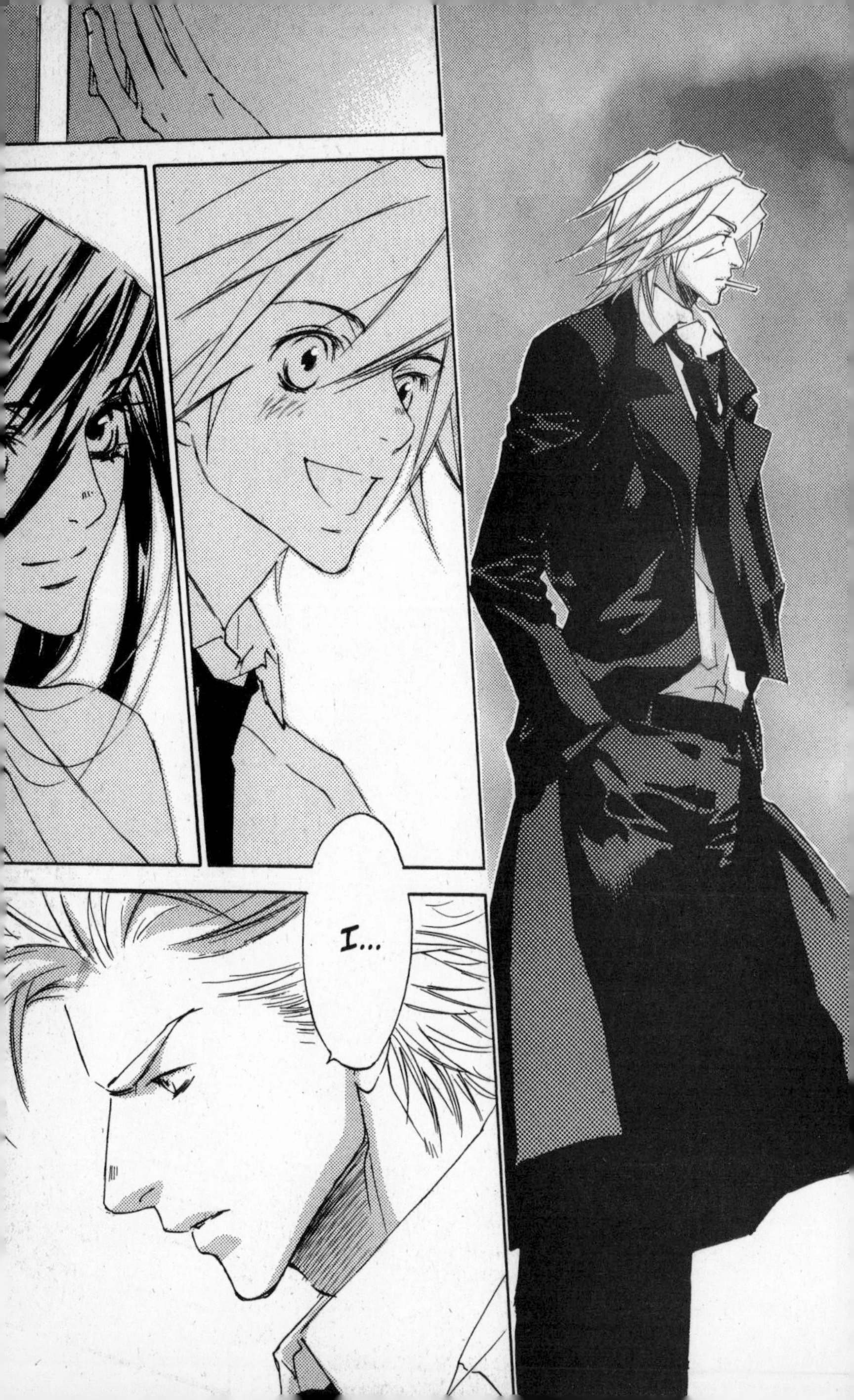
I...

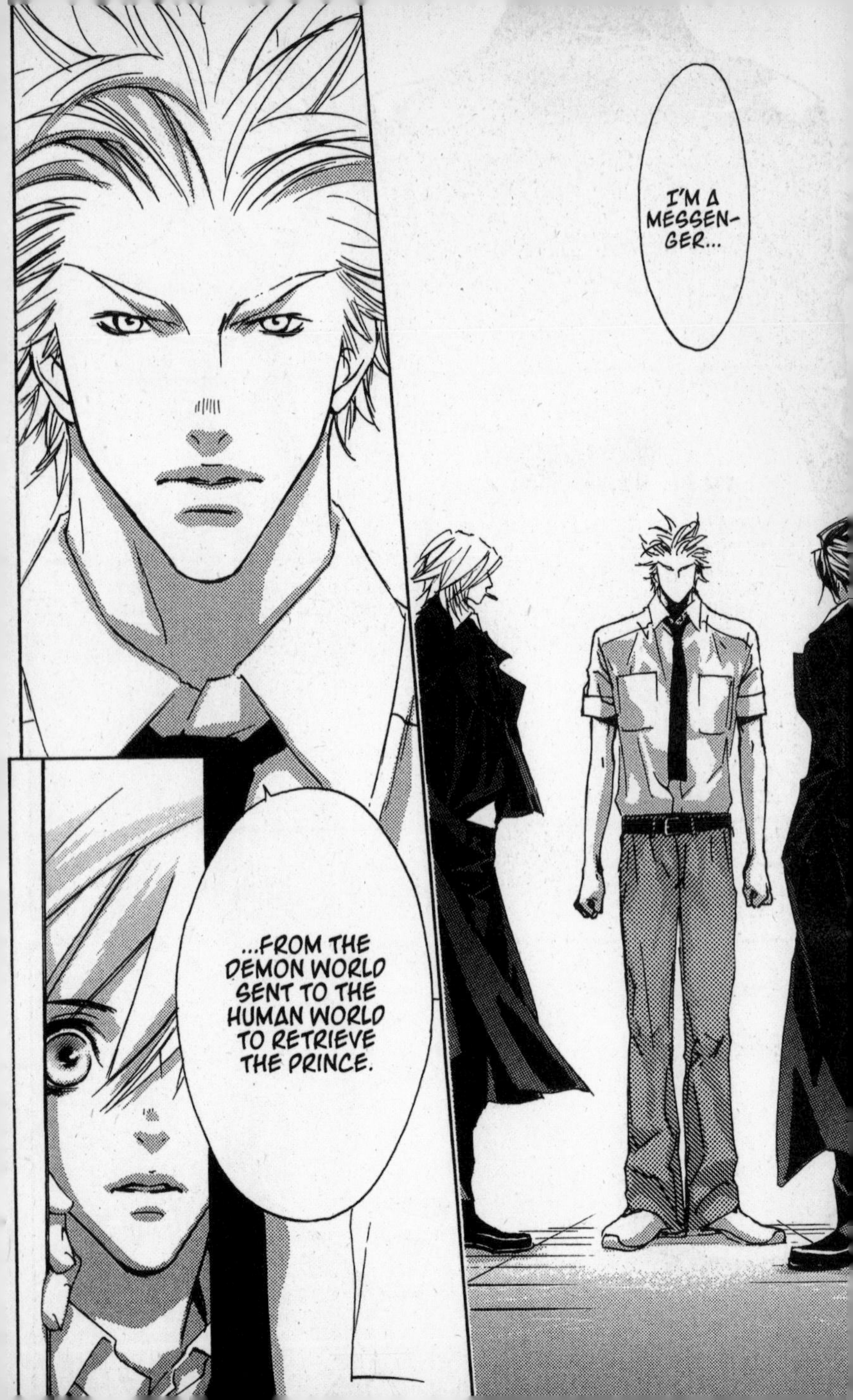
I'M A MESSENGER...
...FROM THE DEMON WORLD SENT TO THE HUMAN WORLD TO RETRIEVE THE PRINCE.

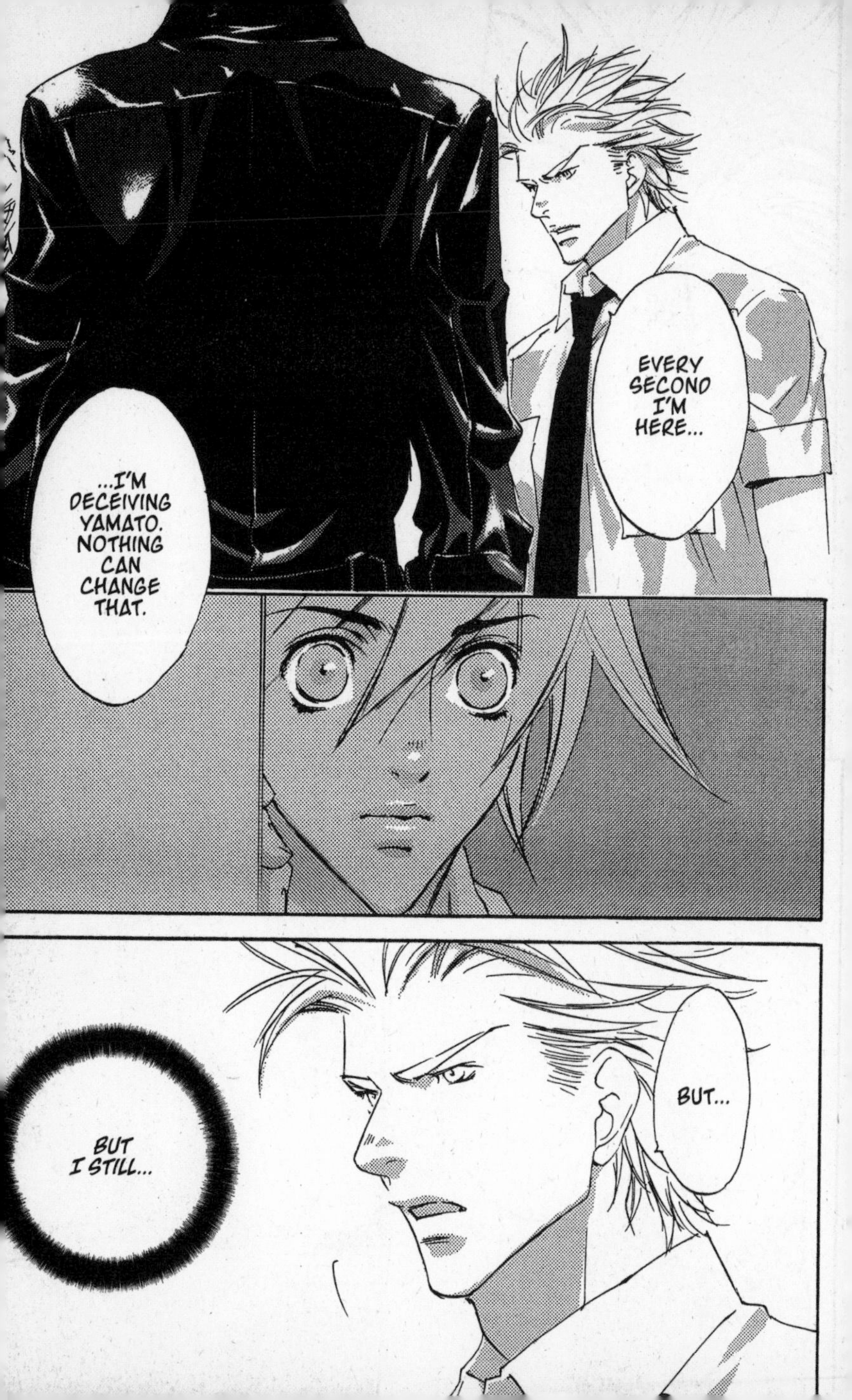
EVERY SECOND I'M HERE...
...I'M DECEIVING YAMATO. NOTHING CAN CHANGE THAT.
BUT...
BUT I STILL...

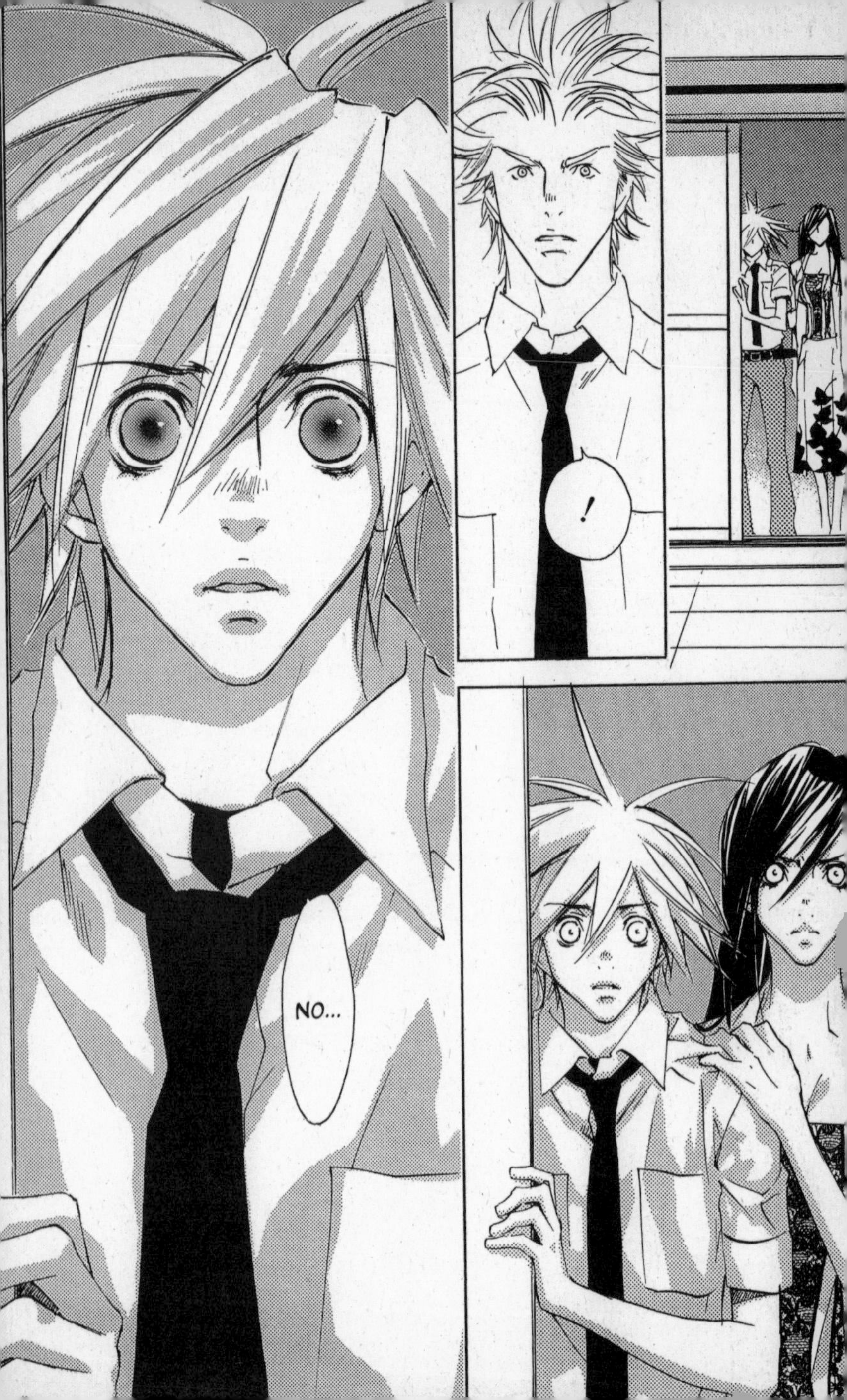
!
NO...

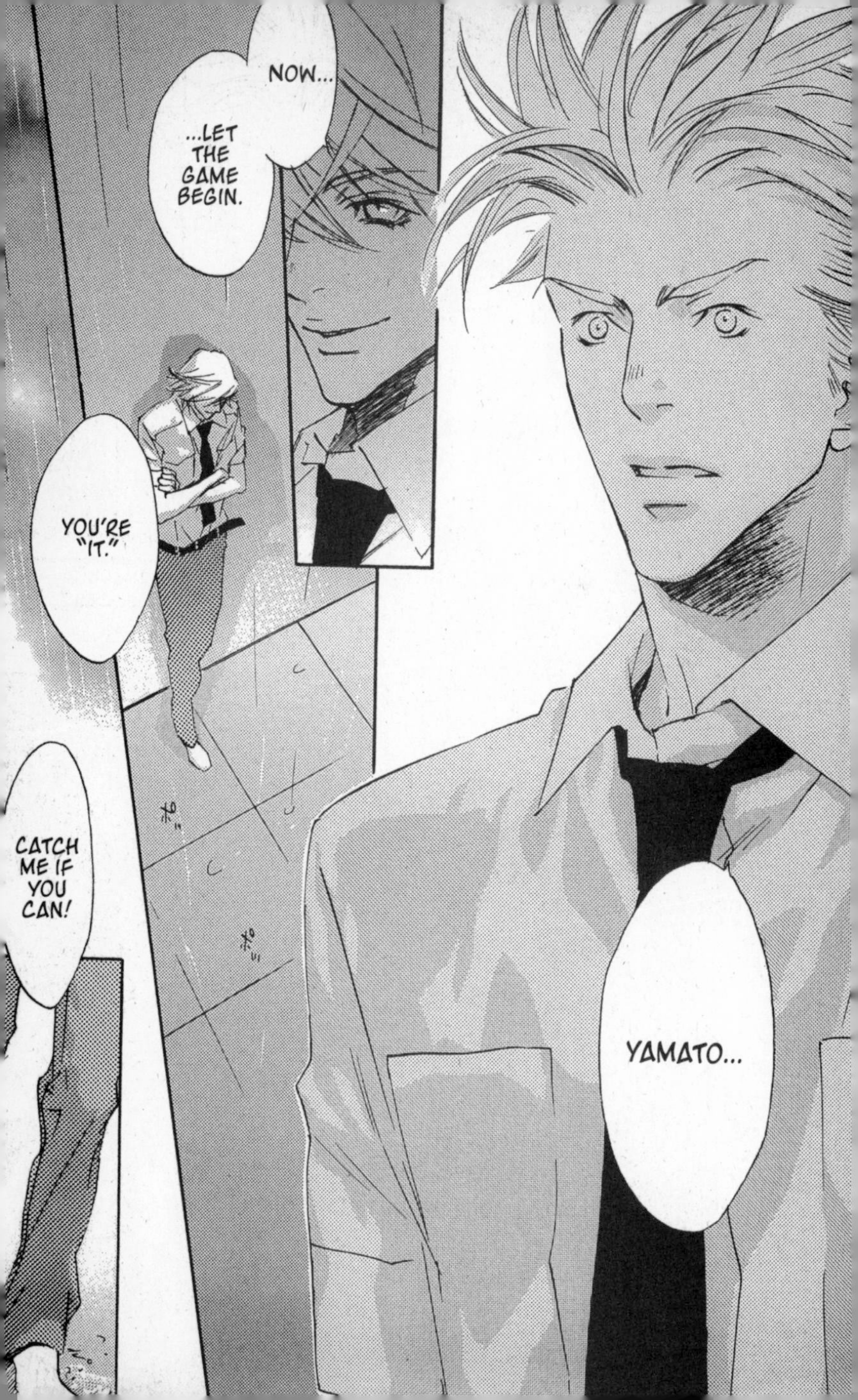
NOW...
...LET THE GAME BEGIN.
YOU'RE "IT."
CATCH ME IF YOU CAN!
YAMATO...

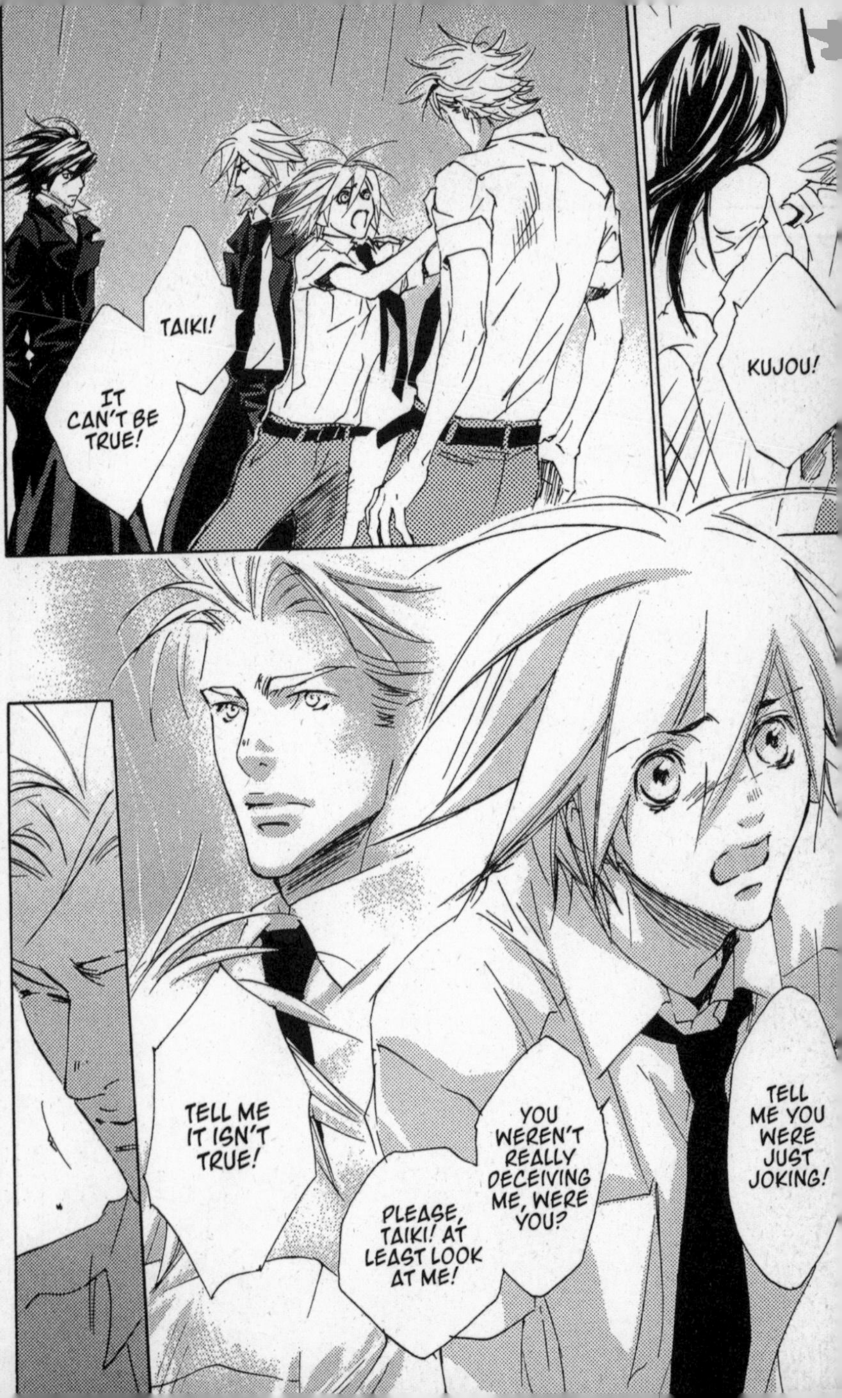
KUJOU!
TAIKI!
IT CAN'T BE TRUE!
TELL ME YOU WERE JUST JOKING!
YOU WEREN'T REALLY DECEIVING ME, WERE YOU?
TELL ME IT ISN'T TRUE!
PLEASE, TAIKI! AT LEAST LOOK AT ME!

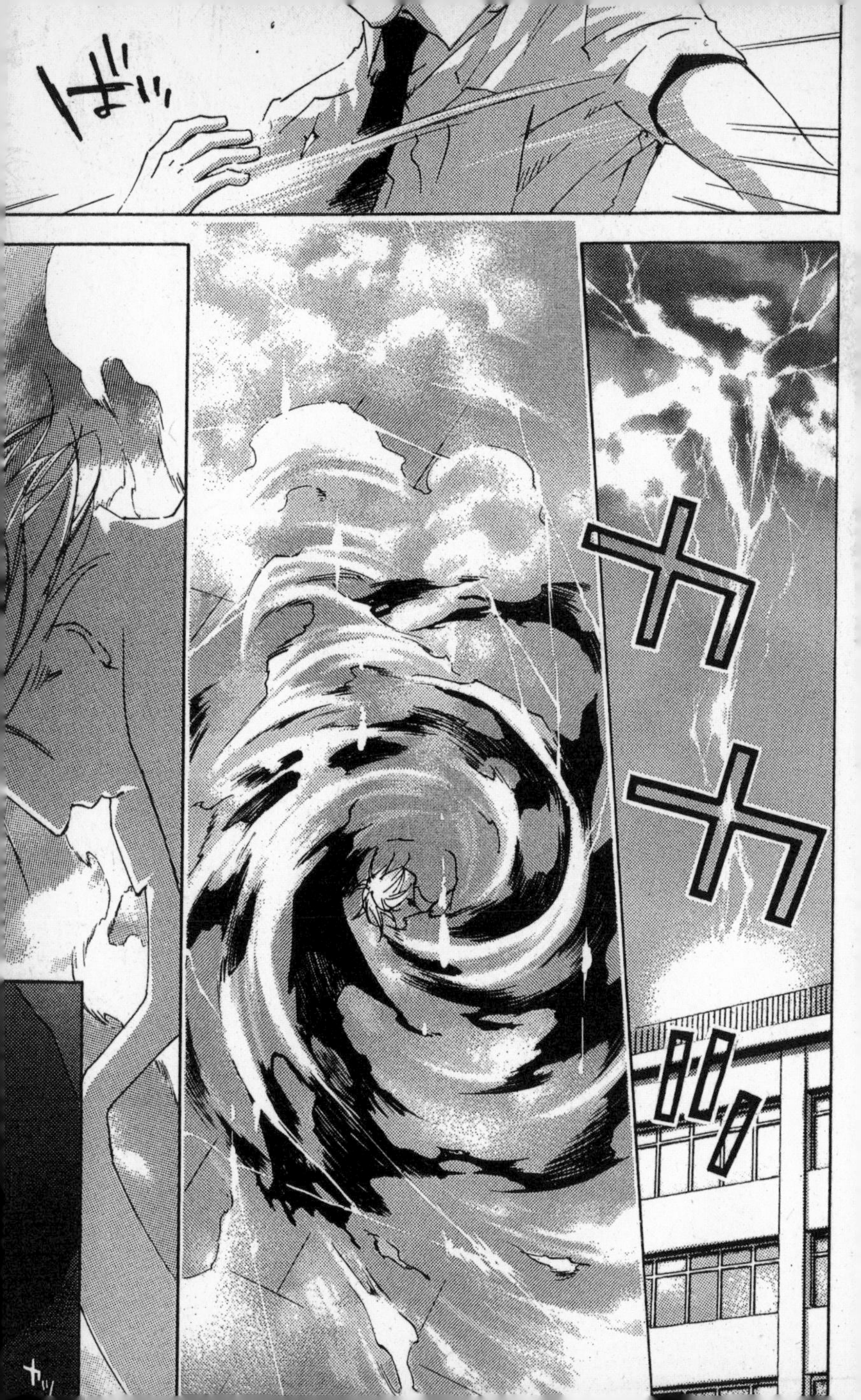
ばっ
カカ
カッ

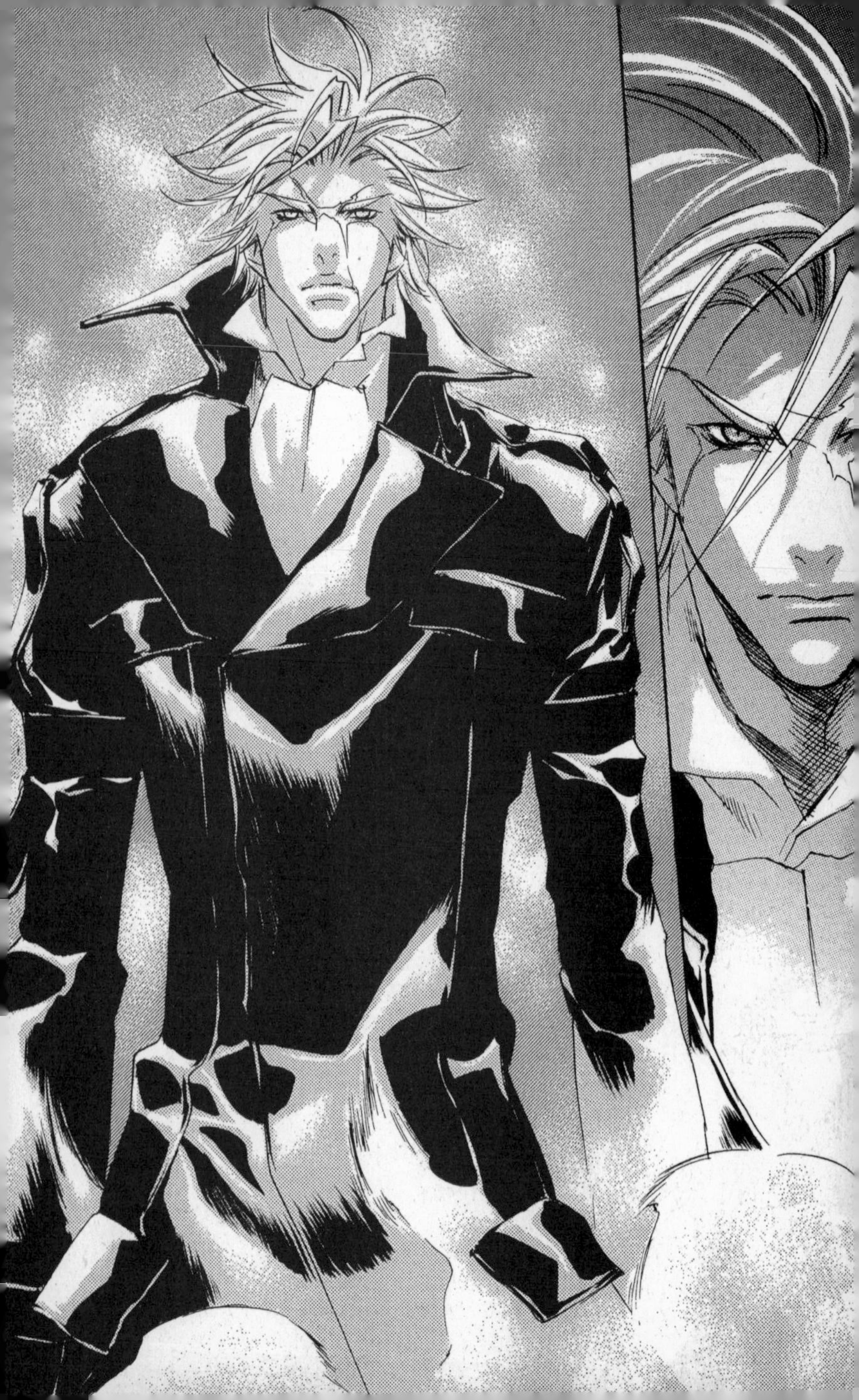

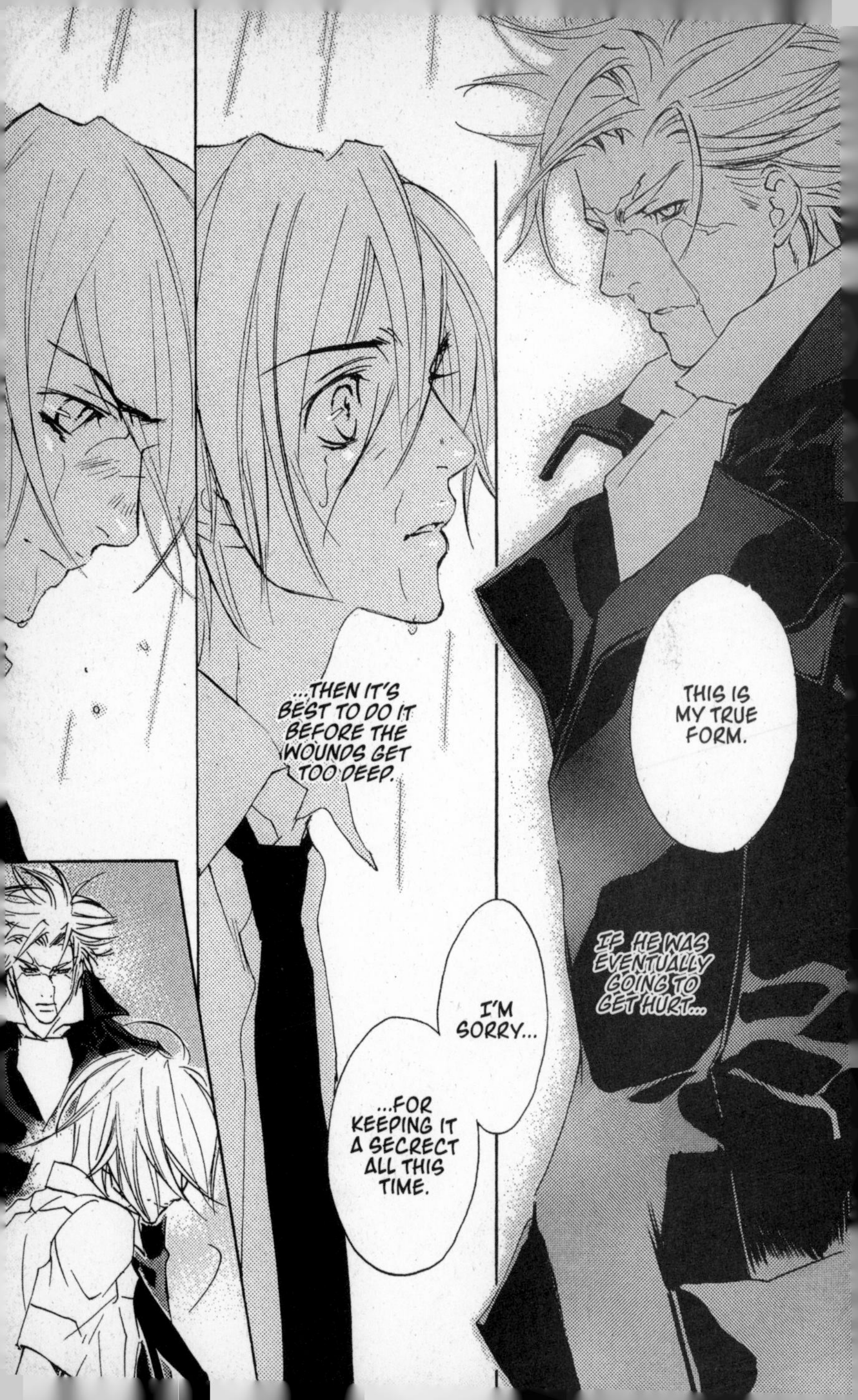
THIS IS MY TRUE FORM.
IF HE WAS EVENTUALLY GOING TO GET HURT...
...THEN IT'S BEST TO DO IT BEFORE THE WOUNDS GET TOO DEEP.
I'M SORRY...
...FOR KEEPING IT A SECRECT ALL THIS TIME.

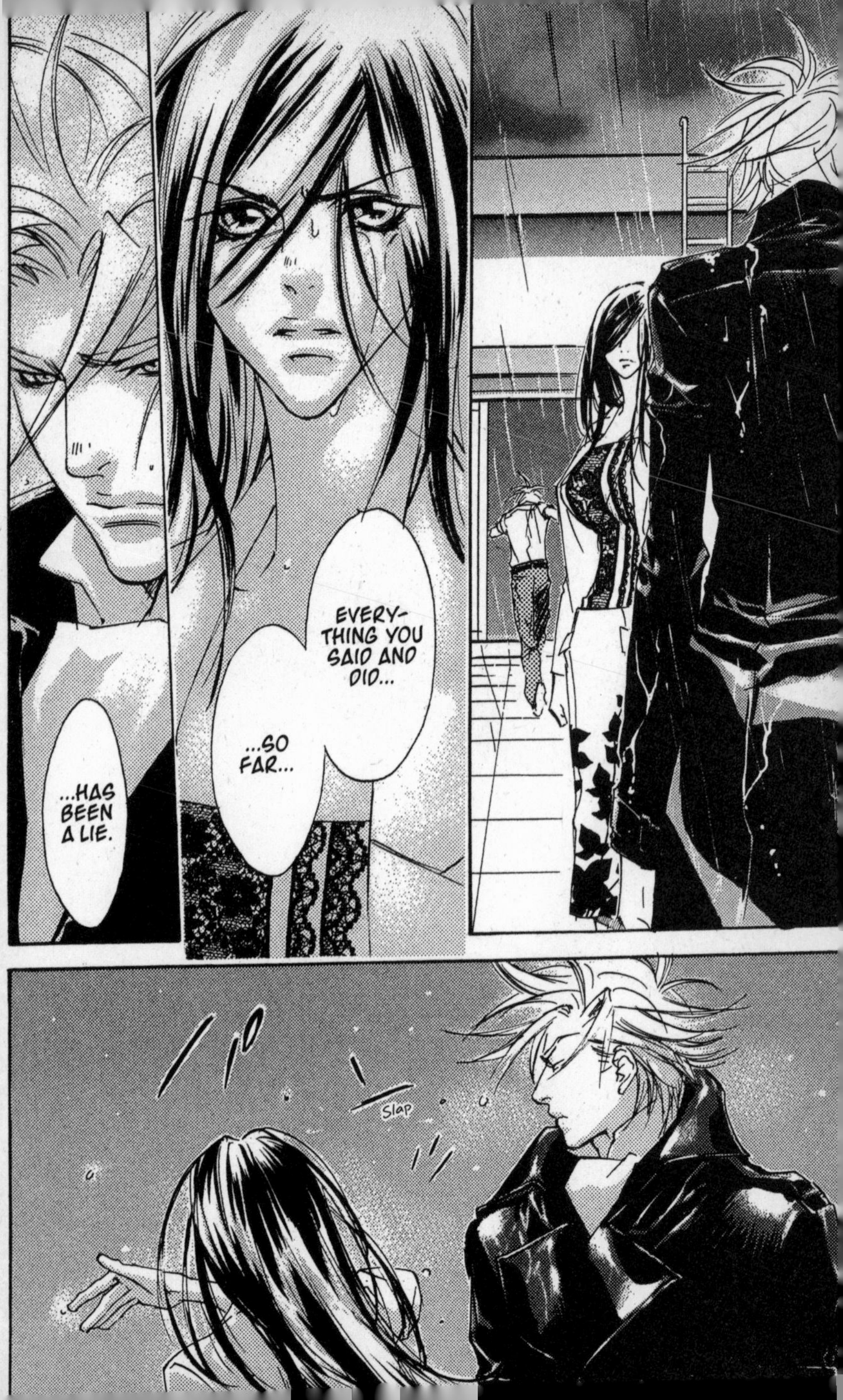
EVERY-THING YOU SAID AND DID...
...SO FAR...
...HAS BEEN A LIE.
Slap

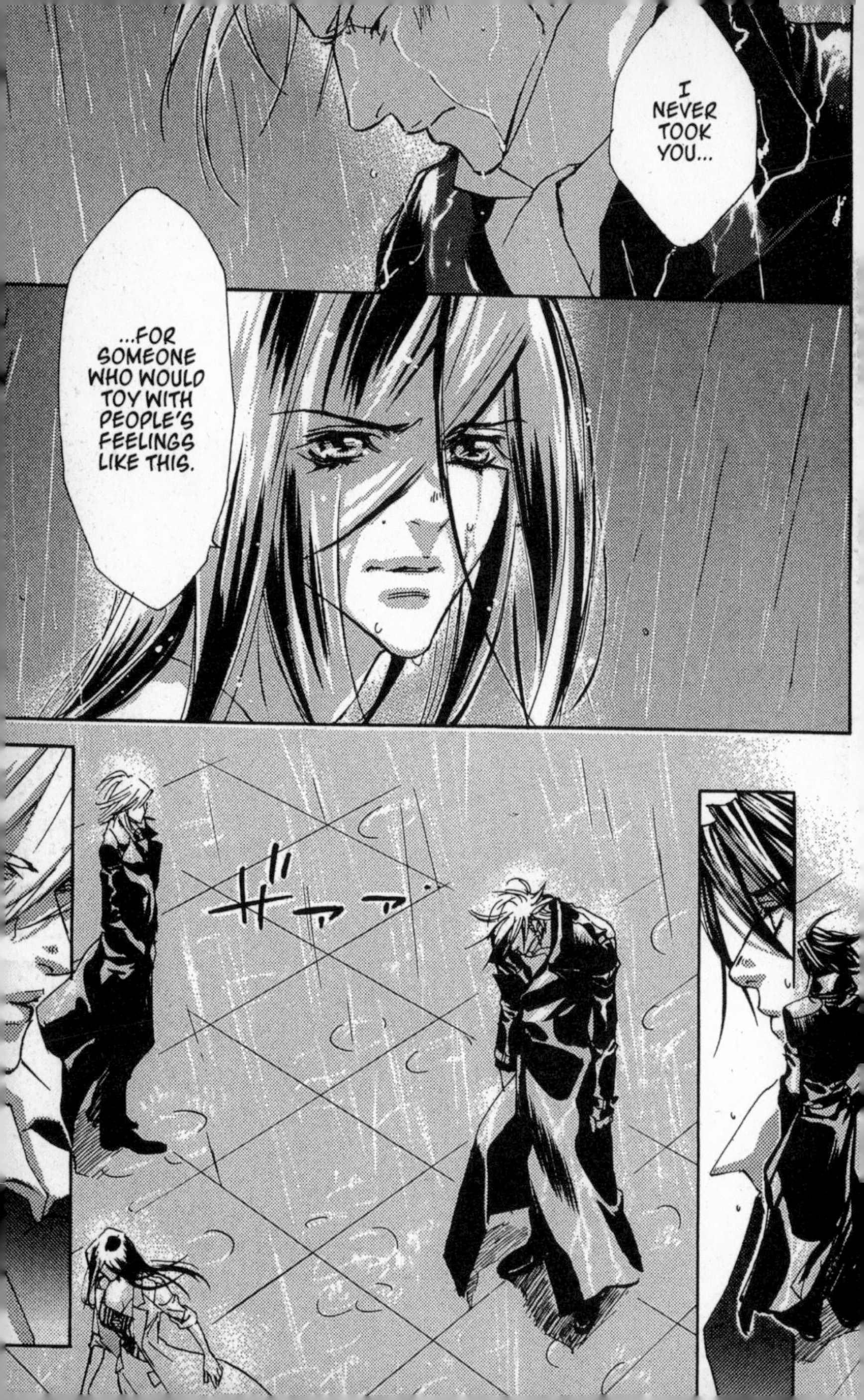
I NEVER TOOK YOU...
...FOR SOMEONE WHO WOULD TOY WITH PEOPLE'S FEELINGS LIKE THIS.
ザァァ

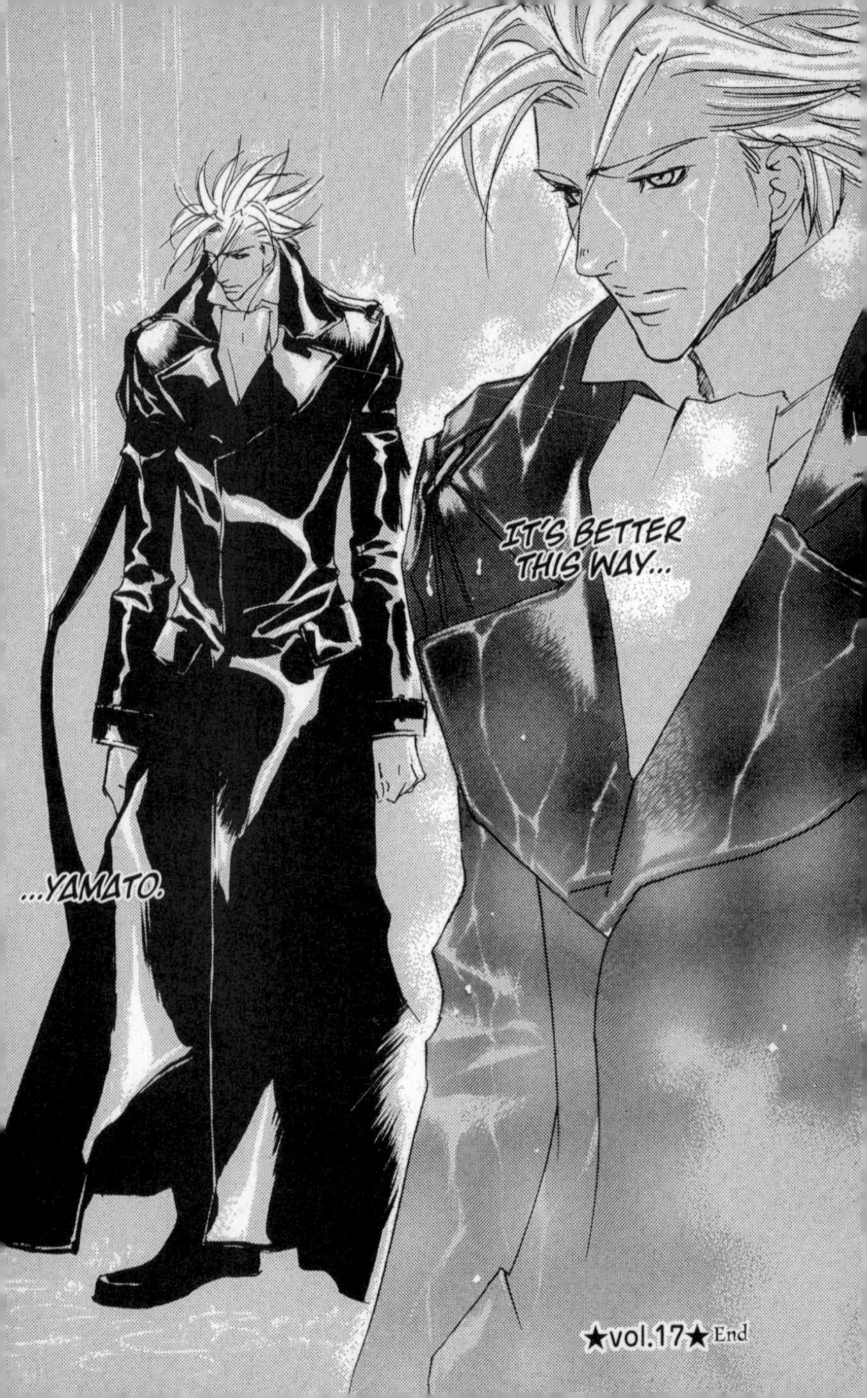
IT'S BETTER THIS WAY...
...YAMATO.
★vol.17★ End

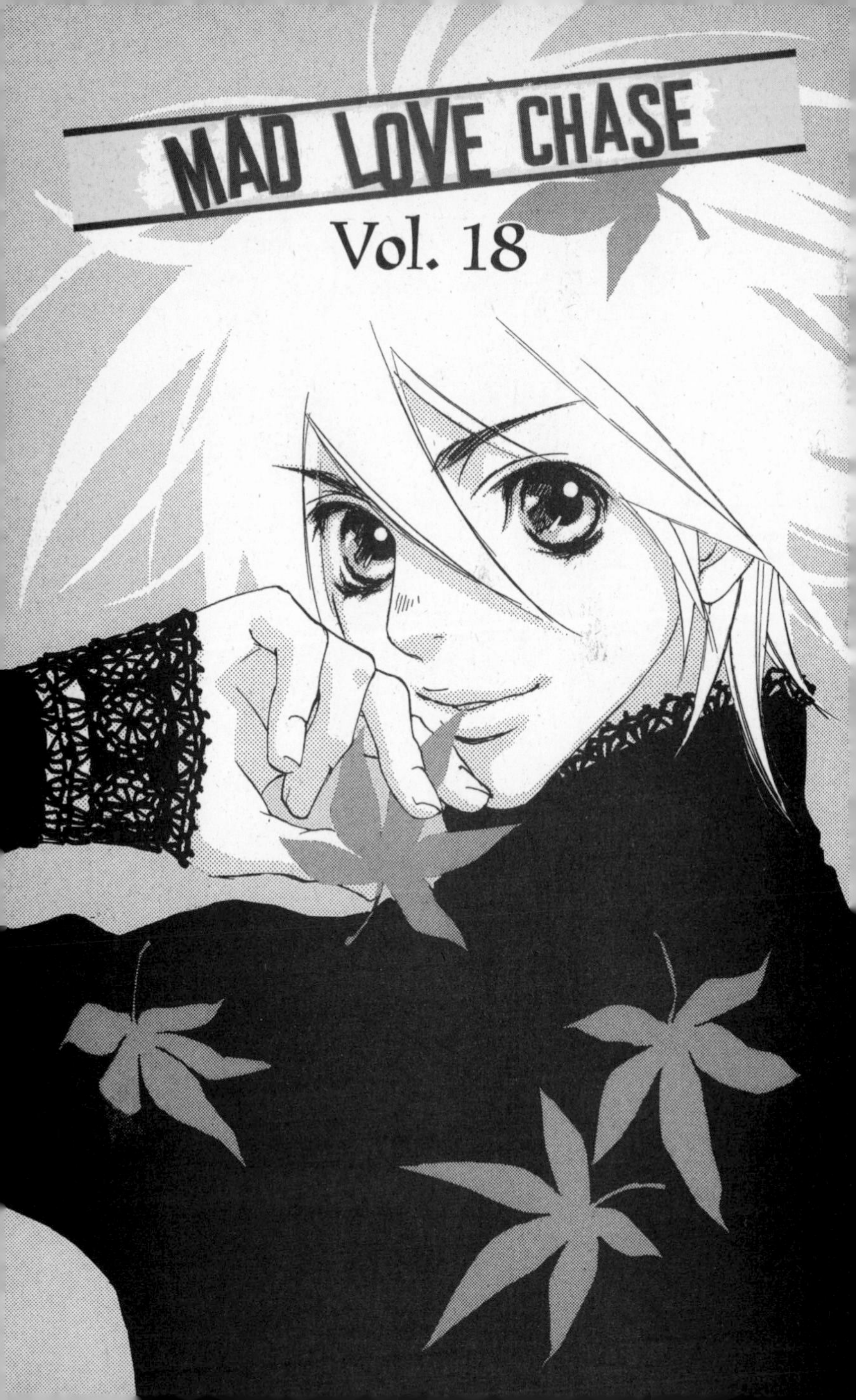
MAD LOVE CHASE
Vol. 18

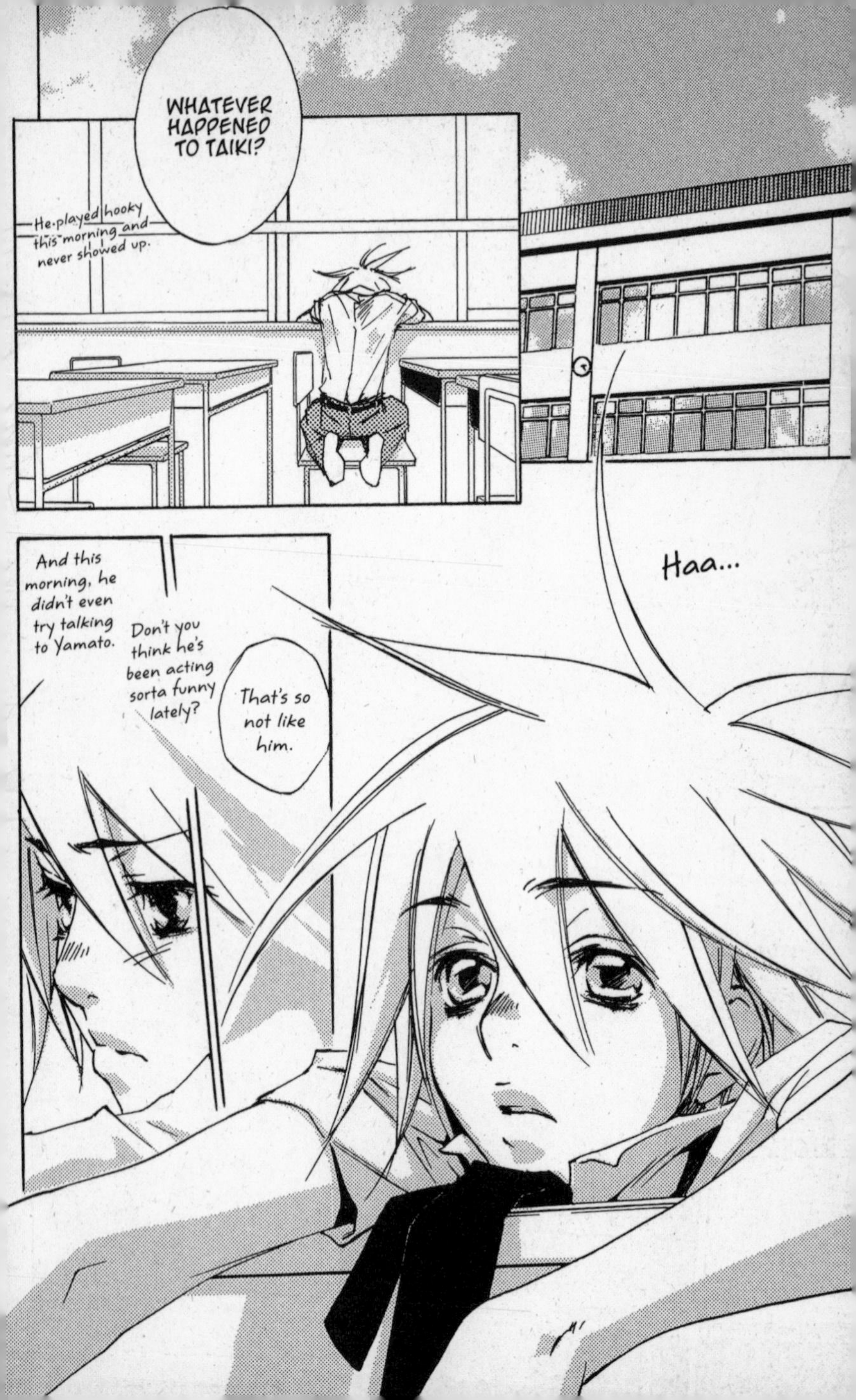
WHATEVER HAPPENED TO TAIKI?
He played hooky this morning and never showed up.
Haa...
Don't you think he's been acting sorta funny lately?
And this morning, he didn't even try talking to Yamato.
That's so not like him.

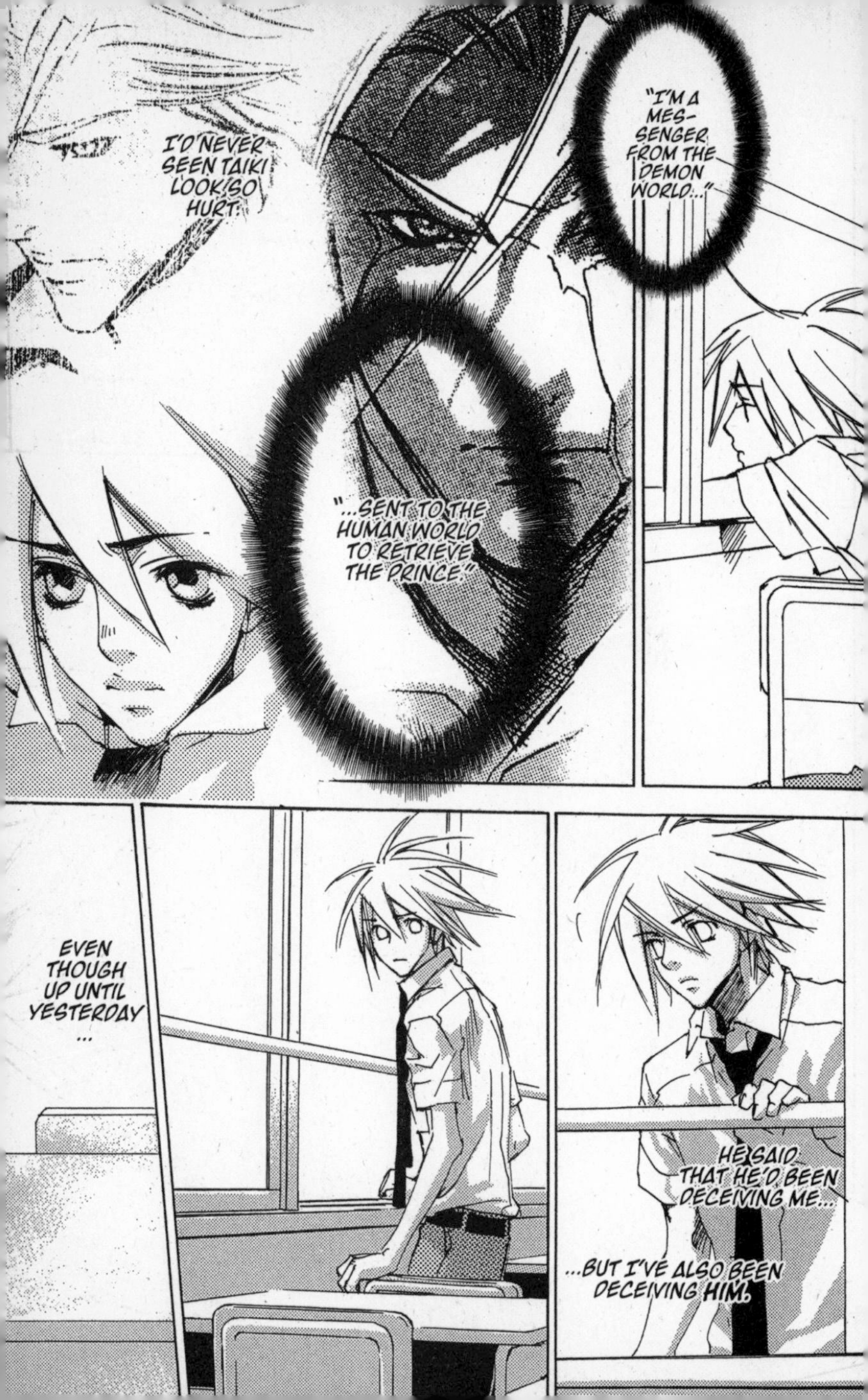
"I'M A MESSENGER FROM THE DEMON WORLD..."
"...SENT TO THE HUMAN WORLD TO RETRIEVE THE PRINCE."
I'D NEVER SEEN TAIKI LOOK SO HURT.
HE SAID THAT HE'D BEEN DECEIVING ME...
...BUT I'VE ALSO BEEN DECEIVING HIM.
EVEN THOUGH UP UNTIL YESTERDAY...

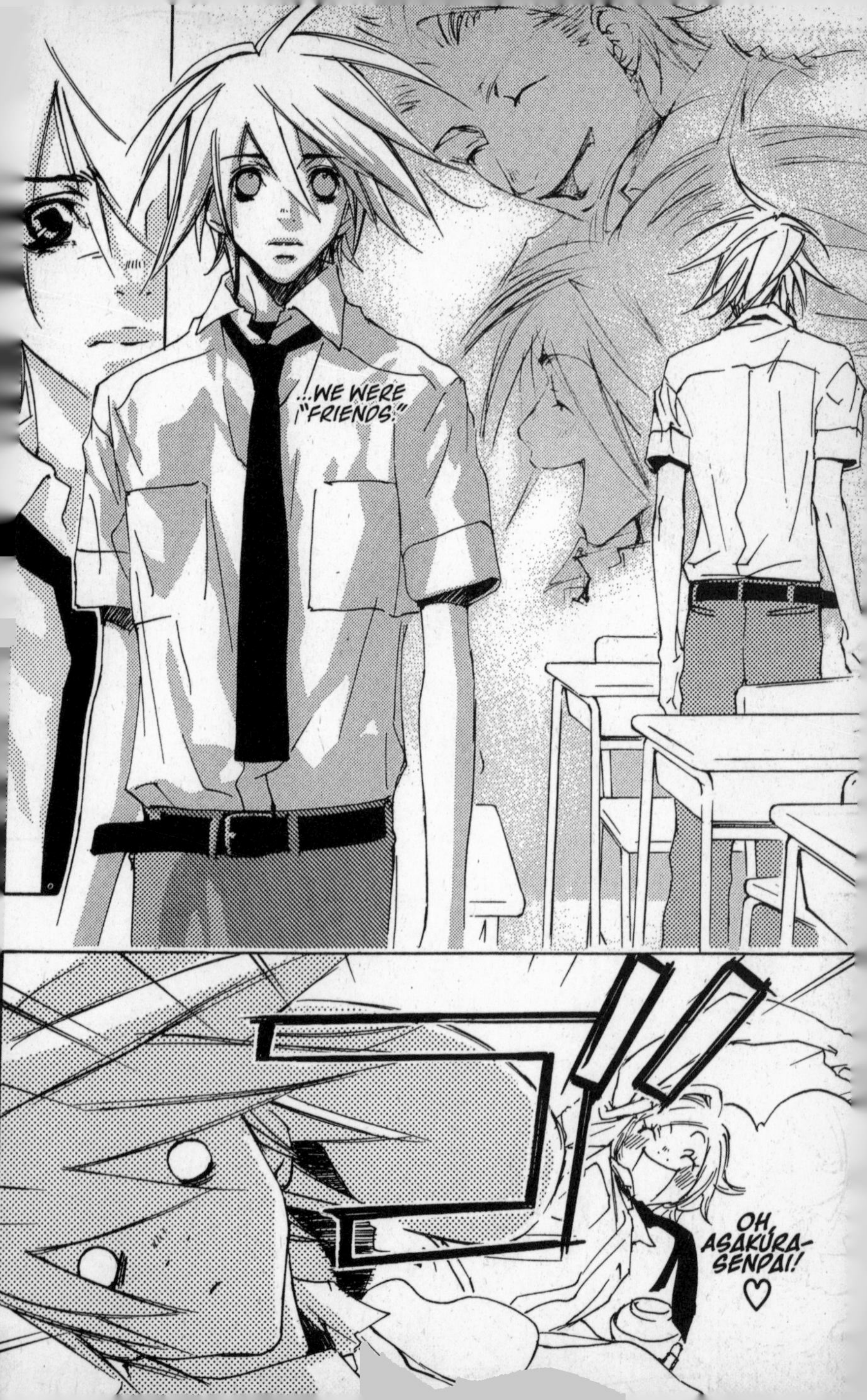
...WE WERE "FRIENDS."
OH, ASAKURA-SENPAI! ♡

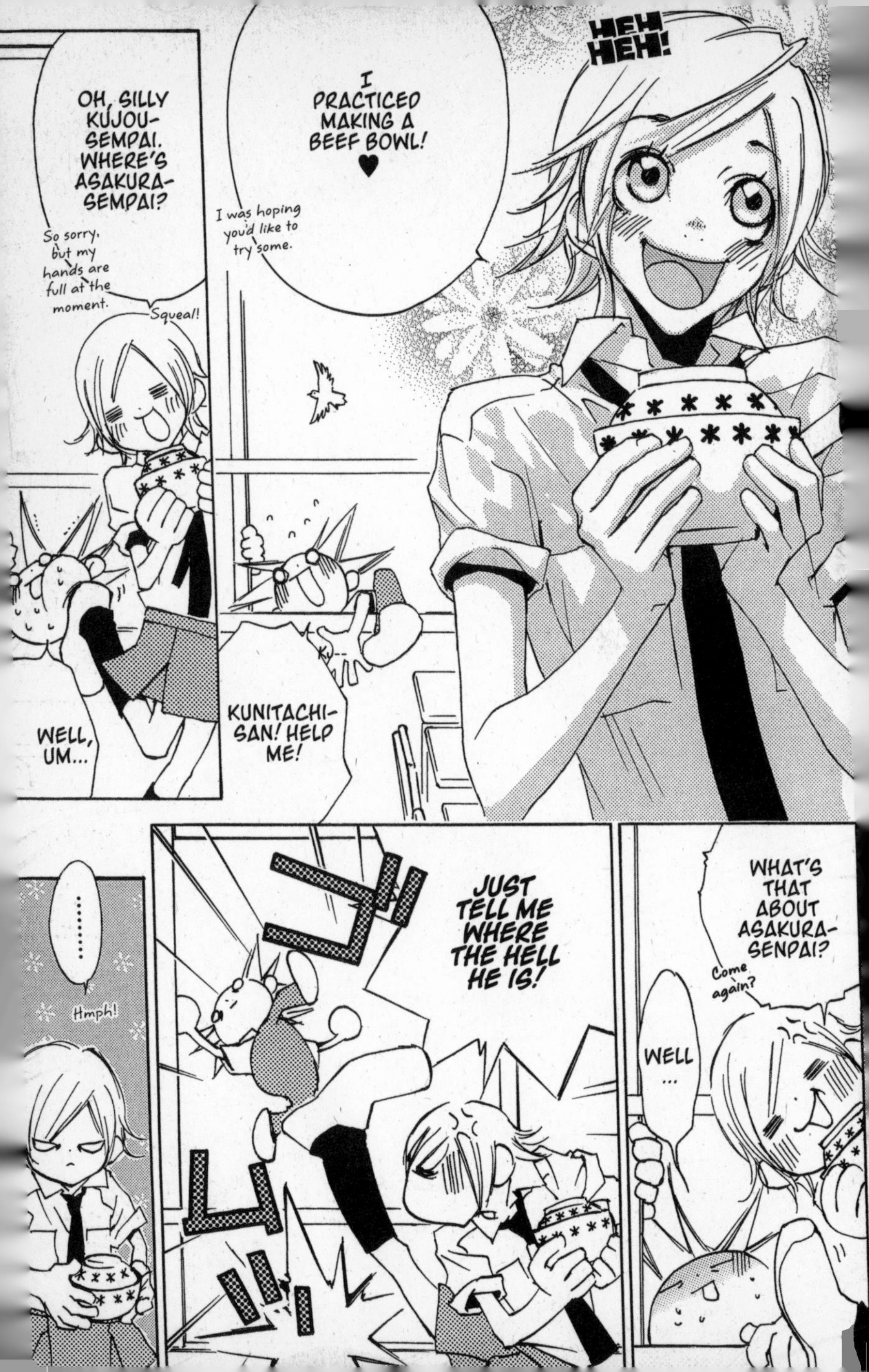
HEH HEH!
I PRACTICED MAKING A BEEF BOWL! ♥
I was hoping you'd like to try some.
KUNITACHI-SAN! HELP ME!
Ku--
OH, SILLY KUJOU-SEMPAI. WHERE'S ASAKURA-SEMPAI?
So sorry, but my hands are full at the moment.
Squeal!
WELL, UM...
WHAT'S THAT ABOUT ASAKURA-SENPAI?
Come again?
WELL...
JUST TELL ME WHERE THE HELL HE IS!
..........
Hmph!

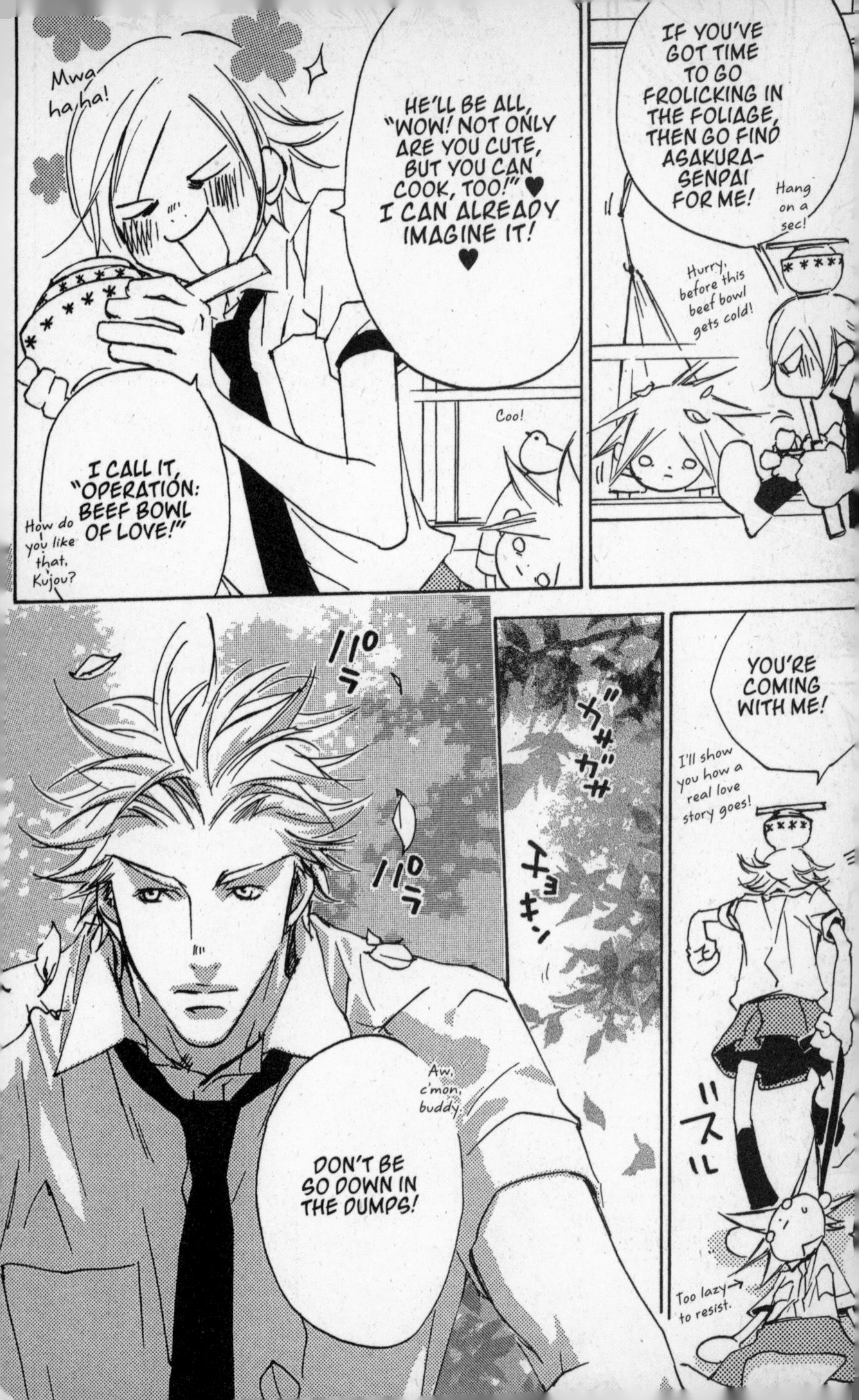
IF YOU'VE GOT TIME TO GO FROLICKING IN THE FOLIAGE, THEN GO FIND ASAKURA-SENPAI FOR ME!
Hang on a sec!
Hurry, before this beef bowl gets cold!
HE'LL BE ALL, "WOW! NOT ONLY ARE YOU CUTE, BUT YOU CAN COOK, TOO!"♥ I CAN ALREADY IMAGINE IT! ♥
Mwa ha ha!
Coo!
I CALL IT, "OPERATION: BEEF BOWL OF LOVE!"
How do you like that, Kujou?
YOU'RE COMING WITH ME!
I'll show you how a real love story goes!
ズル
Too lazy to resist.
ガサガサ
チョキン
パラ
パラ
Aw, c'mon, buddy.
DON'T BE SO DOWN IN THE DUMPS!

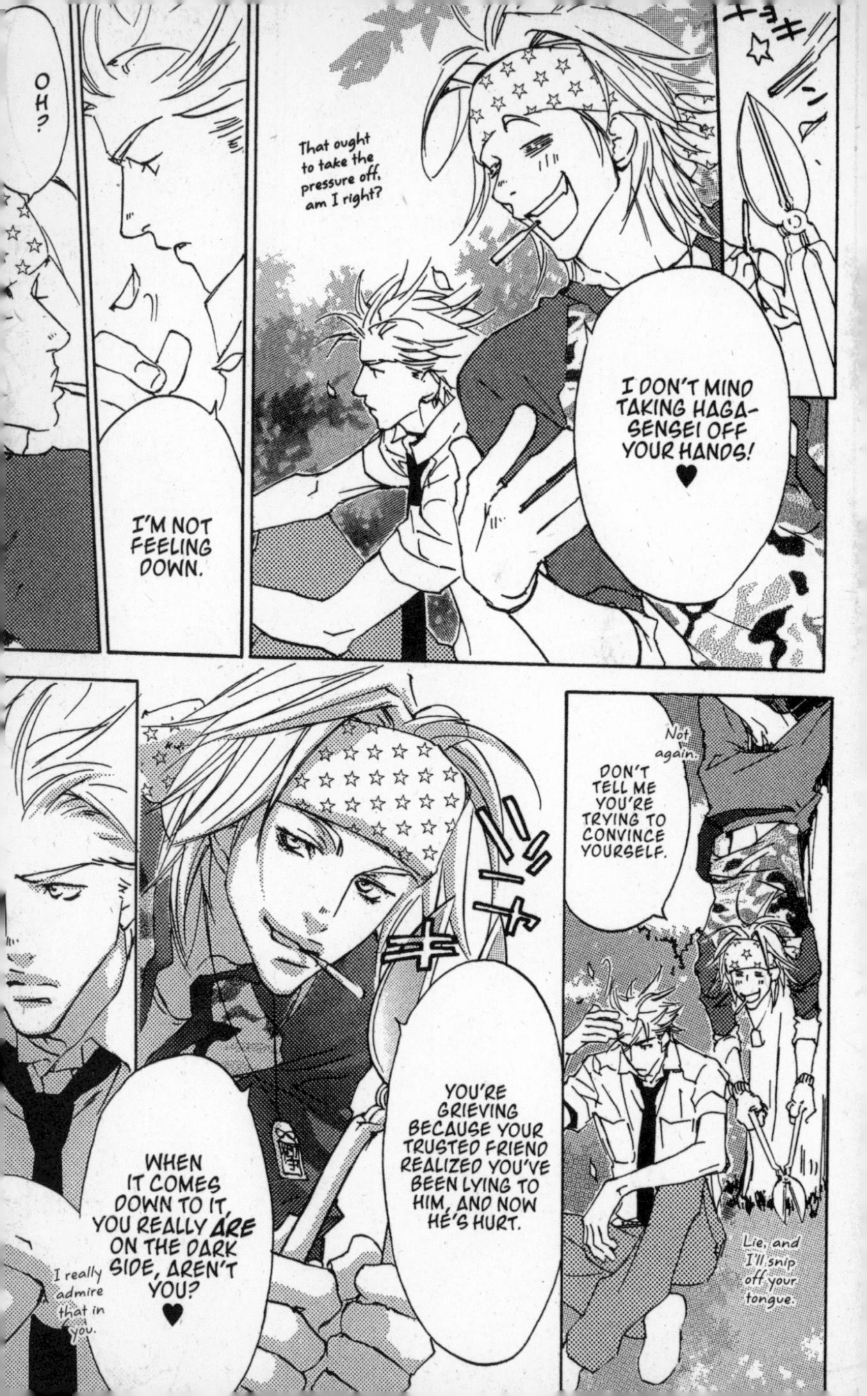
I DON'T MIND TAKING HAGA-SENSEI OFF YOUR HANDS! ♥
That ought to take the pressure off, am I right?
I'M NOT FEELING DOWN.
OH?
Not again.
DON'T TELL ME YOU'RE TRYING TO CONVINCE YOURSELF.
Lie, and I'll snip off your tongue.
YOU'RE GRIEVING BECAUSE YOUR TRUSTED FRIEND REALIZED YOU'VE BEEN LYING TO HIM, AND NOW HE'S HURT.
WHEN IT COMES DOWN TO IT, YOU REALLY *ARE* ON THE DARK SIDE, AREN'T YOU? ♥
I really admire that in you.

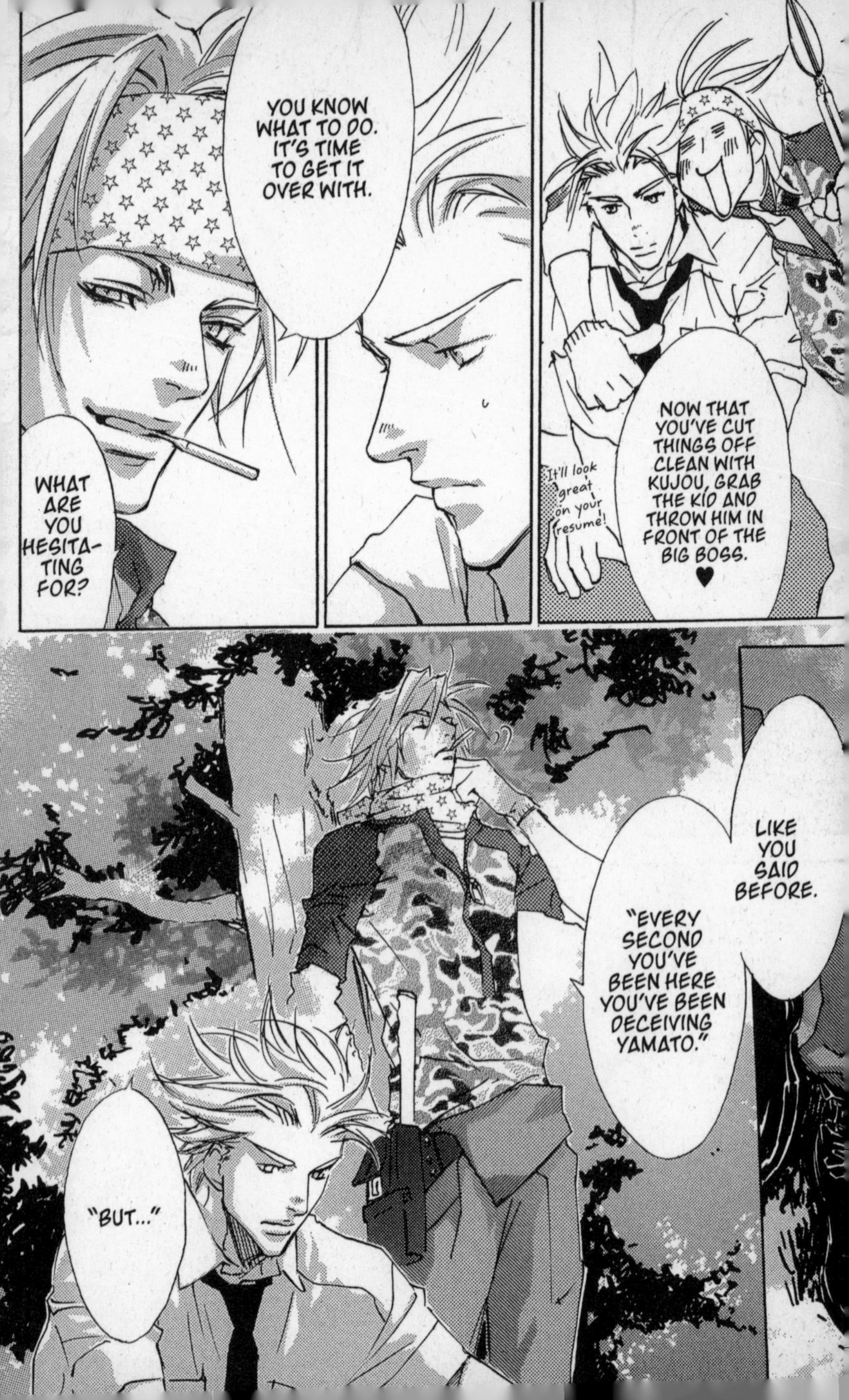
NOW THAT YOU'VE CUT THINGS OFF CLEAN WITH KUJOU, GRAB THE KID AND THROW HIM IN FRONT OF THE BIG BOSS. ♥
It'll look great on your resume!
YOU KNOW WHAT TO DO. IT'S TIME TO GET IT OVER WITH.
WHAT ARE YOU HESITATING FOR?
LIKE YOU SAID BEFORE.
"EVERY SECOND YOU'VE BEEN HERE YOU'VE BEEN DECEIVING YAMATO."
"BUT..."

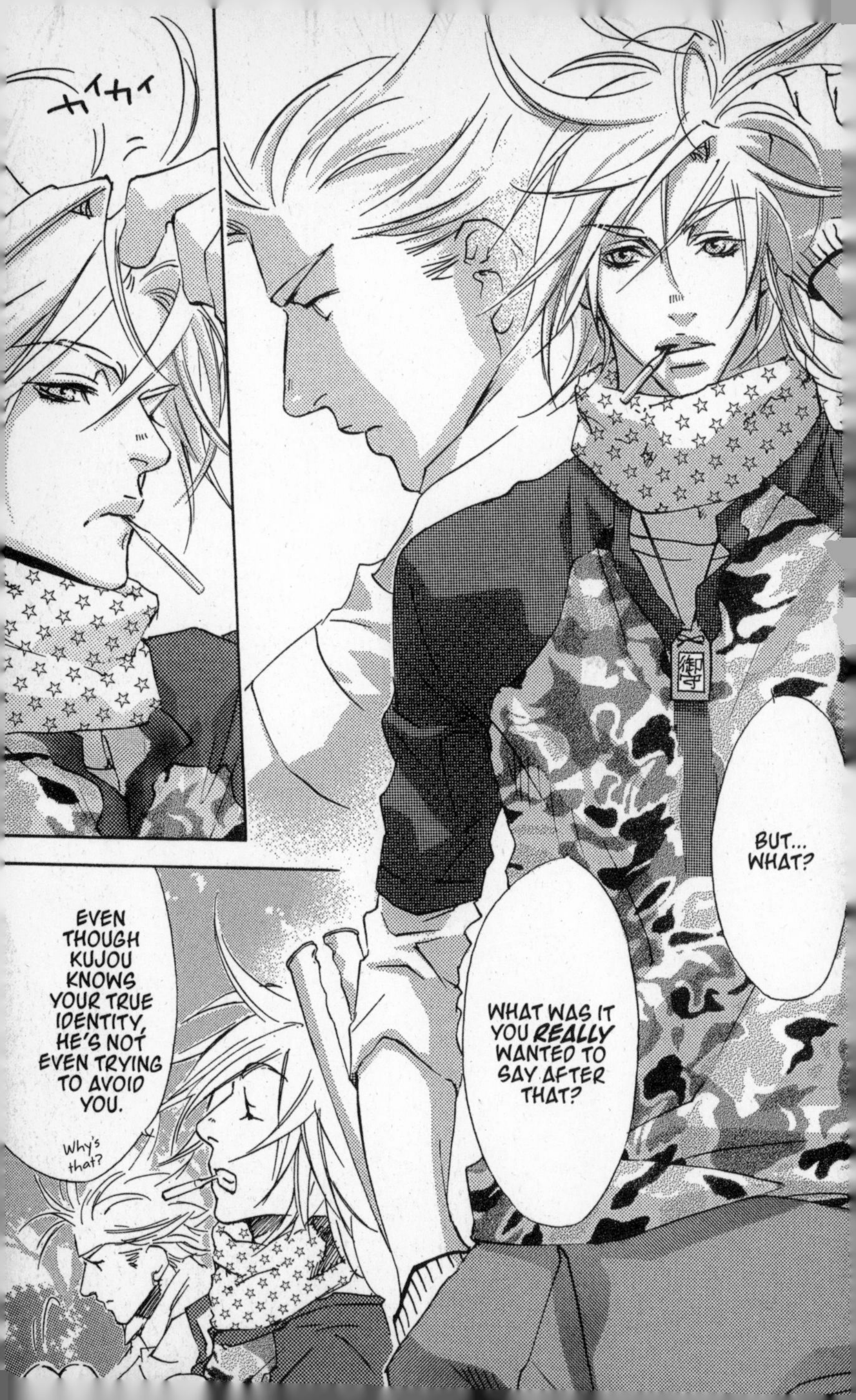
BUT... WHAT?
WHAT WAS IT YOU **REALLY** WANTED TO SAY AFTER THAT?
カイカイ
EVEN THOUGH KUJOU KNOWS YOUR TRUE IDENTITY, HE'S NOT EVEN TRYING TO AVOID YOU.
Why's that?

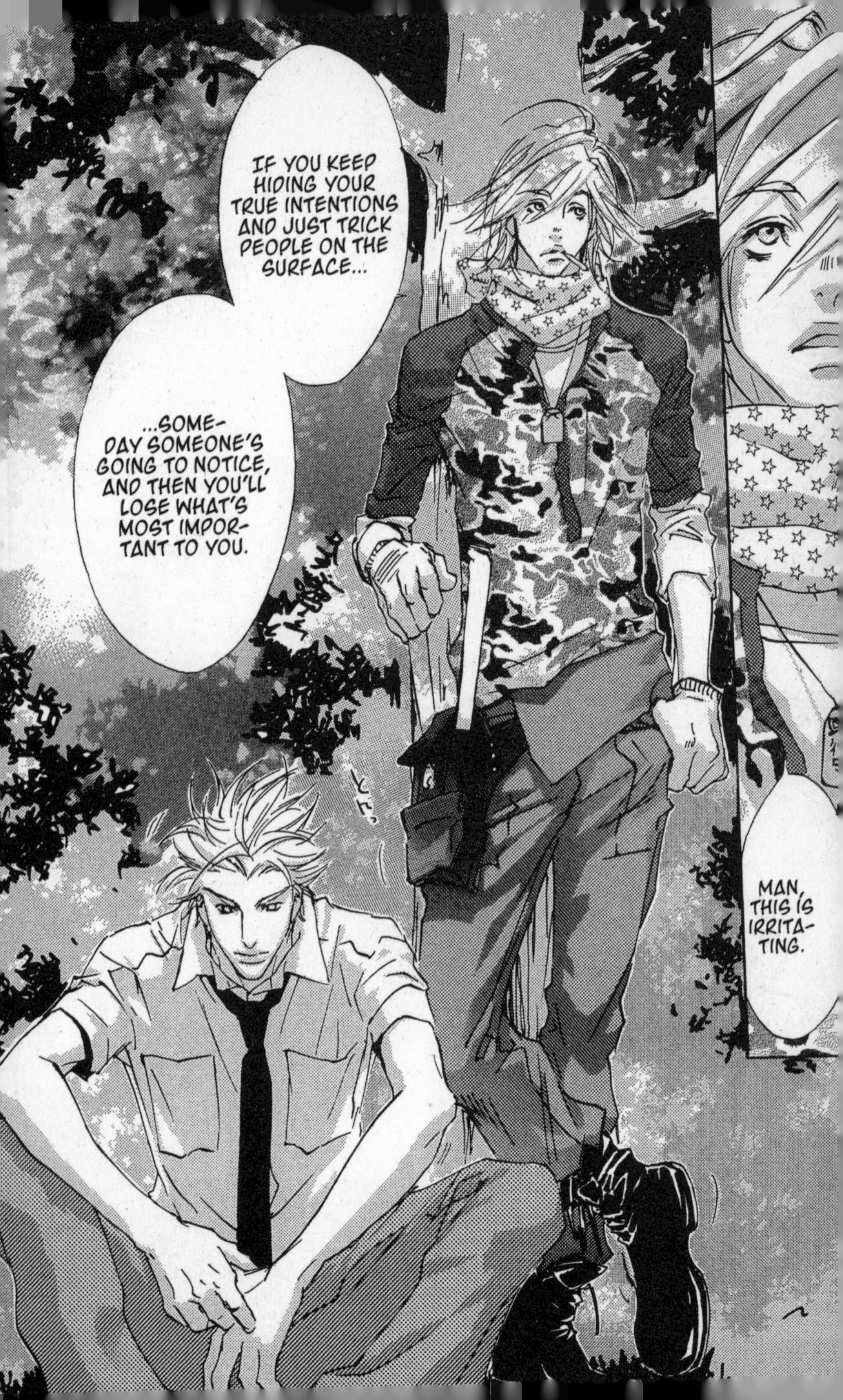
MAN, THIS IS IRRITA-TING.
IF YOU KEEP HIDING YOUR TRUE INTENTIONS AND JUST TRICK PEOPLE ON THE SURFACE...
...SOME-DAY SOMEONE'S GOING TO NOTICE, AND THEN YOU'LL LOSE WHAT'S MOST IMPOR-TANT TO YOU.

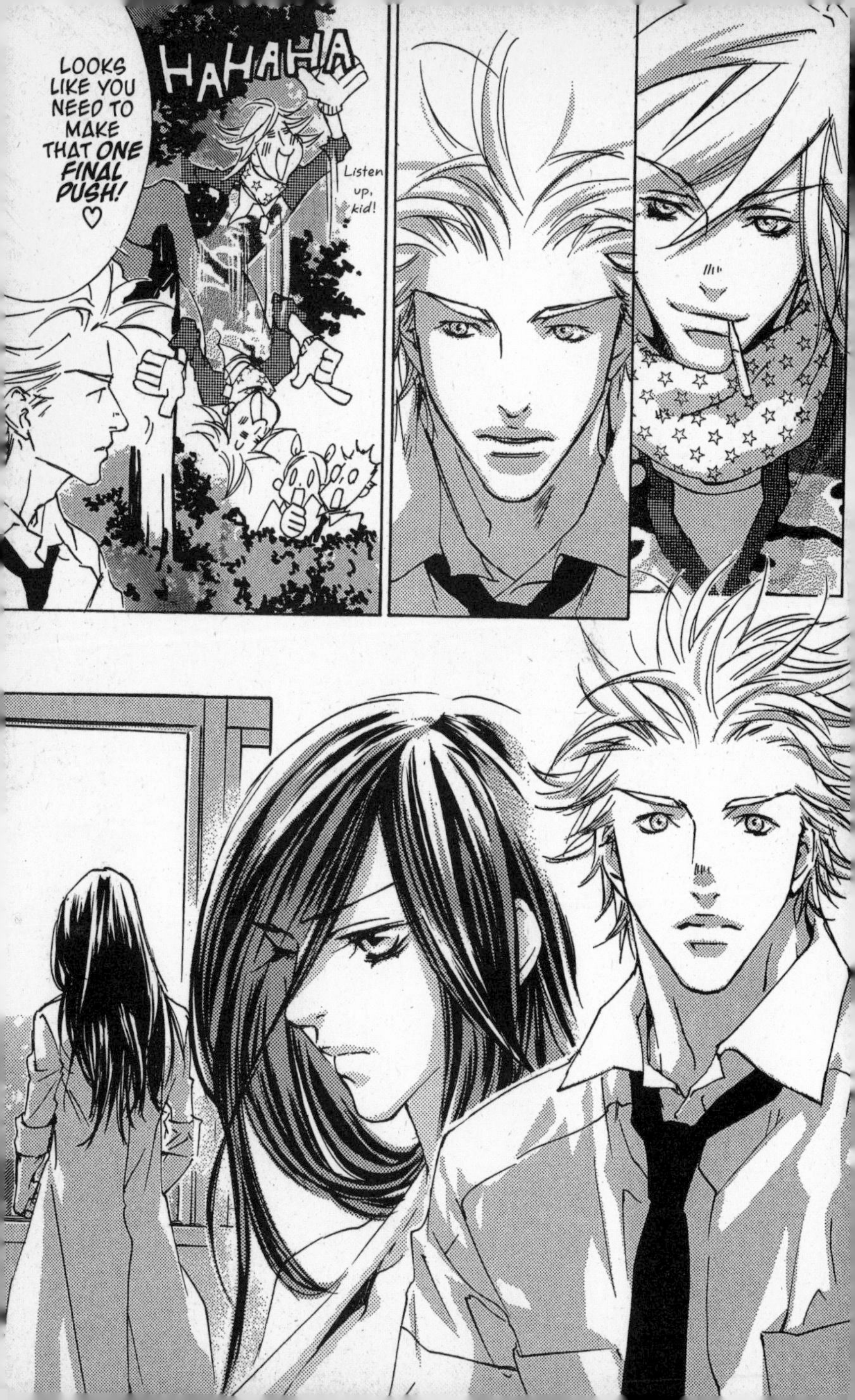
HAHAHA
LOOKS LIKE YOU NEED TO MAKE THAT ONE FINAL PUSH! ♡
Listen up, kid!

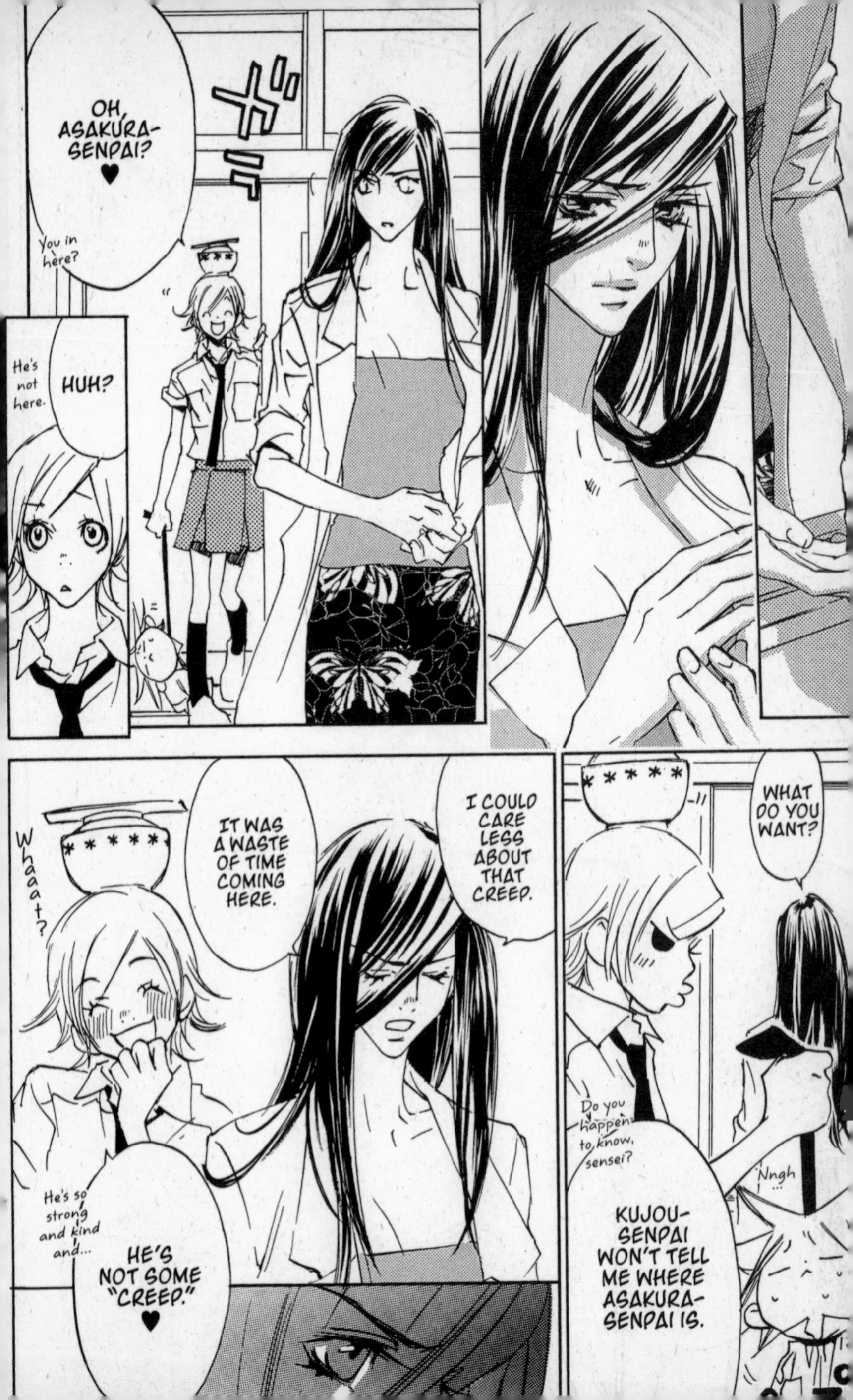

OH, ASAKURA-SENPAI? ♥
You in here?
HUH?
He's not here.
WHAT DO YOU WANT?
Do you happen to know, sensei?
KUJOU-SENPAI WON'T TELL ME WHERE ASAKURA-SENPAI IS.
Nngh...
I COULD CARE LESS ABOUT THAT CREEP.
IT WAS A WASTE OF TIME COMING HERE.
Whaaat?
HE'S NOT SOME "CREEP." ♥
He's so strong and kind and...

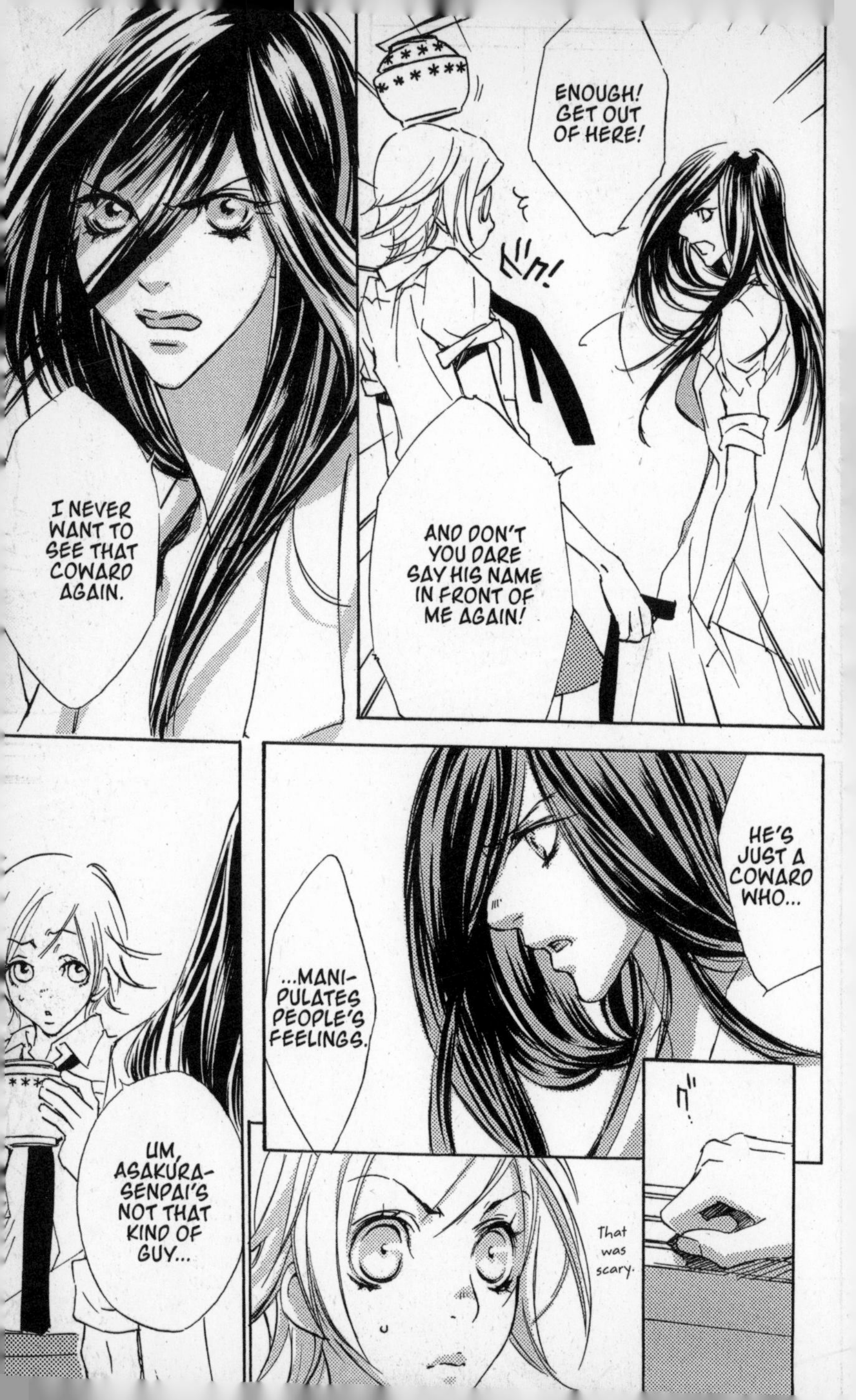
ENOUGH! GET OUT OF HERE!
AND DON'T YOU DARE SAY HIS NAME IN FRONT OF ME AGAIN!
I NEVER WANT TO SEE THAT COWARD AGAIN.
HE'S JUST A COWARD WHO...
...MANI-PULATES PEOPLE'S FEELINGS.
That was scary.
UM, ASAKURA-SENPAI'S NOT THAT KIND OF GUY...

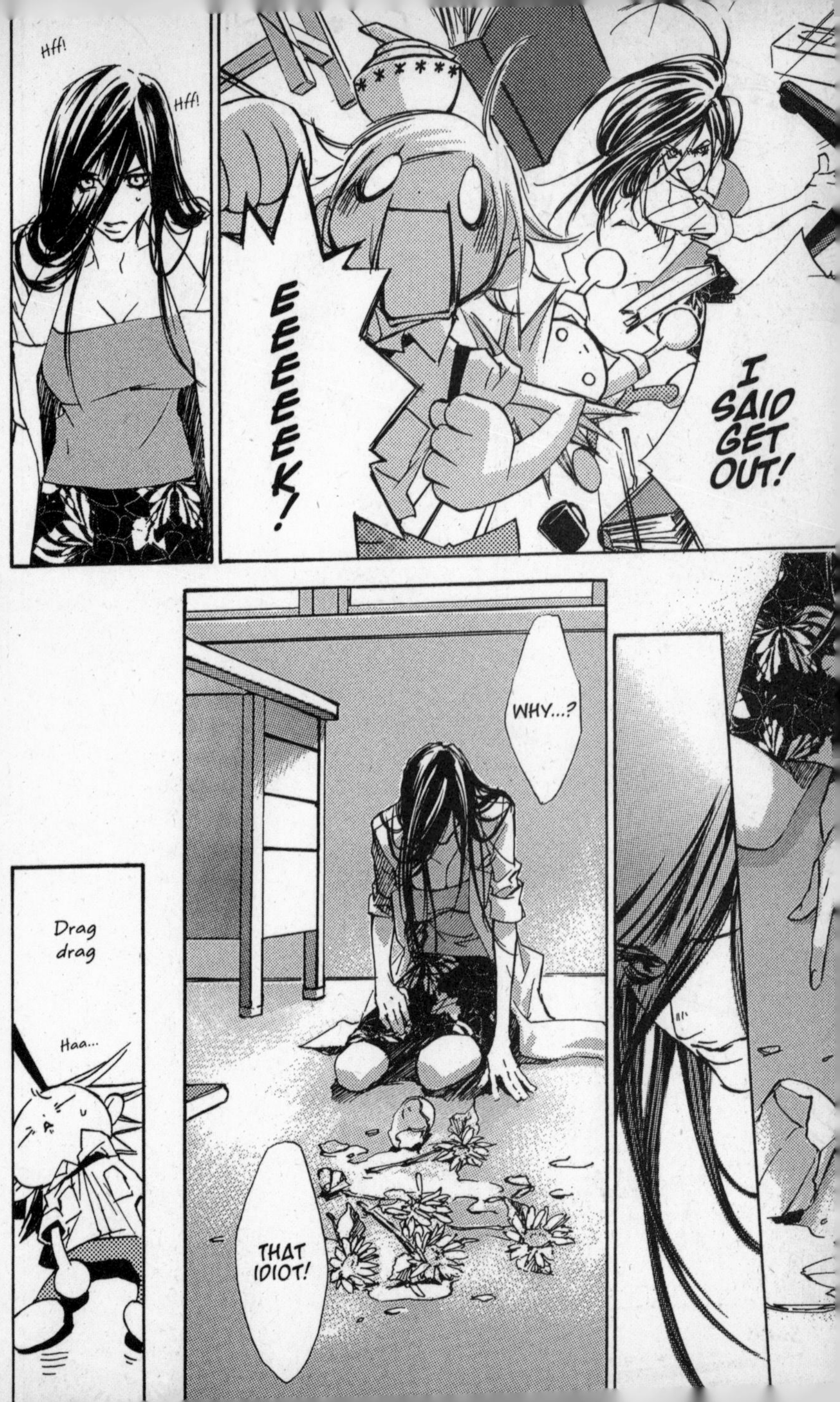
I SAID GET OUT!
EEEEEEEK!
Hff!
Hff!
WHY...?
THAT IDIOT!
Drag drag
Haa...

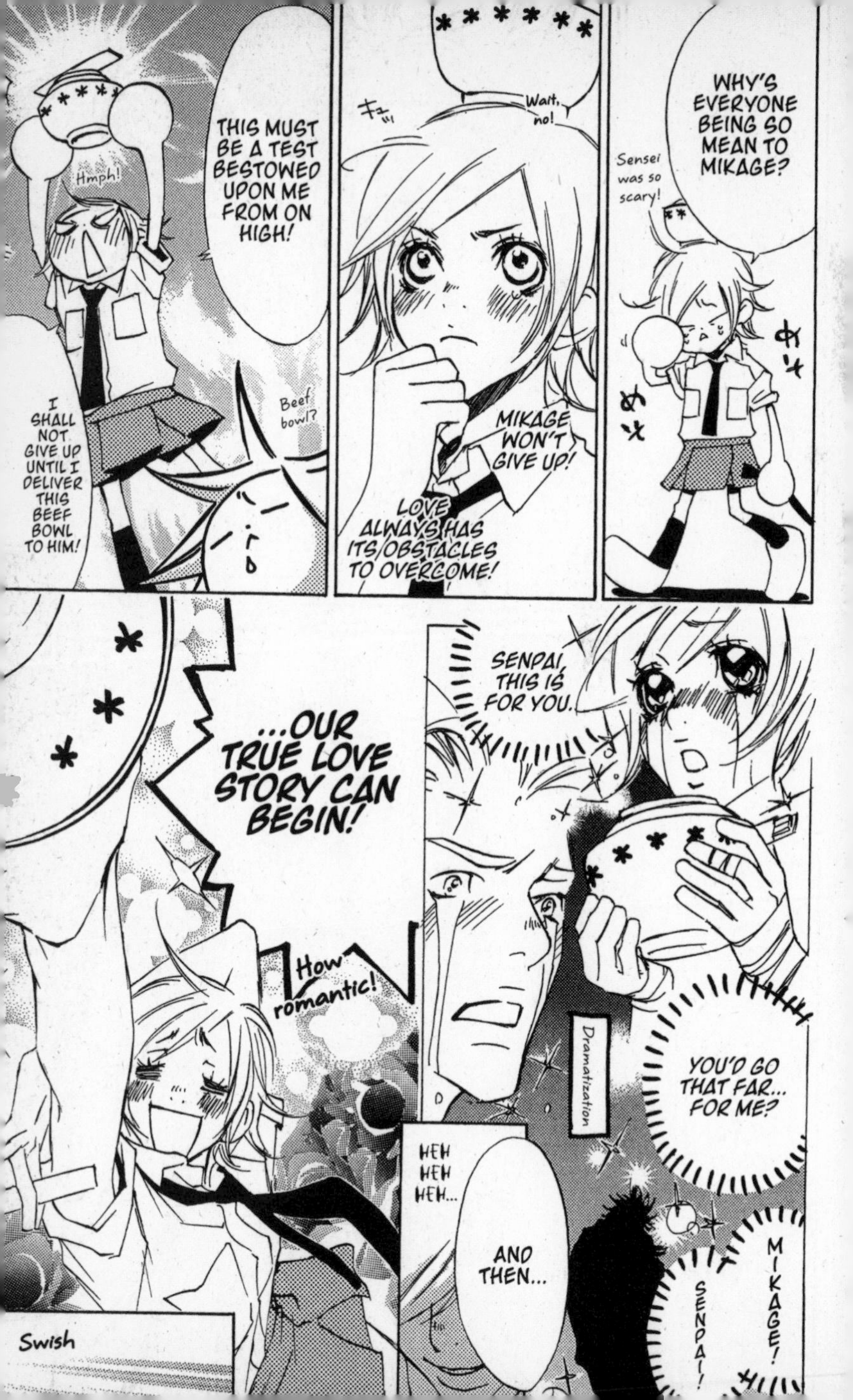
Sensei was so scary!
WHY'S EVERYONE BEING SO MEAN TO MIKAGE?
Wait, no!
MIKAGE WON'T GIVE UP!
LOVE ALWAYS HAS ITS OBSTACLES TO OVERCOME!
Hmph!
THIS MUST BE A TEST BESTOWED UPON ME FROM ON HIGH!
Beef bowl?
I SHALL NOT GIVE UP UNTIL I DELIVER THIS BEEF BOWL TO HIM!
SENPAI, THIS IS FOR YOU.
YOU'D GO THAT FAR... FOR ME?
Dramatization
MIKAGE!
SENPAI!
HEH HEH HEH...
AND THEN...
...OUR TRUE LOVE STORY CAN BEGIN!
How romantic!
Swish

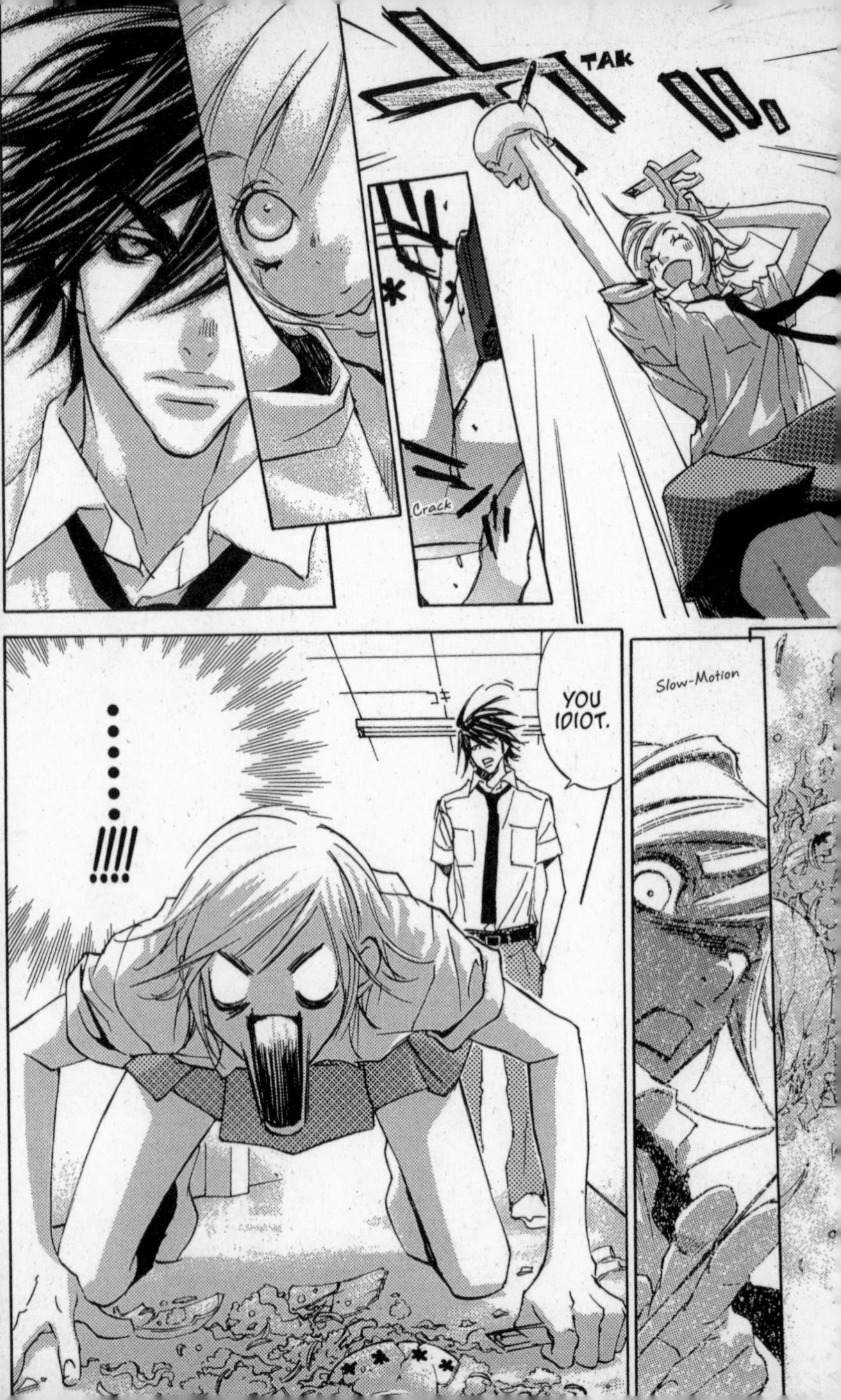
TAK
Crack
Slow-Motion
YOU IDIOT.
......
!!!!

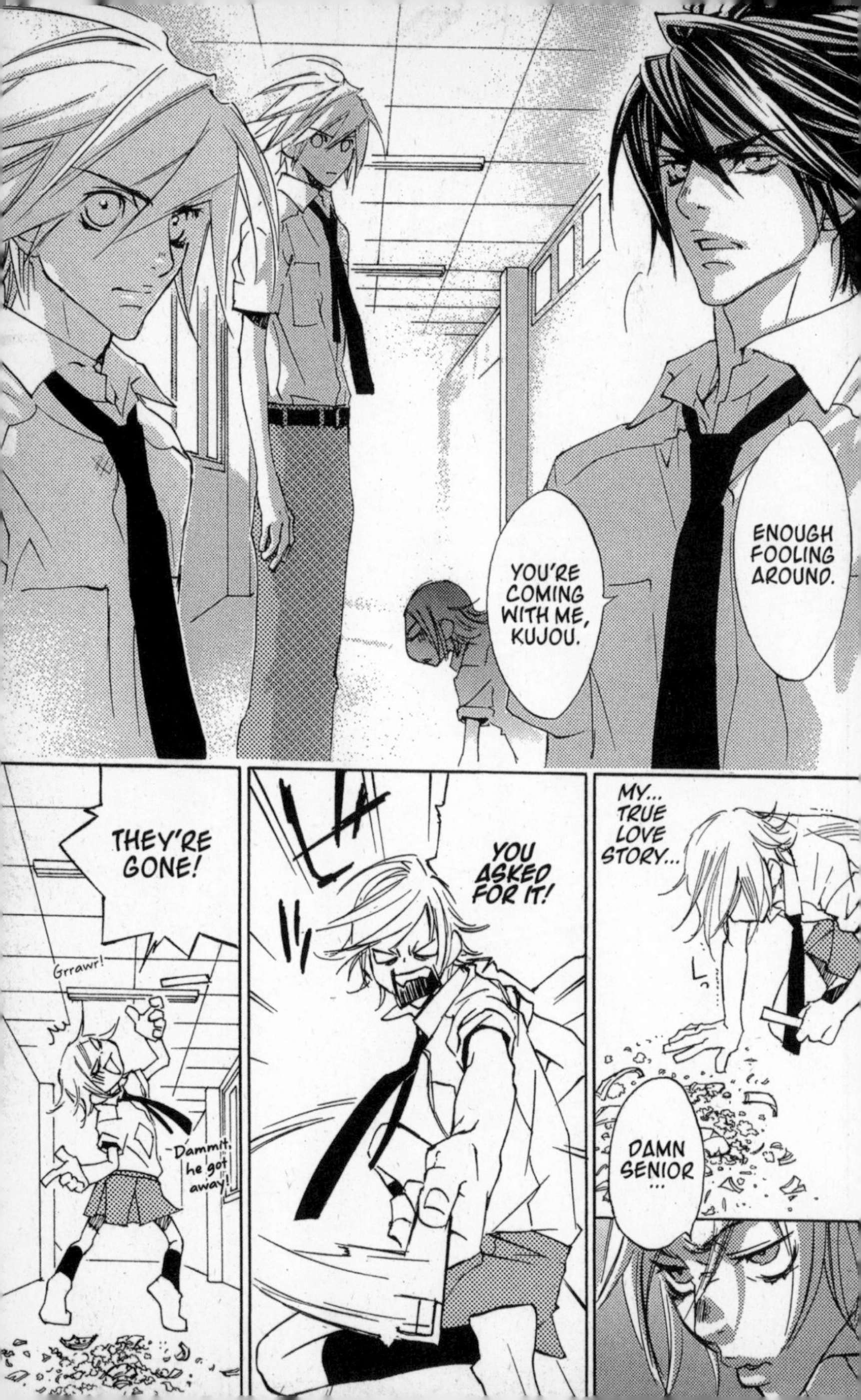
ENOUGH FOOLING AROUND.
YOU'RE COMING WITH ME, KUJOU.
MY... TRUE LOVE STORY...
DAMN SENIOR ...
YOU ASKED FOR IT!
THEY'RE GONE!
Grrawr!
Dammit, he got away!

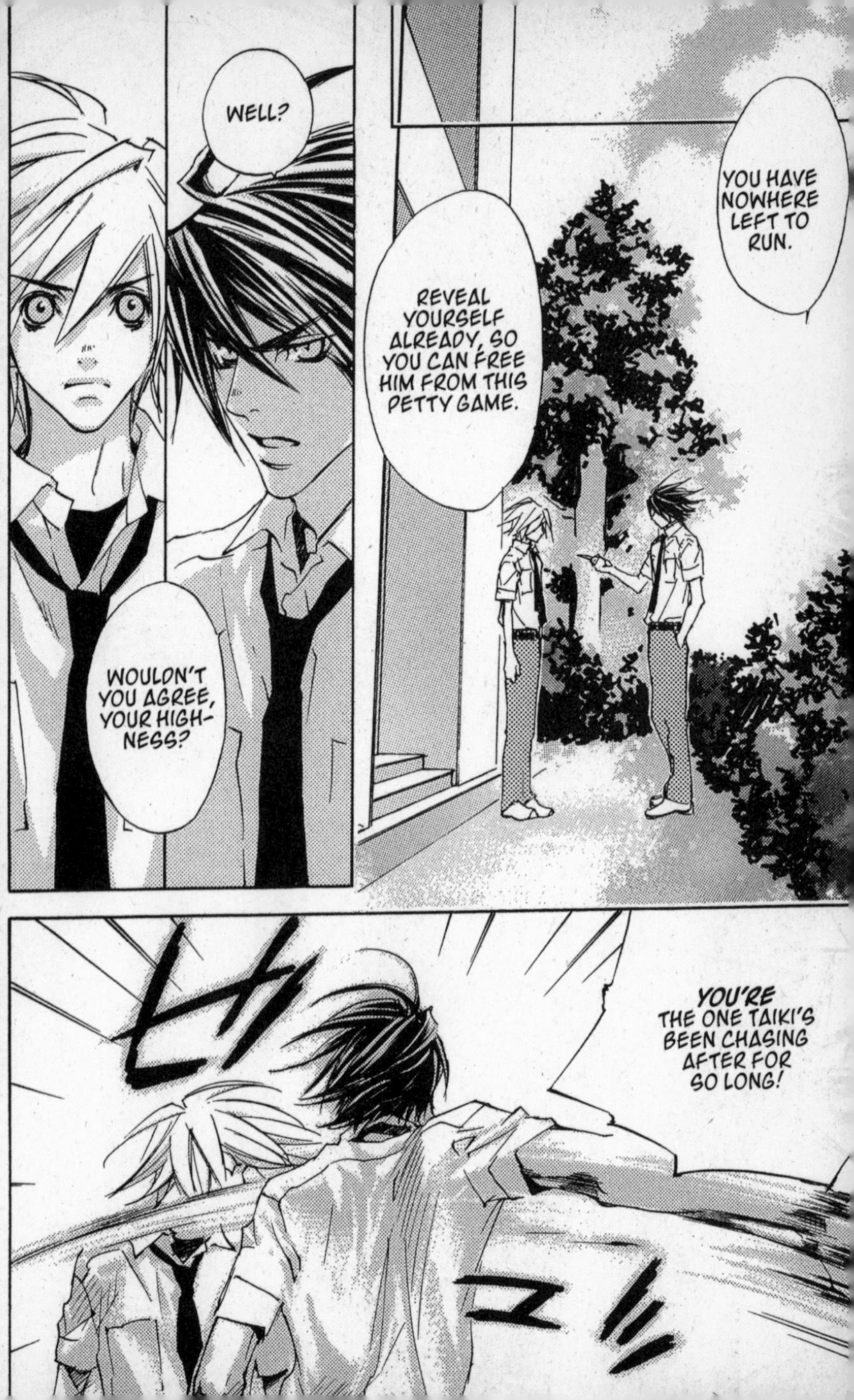
YOU HAVE NOWHERE LEFT TO RUN.
REVEAL YOURSELF ALREADY, SO YOU CAN FREE HIM FROM THIS PETTY GAME.
WELL?
WOULDN'T YOU AGREE, YOUR HIGHNESS?
YOU'RE THE ONE TAIKI'S BEEN CHASING AFTER FOR SO LONG!

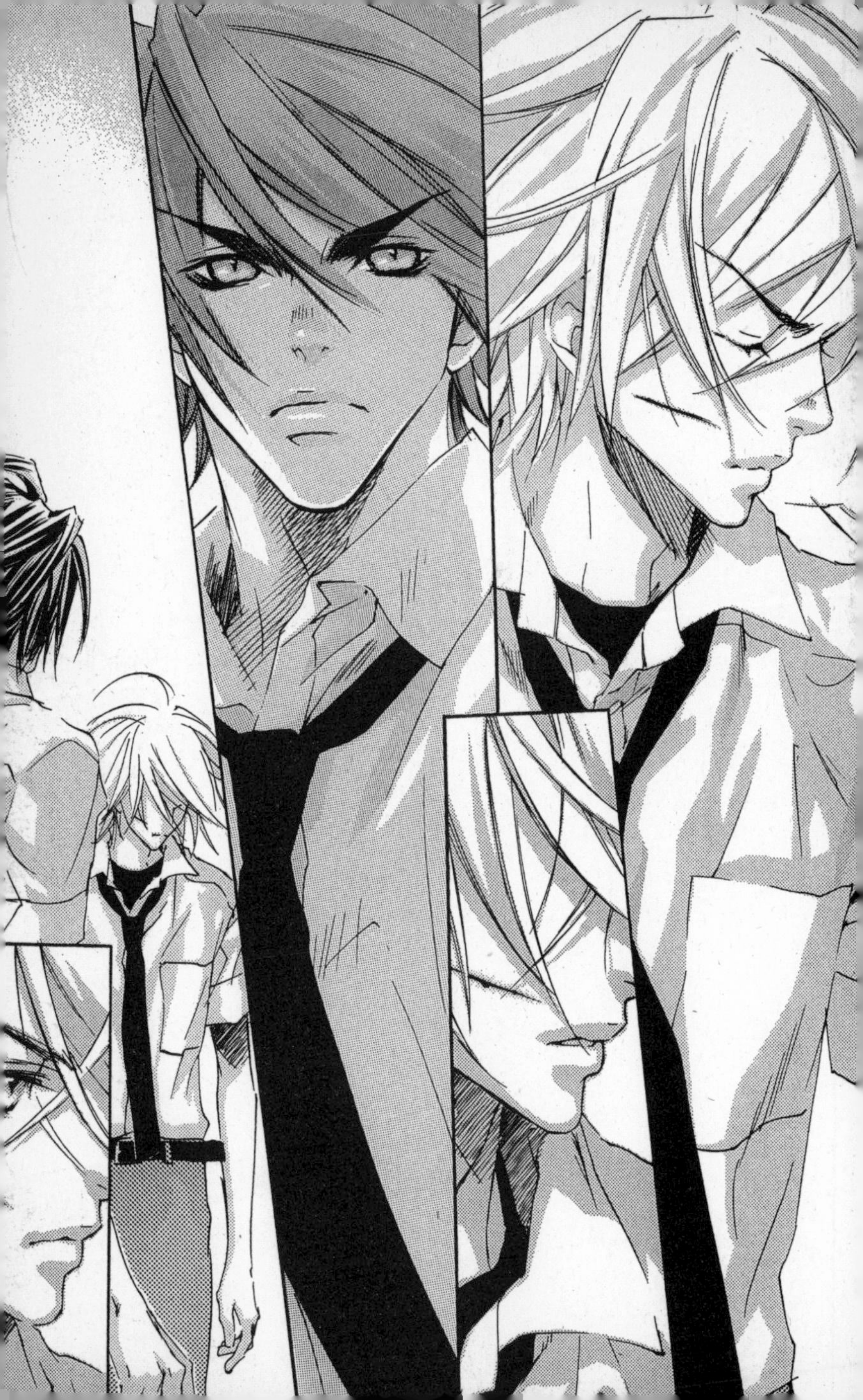

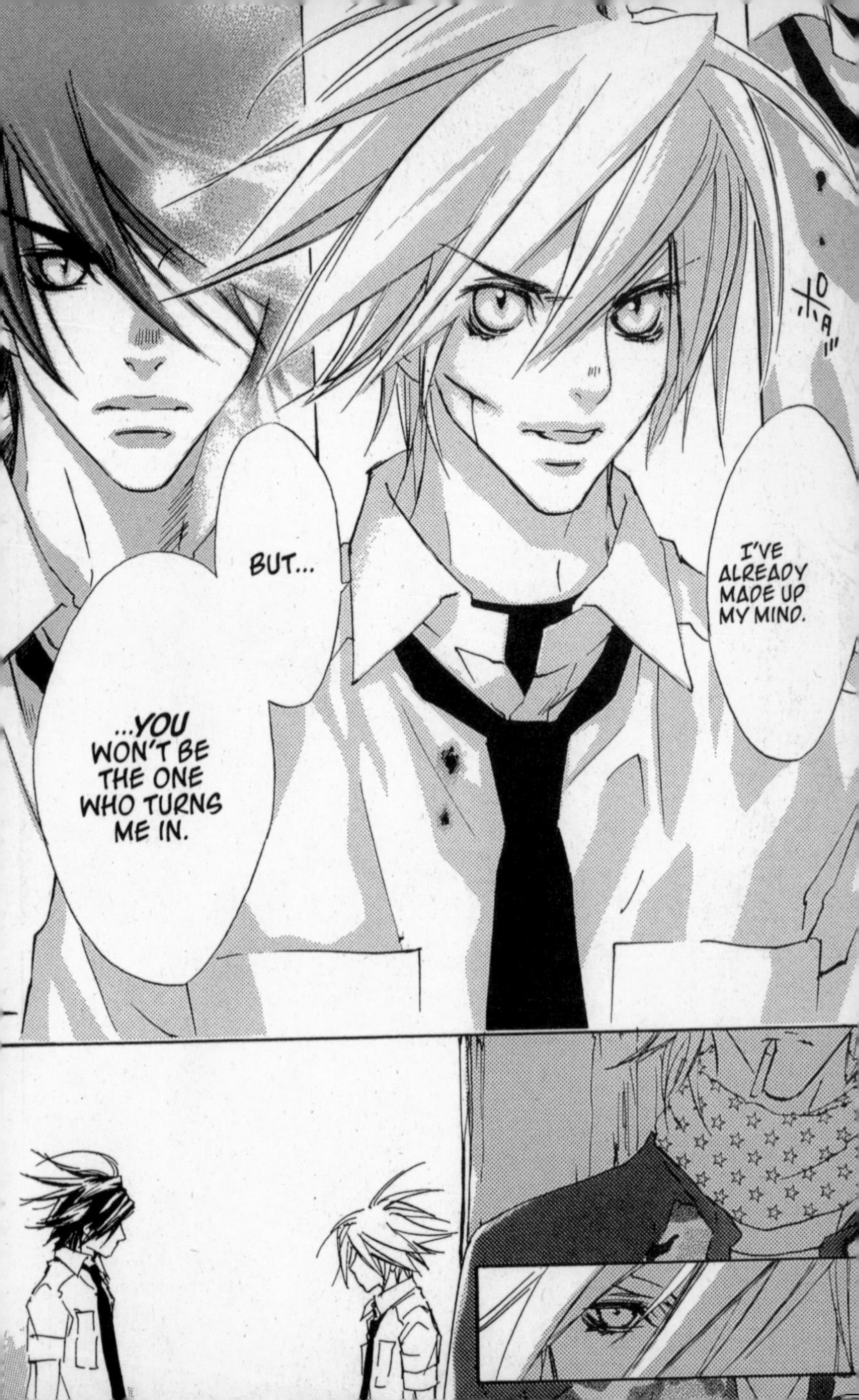
I'VE ALREADY MADE UP MY MIND.
BUT...
...YOU WON'T BE THE ONE WHO TURNS ME IN.

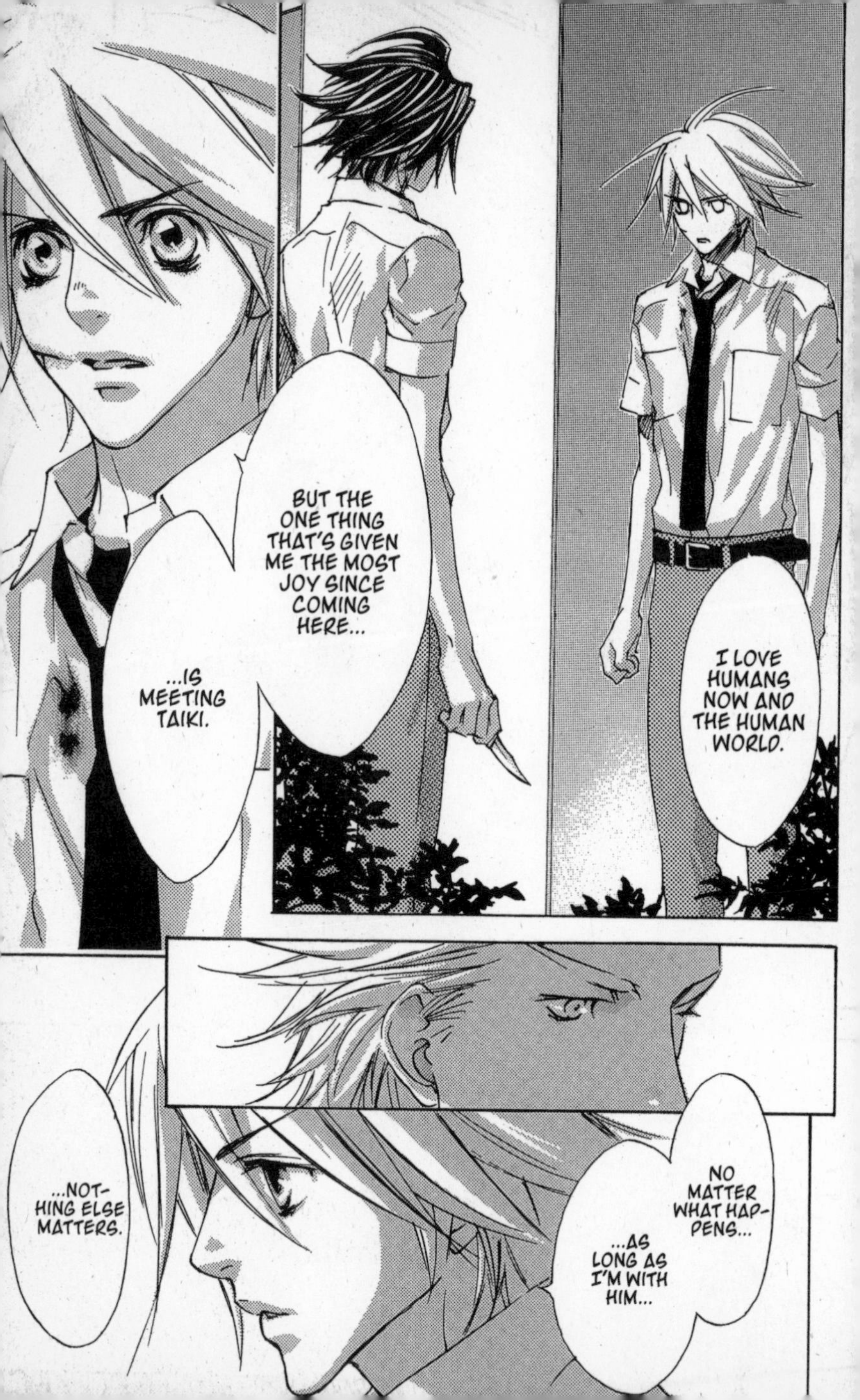
I LOVE HUMANS NOW AND THE HUMAN WORLD.
BUT THE ONE THING THAT'S GIVEN ME THE MOST JOY SINCE COMING HERE...
...IS MEETING TAIKI.
NO MATTER WHAT HAPPENS...
...AS LONG AS I'M WITH HIM...
...NOTHING ELSE MATTERS.

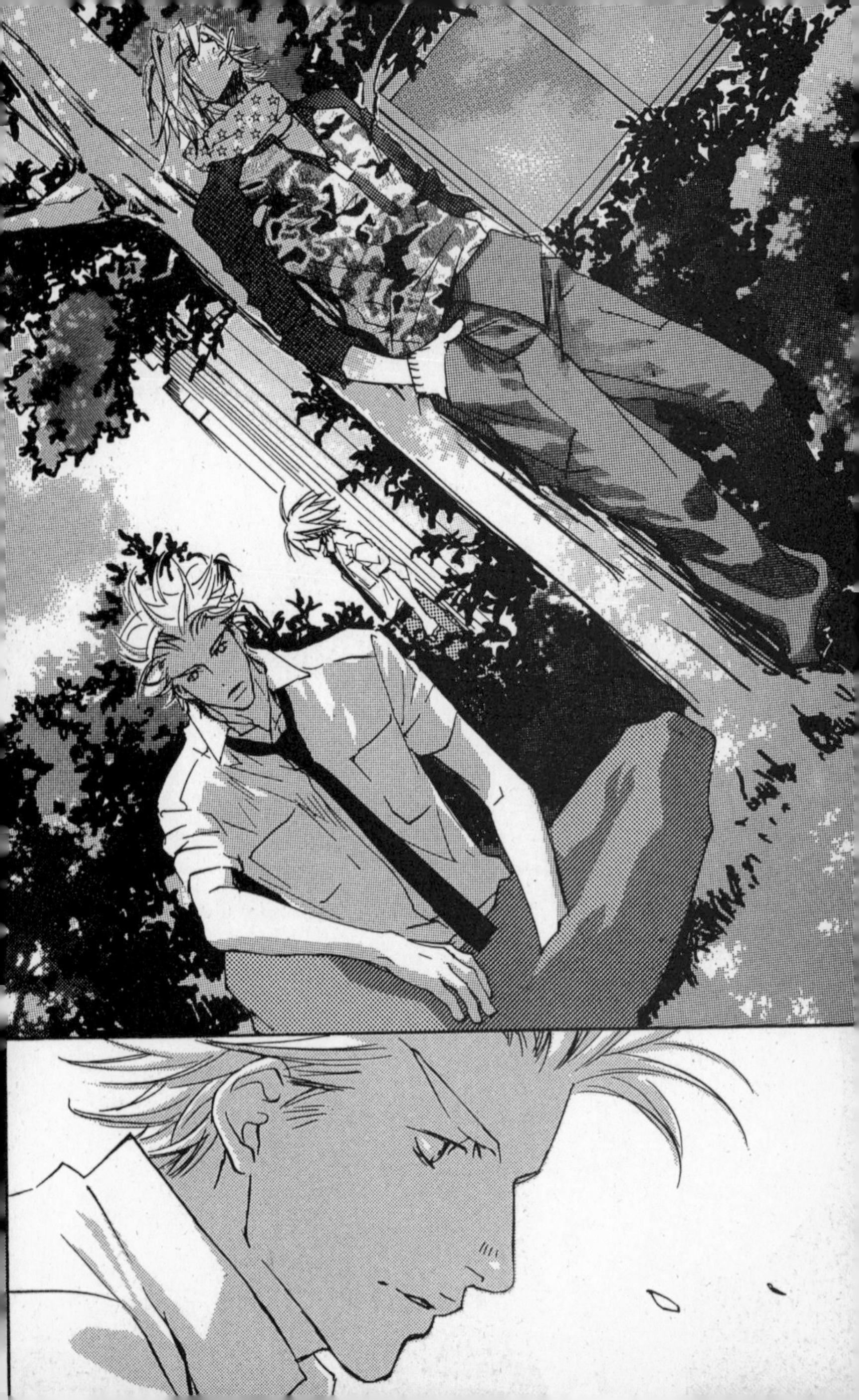

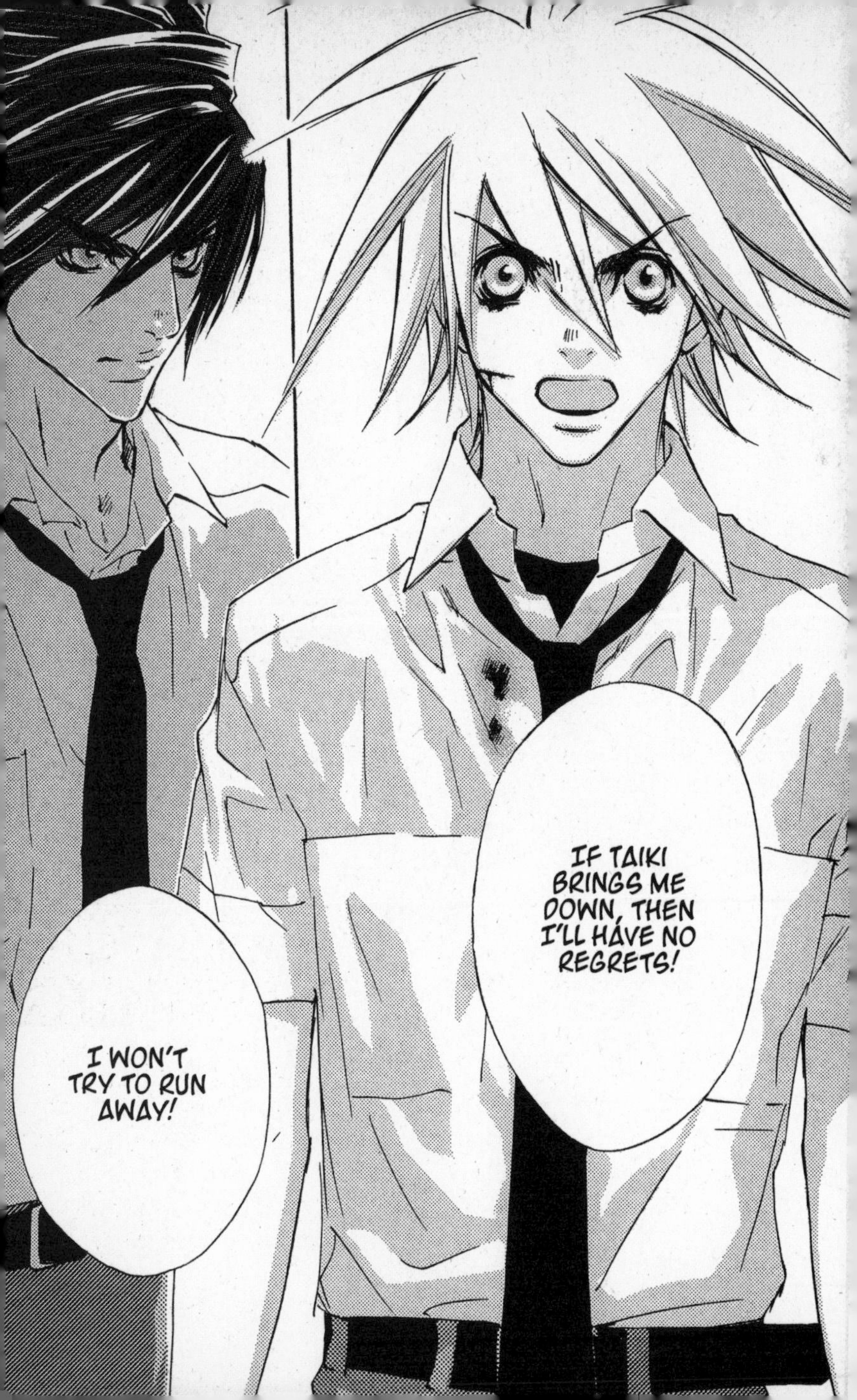
IF TAIKI BRINGS ME DOWN, THEN I'LL HAVE NO REGRETS!
I WON'T TRY TO RUN AWAY!

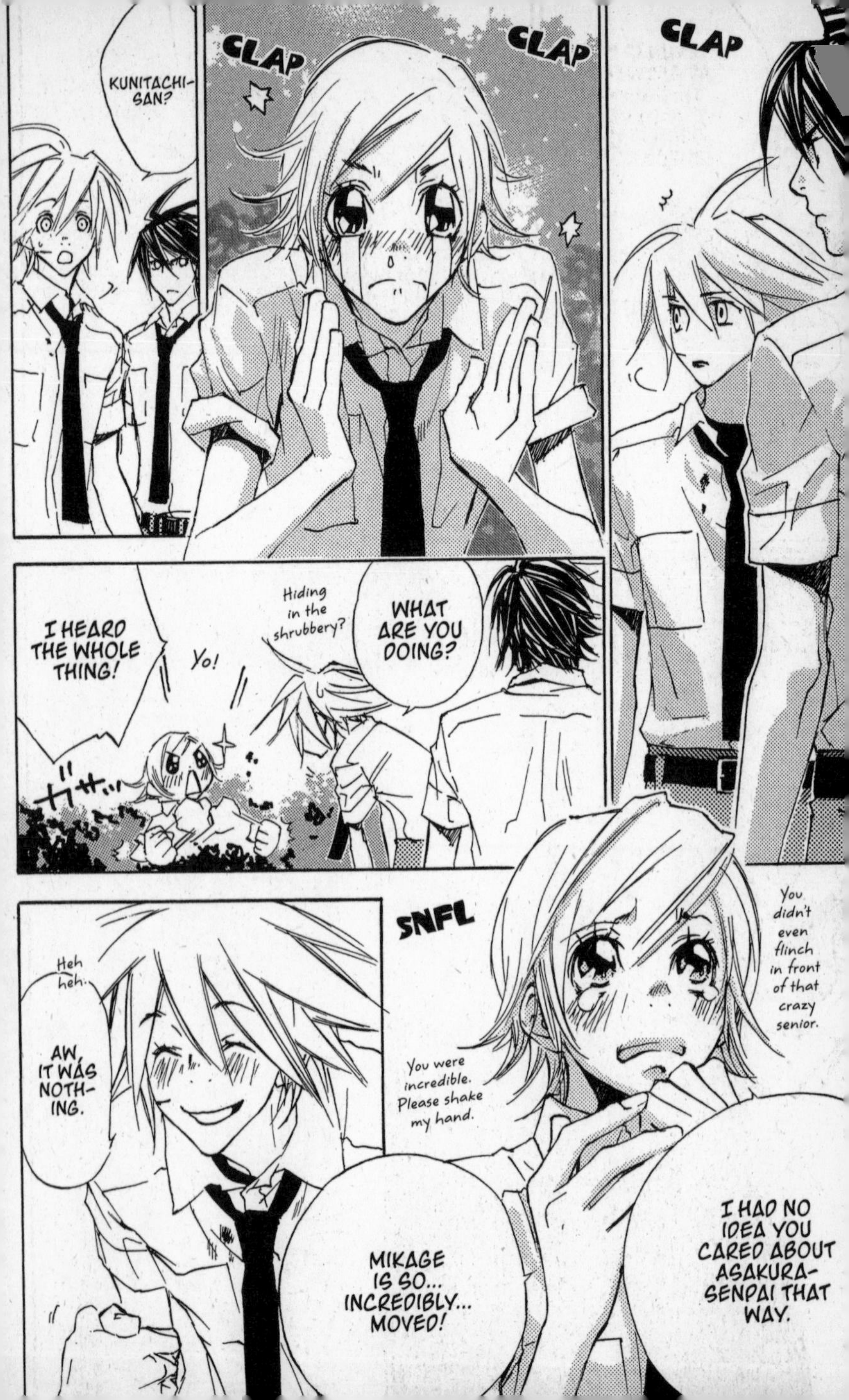
CLAP
CLAP
CLAP
KUNITACHI-SAN?
WHAT ARE YOU DOING?
Hiding in the shrubbery?
Yo!
I HEARD THE WHOLE THING!
You didn't even flinch in front of that crazy senior.
I HAD NO IDEA YOU CARED ABOUT ASAKURA-SENPAI THAT WAY.
SNFL
You were incredible. Please shake my hand.
MIKAGE IS SO... INCREDIBLY... MOVED!
Heh heh.
AW, IT WAS NOTHING.

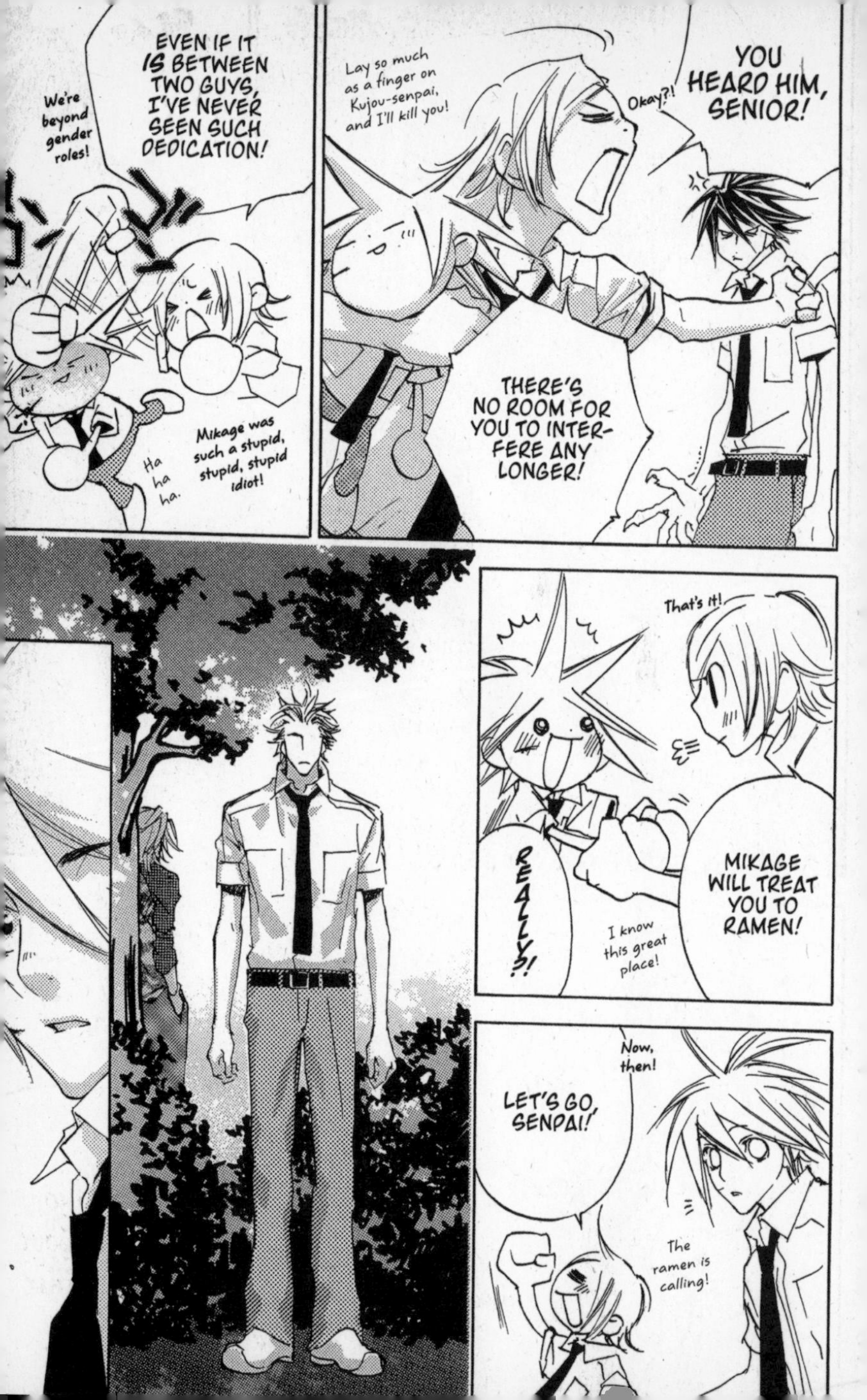
YOU HEARD HIM, SENIOR!
Okay?!
Lay so much as a finger on Kujou-senpai, and I'll kill you!
THERE'S NO ROOM FOR YOU TO INTERFERE ANY LONGER!
EVEN IF IT IS BETWEEN TWO GUYS, I'VE NEVER SEEN SUCH DEDICATION!
We're beyond gender roles!
Mikage was such a stupid, stupid, stupid idiot!
Ha ha ha.
That's it!
MIKAGE WILL TREAT YOU TO RAMEN!
I know this great place!
REALLY?!
Now, then!
LET'S GO, SENPAI!
The ramen is calling!

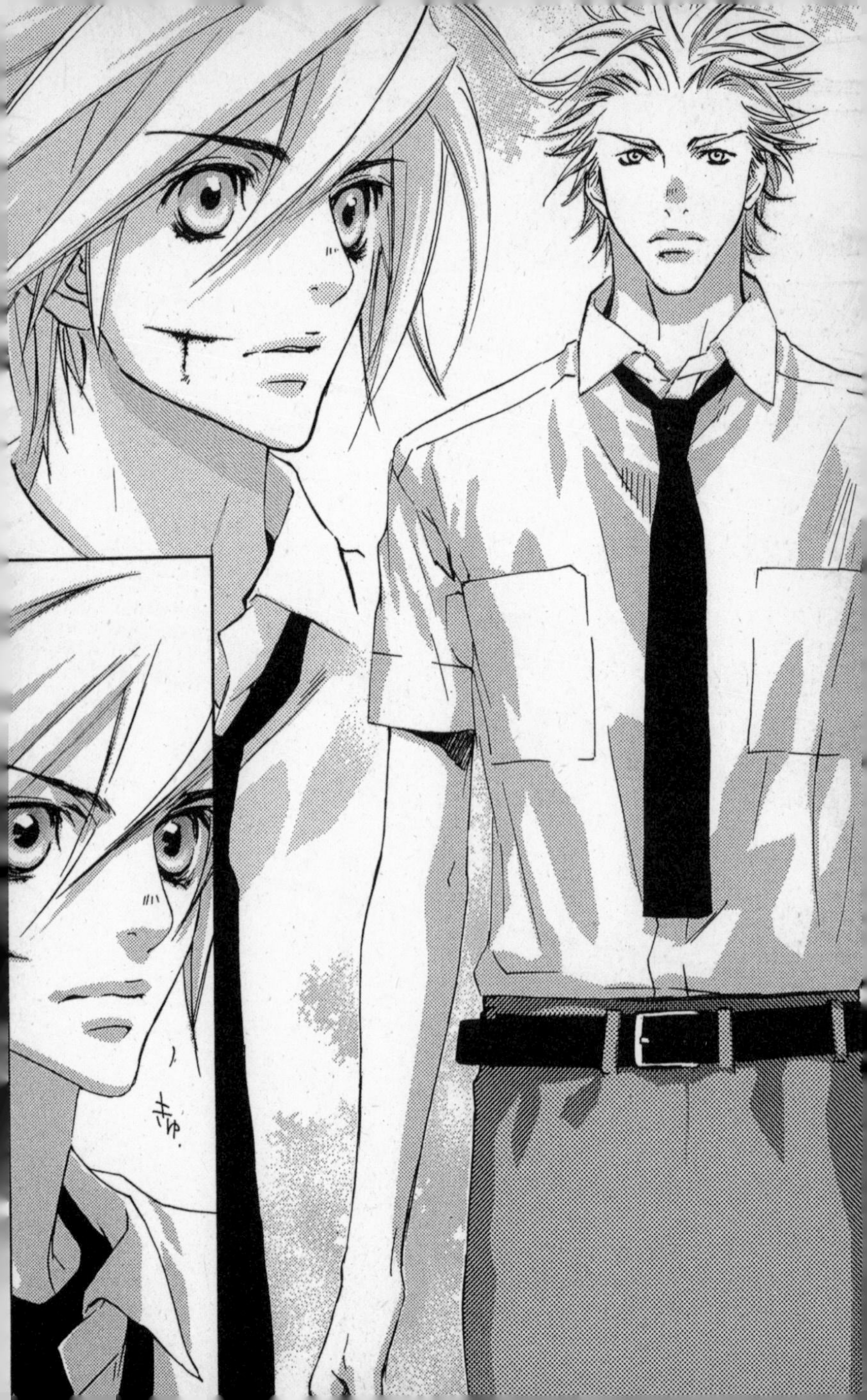
きゅ.

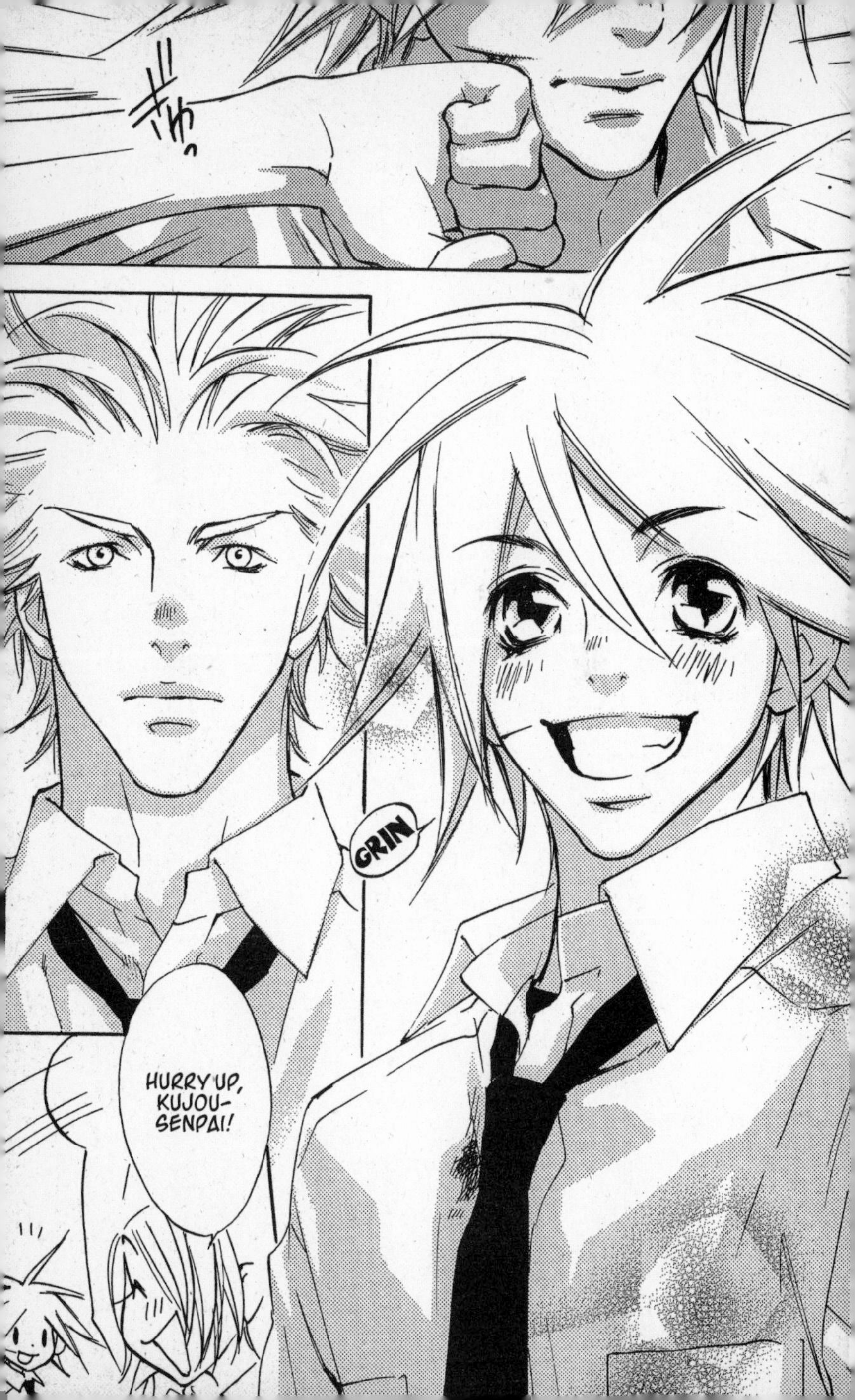
ぎゅっ
GRIN
HURRY UP, KUJOU-SENPAI!

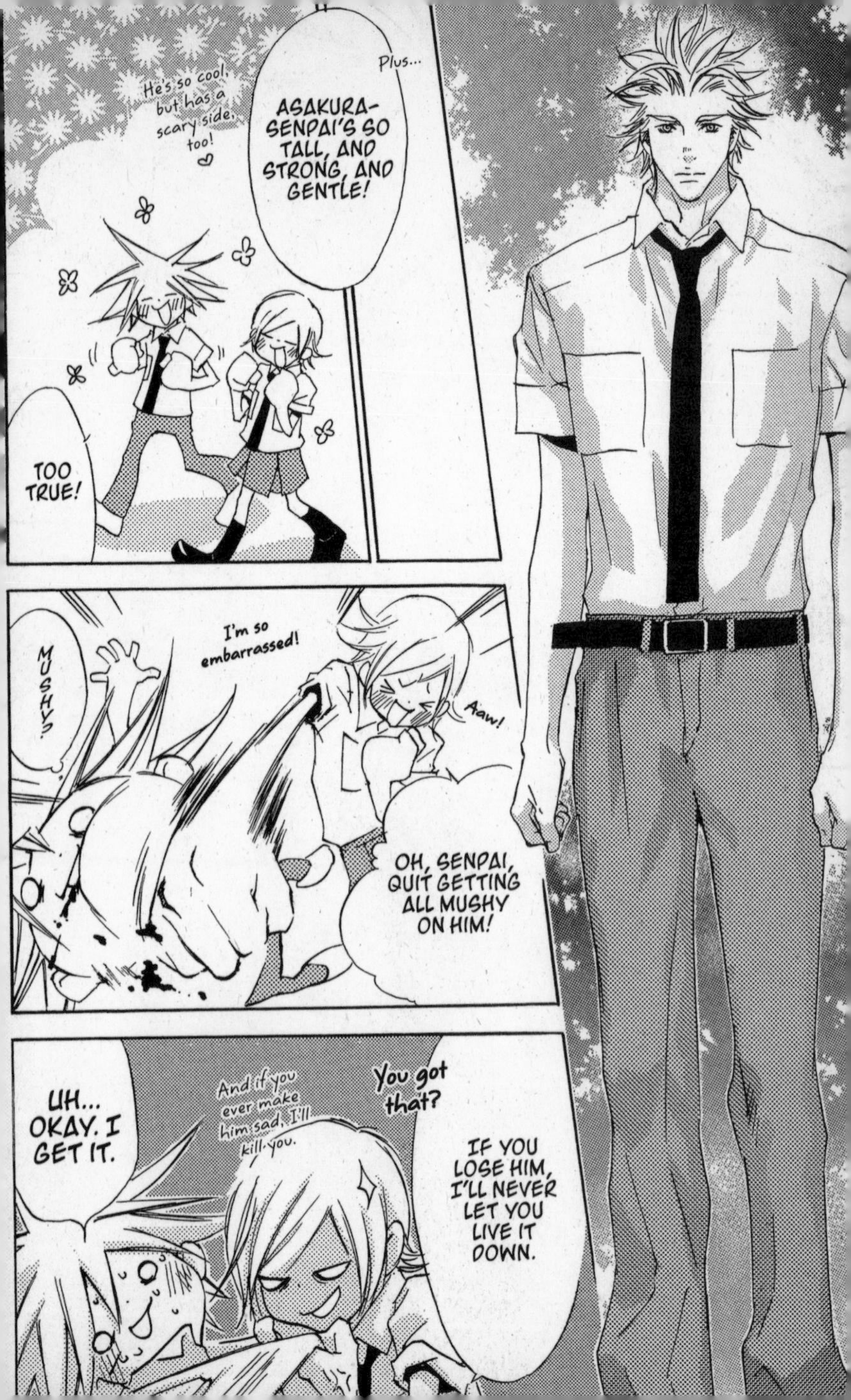
Plus...
ASAKURA-SENPAI'S SO TALL, AND STRONG, AND GENTLE!
He's so cool, but has a scary side, too!
TOO TRUE!
OH, SENPAI, QUIT GETTING ALL MUSHY ON HIM!
Aaw!
I'm so embarrassed!
MUSHY!?
You got that?
IF YOU LOSE HIM, I'LL NEVER LET YOU LIVE IT DOWN.
And if you ever make him sad, I'll kill you.
UH... OKAY. I GET IT.

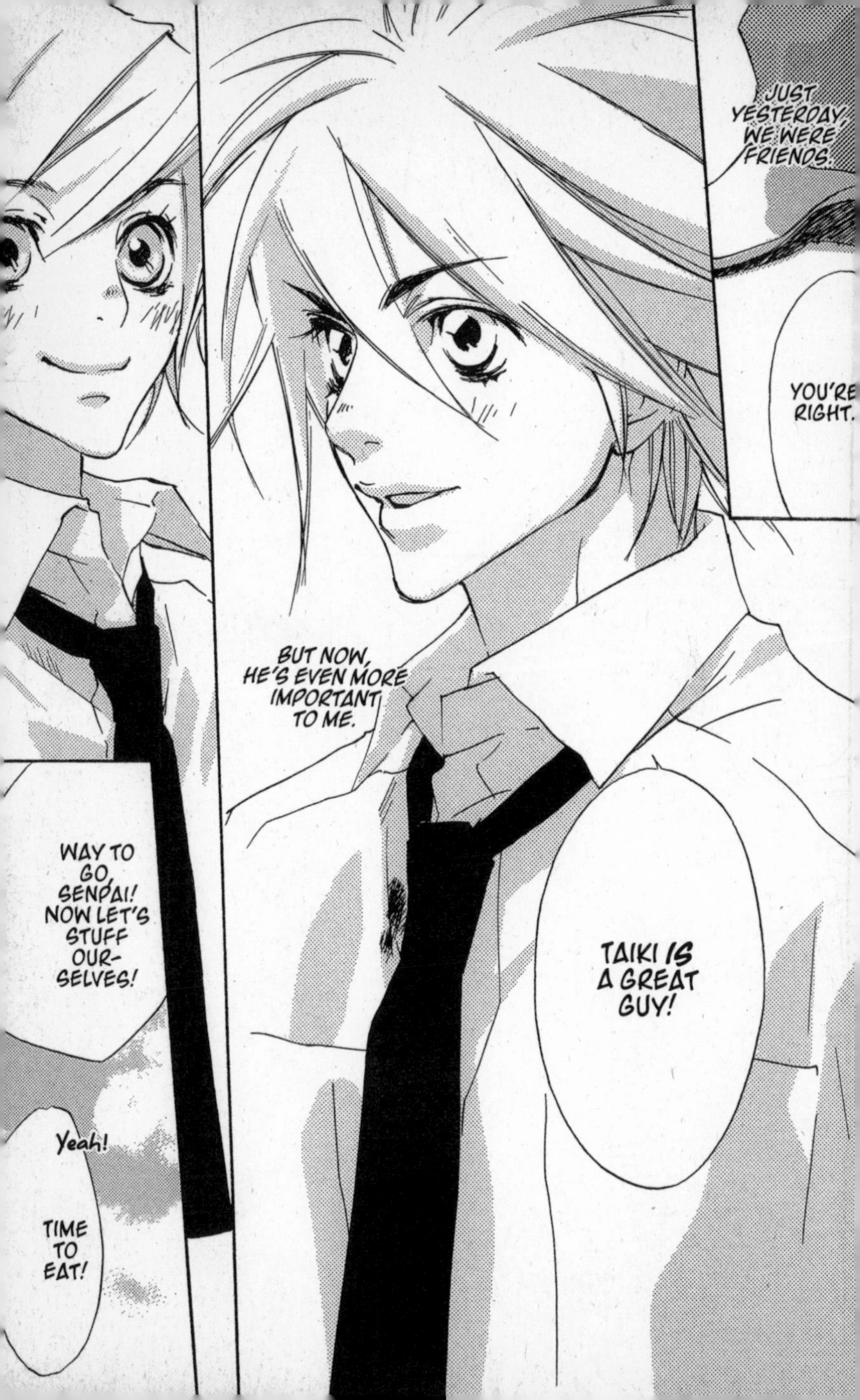

JUST YESTERDAY, WE WERE FRIENDS.
YOU'RE RIGHT.
TAIKI IS A GREAT GUY!
BUT NOW, HE'S EVEN MORE IMPORTANT TO ME.
WAY TO GO, SENPAI! NOW LET'S STUFF OUR-SELVES!
Yeah!
TIME TO EAT!

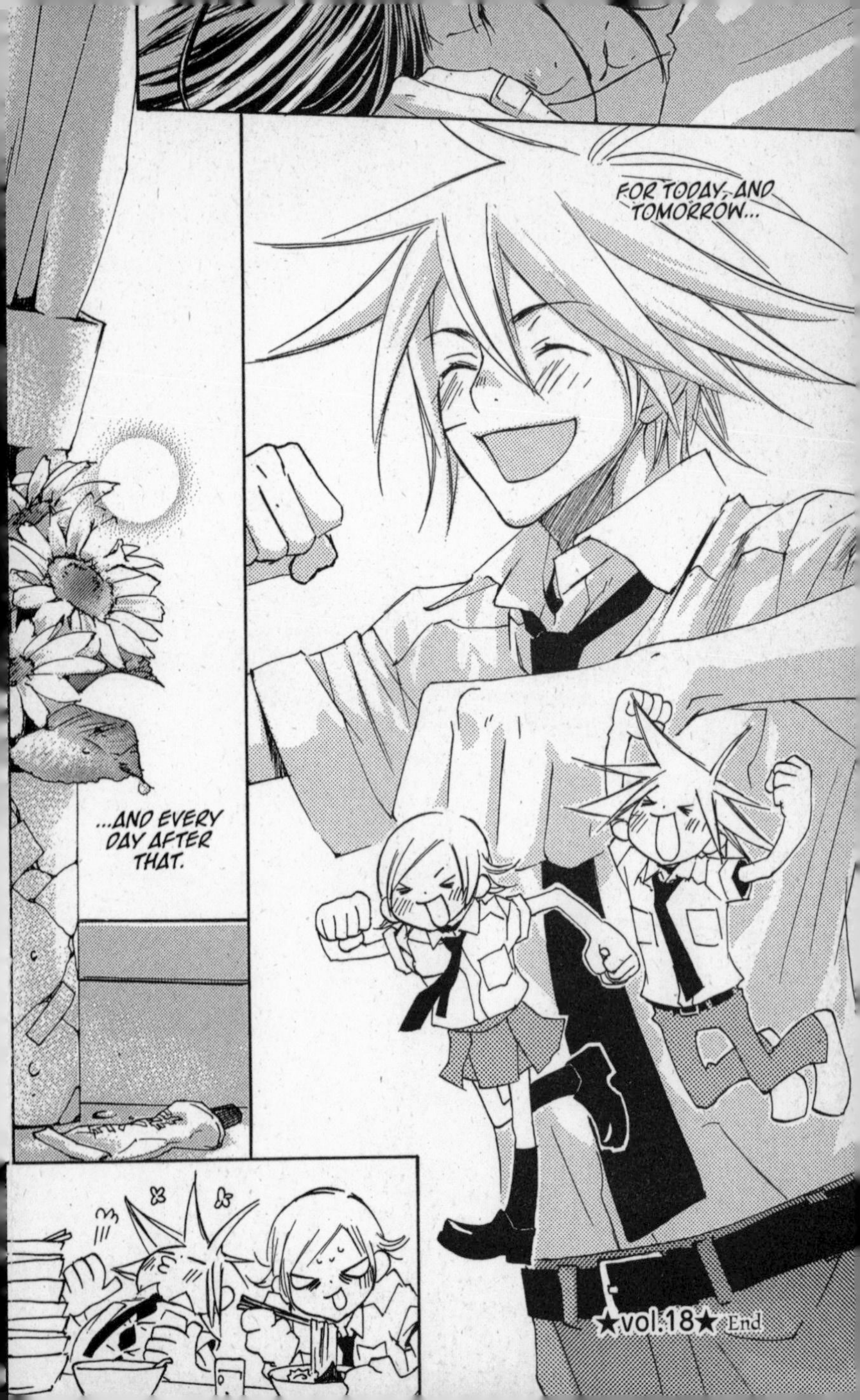
FOR TODAY, AND TOMORROW...
...AND EVERY DAY AFTER THAT.
★vol.18★ End

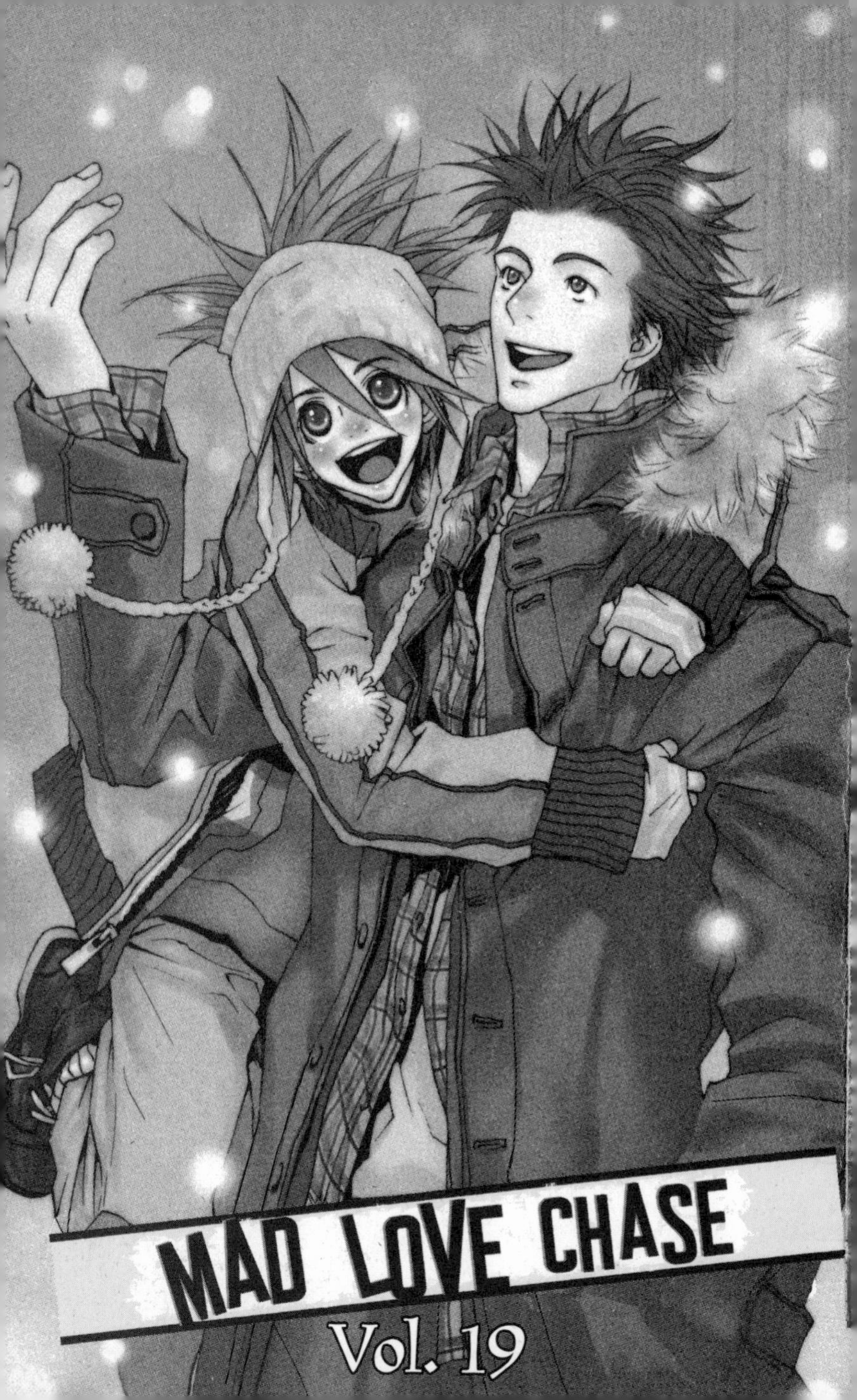
MAD LOVE CHASE
Vol. 19

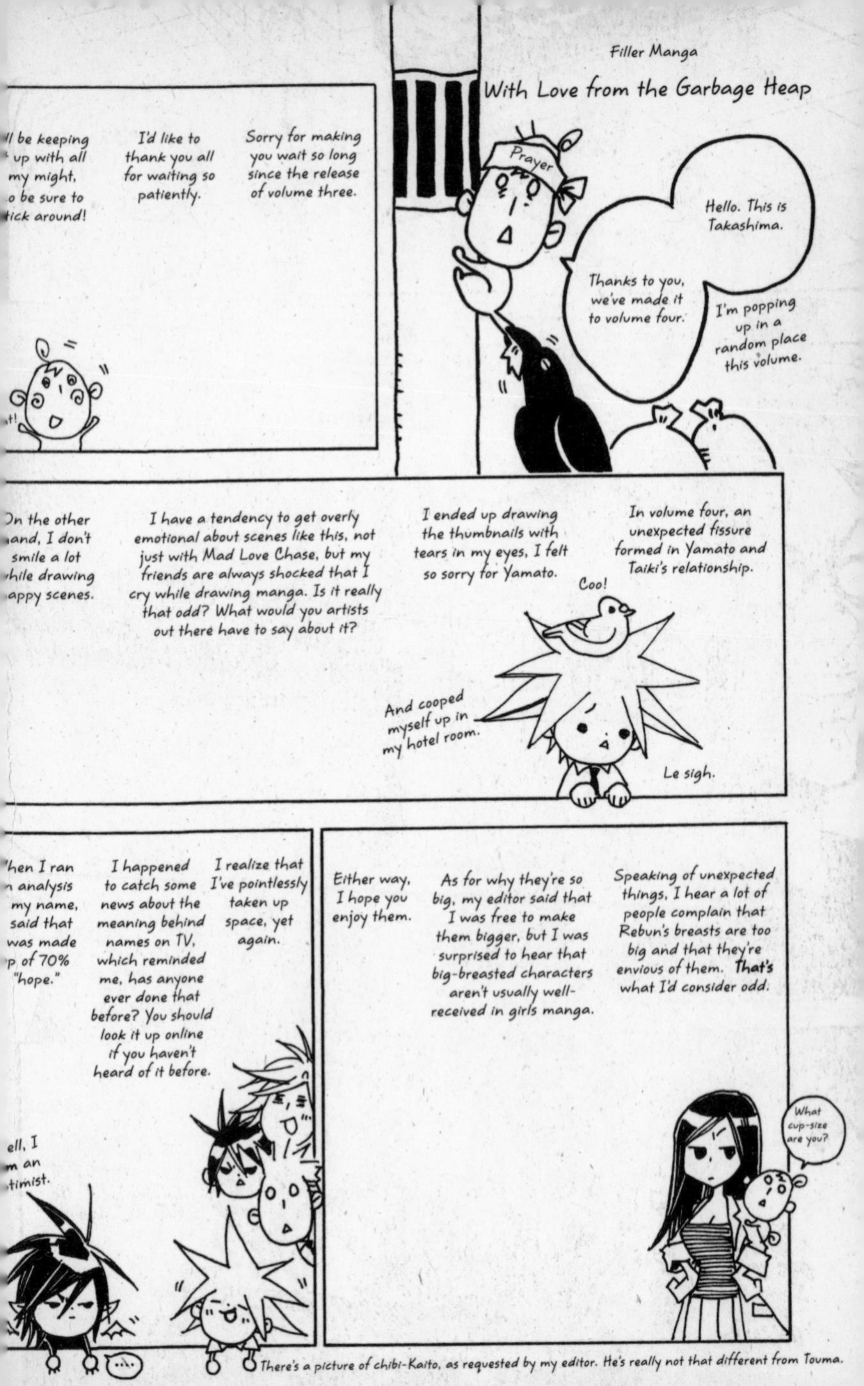
Filler Manga
With Love from the Garbage Heap
Prayer
Hello. This is Takashima.
Thanks to you, we've made it to volume four.
I'm popping up in a random place this volume.
Sorry for making you wait so long since the release of volume three.
I'd like to thank you all for waiting so patiently.
ll be keeping up with all my might, o be sure to tick around!
t!
In volume four, an unexpected fissure formed in Yamato and Taiki's relationship.
I ended up drawing the thumbnails with tears in my eyes, I felt so sorry for Yamato.
Coo!
I have a tendency to get overly emotional about scenes like this, not just with Mad Love Chase, but my friends are always shocked that I cry while drawing manga. Is it really that odd? What would you artists out there have to say about it?
On the other and, I don't smile a lot hile drawing appy scenes.
And cooped myself up in my hotel room.
Le sigh.
Speaking of unexpected things, I hear a lot of people complain that Rebun's breasts are too big and that they're envious of them. That's what I'd consider odd.
As for why they're so big, my editor said that I was free to make them bigger, but I was surprised to hear that big-breasted characters aren't usually well-received in girls manga.
Either way, I hope you enjoy them.
What cup-size are you?
I realize that I've pointlessly taken up space, yet again.
I happened to catch some news about the meaning behind names on TV, which reminded me, has anyone ever done that before? You should look it up online if you haven't heard of it before.
hen I ran n analysis my name, said that was made p of 70% "hope."
ell, I m an timist.
...

There's a picture of chibi-Kaito, as requested by my editor. He's really not that different from Touma.

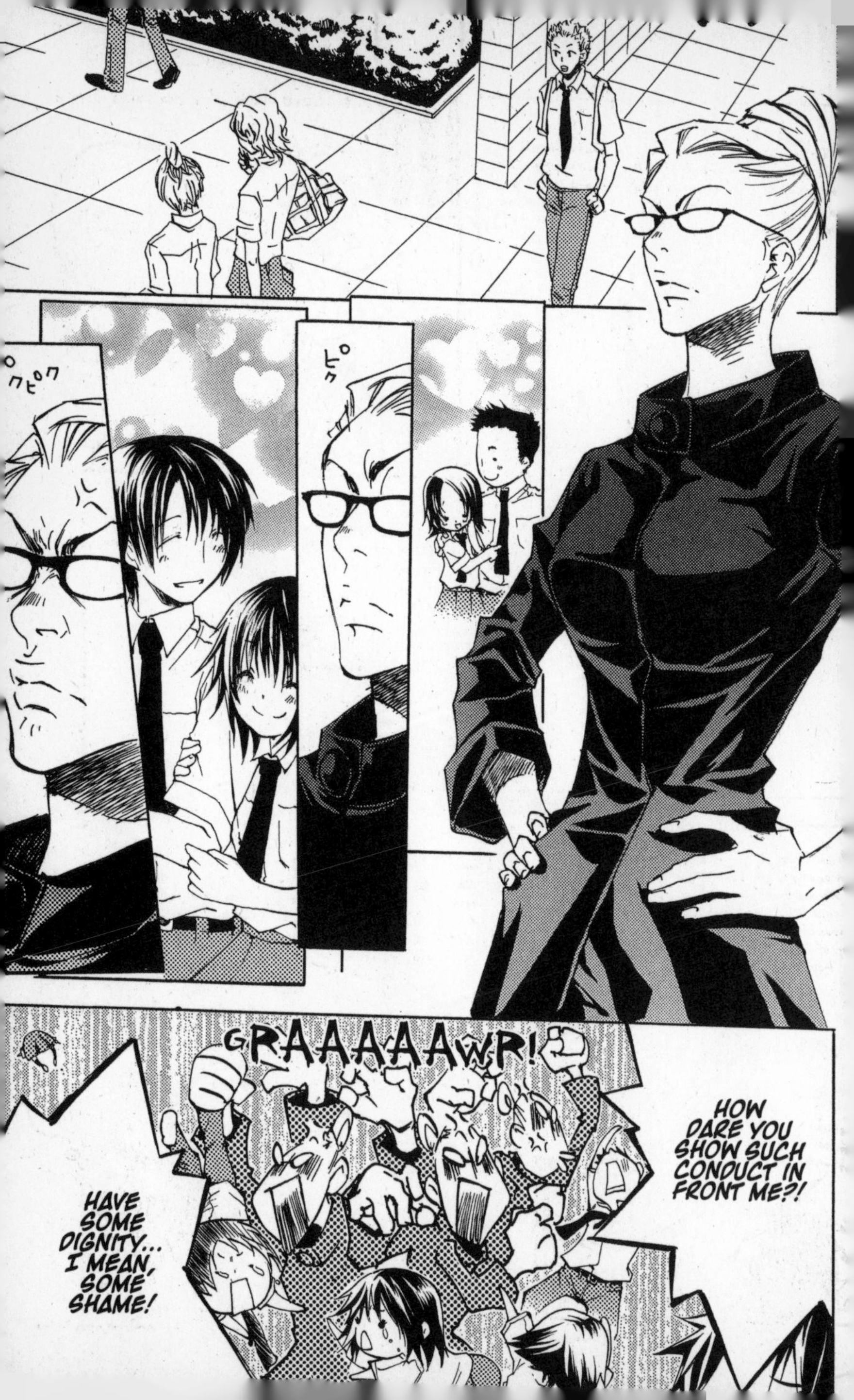
ピク
ピクピク
HOW DARE YOU SHOW SUCH CONDUCT IN FRONT ME?!
GRAAAAAAWR!
HAVE SOME DIGNITY... I MEAN, SOME SHAME!

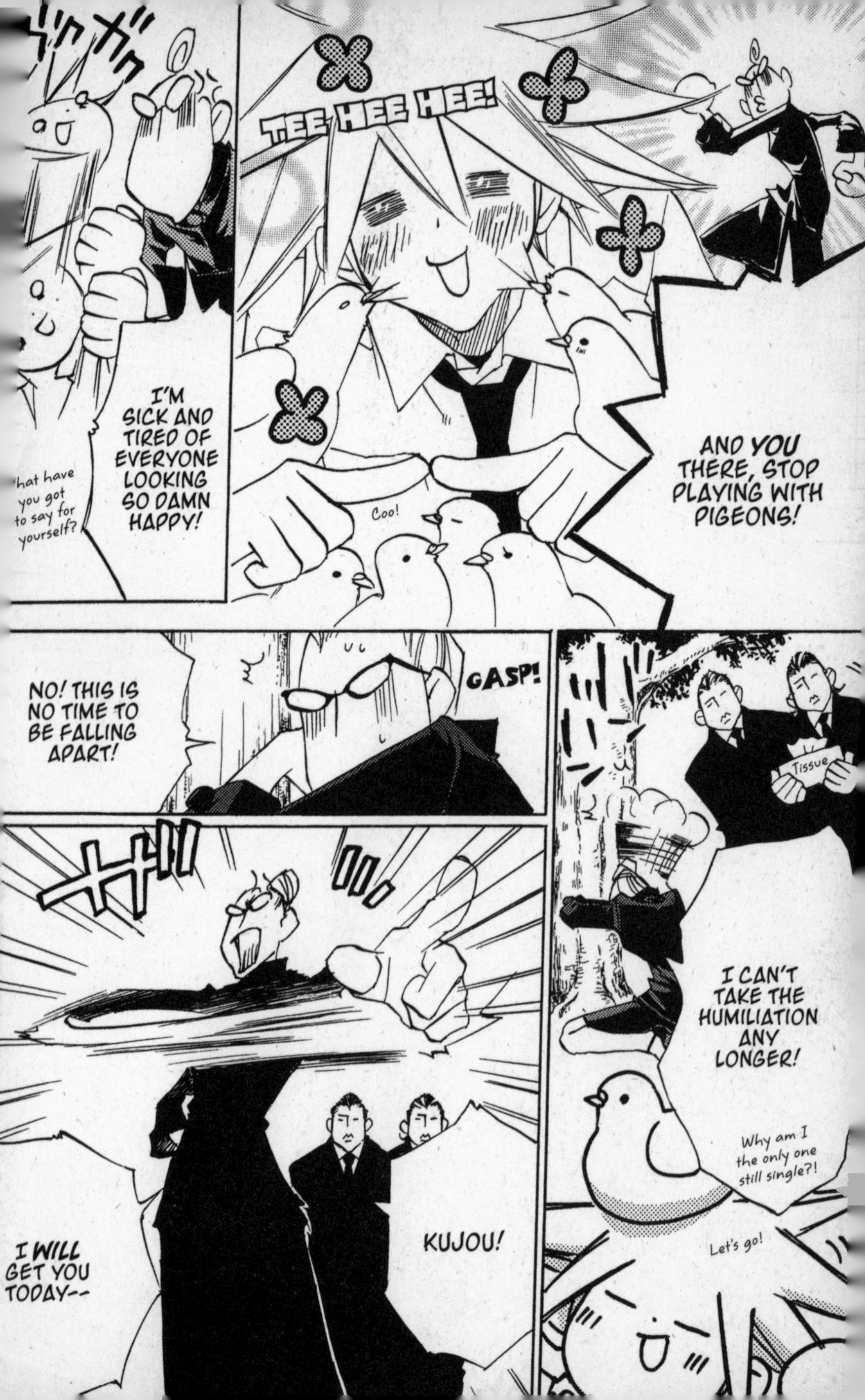
TEE HEE HEE!
AND YOU THERE, STOP PLAYING WITH PIGEONS!
Coo!
I'M SICK AND TIRED OF EVERYONE LOOKING SO DAMN HAPPY!
hat have you got to say for yourself?
Tissue
I CAN'T TAKE THE HUMILIATION ANY LONGER!
Why am I the only one still single?!
Let's go!
GASP!
NO! THIS IS NO TIME TO BE FALLING APART!
KUJOU!
I WILL GET YOU TODAY--

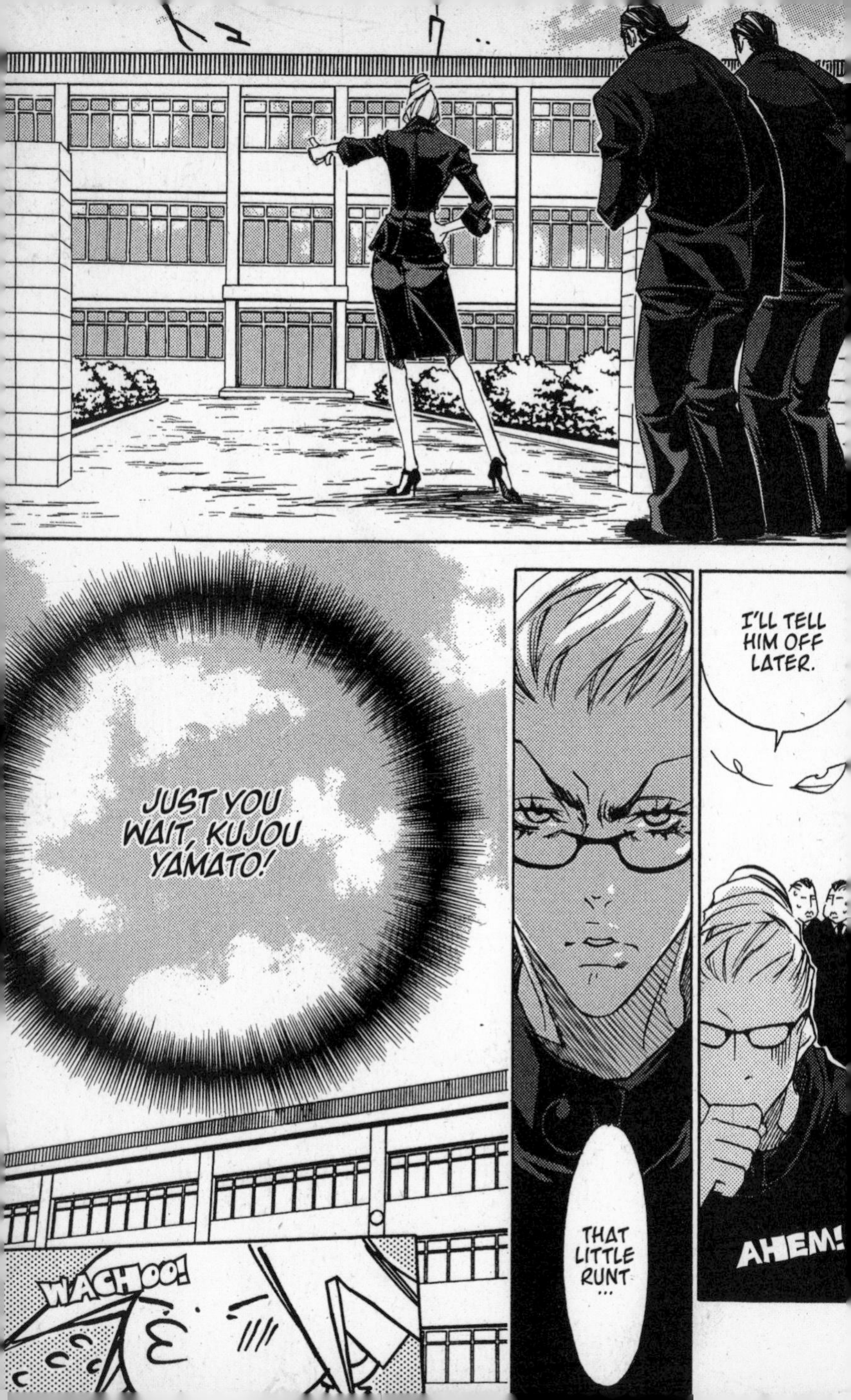
I'LL TELL HIM OFF LATER.
AHEM!
THAT LITTLE RUNT ...
JUST YOU WAIT, KUJOU YAMATO!
WACHOO!

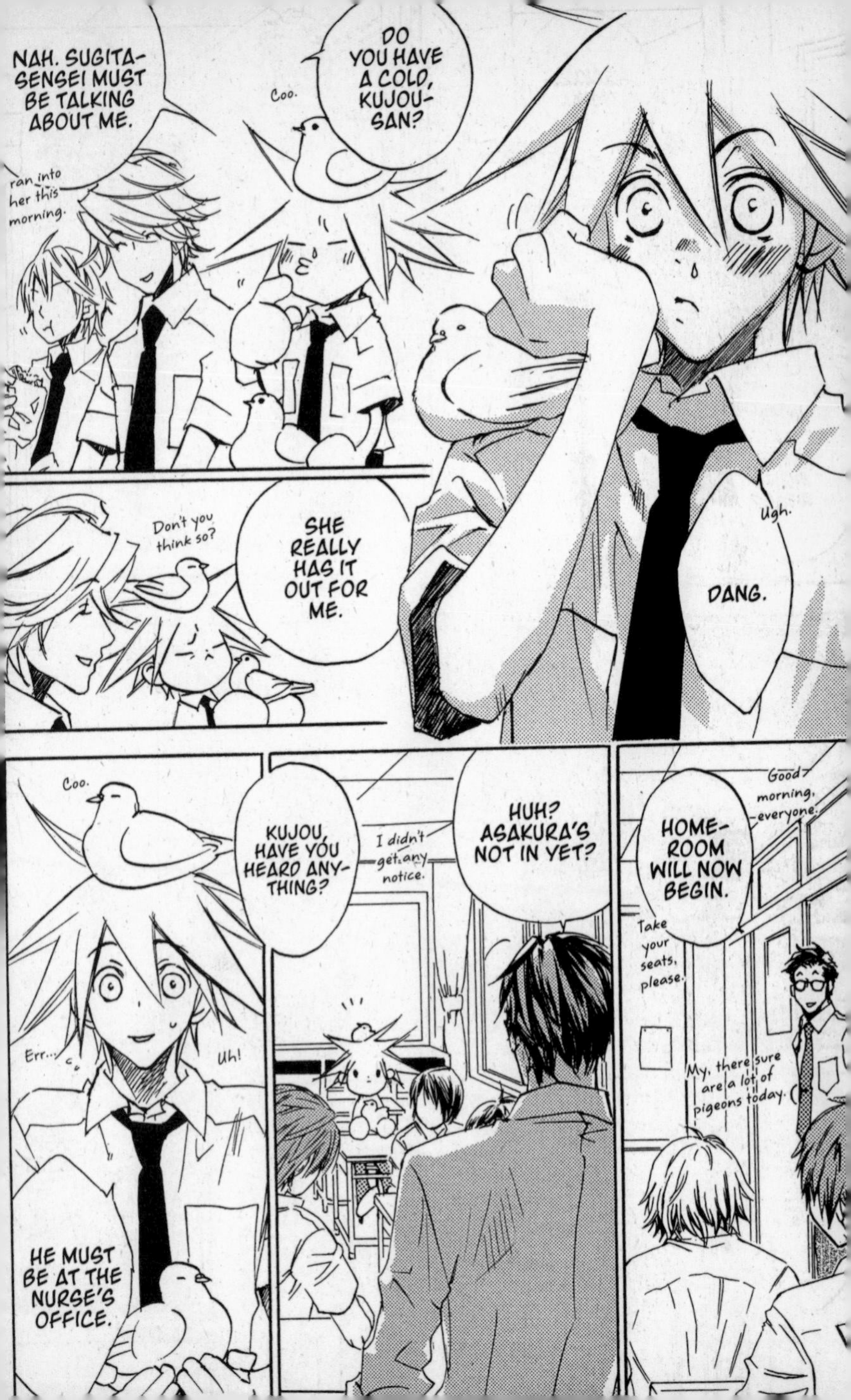
Ugh.
DANG.
DO YOU HAVE A COLD, KUJOU-SAN?
Coo.
NAH. SUGITA-SENSEI MUST BE TALKING ABOUT ME.
ran into her this morning.
SHE REALLY HAS IT OUT FOR ME.
Don't you think so?
Good morning, everyone.
HOME-ROOM WILL NOW BEGIN.
Take your seats, please.
My, there sure are a lot of pigeons today.
HUH? ASAKURA'S NOT IN YET?
KUJOU, HAVE YOU HEARD ANYTHING?
I didn't get any notice.
Coo.
Uh!
Err...
HE MUST BE AT THE NURSE'S OFFICE.

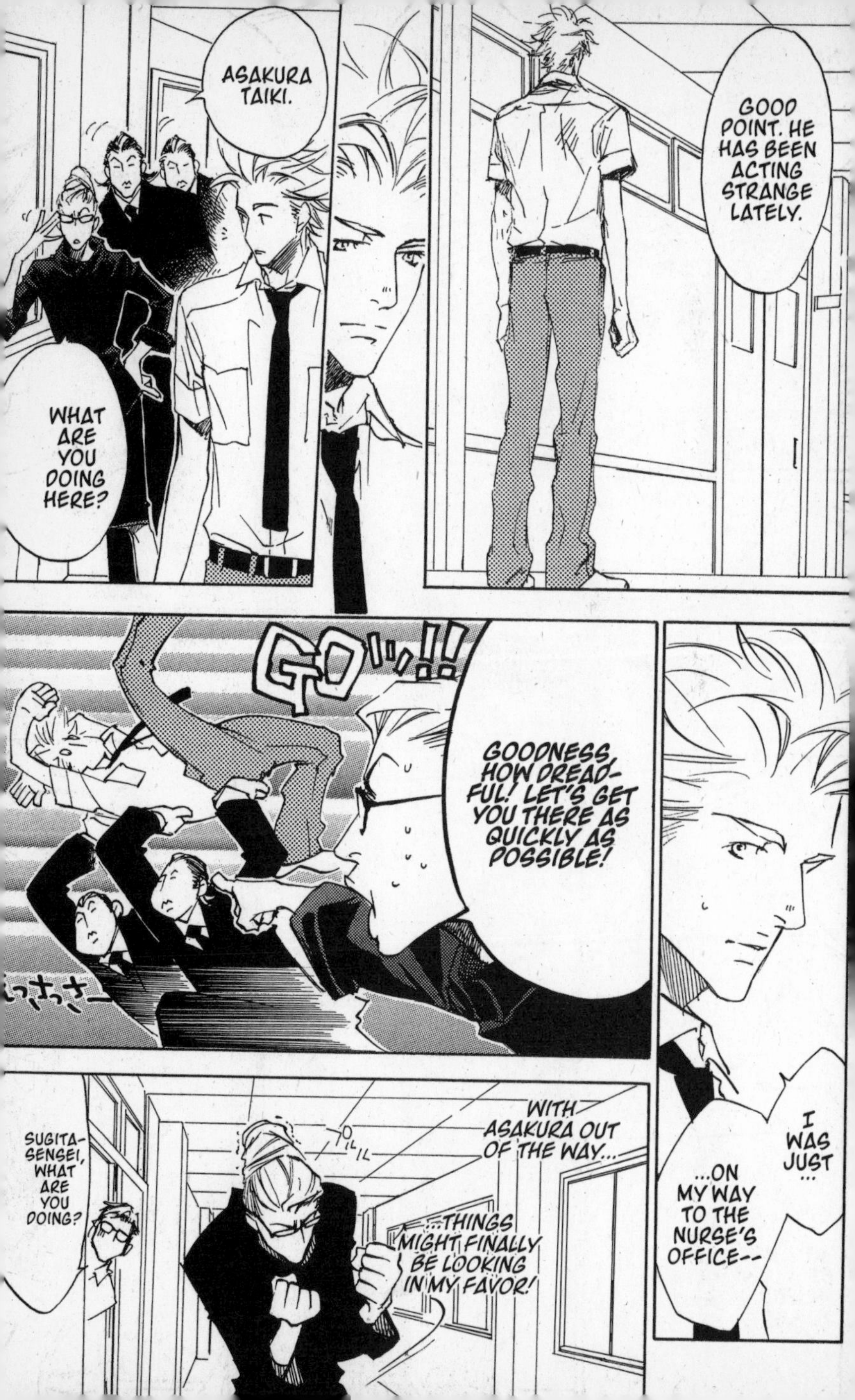
GOOD POINT. HE HAS BEEN ACTING STRANGE LATELY.
ASAKURA TAIKI.
WHAT ARE YOU DOING HERE?
I WAS JUST...
...ON MY WAY TO THE NURSE'S OFFICE--
GO!!
GOODNESS HOW DREAD-FUL! LET'S GET YOU THERE AS QUICKLY AS POSSIBLE!
WITH ASAKURA OUT OF THE WAY...
...THINGS MIGHT FINALLY BE LOOKING IN MY FAVOR!
SUGITA-SENSEI, WHAT ARE YOU DOING?

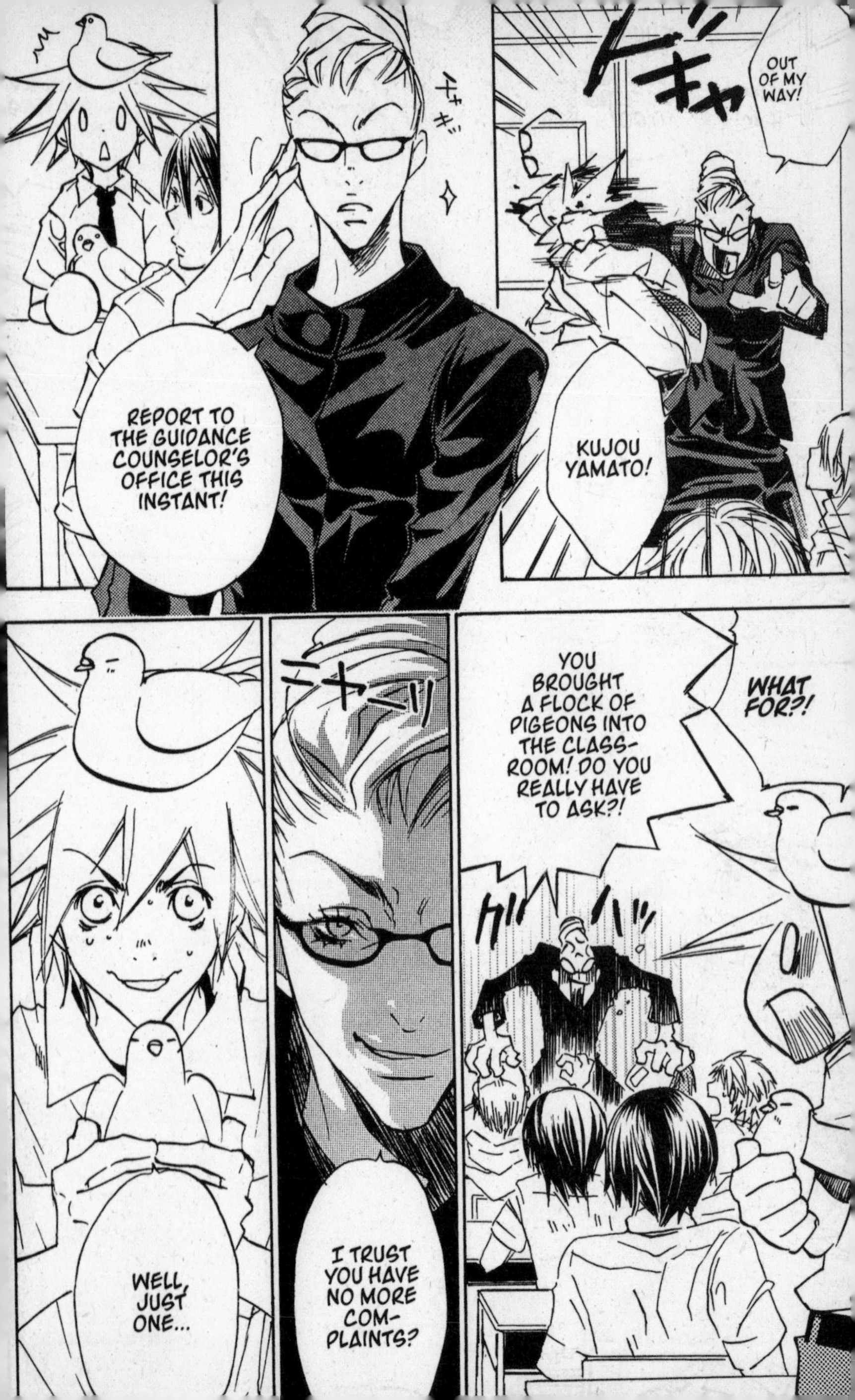
OUT OF MY WAY!
KUJOU YAMATO!
REPORT TO THE GUIDANCE COUNSELOR'S OFFICE THIS INSTANT!
WHAT FOR?!
YOU BROUGHT A FLOCK OF PIGEONS INTO THE CLASS-ROOM! DO YOU REALLY HAVE TO ASK?!
I TRUST YOU HAVE NO MORE COM-PLAINTS?
WELL, JUST ONE...

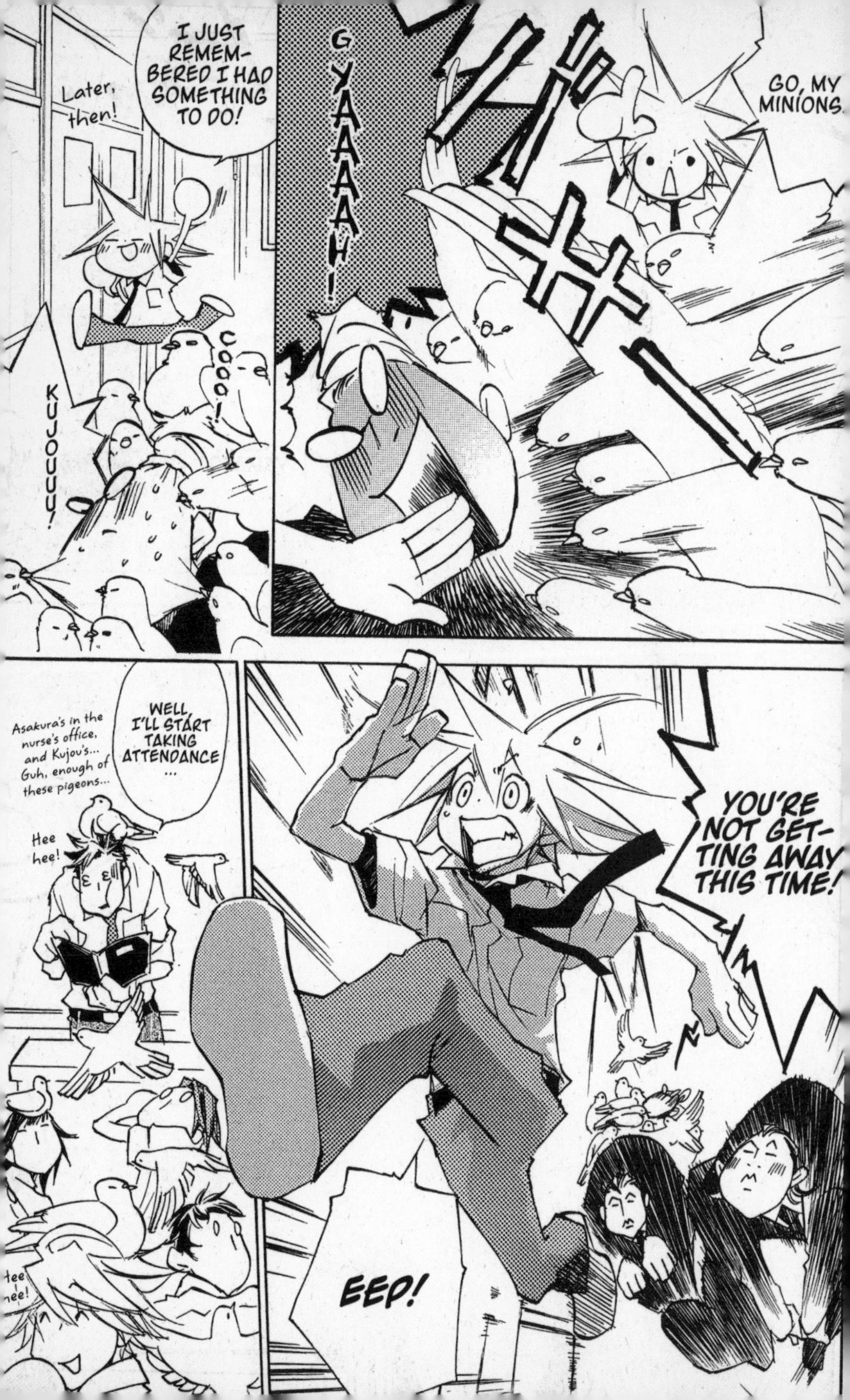
GO, MY MINIONS.
GYAAAAH!
I JUST REMEMBERED I HAD SOMETHING TO DO!
Later, then!
COOOO!
KUJOUUU!
YOU'RE NOT GETTING AWAY THIS TIME!
EEP!
WELL, I'LL START TAKING ATTENDANCE...
Asakura's in the nurse's office, and Kujou's... Guh, enough of these pigeons...
Hee hee!
tee hee!

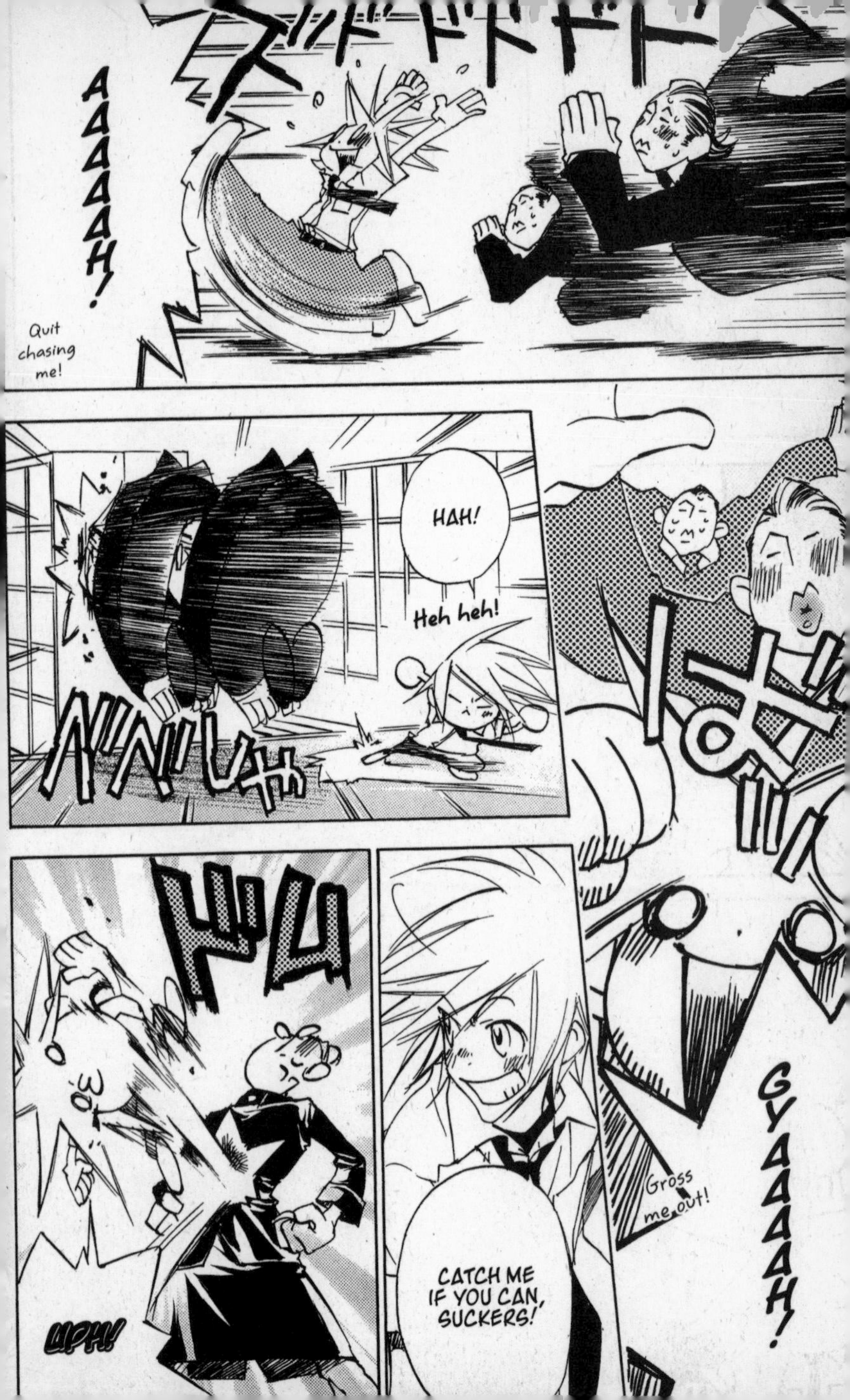
ズドドドドドン
AAAAAAH!
Quit chasing me!
GYAAAAAH!
Gross me out!
HAH!
Heh heh!
CATCH ME IF YOU CAN, SUCKERS!
UPH!

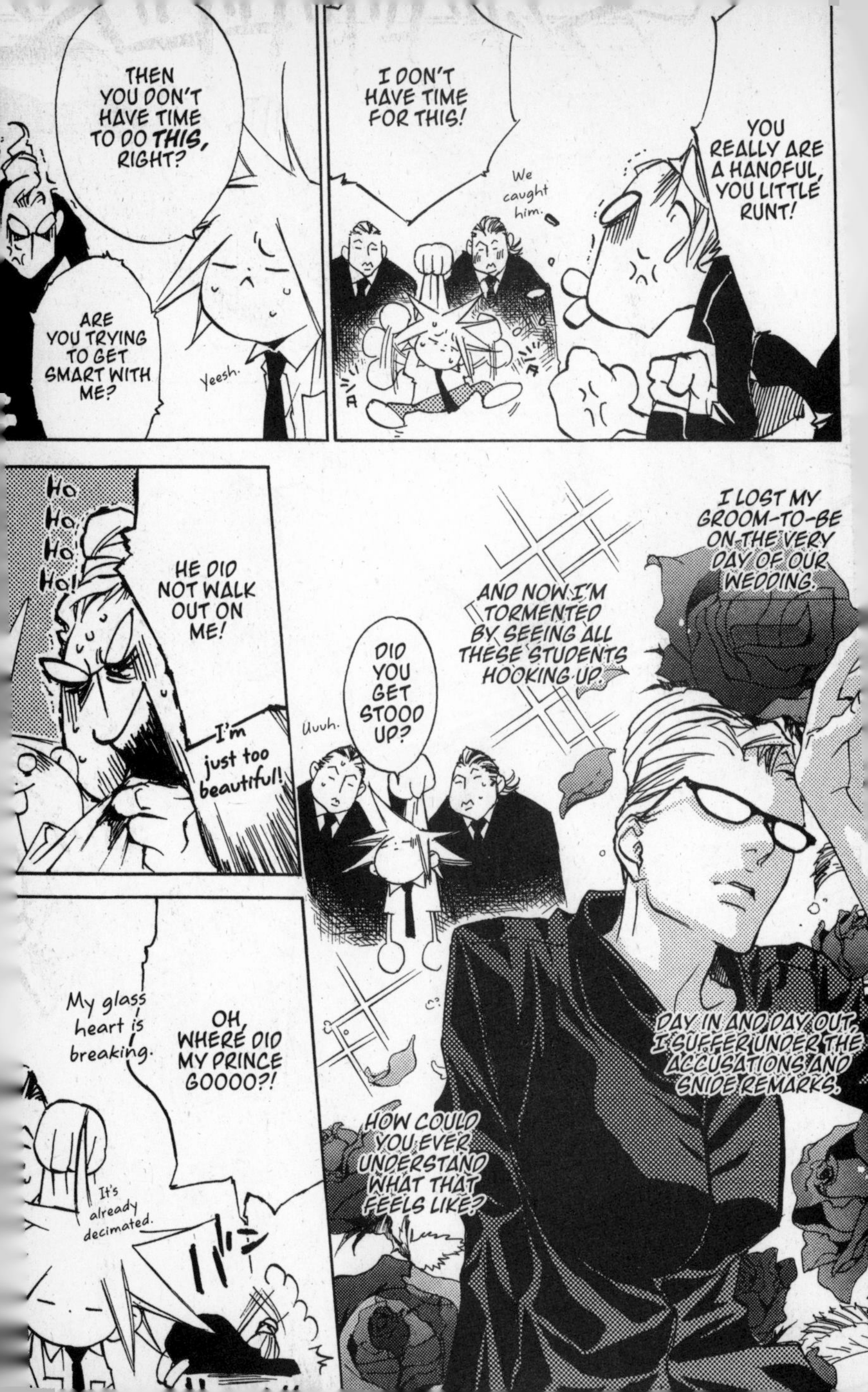
We caught him.
YOU REALLY ARE A HANDFUL, YOU LITTLE RUNT!
I DON'T HAVE TIME FOR THIS!
THEN YOU DON'T HAVE TIME TO DO **THIS**, RIGHT?
Yeesh.
ARE YOU TRYING TO GET SMART WITH ME?
I LOST MY GROOM-TO-BE ON THE VERY DAY OF OUR WEDDING.
AND NOW I'M TORMENTED BY SEEING ALL THESE STUDENTS HOOKING UP.
DID YOU GET STOOD UP?
Uuuh.
DAY IN AND DAY OUT, I SUFFER UNDER THE ACCUSATIONS AND SNIDE REMARKS.
HOW COULD YOU EVER UNDERSTAND WHAT THAT FEELS LIKE?
Ho Ho Ho Ho!
HE DID NOT WALK OUT ON ME!
I'm just too beautiful!
OH, WHERE DID MY PRINCE GOOOO?!
My glass heart is breaking.
It's already decimated.

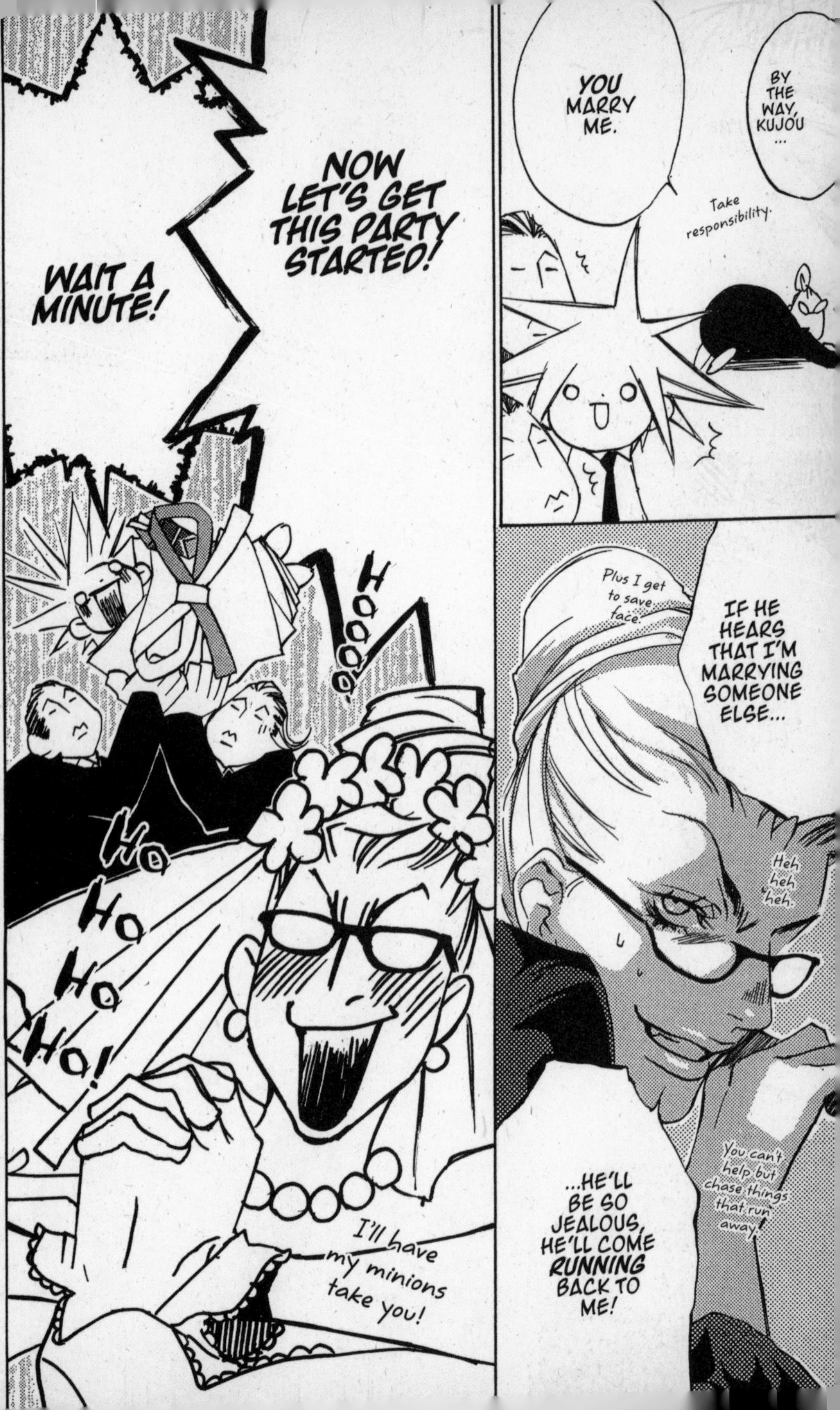

BY THE WAY, KUJOU...
YOU MARRY ME.
Take responsibility.
IF HE HEARS THAT I'M MARRYING SOMEONE ELSE...
Plus I get to save face.
Heh heh heh.
...HE'LL BE SO JEALOUS, HE'LL COME RUNNING BACK TO ME!
You can't help but chase things that run away.
NOW LET'S GET THIS PARTY STARTED!
WAIT A MINUTE!
HOOOOO
HO HO HO HO!
I'll have my minions take you!

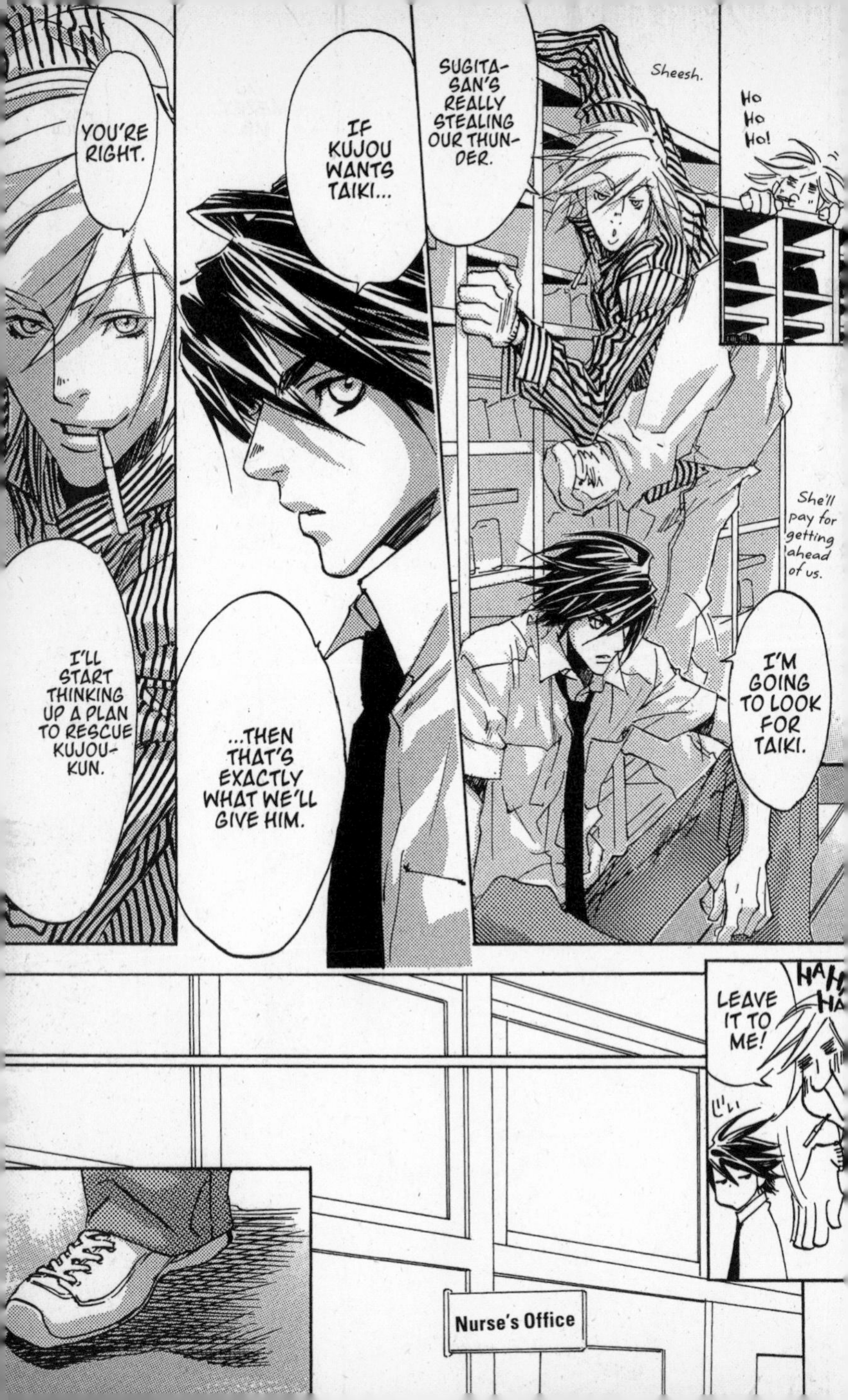

Ho Ho Ho!
Sheesh.
SUGITA-SAN'S REALLY STEALING OUR THUNDER.
She'll pay for getting ahead of us.
I'M GOING TO LOOK FOR TAIKI.
IF KUJOU WANTS TAIKI...
...THEN THAT'S EXACTLY WHAT WE'LL GIVE HIM.
YOU'RE RIGHT.
I'LL START THINKING UP A PLAN TO RESCUE KUJOU-KUN.
LEAVE IT TO ME!
Nurse's Office

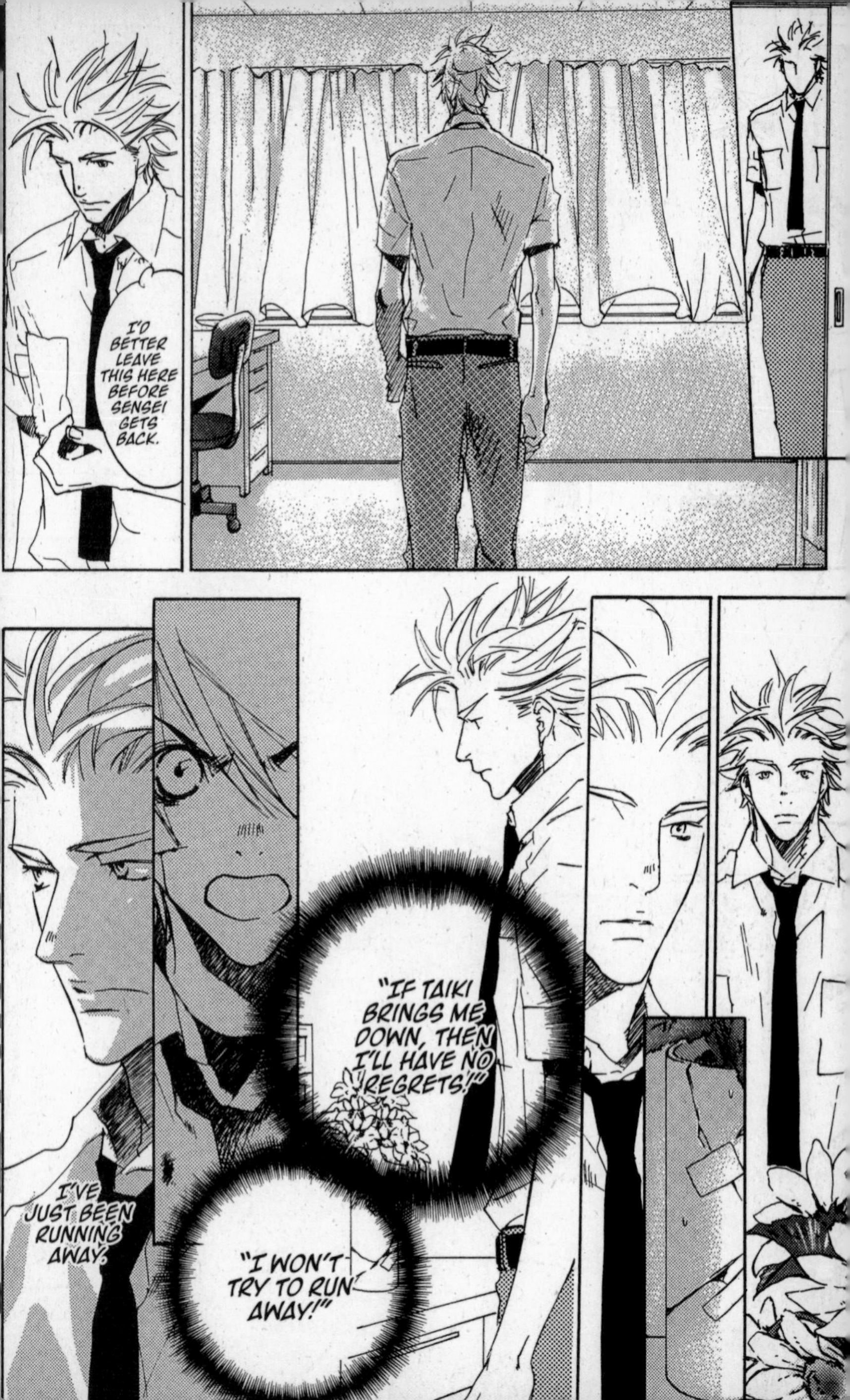
I'D BETTER LEAVE THIS HERE BEFORE SENSEI GETS BACK.
"IF TAIKI BRINGS ME DOWN, THEN I'LL HAVE NO REGRETS!"
"I WON'T TRY TO RUN AWAY!"
I'VE JUST BEEN RUNNING AWAY.

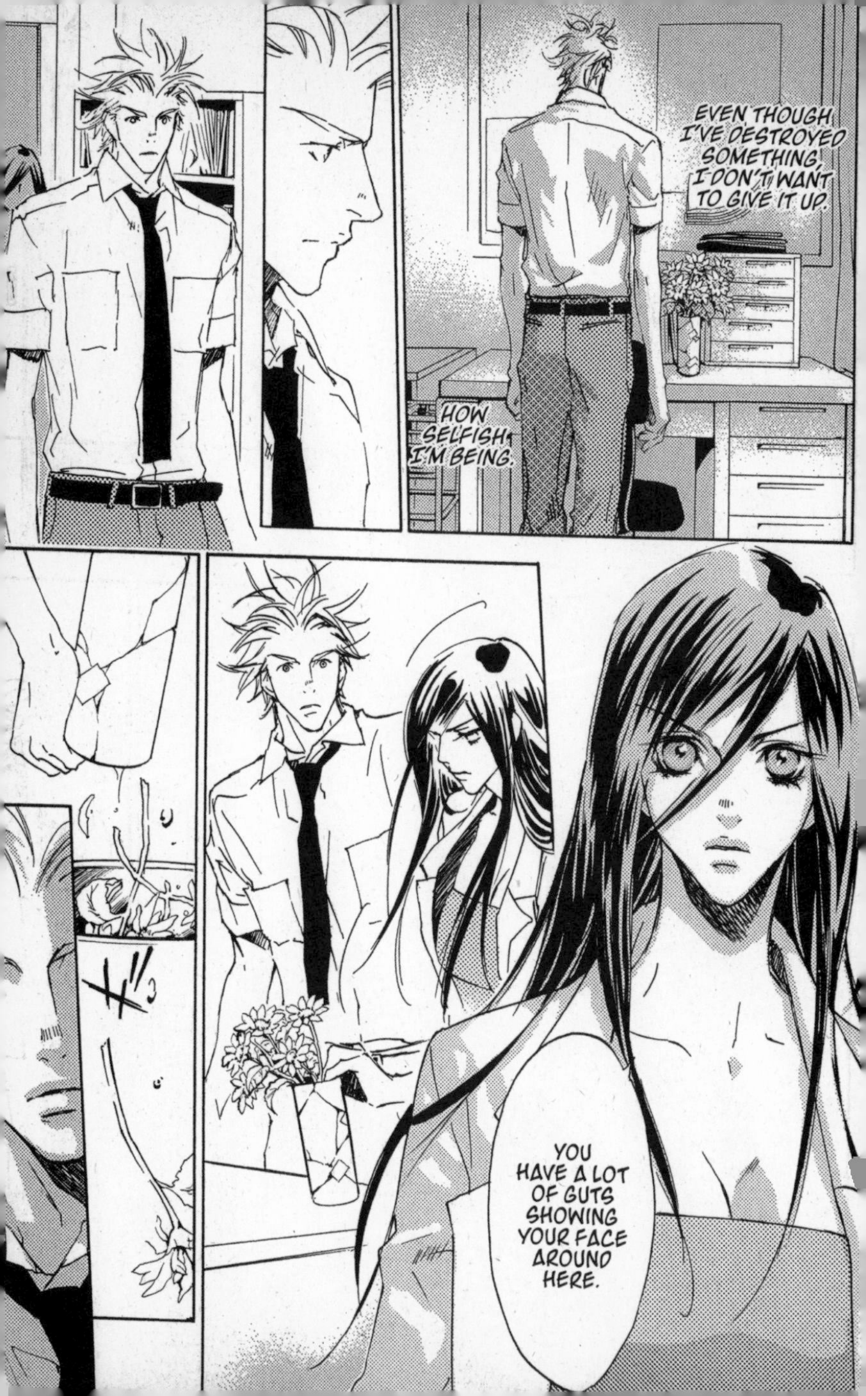
EVEN THOUGH I'VE DESTROYED SOMETHING, I DON'T WANT TO GIVE IT UP.
HOW SELFISH I'M BEING.
YOU HAVE A LOT OF GUTS SHOWING YOUR FACE AROUND HERE.

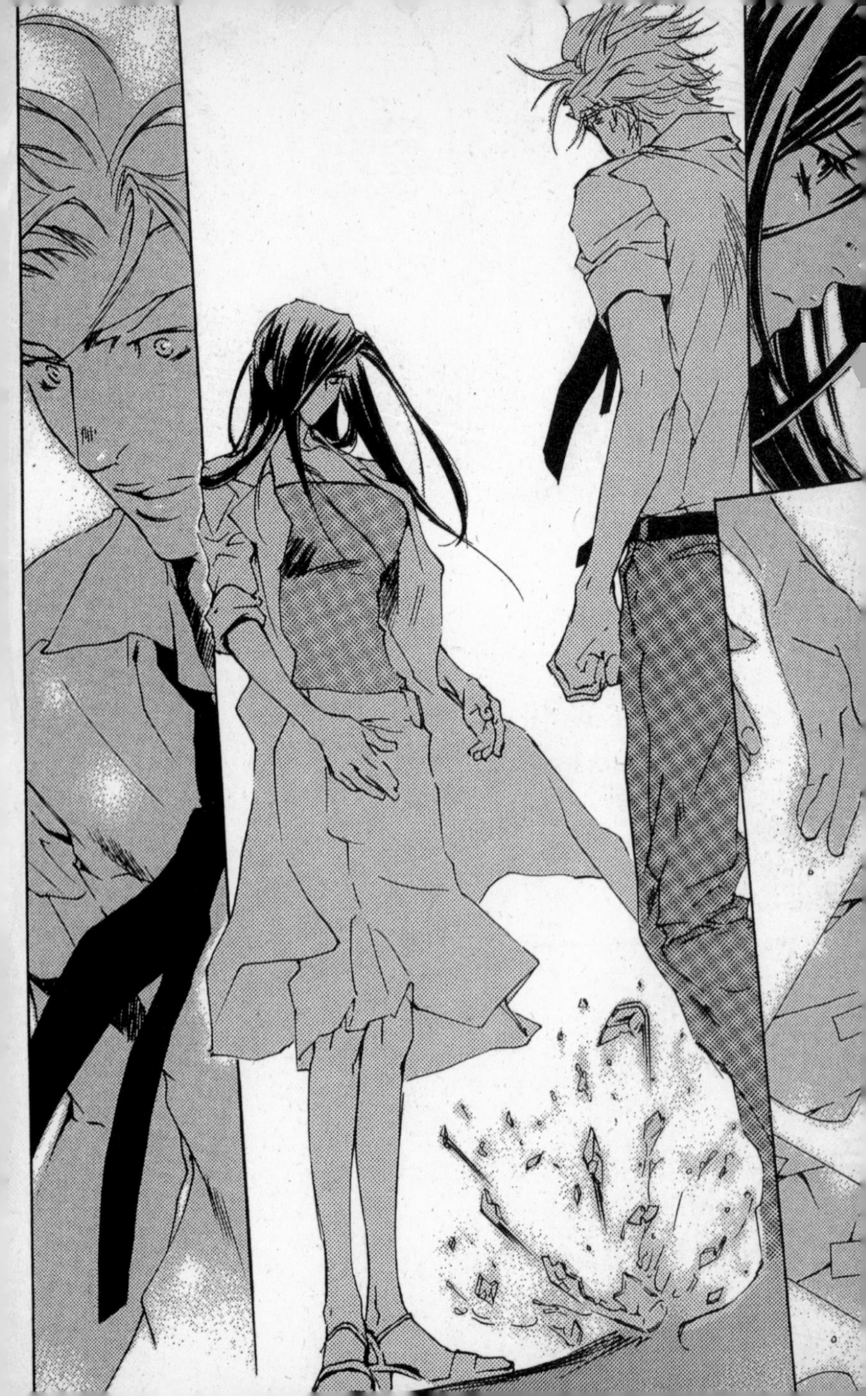

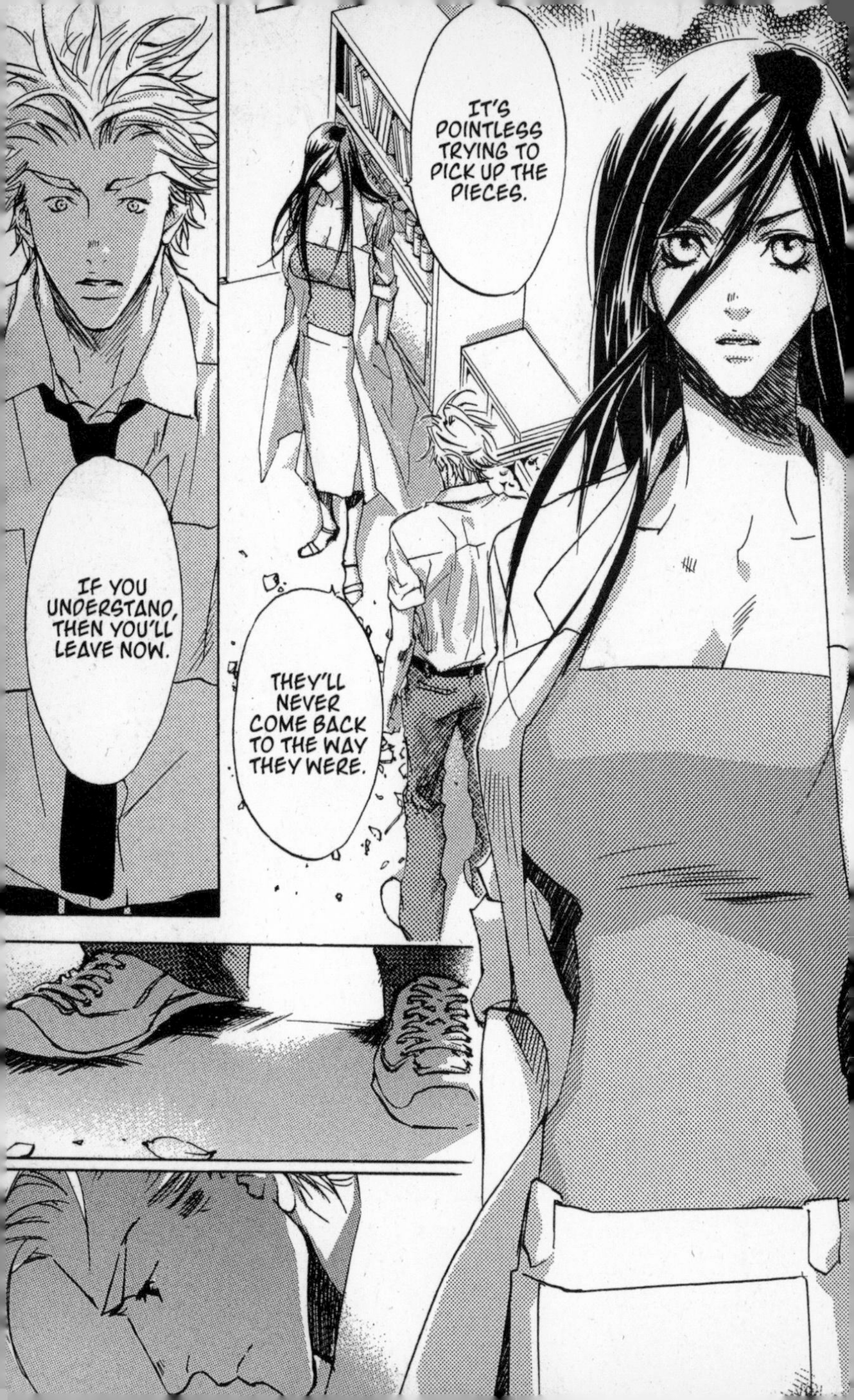
IT'S POINTLESS TRYING TO PICK UP THE PIECES.
THEY'LL NEVER COME BACK TO THE WAY THEY WERE.
IF YOU UNDERSTAND, THEN YOU'LL LEAVE NOW.

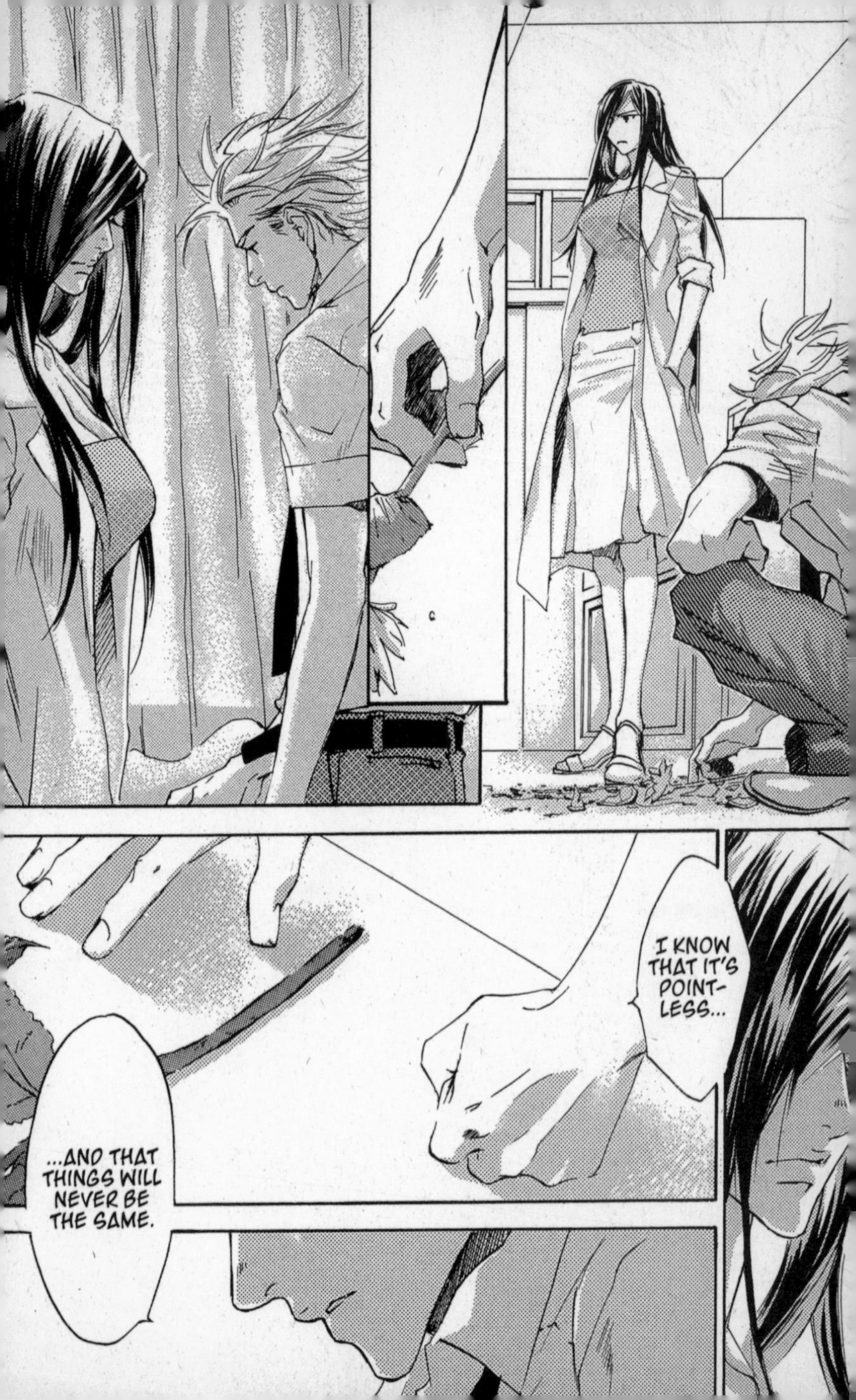
I KNOW THAT IT'S POINT-LESS...
...AND THAT THINGS WILL NEVER BE THE SAME.

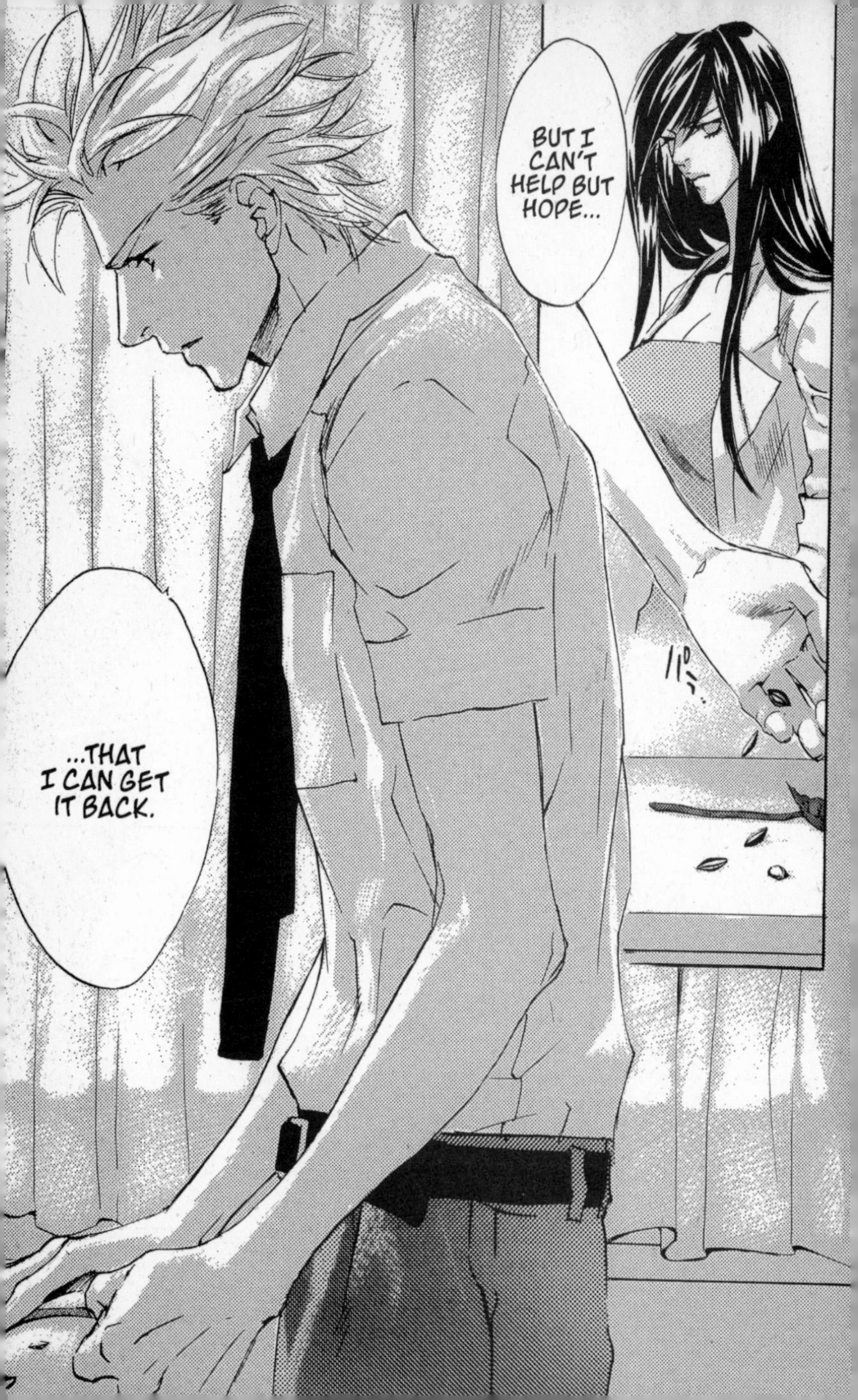
BUT I CAN'T HELP BUT HOPE...
...THAT I CAN GET IT BACK.

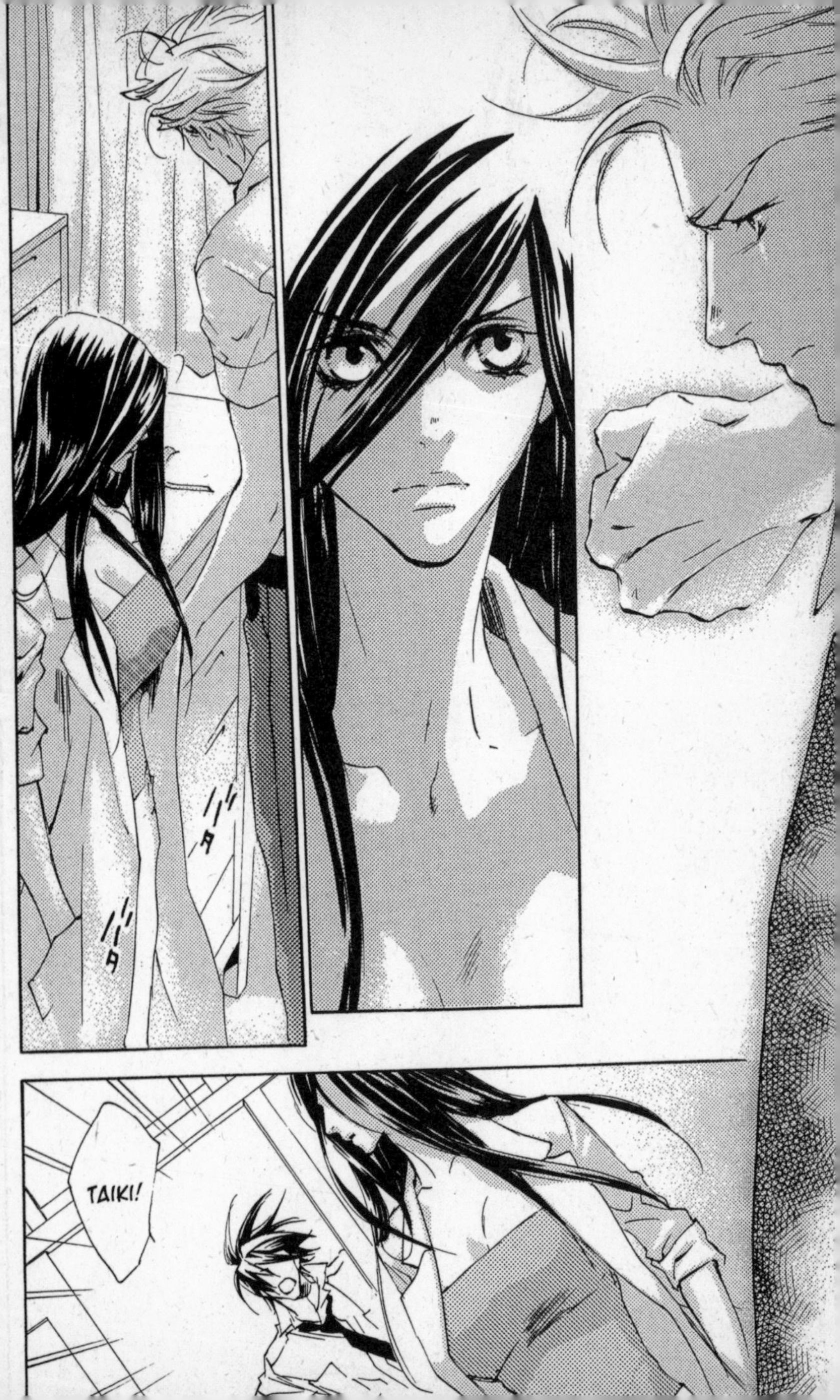
TAIKI!

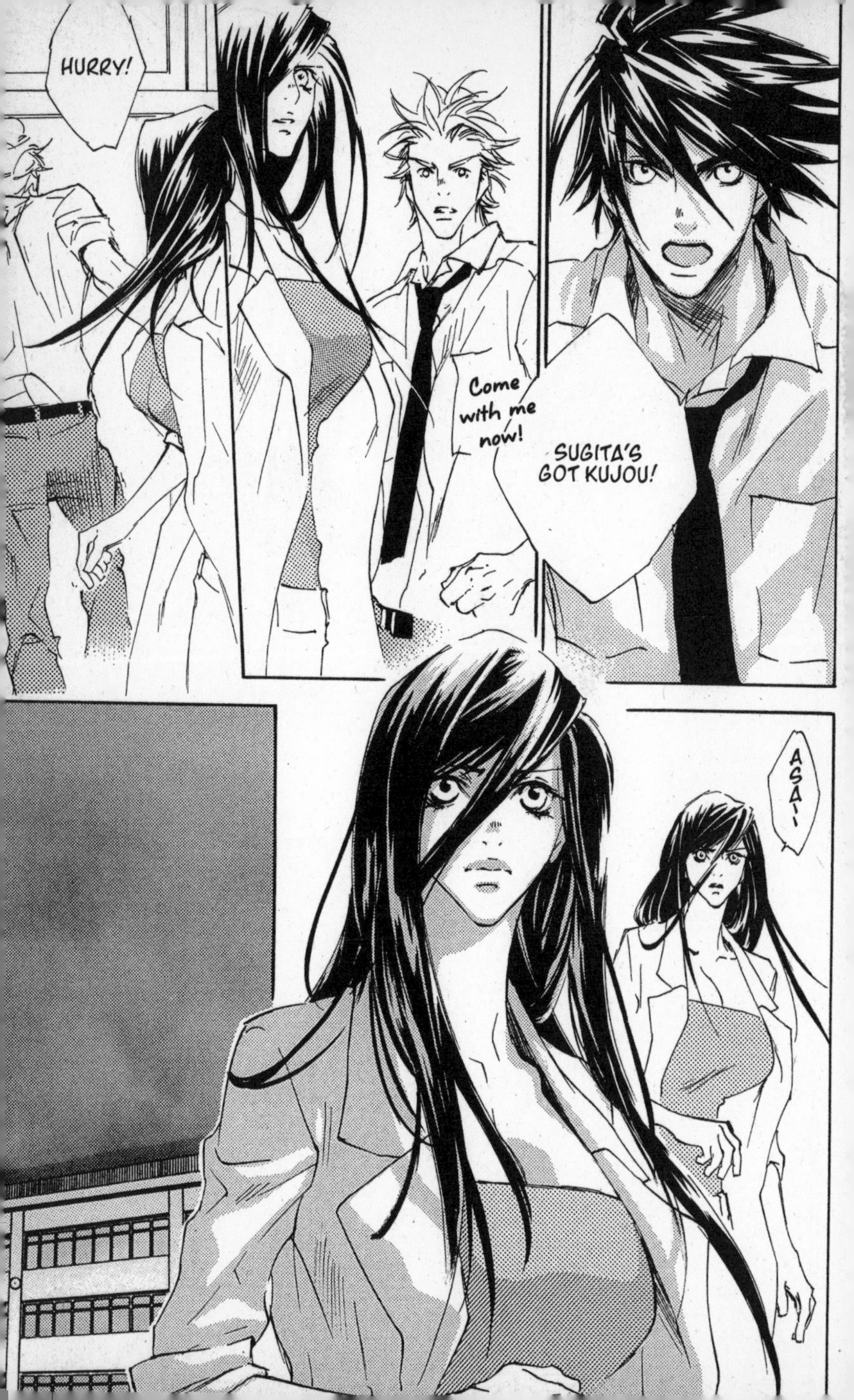
SUGITA'S GOT KUJOU!
Come with me now!
HURRY!
ASAI...

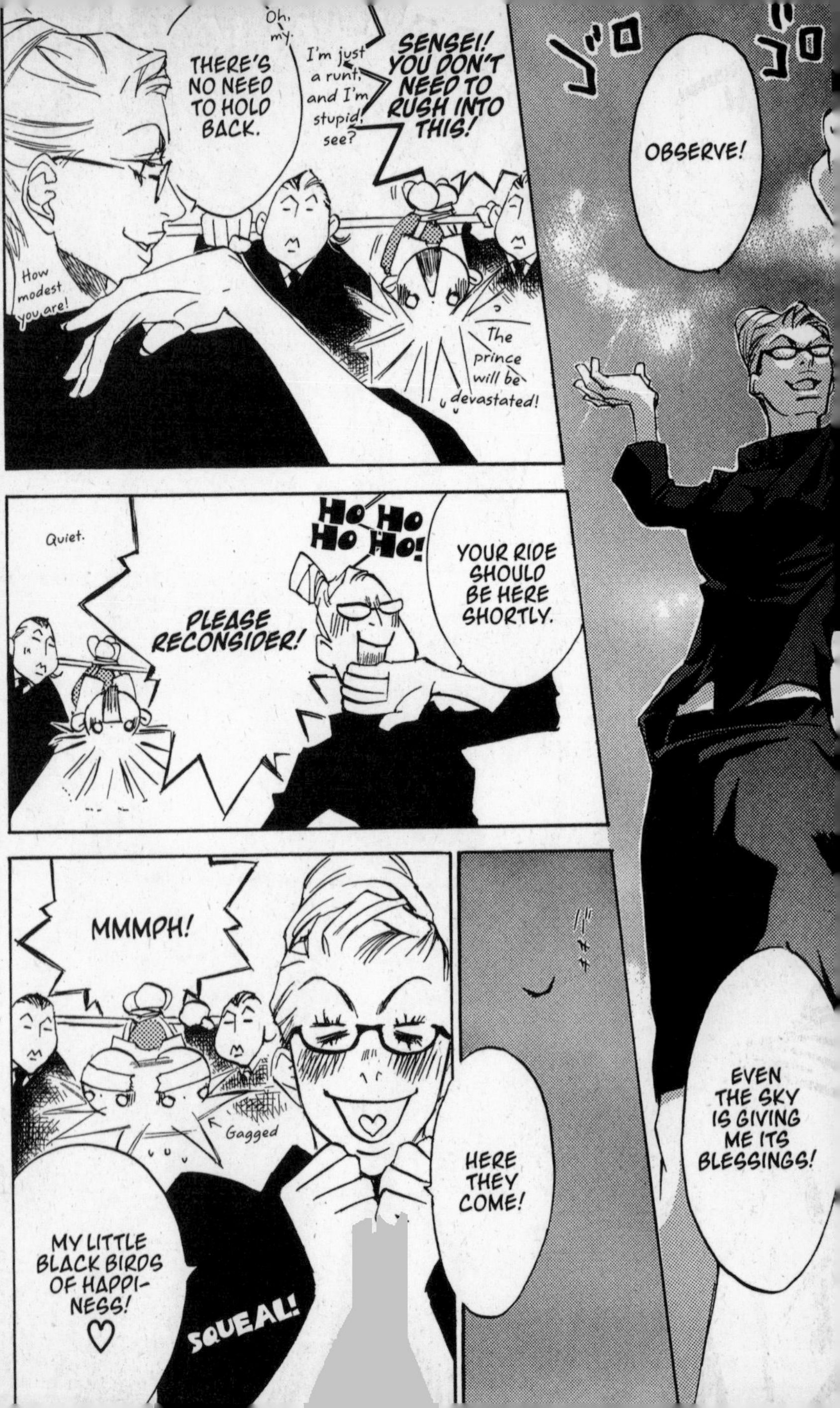
ゴロ
ゴロ
OBSERVE!
EVEN THE SKY IS GIVING ME ITS BLESSINGS!
SENSEI! YOU DON'T NEED TO RUSH INTO THIS!
I'm just a runt, and I'm stupid! see?
Oh, my.
THERE'S NO NEED TO HOLD BACK.
How modest you are!
The prince will be devastated!
YOUR RIDE SHOULD BE HERE SHORTLY.
HO HO HO HO!
PLEASE RECONSIDER!
Quiet.
HERE THEY COME!
MMMPH!
Gagged
MY LITTLE BLACK BIRDS OF HAPPI-NESS! ♡
SQUEAL!

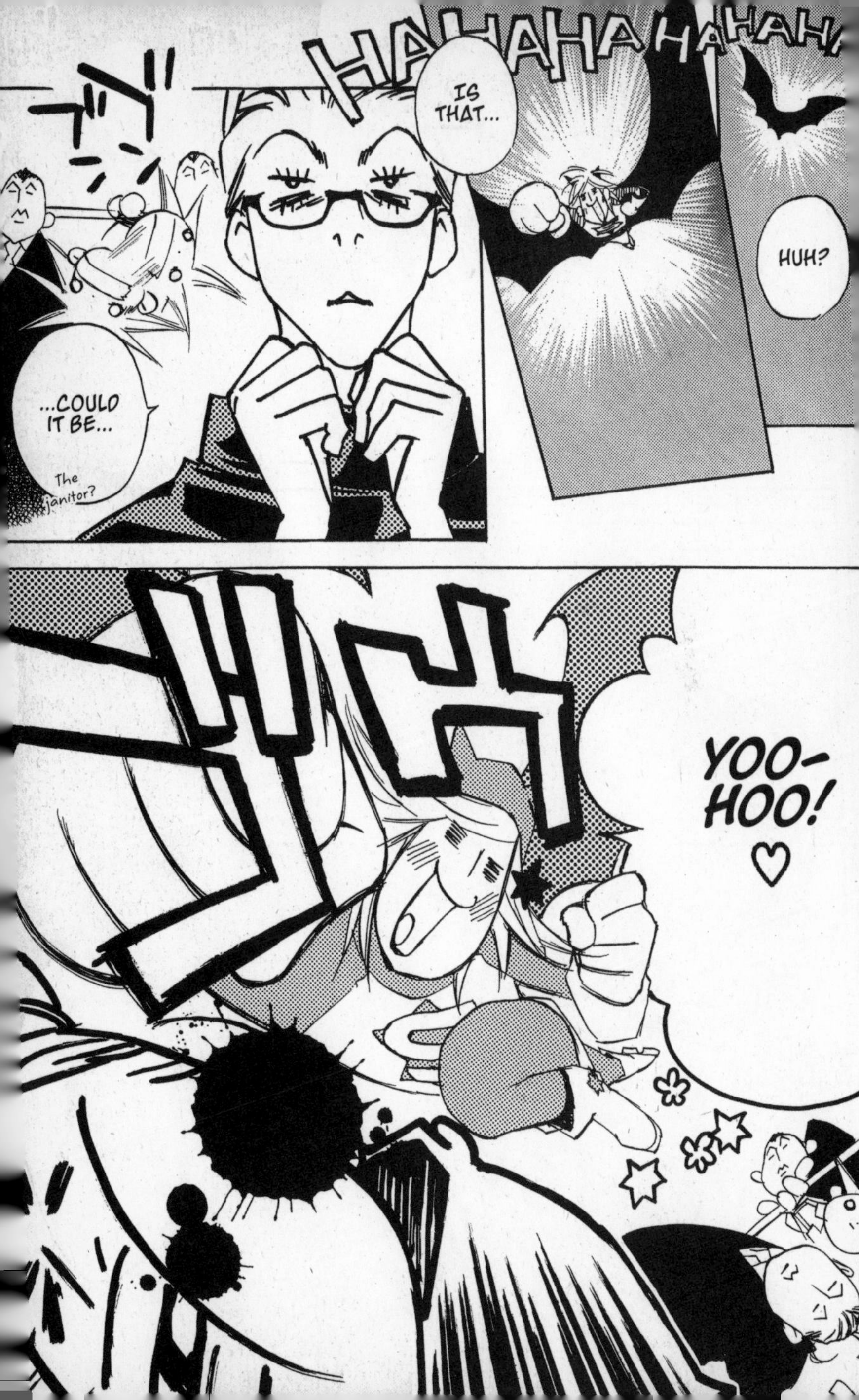
HUH?
HAHAHAHAHAHA
IS THAT...
...COULD IT BE...
The janitor?
YOO-HOO! ♥

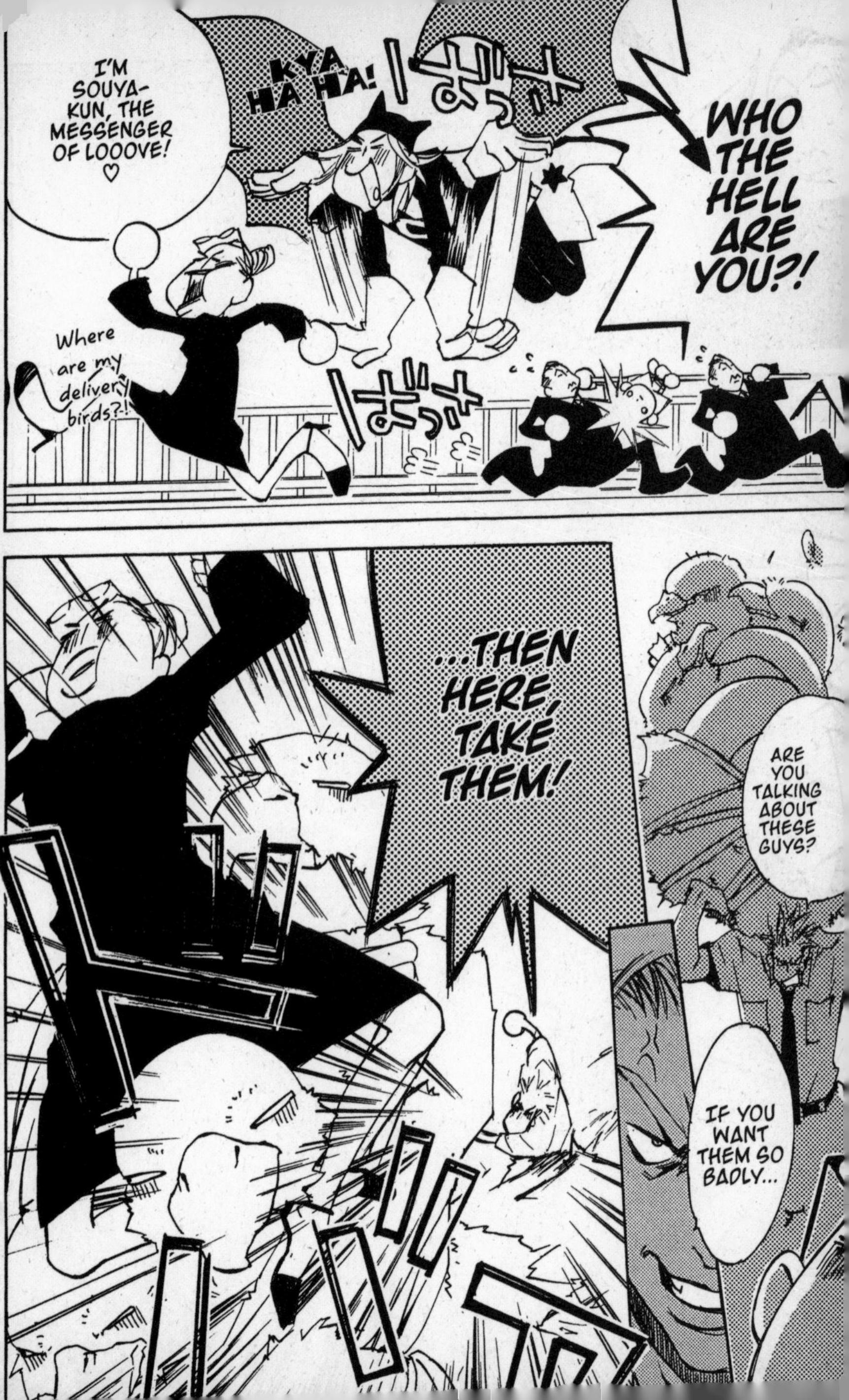
WHO THE HELL ARE YOU?!
KYA HA HA!
I'M SOUYA-KUN, THE MESSENGER OF LOOOVE! ♡
Where are my delivery birds?!
ARE YOU TALKING ABOUT THESE GUYS?
IF YOU WANT THEM SO BADLY...
...THEN HERE, TAKE THEM!

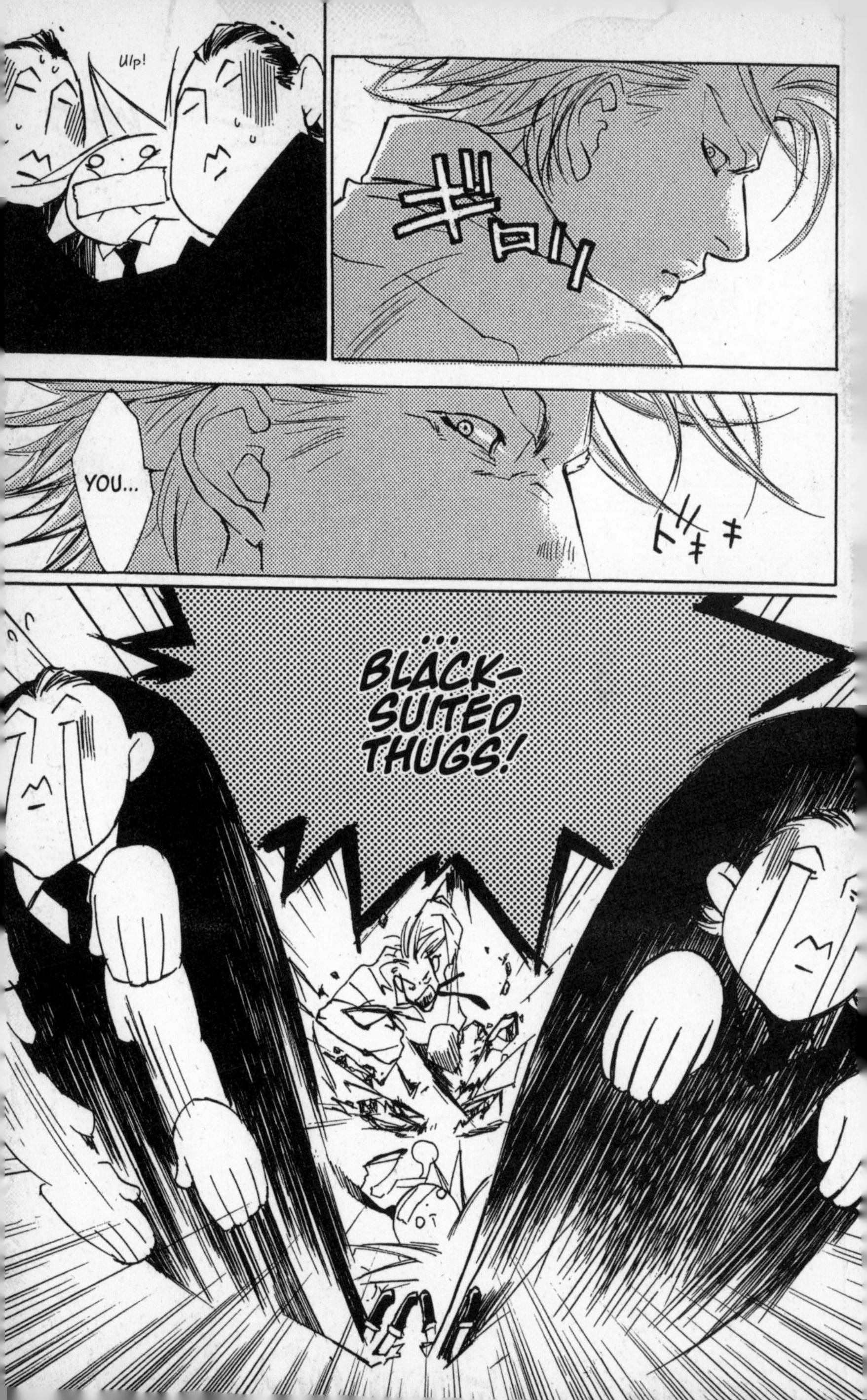
ギロッ
Ulp!
YOU...
ドキ
BLACK-SUITED THUGS!

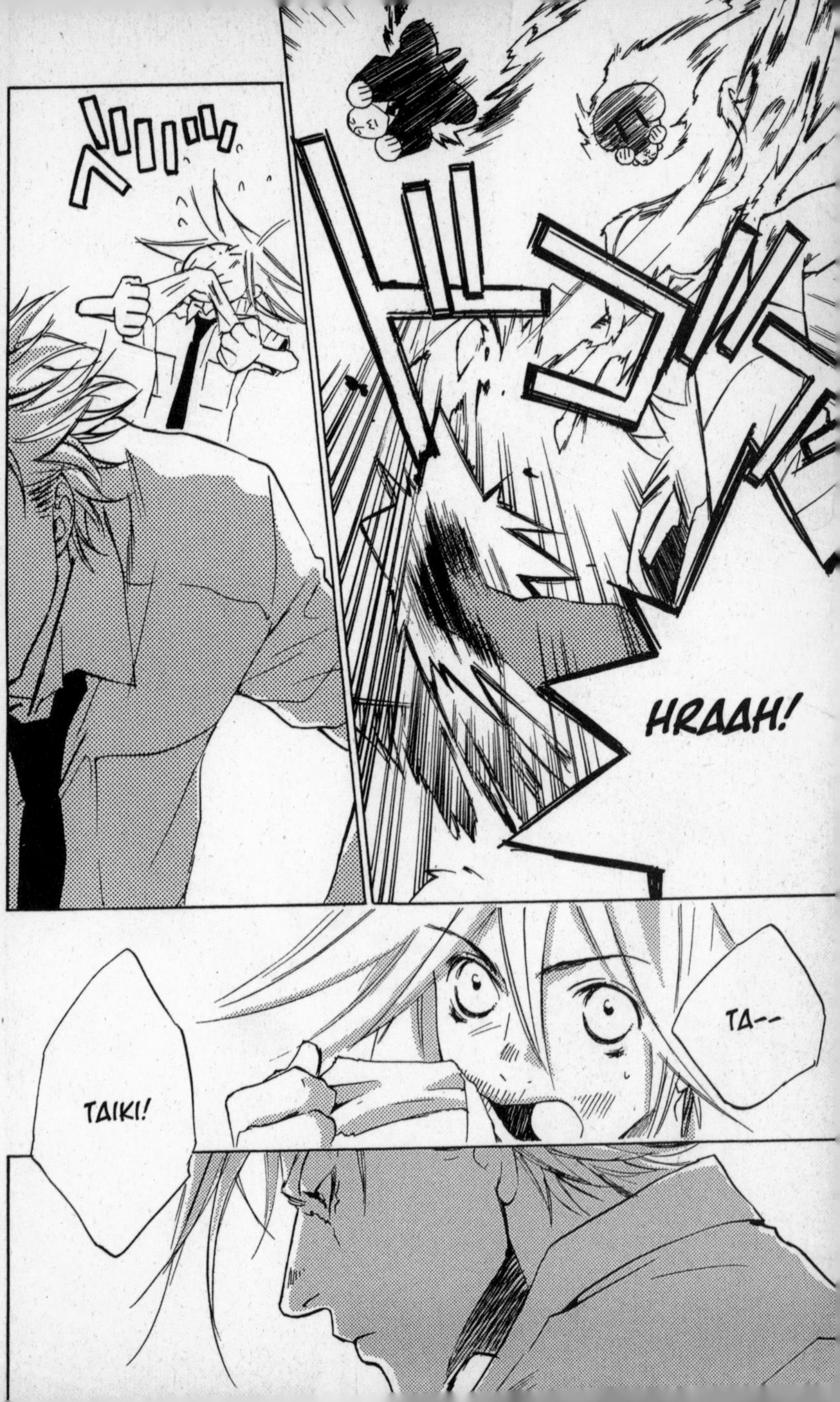
HRAAH!
TA--
TAIKI!

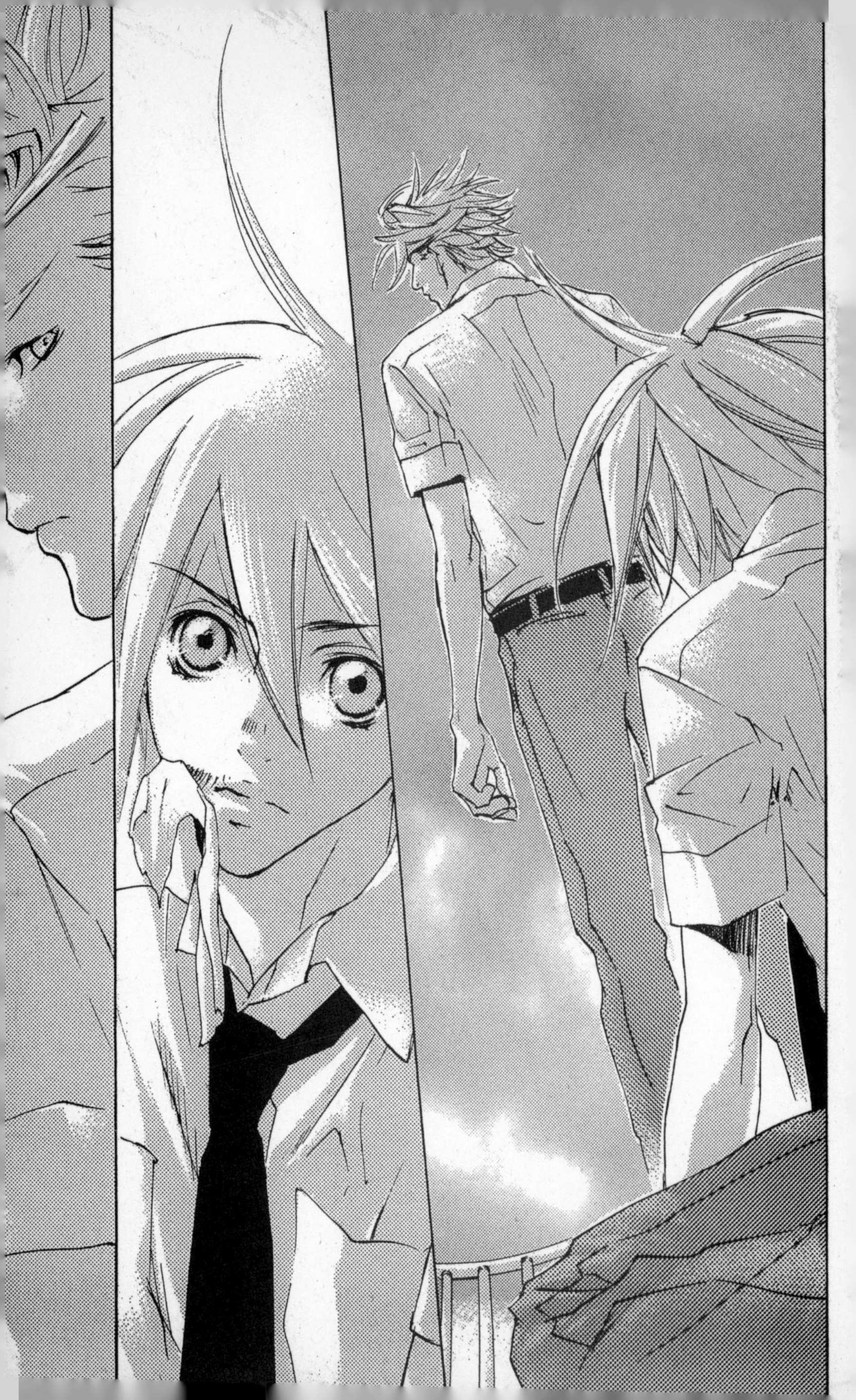

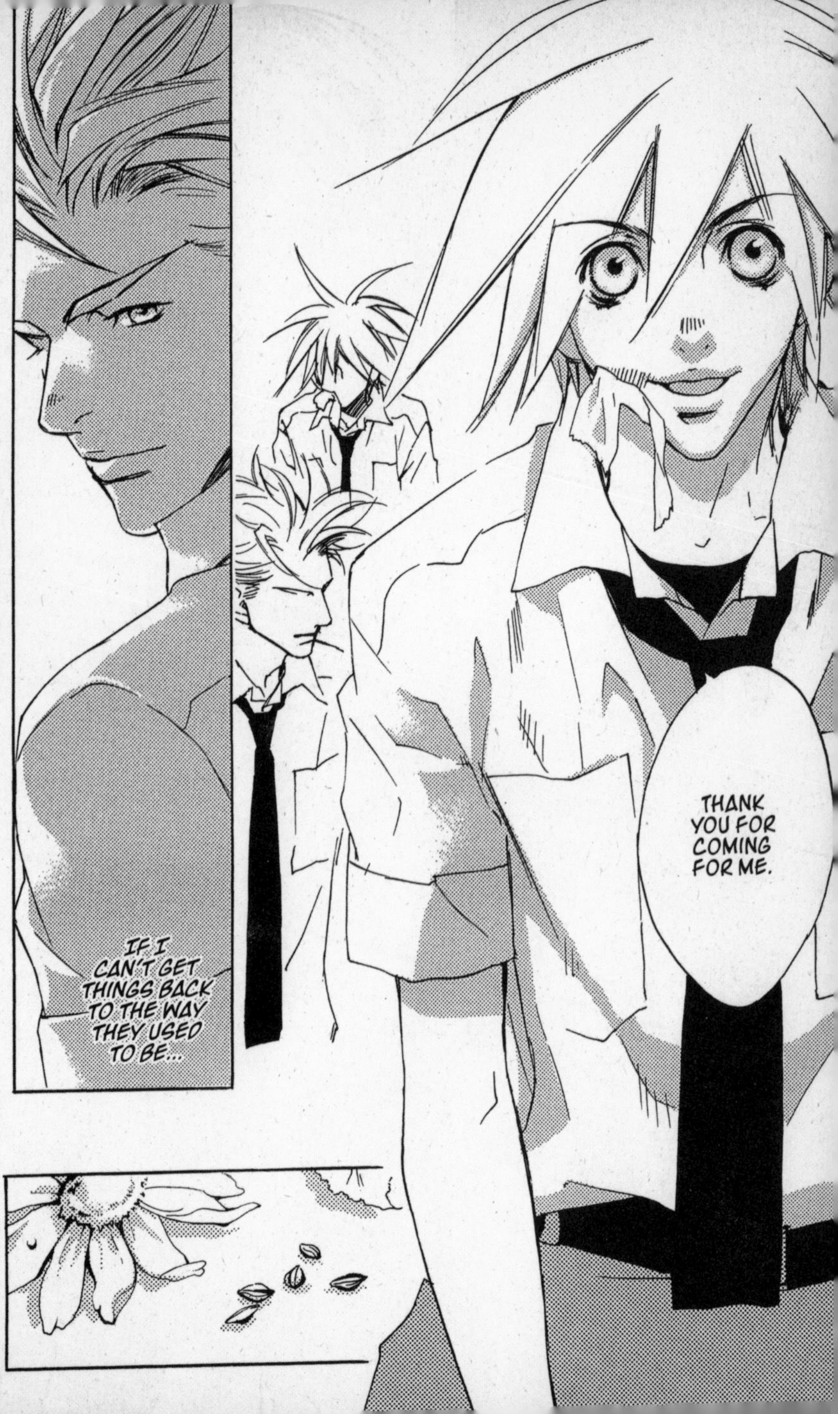
THANK YOU FOR COMING FOR ME.
IF I CAN'T GET THINGS BACK TO THE WAY THEY USED TO BE...

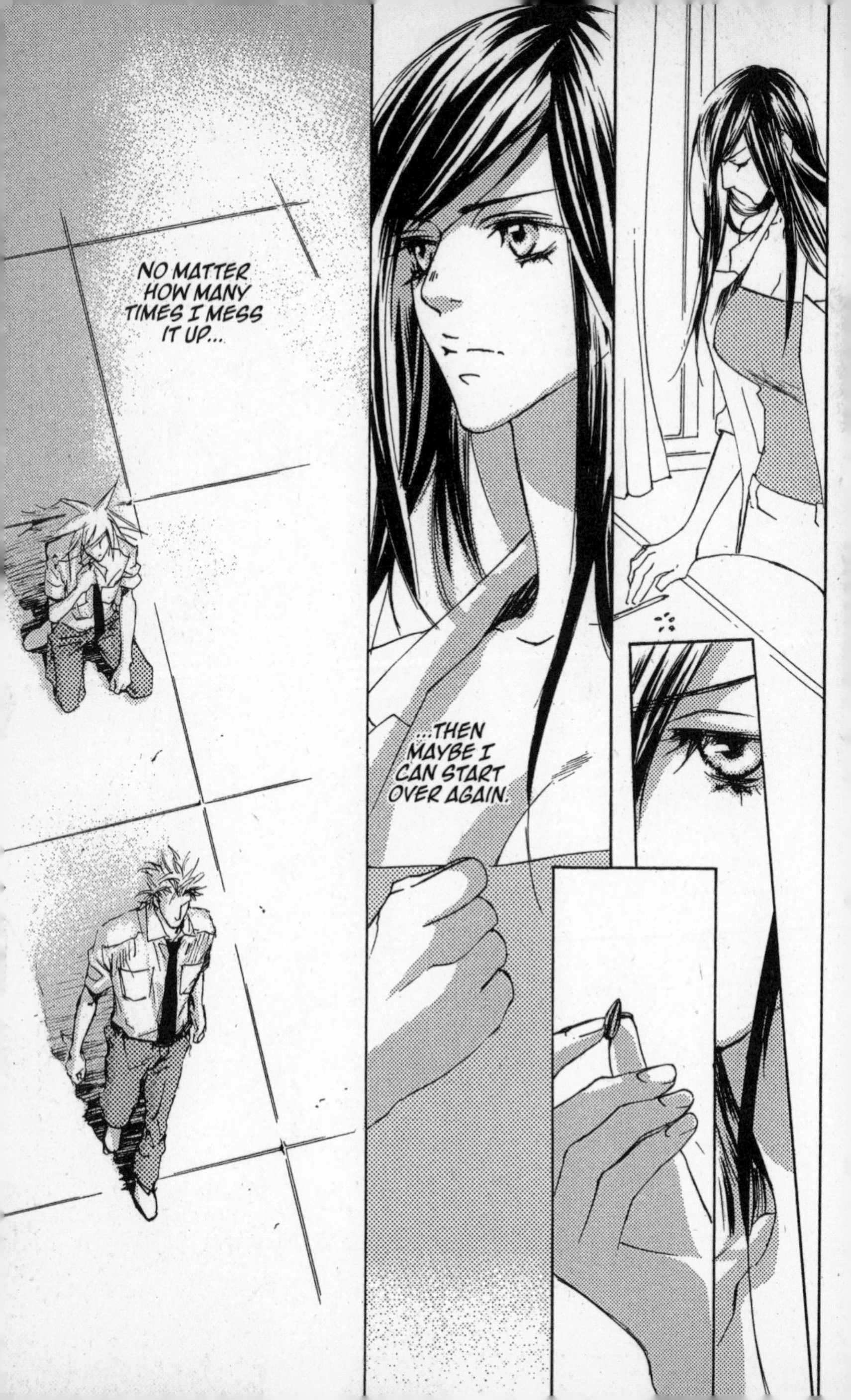
NO MATTER HOW MANY TIMES I MESS IT UP...
...THEN MAYBE I CAN START OVER AGAIN.

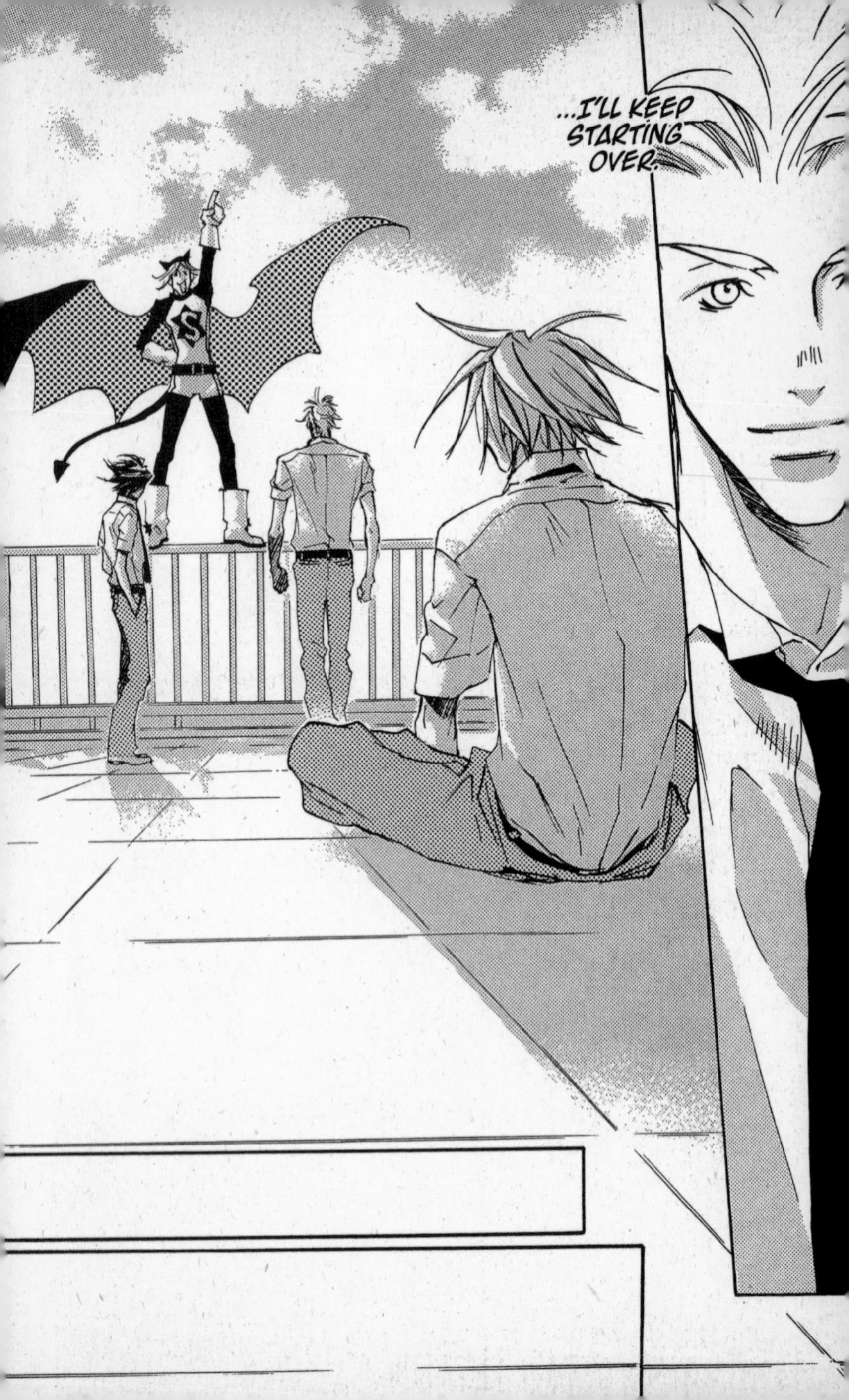
...I'LL KEEP STARTING OVER.

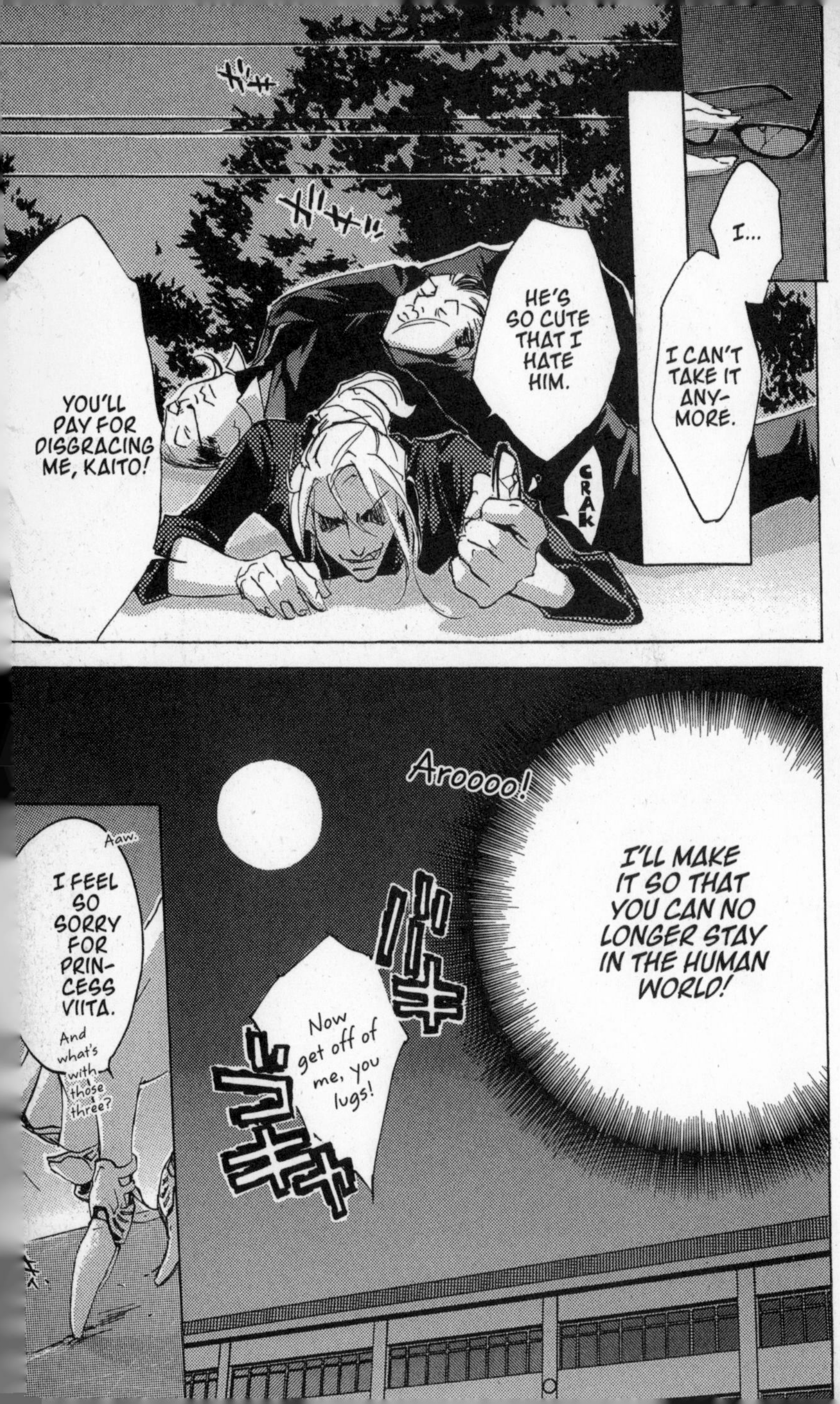
I...
I CAN'T TAKE IT ANYMORE.
HE'S SO CUTE THAT I HATE HIM.
CRAK
YOU'LL PAY FOR DISGRACING ME, KAITO!
Aroooo!
I'LL MAKE IT SO THAT YOU CAN NO LONGER STAY IN THE HUMAN WORLD!
Now get off of me, you lugs!
Aaw.
I FEEL SO SORRY FOR PRINCESS VIITA.
And what's with those three?

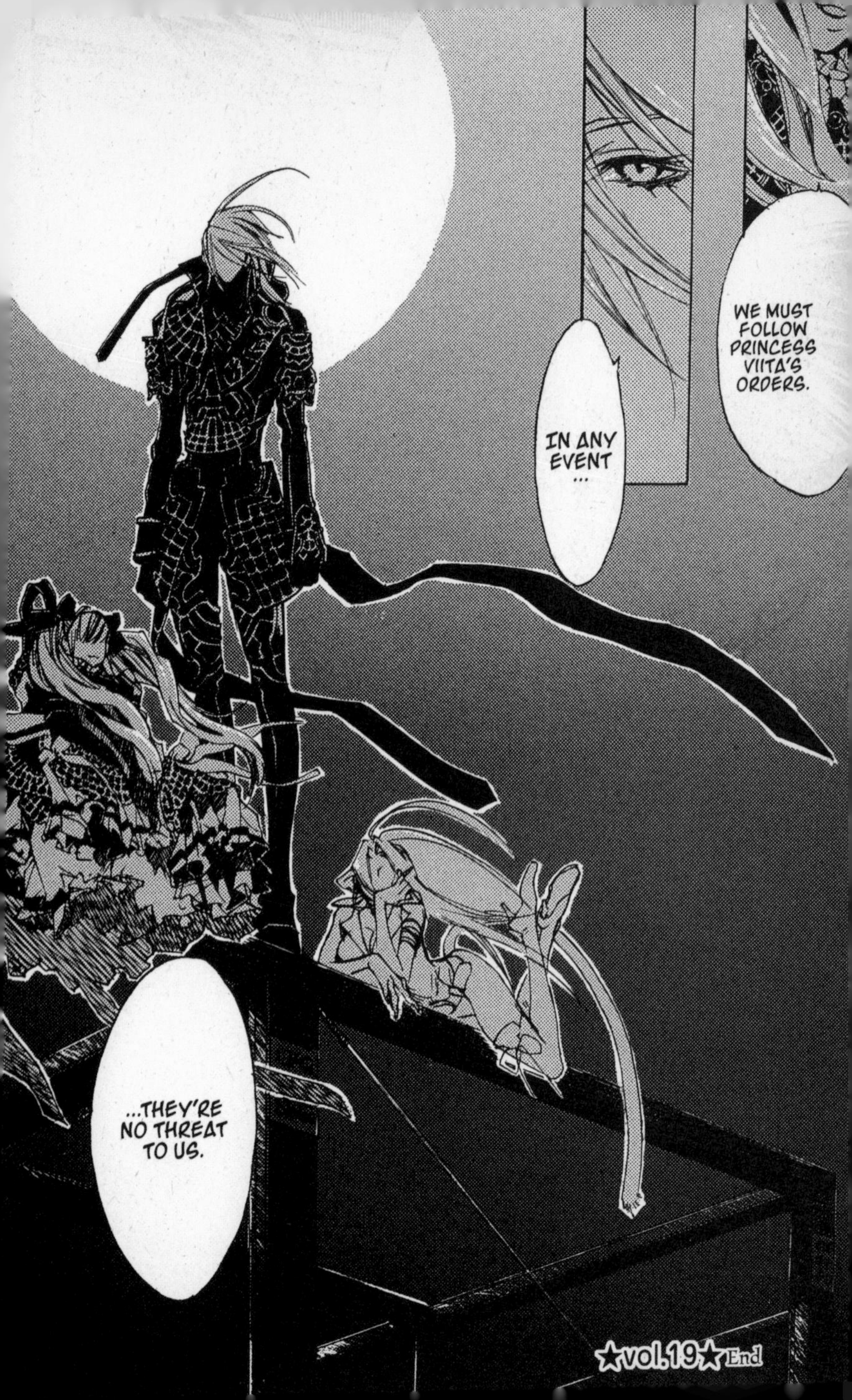
WE MUST FOLLOW PRINCESS VIITA'S ORDERS.
IN ANY EVENT...
...THEY'RE NO THREAT TO US.
★vol.19★ End

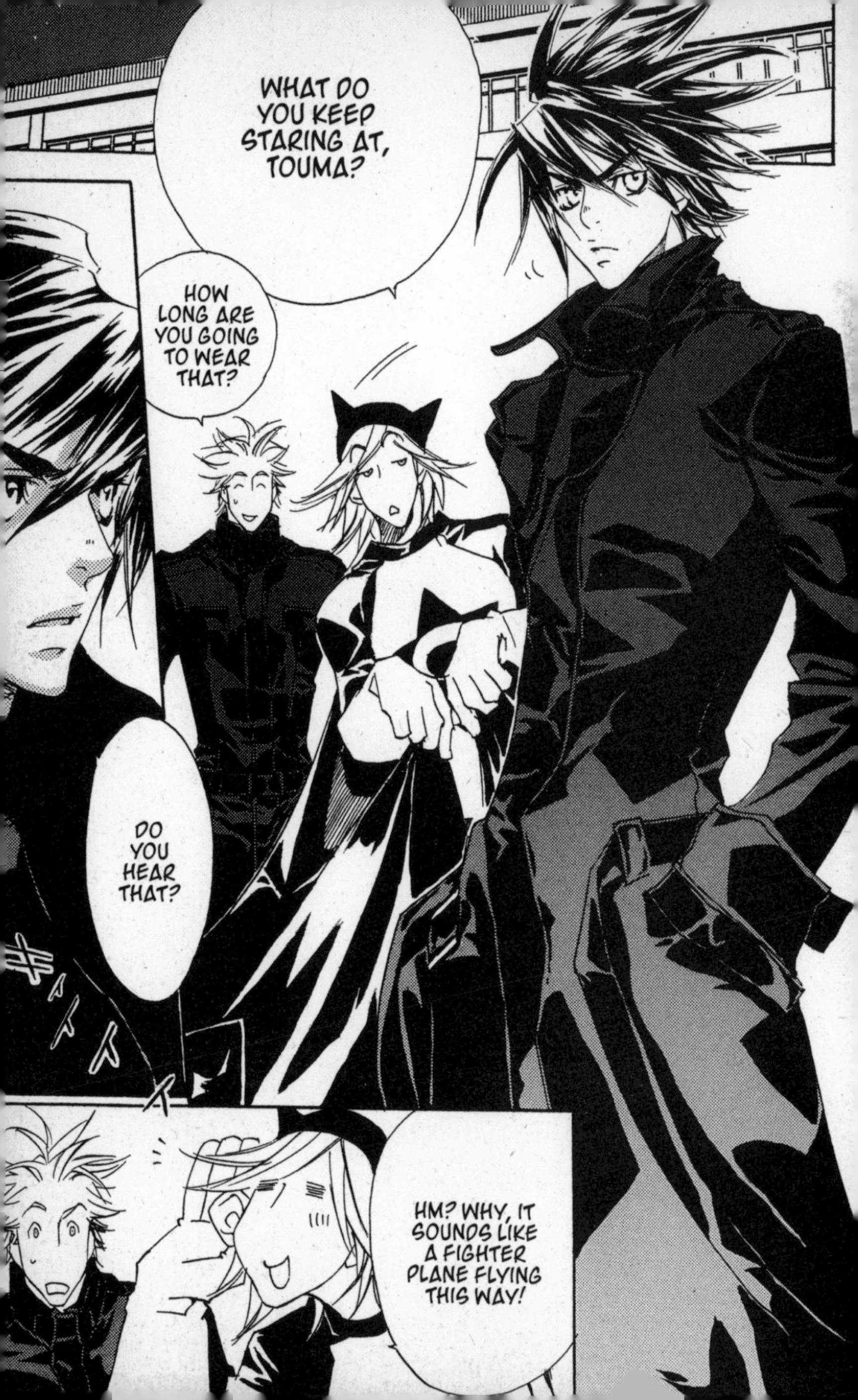
WHAT DO YOU KEEP STARING AT, TOUMA?
HOW LONG ARE YOU GOING TO WEAR THAT?
DO YOU HEAR THAT?
HM? WHY, IT SOUNDS LIKE A FIGHTER PLANE FLYING THIS WAY!

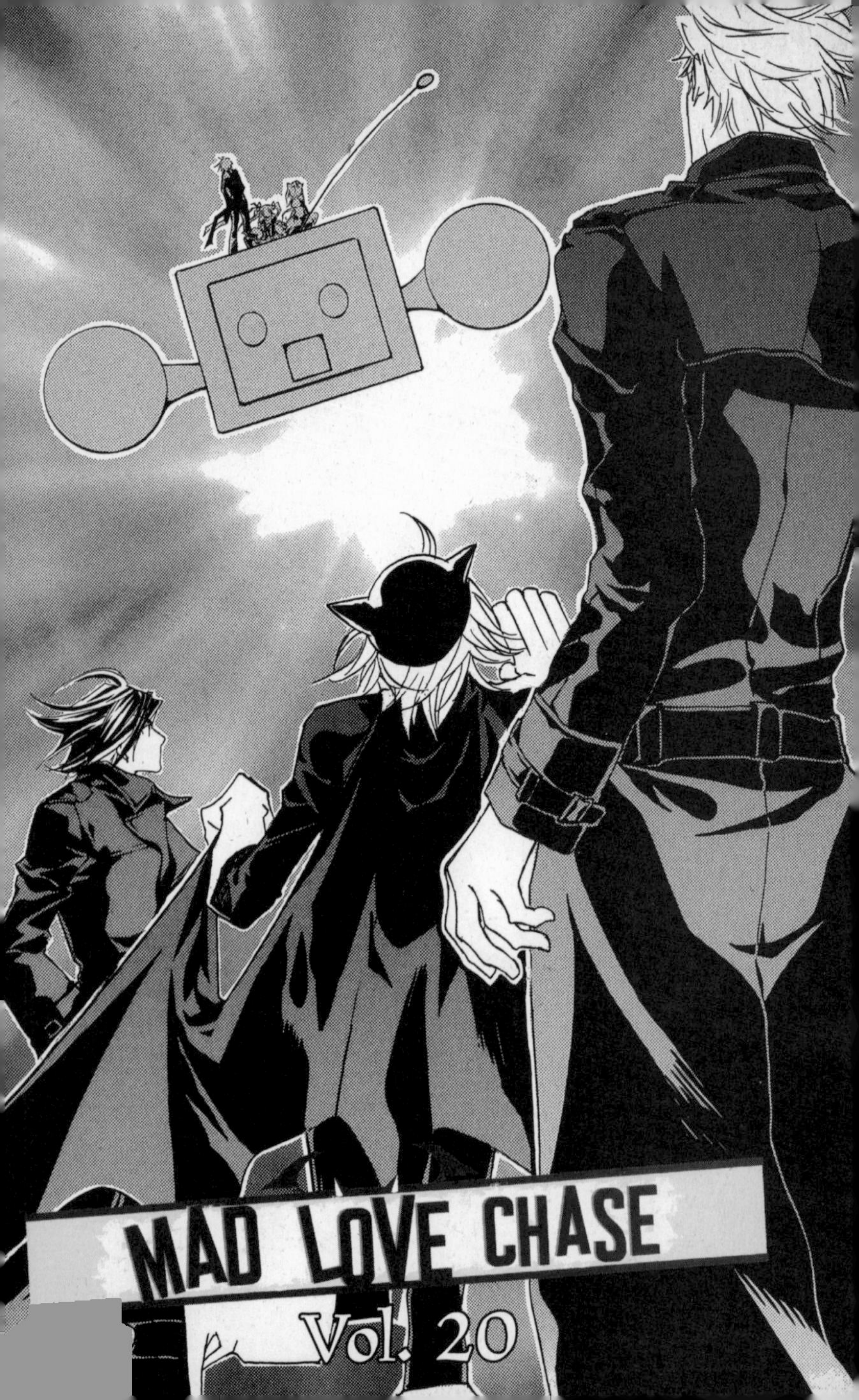
MAD LOVE CHASE
Vol. 20

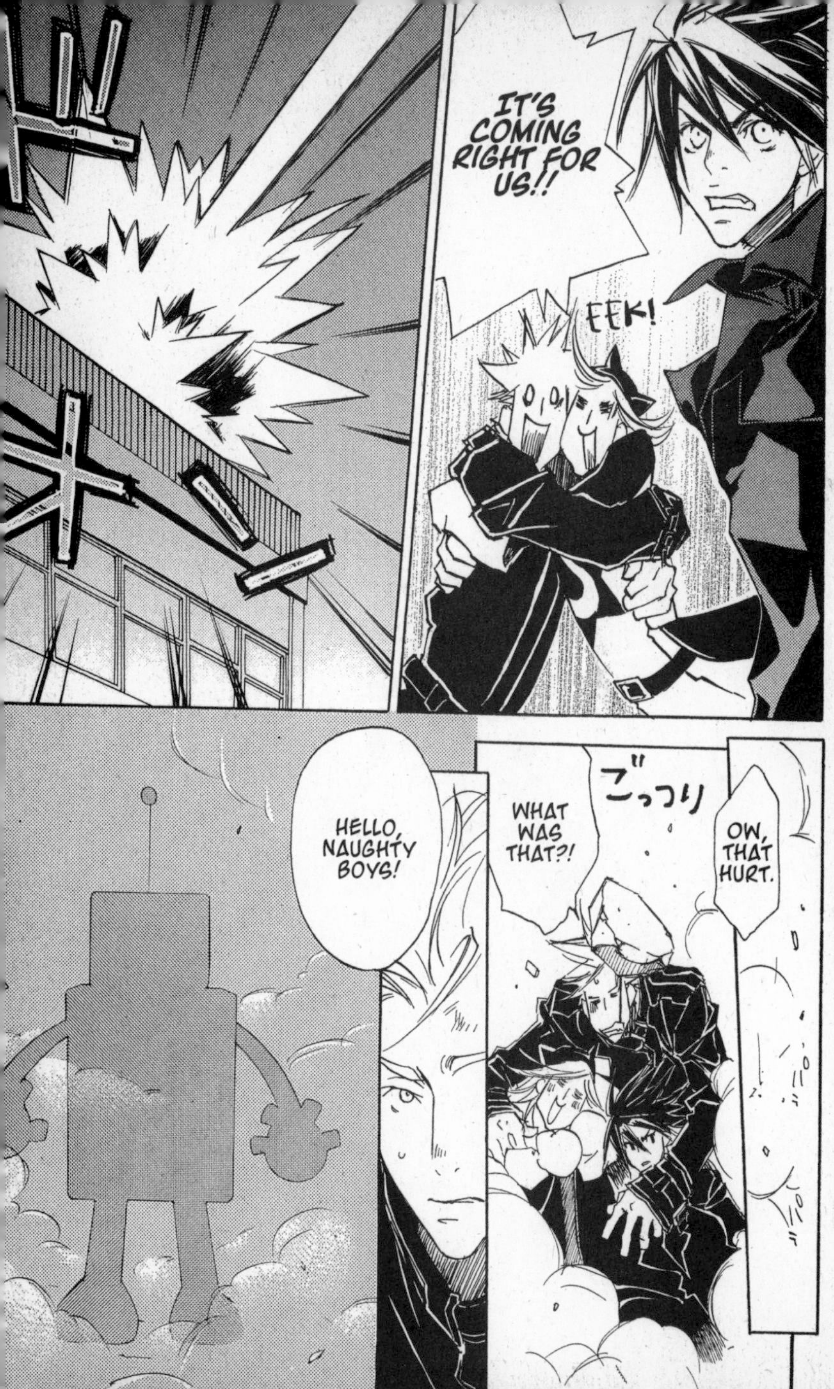
IT'S COMING RIGHT FOR US!!
EEK!
OW, THAT HURT.
ごっつり
WHAT WAS THAT?!
HELLO, NAUGHTY BOYS!

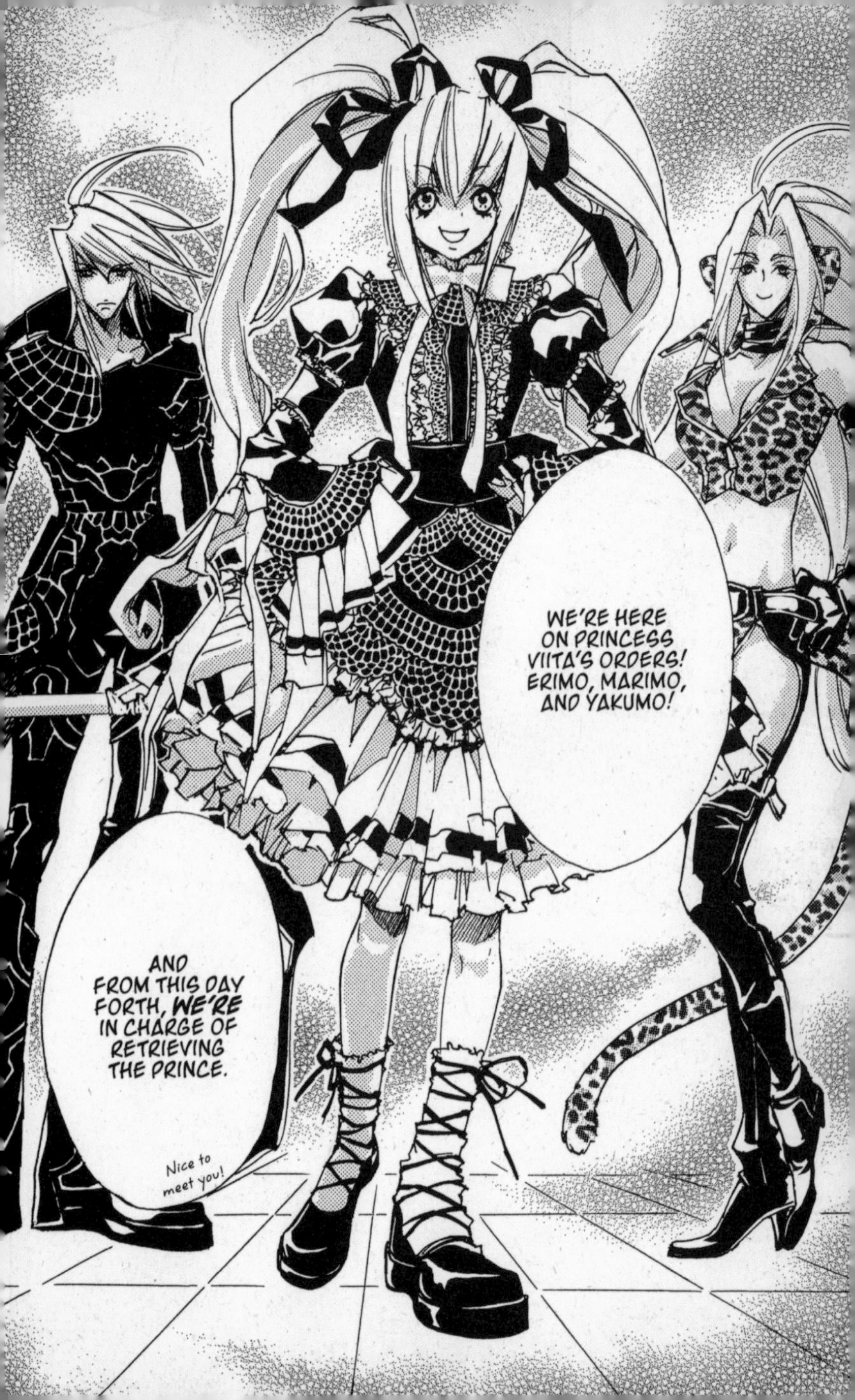
WE'RE HERE ON PRINCESS VIITA'S ORDERS! ERIMO, MARIMO, AND YAKUMO!
AND FROM THIS DAY FORTH, **WE'RE** IN CHARGE OF RETRIEVING THE PRINCE.
Nice to meet you!

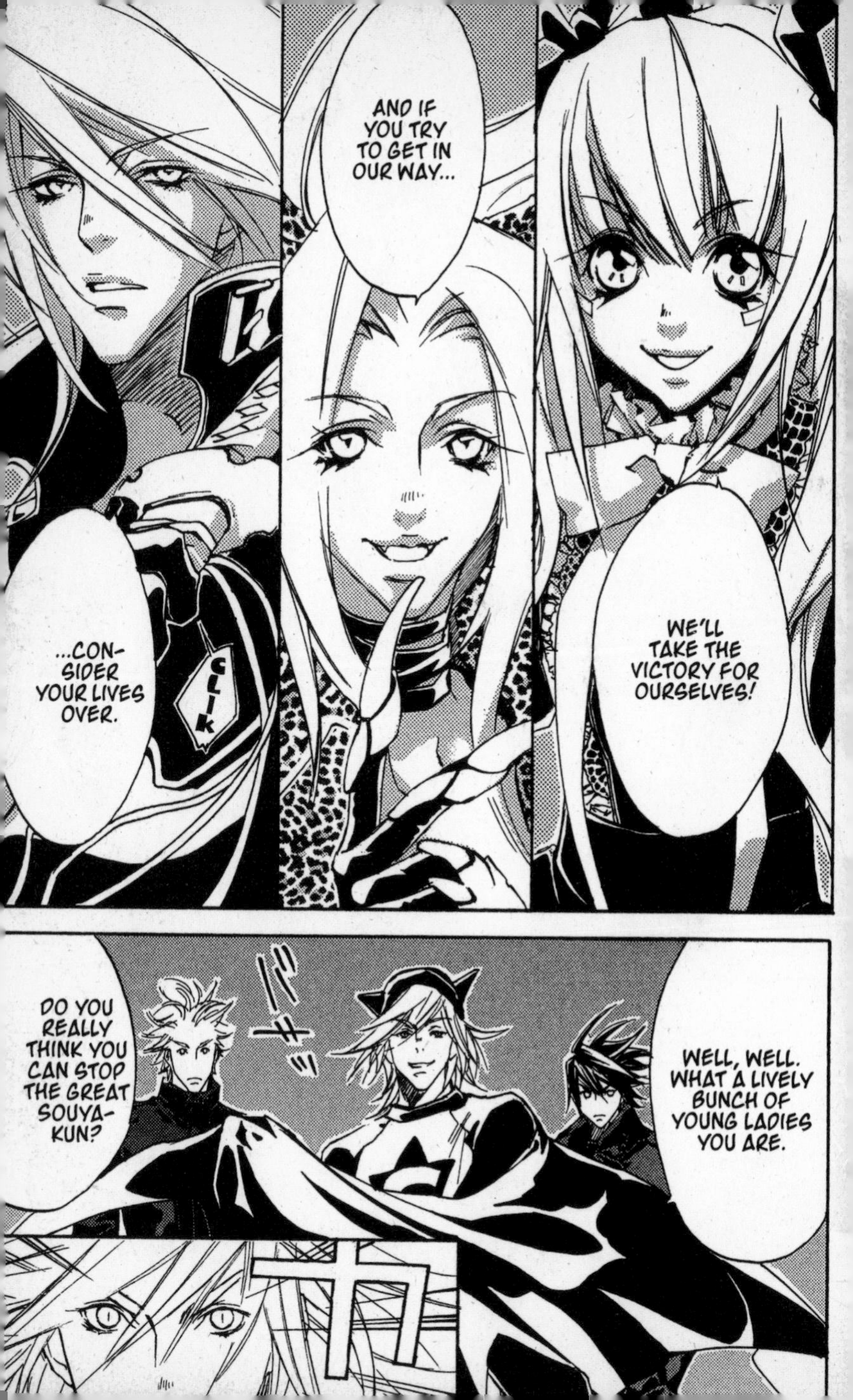
WE'LL TAKE THE VICTORY FOR OURSELVES!
AND IF YOU TRY TO GET IN OUR WAY...
...CON-SIDER YOUR LIVES OVER.
CLIK
WELL, WELL. WHAT A LIVELY BUNCH OF YOUNG LADIES YOU ARE.
DO YOU REALLY THINK YOU CAN STOP THE GREAT SOUYA-KUN?

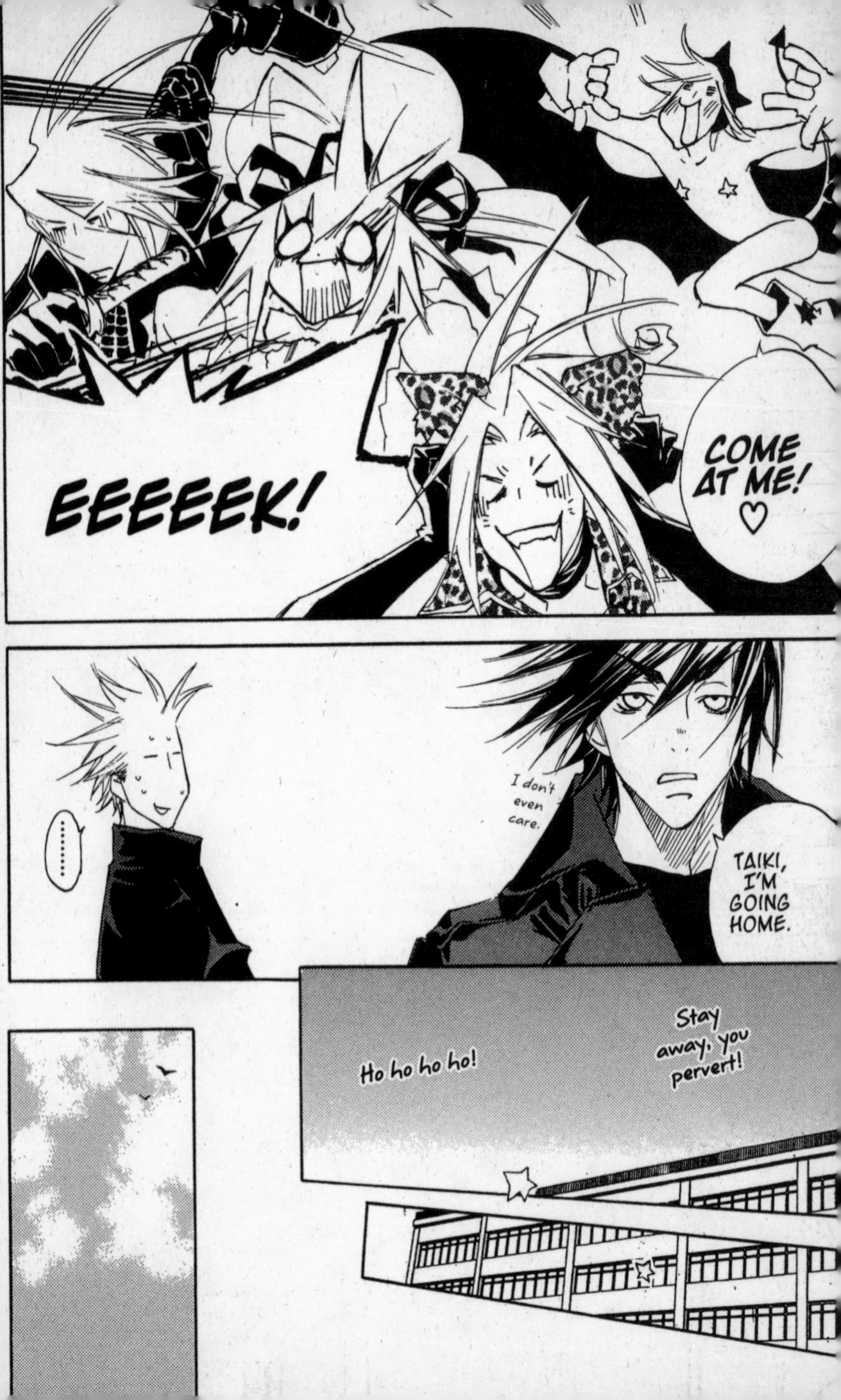
COME AT ME! ♡
EEEEEK!
TAIKI, I'M GOING HOME.
I don't even care.
......
Stay away, you pervert!
Ho ho ho ho!

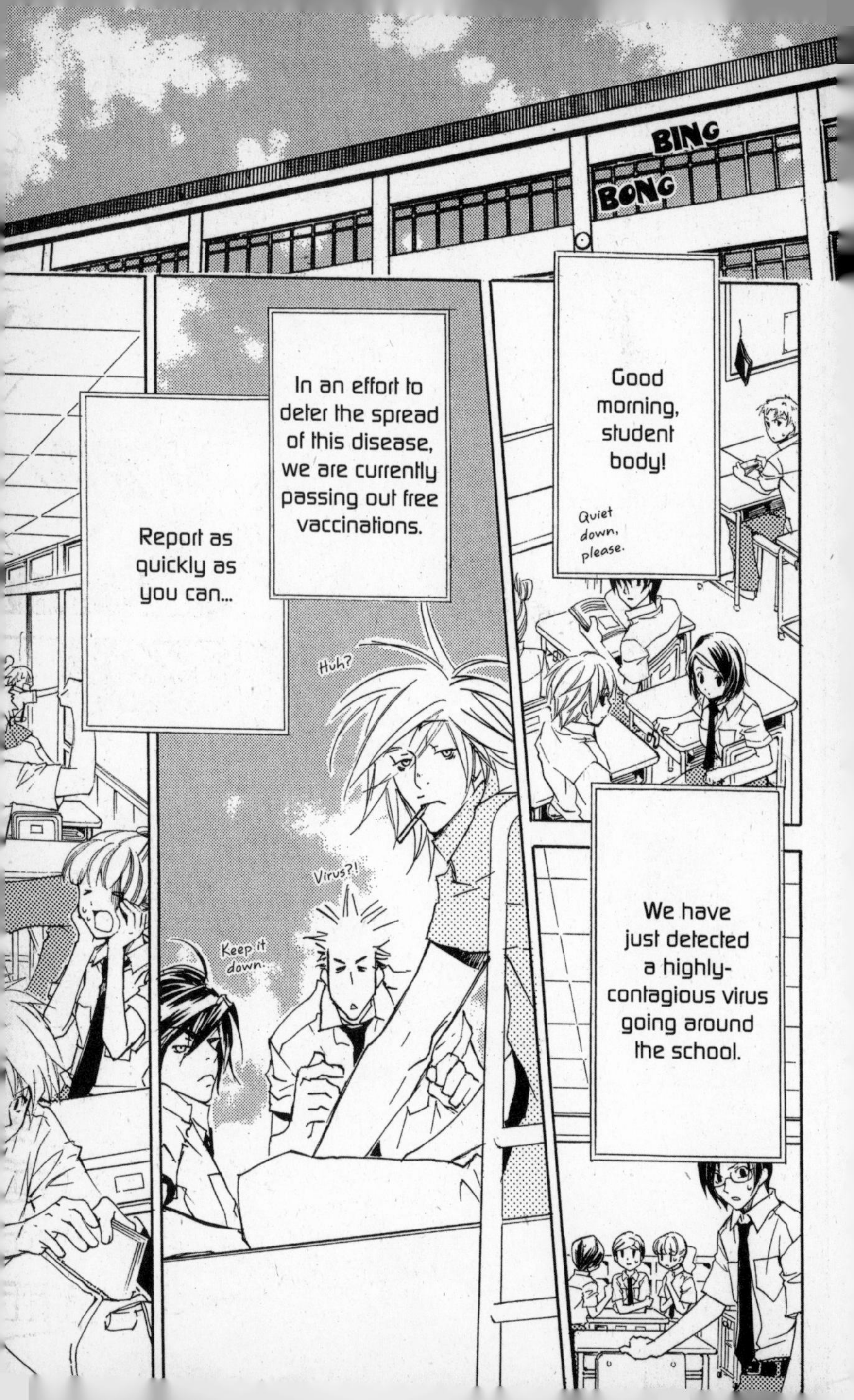
BING
BONG
Good morning, student body!
Quiet down, please.
We have just detected a highly-contagious virus going around the school.
In an effort to deter the spread of this disease, we are currently passing out free vaccinations.
Huh?
Virus?!
Keep it down.
Report as quickly as you can...

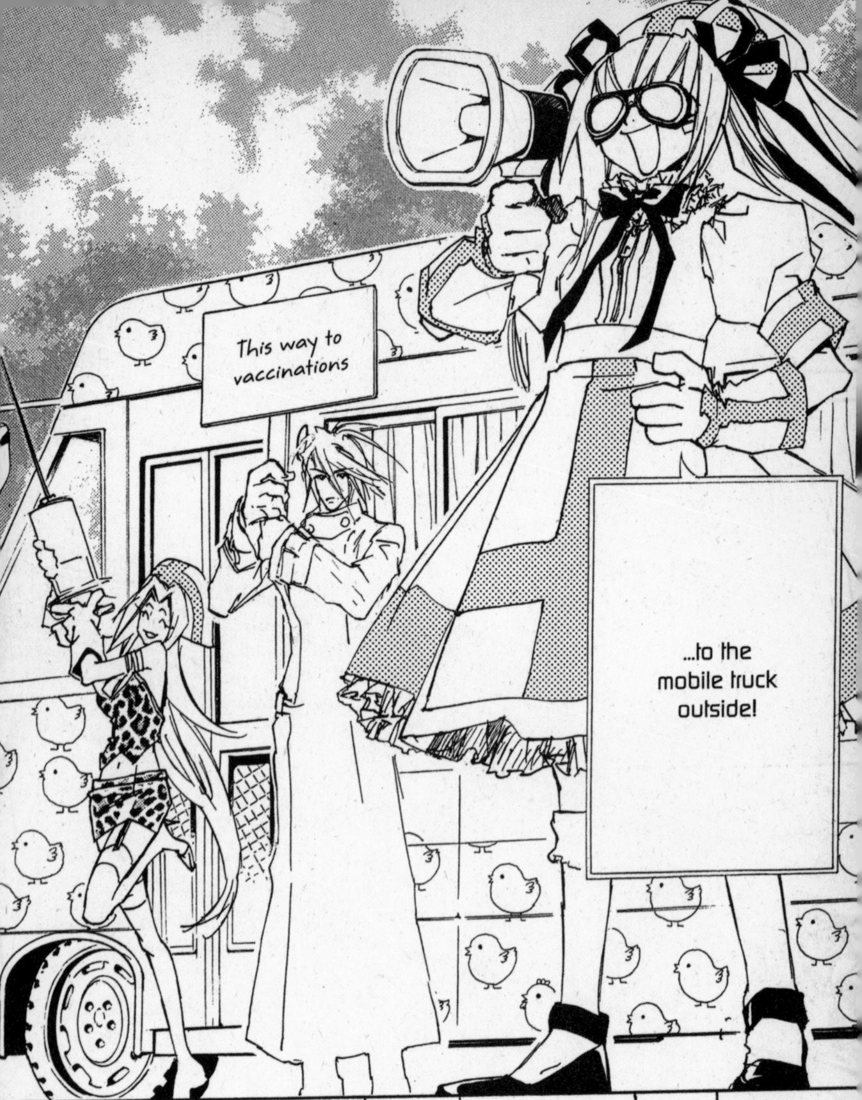
...to the mobile truck outside!
This way to vaccinations

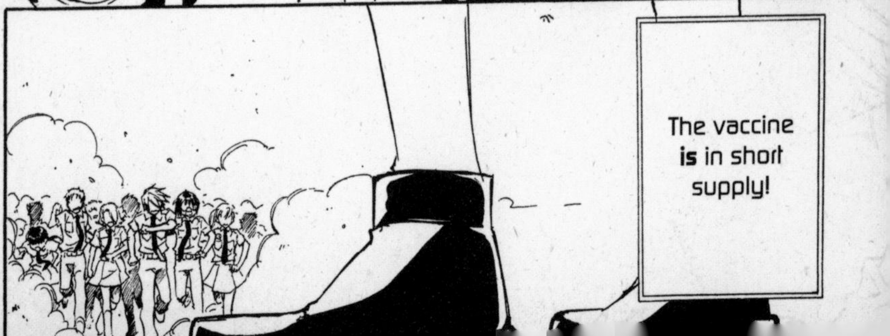
The vaccine **is** in short supply!

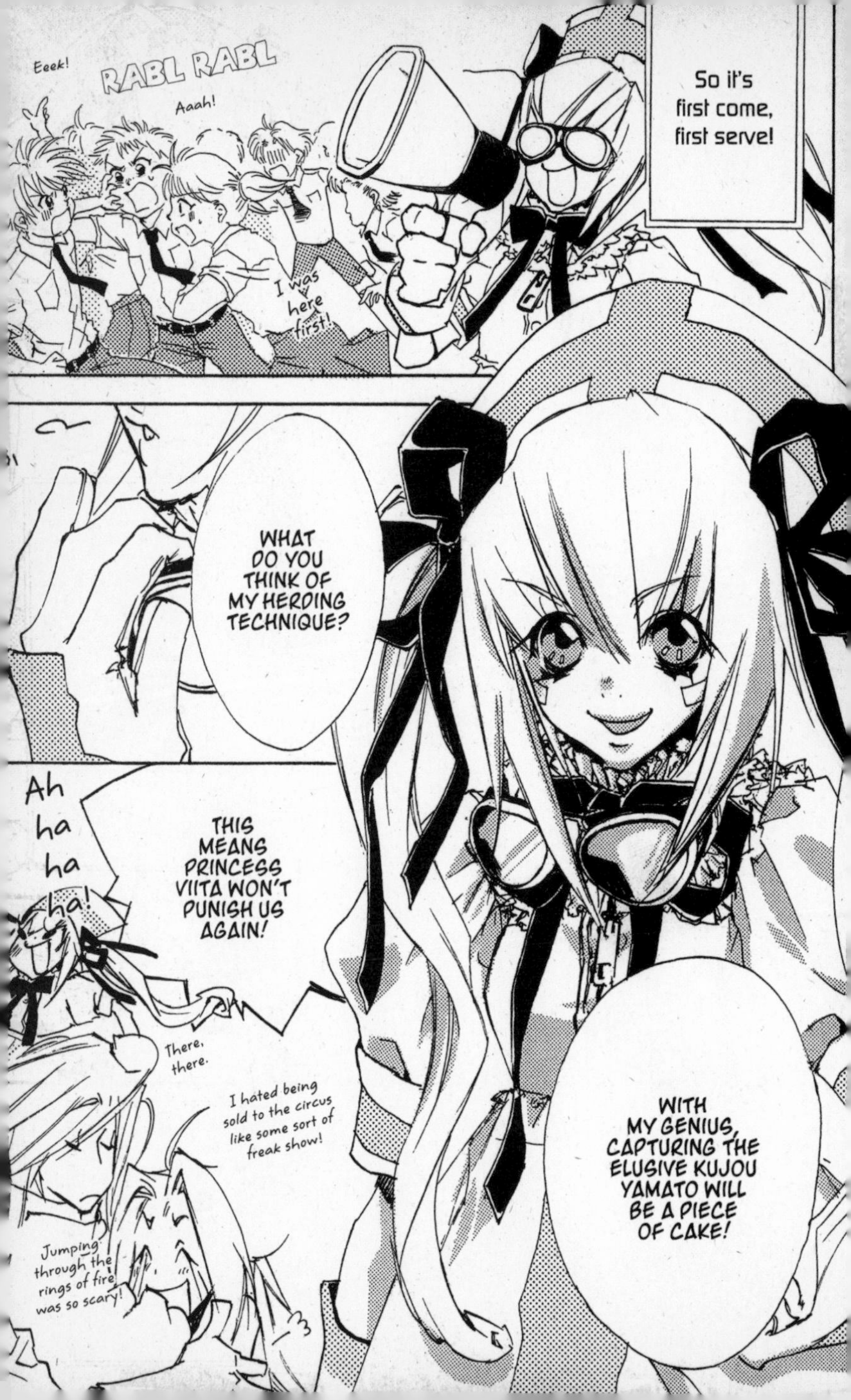
So it's first come, first serve!
RABL RABL
Aaah!
Eeek!
I was here first!
WHAT DO YOU THINK OF MY HERDING TECHNIQUE?
WITH MY GENIUS, CAPTURING THE ELUSIVE KUJOU YAMATO WILL BE A PIECE OF CAKE!
THIS MEANS PRINCESS VIITA WON'T PUNISH US AGAIN!
Ah ha ha ha!
There, there.
I hated being sold to the circus like some sort of freak show!
Jumping through the rings of fire was so scary!

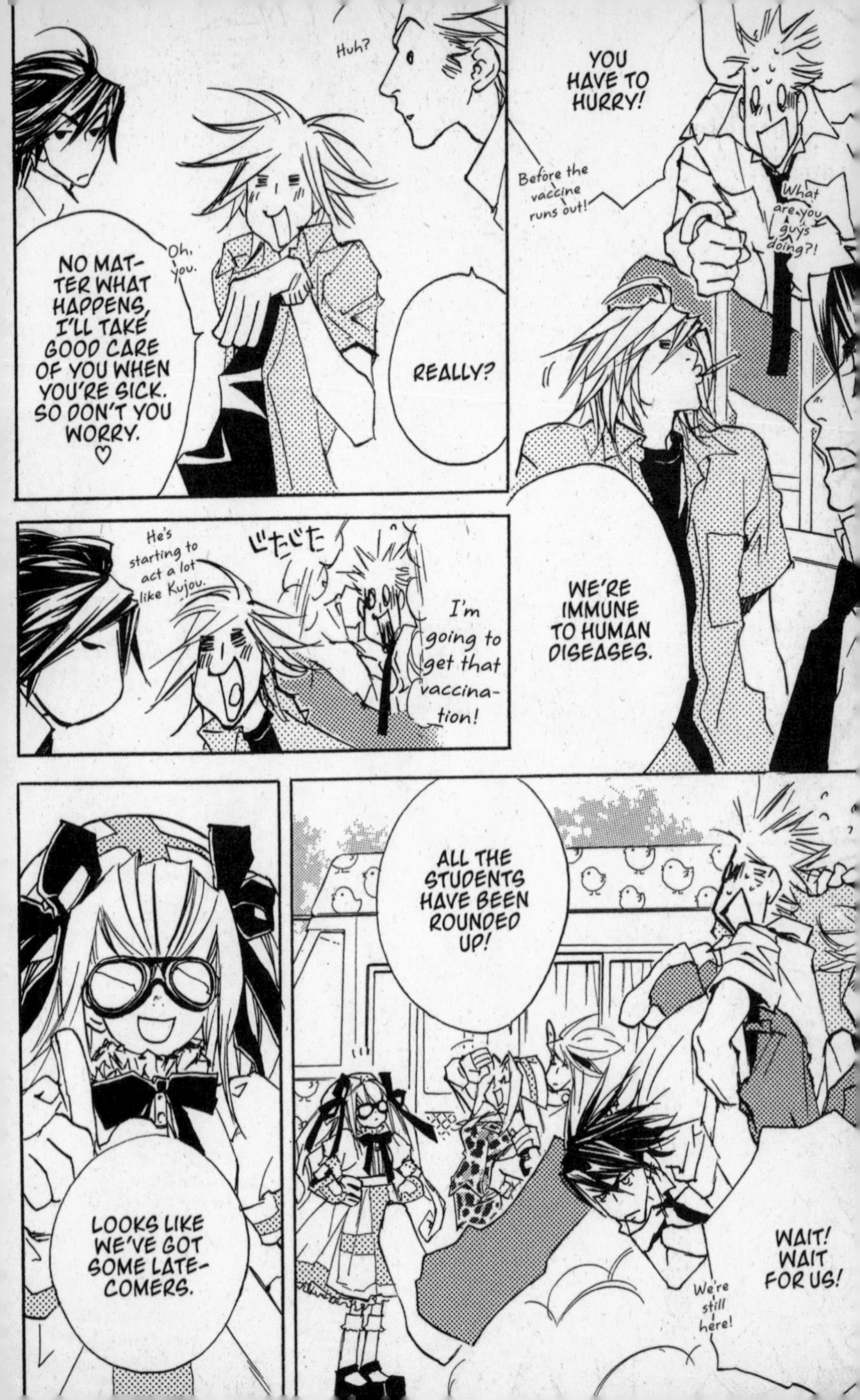
YOU HAVE TO HURRY!
Before the vaccine runs out!
What are you guys doing?!
WE'RE IMMUNE TO HUMAN DISEASES.
Huh?
Oh, you.
NO MATTER WHAT HAPPENS, I'LL TAKE GOOD CARE OF YOU WHEN YOU'RE SICK. SO DON'T YOU WORRY. ♡
REALLY?
I'm going to get that vaccination!
じたばた
He's starting to act a lot like Kujou.
ALL THE STUDENTS HAVE BEEN ROUNDED UP!
WAIT! WAIT FOR US!
We're still here!
LOOKS LIKE WE'VE GOT SOME LATE-COMERS.

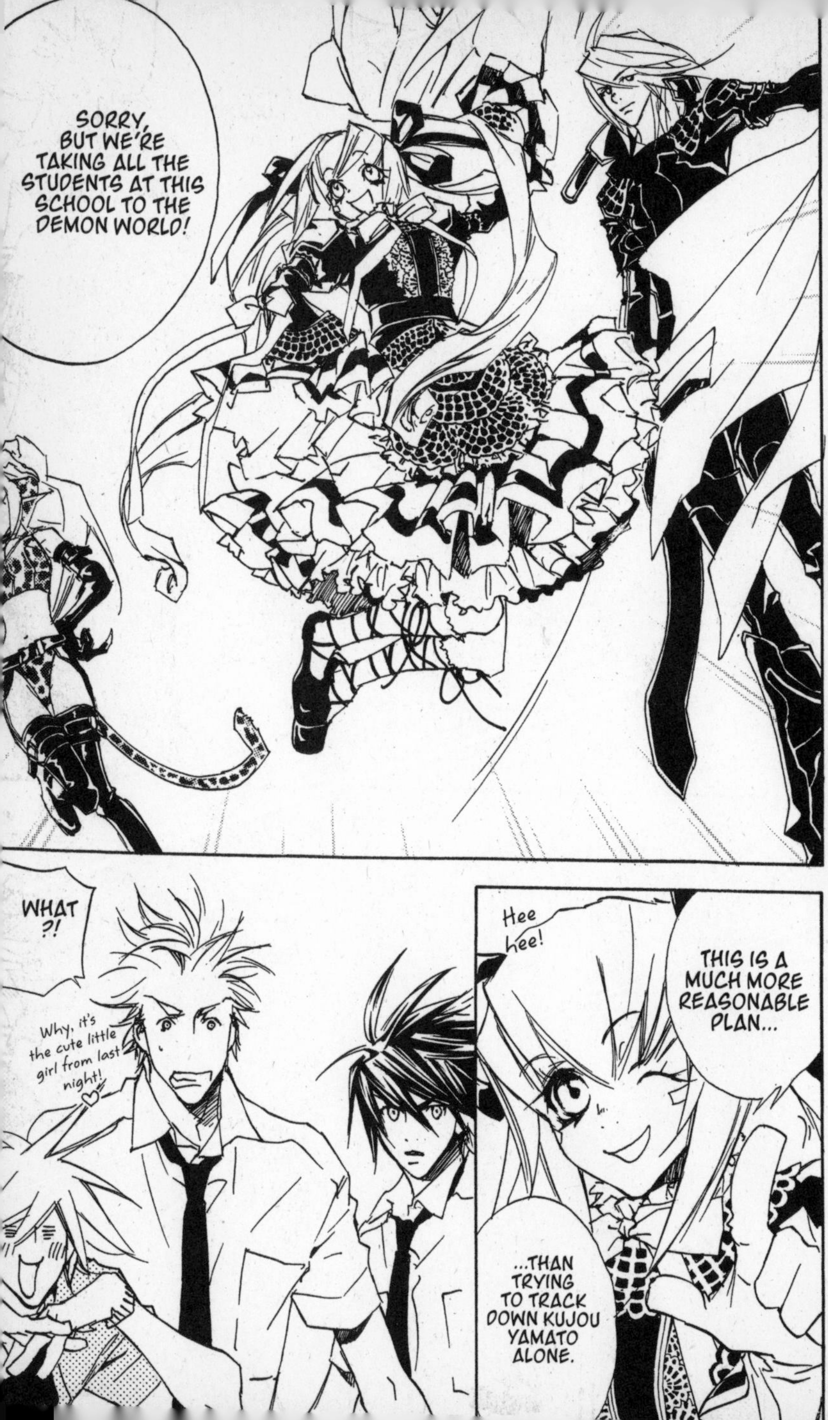
SORRY, BUT WE'RE TAKING ALL THE STUDENTS AT THIS SCHOOL TO THE DEMON WORLD!
Hee hee!
THIS IS A MUCH MORE REASONABLE PLAN...
...THAN TRYING TO TRACK DOWN KUJOU YAMATO ALONE.
WHAT?!
Why, it's the cute little girl from last night!

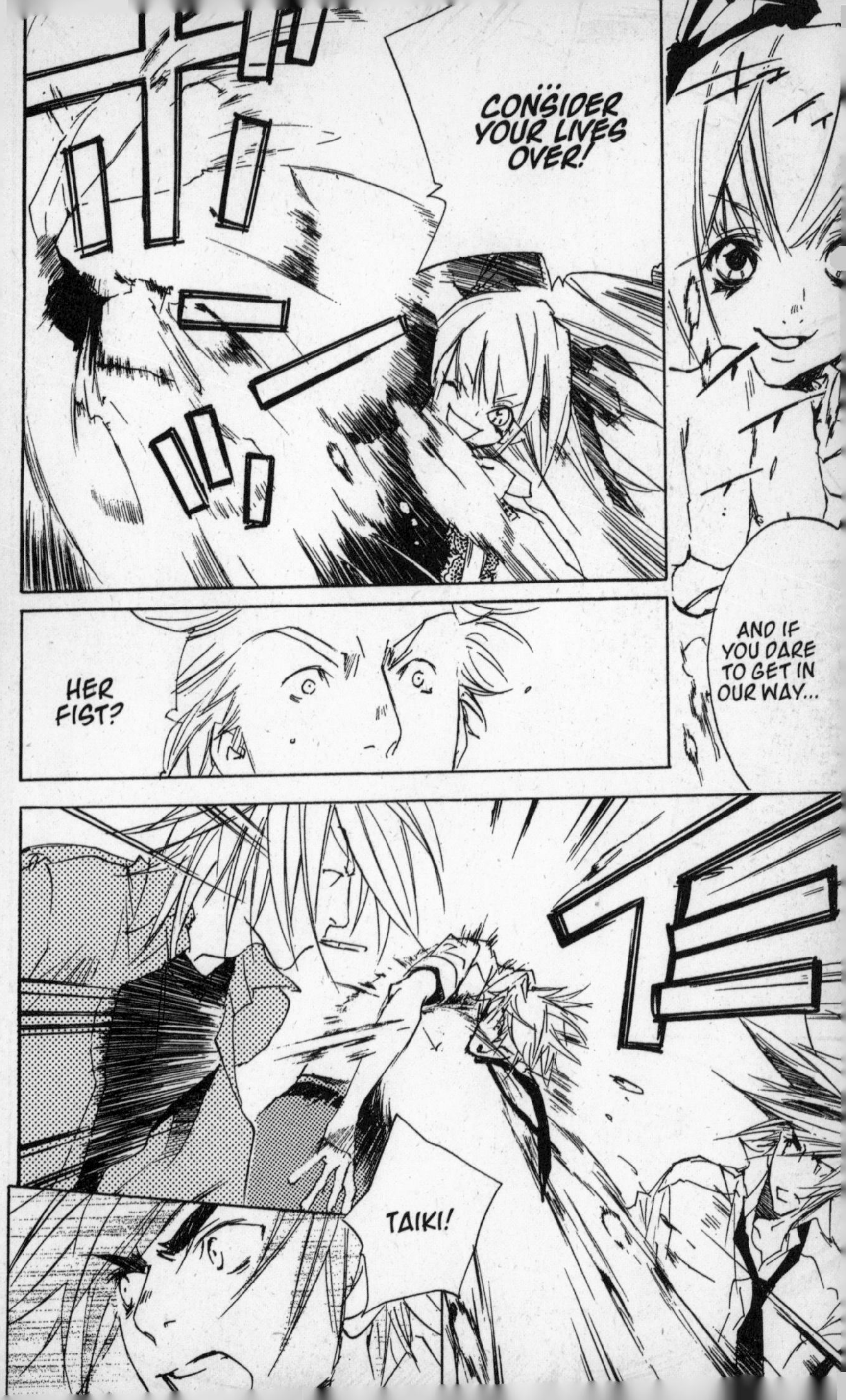
AND IF YOU DARE TO GET IN OUR WAY...
...CONSIDER YOUR LIVES OVER!
HER FIST?
TAIKI!

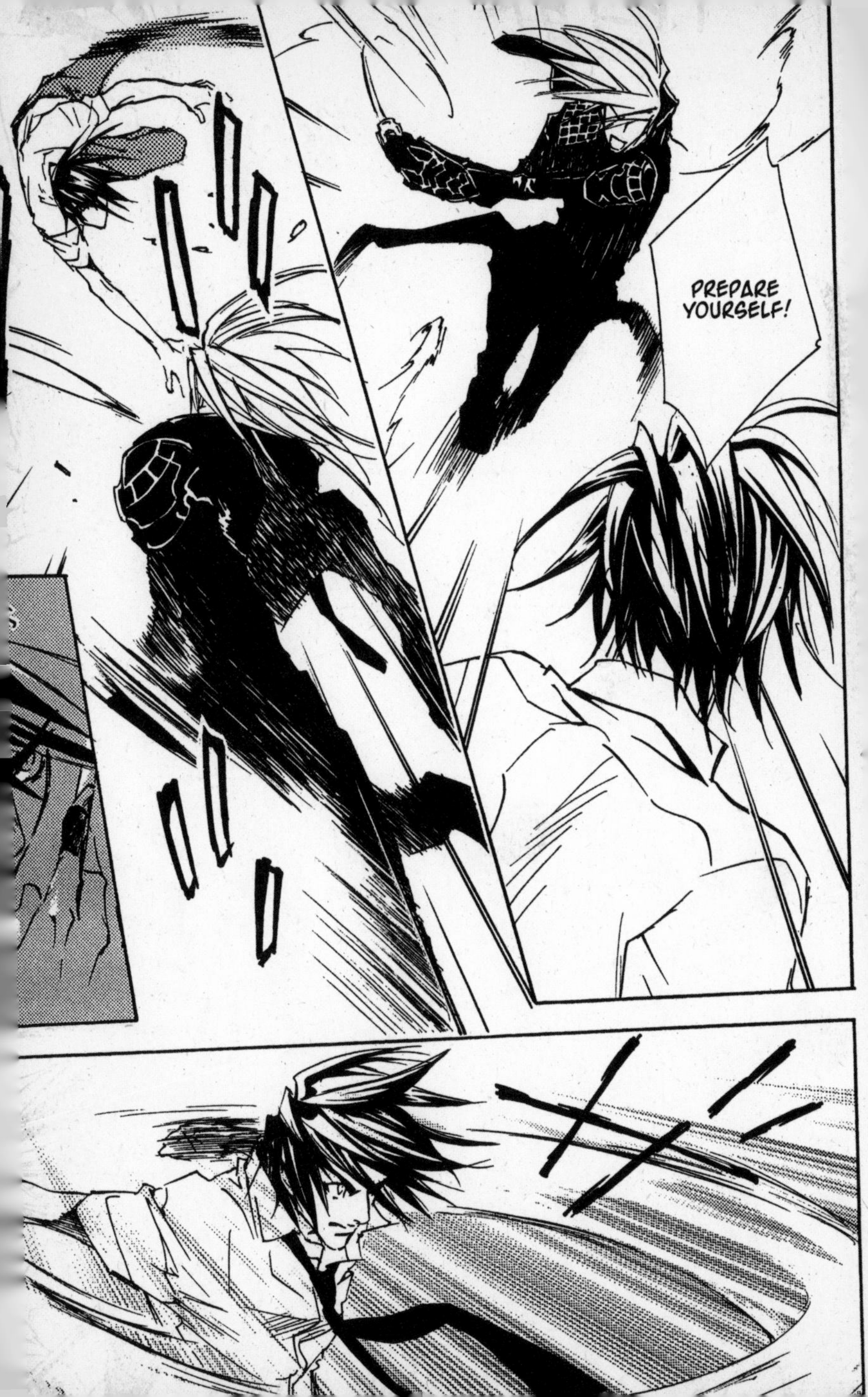
PREPARE YOURSELF!

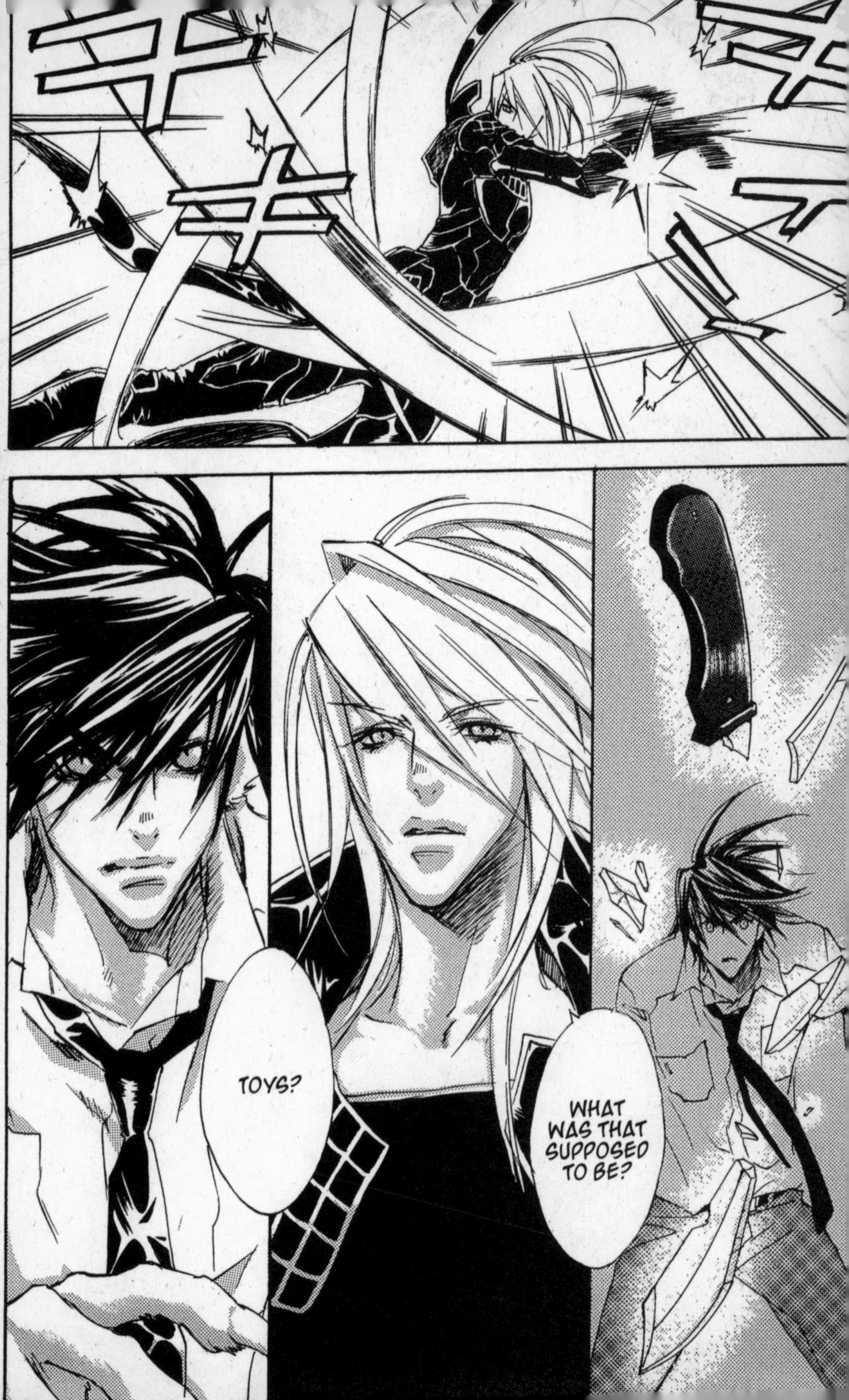
WHAT WAS THAT SUPPOSED TO BE?
TOYS?

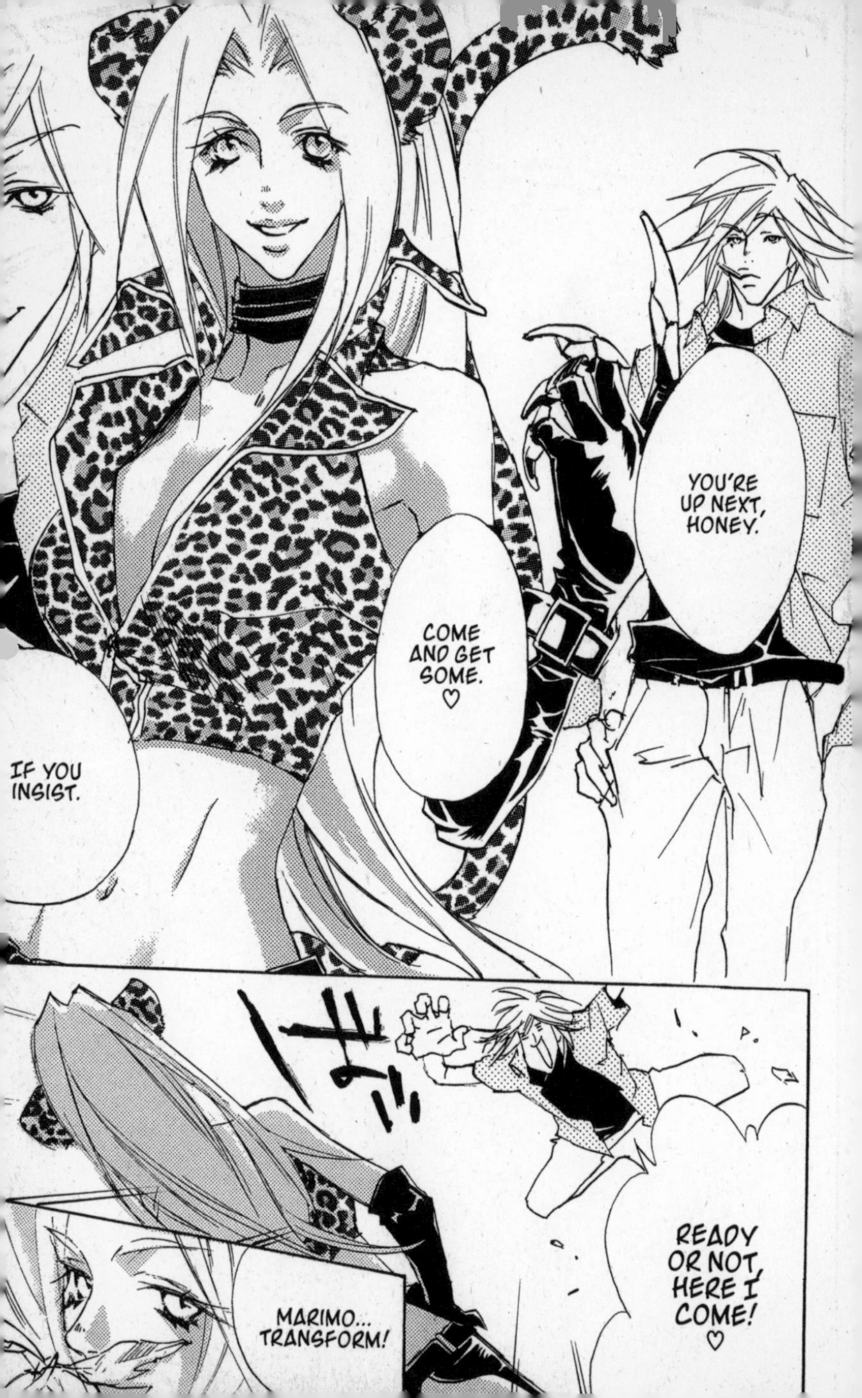
YOU'RE UP NEXT, HONEY.
COME AND GET SOME. ♡
IF YOU INSIST.
READY OR NOT, HERE I COME! ♡
MARIMO... TRANSFORM!

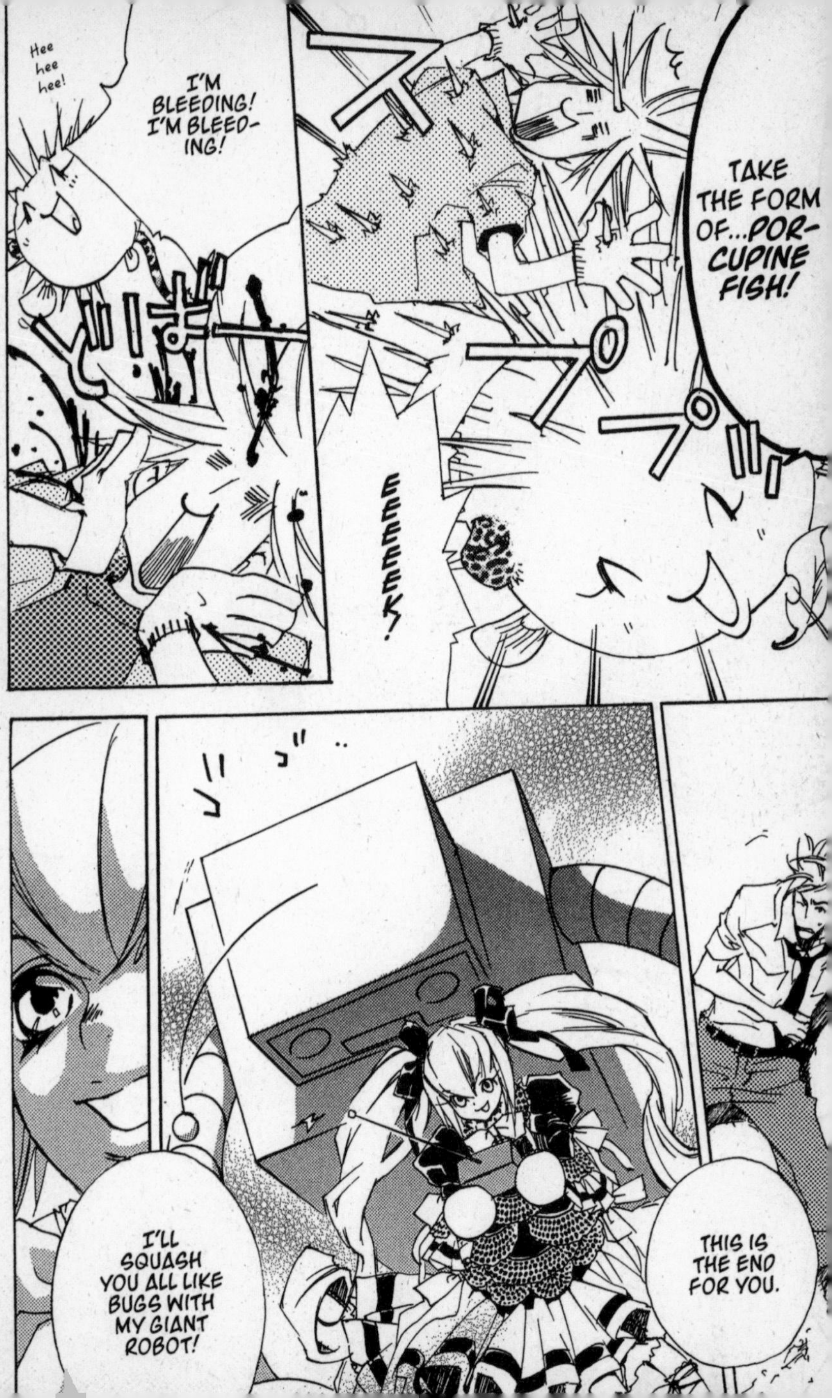
TAKE THE FORM OF...POR-CUPINE FISH!
EEEEEEK!
I'M BLEEDING! I'M BLEED-ING!
Hee hee hee!
THIS IS THE END FOR YOU.
I'LL SQUASH YOU ALL LIKE BUGS WITH MY GIANT ROBOT!

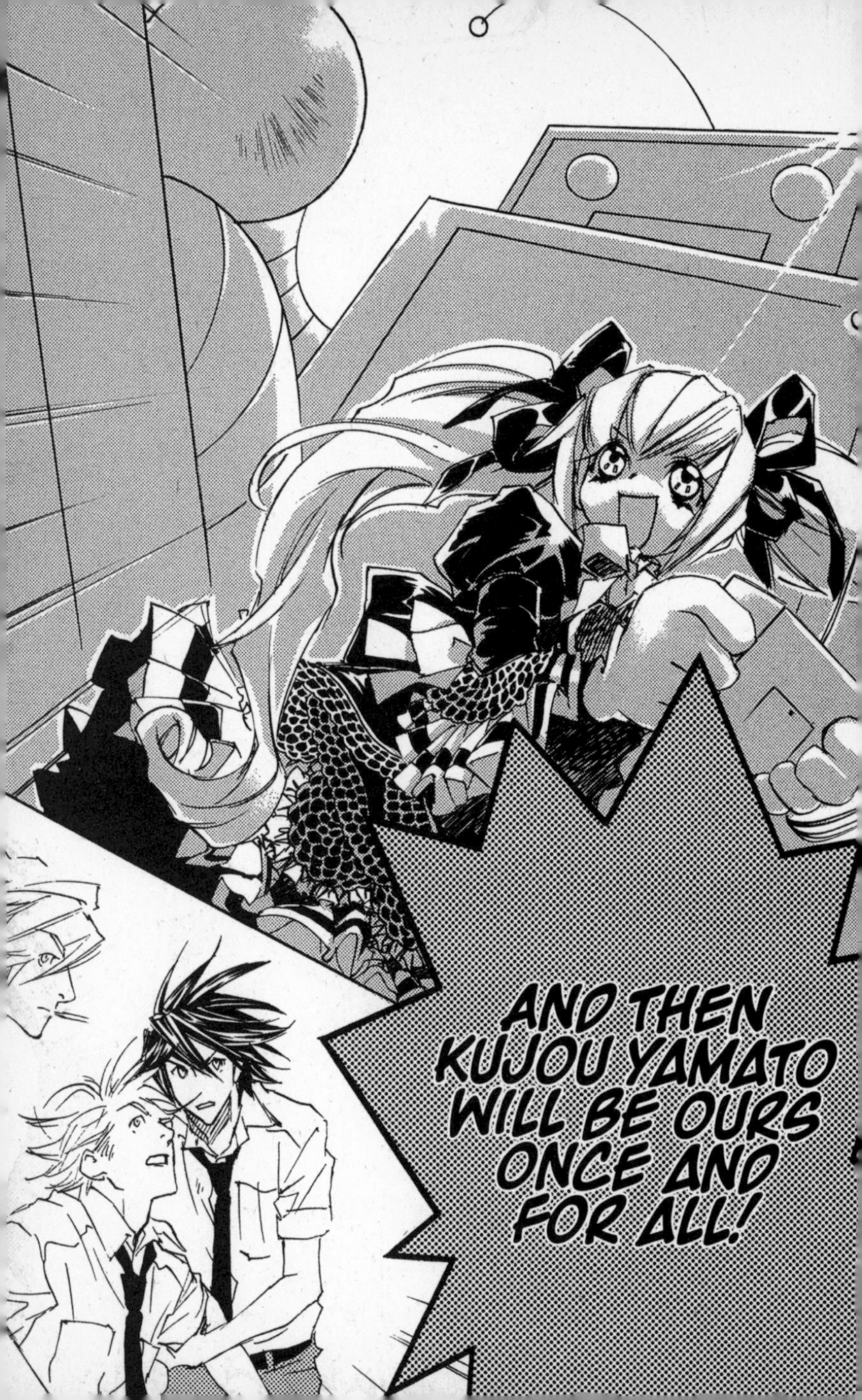
AND THEN KUJOU YAMATO WILL BE OURS ONCE AND FOR ALL!

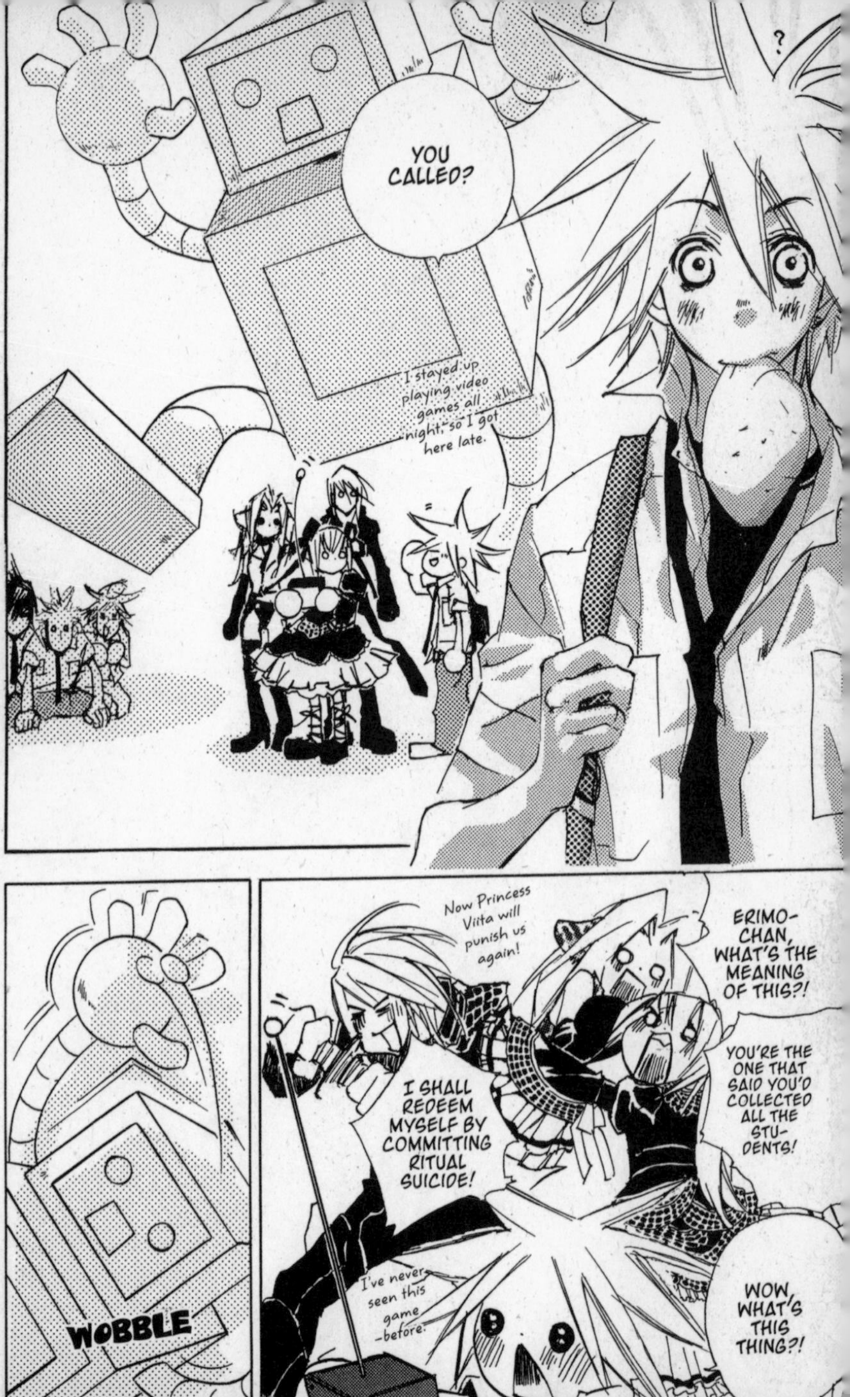
?
YOU CALLED?
I stayed up playing video games all night, so I got here late.
ERIMO-CHAN, WHAT'S THE MEANING OF THIS?!
YOU'RE THE ONE THAT SAID YOU'D COLLECTED ALL THE STU-DENTS!
Now Princess Viita will punish us again!
I SHALL REDEEM MYSELF BY COMMITTING RITUAL SUICIDE!
WOW, WHAT'S THIS THING?!
I've never seen this game before.
WOBBLE

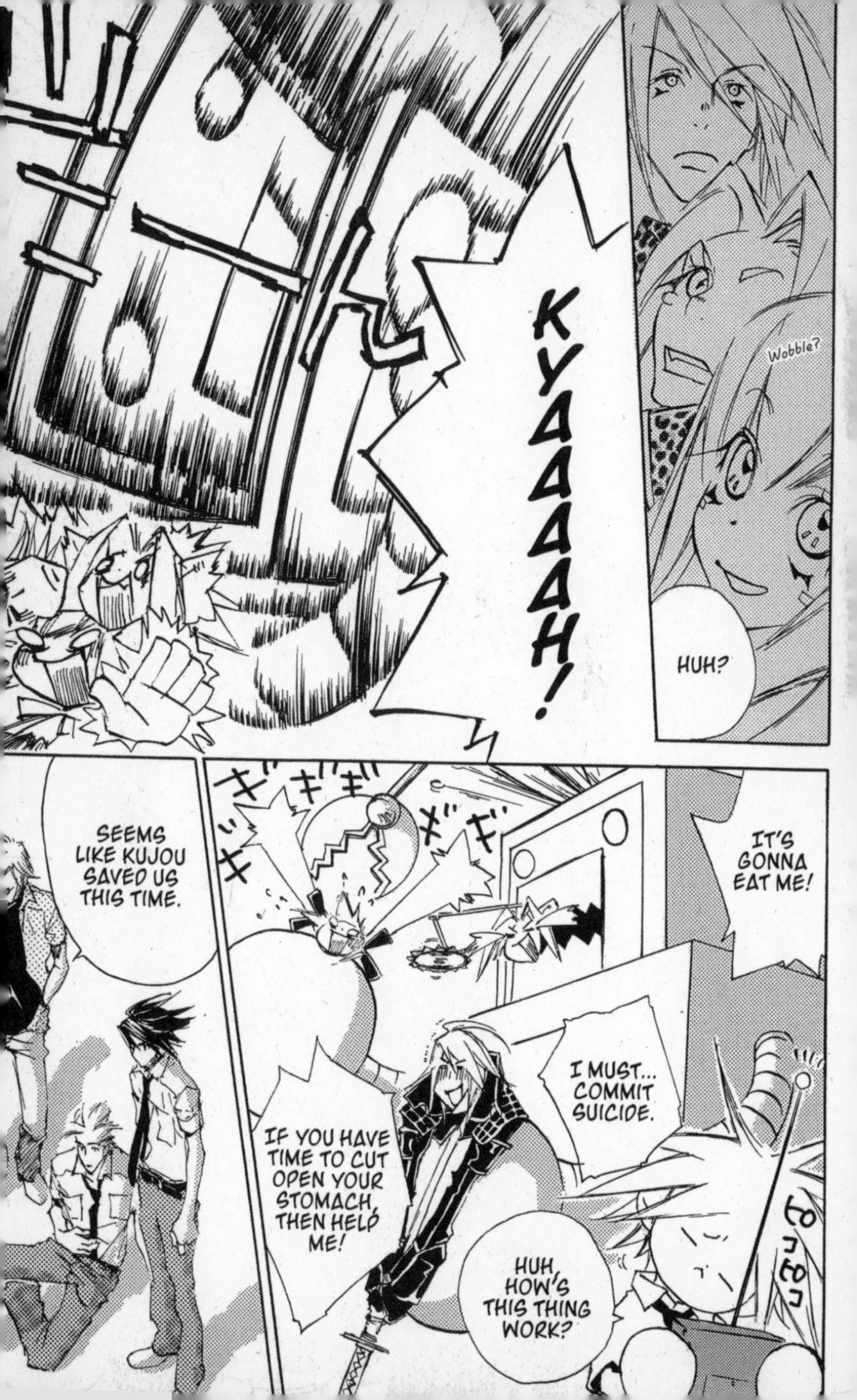
Wobble?
HUH?
KYAAAAH!
IT'S GONNA EAT ME!
I MUST... COMMIT SUICIDE.
HUH, HOW'S THIS THING WORK?
IF YOU HAVE TIME TO CUT OPEN YOUR STOMACH, THEN HELP ME!
SEEMS LIKE KUJOU SAVED US THIS TIME.

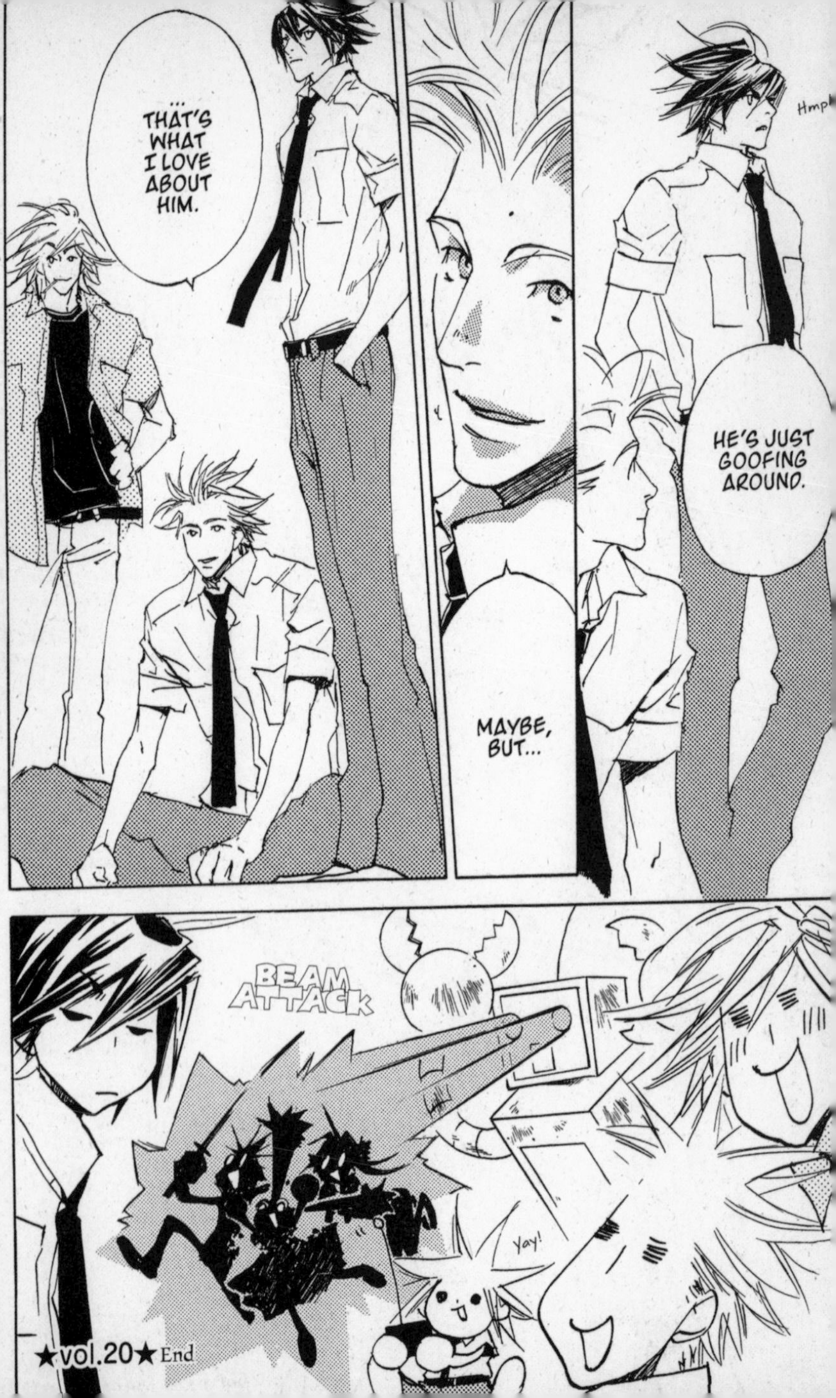
Hmph
HE'S JUST GOOFING AROUND.
MAYBE, BUT...
... THAT'S WHAT I LOVE ABOUT HIM.
BEAM ATTACK
Yay!
★vol.20★ End

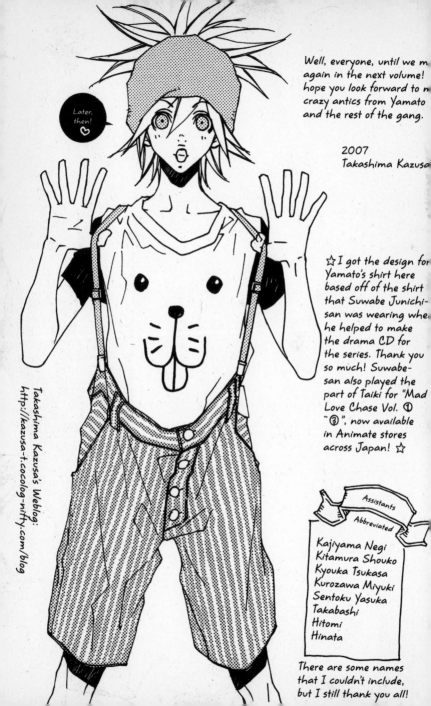

Later, then! ♡

Well, everyone, until we m
again in the next volume! I
hope you look forward to n
crazy antics from Yamato
and the rest of the gang.

2007
Takashima Kazusa

☆ I got the design for
Yamato's shirt here
based off of the shirt
that Suwabe Junichi-
san was wearing whe
he helped to make
the drama CD for
the series. Thank you
so much! Suwabe-
san also played the
part of Taiki for "Mad
Love Chase Vol. ①
~③", now available
in Animate stores
across Japan! ☆

Assistants
Abbreviated

Kajiyama Negi
Kitamura Shouko
Kyouka Tsukasa
Kurozawa Miyuki
Sentoku Yasuka
Takabashi
Hitomi
Hinata

There are some names
that I couldn't include,
but I still thank you all!

Takashima Kazusa's Weblog:
http://kazusa-t.cocolog-nifty.com/blog

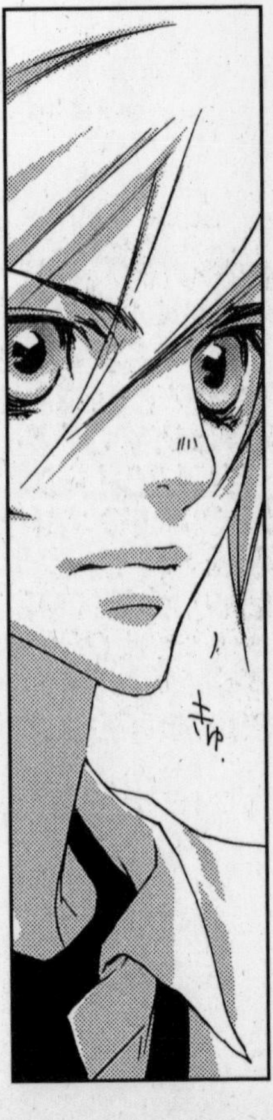
きゅ.

IN THE NEXT VOLUME...

# MAD LOVE CHASE

IT'S ALL FUN AND GAMES UNTIL SOMEONE GETS ARRESTED AND CHARGED WITH TREASON! WORD FINALLY LEAKS OUT IN THE DEMON WORLD THAT PRINCE KAITO IS MISSING, AND THE KING IS FORCED TO PLAY HIS TRUMP CARD—HE SUMMONS TAIKI AND CO. BACK UNDER PENALTY OF DEATH, CHARGED WITH OBSTRUCTING THE SEARCH FOR THE LOST PRINCE. THE THREE AREN'T ABOUT TO TAKE THE SITUATION LYING DOWN, BUT WITH DEMON FORCES INVADING THE SCHOOL, THEY MAY NOT HAVE MUCH OF A CHOICE... AND YAMATO IS FORCED TO MAKE A DECISION BETWEEN HIS FREEDOM...AND HIS FRIENDS. STAY TUNED FOR THE HEART-WRENCHING, PULSE-POUNDING CONCLUSION OF MAD LOVE CHASE!

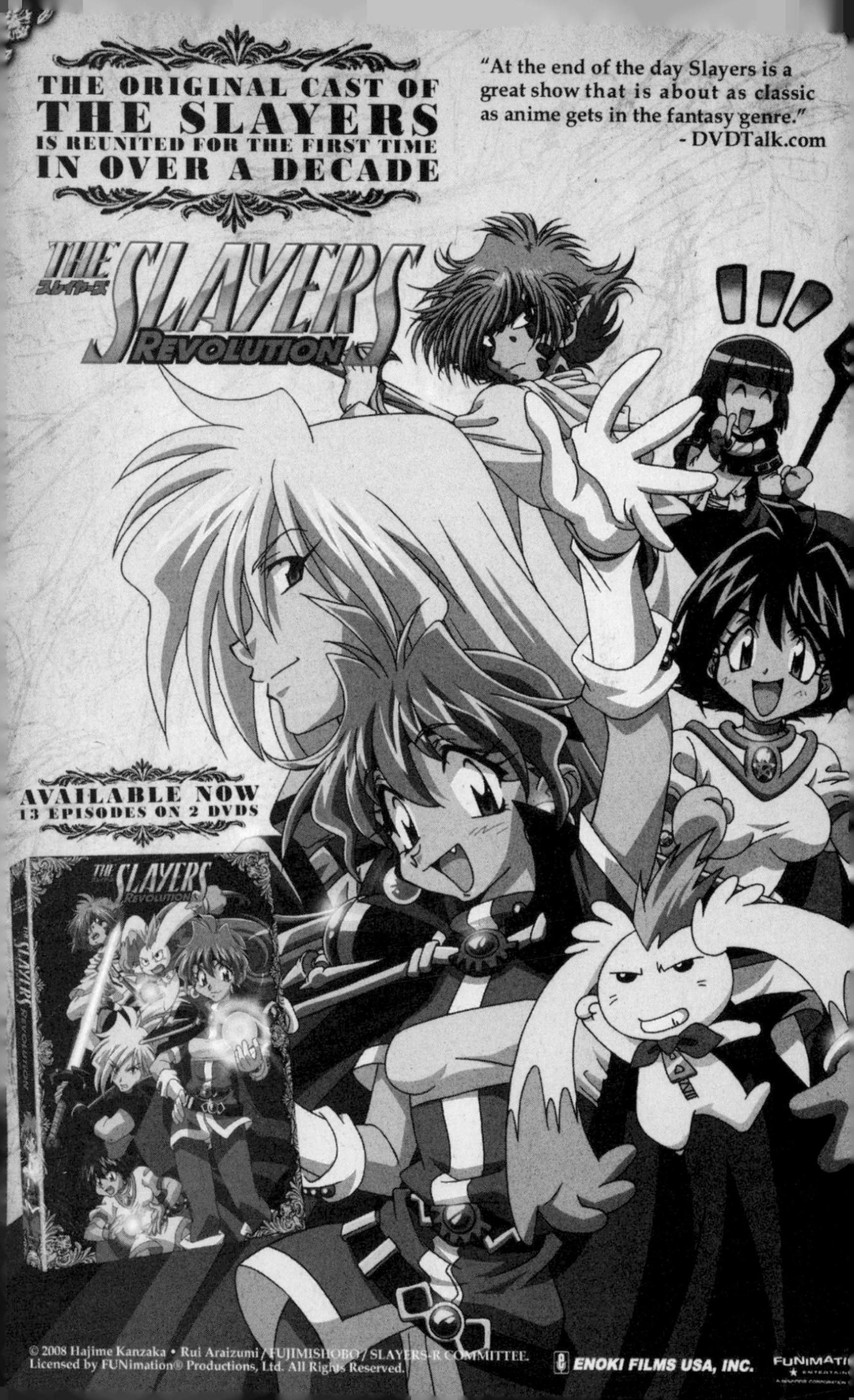
THE ORIGINAL CAST OF
THE SLAYERS
IS REUNITED FOR THE FIRST TIME
IN OVER A DECADE
"At the end of the day Slayers is a great show that is about as classic as anime gets in the fantasy genre."
- DVDTalk.com
THE SLAYERS
スレイヤーズ
REVOLUTION
AVAILABLE NOW
13 EPISODES ON 2 DVDS
THE SLAYERS REVOLUTION
© 2008 Hajime Kanzaka • Rui Araizumi / FUJIMISHOBO / SLAYERS-R COMMITTEE.
Licensed by FUNimation® Productions, Ltd. All Rights Reserved.
ENOKI FILMS USA, INC.

# *Naruto* star Yuri Lowenthal is VAN VON HUNTER

## Featuring

### Shoji Kawamori

• Anime master
*(Macross, The Vision of Escaflowne)*

### Stu Levy

• TOKYOPOP Founder and CEO
*(Princess Ai, Juror 13)*

Get ready for a hilarious, VANtastic adventure as the out-of-work evil vanquisher Van Von Hunter unravels the mysteries of manga, anime, and Japanese "pop" culture in order to save the world.

PUTTING THE VAN IN VANQUISH
VAN VON HUNTER

## Get your DVD now at www.createspace.com/283456

facebook
Van Von Hunter on Facebook
Become a Fan

To watch the trailer, hear original music from the film, become a VAN FAN, and more, visit: www.facebook.com/vanvonhunter

AVAILABLE FOR PURCHASE ON DVD NOW
AND SCREENING AT FAN CONVENTIONS AROUND THE WORLD!

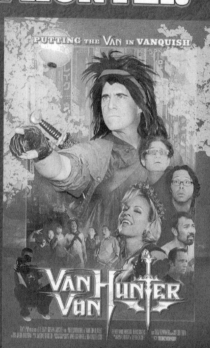

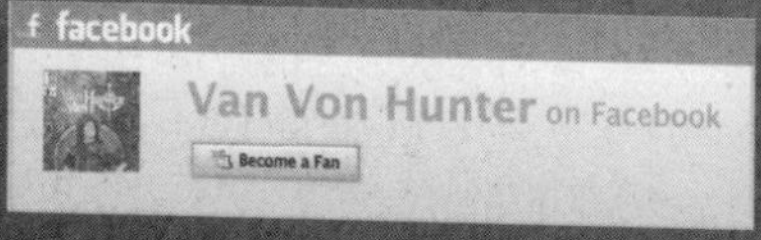

# DEADMAN WONDERLAND

*Where survival comes at an unthinkable price.*

Ten years have passed since the Great Tokyo Earthquake, and the people's memories of the disaster have
Igarashi, a mi
evacuee, has
a normal life..
"Red Man" ap
and Ganta's f
forever. His e
brutally murde
innocent of the crime, Ganta is sentenced to death and sent to the bizarre prison known as "Deadman Wonderland.

DEADMAN
WONDERLAND
TOKYOPOP
[BY] JINSEI KATAOKA
KAZUMA KONDOU

Let the insane and brutal game of prison survival begin!

## WATCH THE TRAILER AT

www.TOKYOPOP.com/DeadmanTrailer

OT OLDER TEEN AGE 16+

ACTION

**BE SURE TO VISIT WWW.TOKYOPOP.COM/SHOP FOR EVERYTHING YOU COULD EVER WANT!**

# STOP!

## This is the back of the book.
## You wouldn't want to spoil a great ending!

This book is printed "manga-style," in the authentic Japanese right-to-left format. Since none of the artwork has been flipped or altered, readers get to experience the story just as the creator intended. You've been asking for it, so TOKYOPOP® delivered: authentic, hot-off-the-press, and far more fun!

1
2
3
4
5
6
7
8
9
10

# DIRECTIONS

If this is your first time reading manga-style, here's a quick guide to help you understand how it works.

It's easy... just start in the top right panel and follow the numbers. Have fun, and look for more 100% authentic manga from TOKYOPOP®!

THE MANGA REVOLUTION • LEADING THE MANGA REVOLUTION • LEADING
漫画革命